Lethal Autonomous Weapons

The Oxford Series in Ethics, National Security, and the Rule of Law

Series Editors
Claire Finkelstein and Jens David Ohlin

Oxford University Press

About the Series

The *Oxford Series in Ethics, National Security, and the Rule of Law* is an interdisciplinary book series designed to address abiding questions at the intersection of national security, moral and political philosophy, and practical ethics. It seeks to illuminate both ethical and legal dilemmas that arise in democratic nations as they grapple with national security imperatives. The synergy the series creates between academic researchers and policy practitioners seeks to protect and augment the rule of law in the context of contemporary armed conflict and national security.

The book series grew out of the work of the Center for Ethics and the Rule of Law (CERL) at the University of Pennsylvania. CERL is a nonpartisan interdisciplinary institute dedicated to the preservation and promotion of the rule of law in twenty-first century warfare and national security. The only Center of its kind housed within a law school, CERL draws from the study of law, philosophy, and ethics to answer the difficult questions that arise in times of war and contemporary transnational conflicts.

Lethal Autonomous Weapons

Re-Examining the Law and Ethics of Robotic Warfare

EDITED BY JAI GALLIOTT
DUNCAN MACINTOSH
& JENS DAVID OHLIN

OXFORD
UNIVERSITY PRESS

OXFORD
UNIVERSITY PRESS

Oxford University Press is a department of the University of Oxford. It furthers the University's objective of excellence in research, scholarship, and education by publishing worldwide. Oxford is a registered trade mark of Oxford University Press in the UK and certain other countries.

Published in the United States of America by Oxford University Press
198 Madison Avenue, New York, NY 10016, United States of America.

Library of Congress Cataloging-in-Publication Data
Names: Galliott, Jai, author. | MacIntosh, Duncan (Writer on autonomous weapons), author. | Ohlin, Jens David, author.
Title: Lethal autonomous weapons : re-examining the law and ethics of robotic warfare / Jai Galliott, Duncan MacIntosh & Jens David Ohlin.
Description: New York, NY : Oxford University Press, [2021]
Identifiers: LCCN 2020032678 (print) | LCCN 2020032679 (ebook) | ISBN 9780197546048 (hardback) | ISBN 9780197546062 (epub) | ISBN 9780197546055 (UPDF) | ISBN 9780197546079 (Digital-Online)
Subjects: LCSH: Military weapons (International law) | Military weapons—Law and legislation—United States. | Weapons systems—Automation. | Autonomous robots—Law and legislation. | Uninhabited combat aerial vehicles (International law) | Autonomous robots—Moral and ethical aspects. | Drone aircraft—Moral and ethical aspects. | Humanitarian law.
Classification: LCC KZ5624 .G35 2020 (print) | LCC KZ5624 (ebook) | DDC 172/.42—dc23
LC record available at https://lccn.loc.gov/2020032678
LC ebook record available at https://lccn.loc.gov/2020032679

DOI: 10.1093/oso/9780197546048.001.0001

9 8 7 6 5 4 3 2

Printed by Integrated Books International, United States of America

TABLE OF CONTENTS

LIST OF CONTRIBUTORS

Bianca Baggiarini is a Political Sociologist and Senior Lecturer at UNSW, Canberra. She obtained her PhD (2018) in sociology from York University in Toronto. Her research is broadly concerned with the sociopolitical effects of autonomy in the military. To that end, she has previously examined the figure of the citizen-soldier considering high-technology warfare, security privatization, neoliberal governmentality, and theories of military sacrifice. Her current work is focused on military attitudes toward autonomous systems.

Deane-Peter Baker is an Associate Professor of International and Political Studies and Co-Convener (with Prof. David Kilcullen) of the Future Operations Research Group in the School of Humanities and Social Sciences at the UNSW Canberra. A specialist in both the ethics of armed conflict and military strategy, Dr. Baker's research straddles philosophy, ethics, and security studies.

Dr. Baker previously held positions as an Assistant Professor of Ethics in the Department of Leadership, Ethics and Law at the United States Naval Academy and as an Associate Professor of Ethics at the University of KwaZulu-Natal in South Africa. He has also held visiting research fellow positions at the Triangle Institute for Security Studies at Duke University, and the US Army War College's Strategic Studies Institute. From 2017 to 2018, Dr. Baker served as a panelist on the International Panel on the Regulation of Autonomous Weapons.

Steven J. Barela is an Assistant Professor at the Global Studies Institute and a member of the law faculty at the University of Geneva. He has taught at the Korbel School of International Studies at Denver University and lectured for *l'Université Laval (Québec), Sciences Po Bordeaux*, UCLA, and the Geneva Academy of International Humanitarian Law and Human Rights. In addition to his PhD in law from the University of Geneva, Dr. Barela holds three master's degrees: MA degrees in Latin American Studies and International Studies, along with an LLM in international humanitarian law and human rights. Dr. Barela has published in respected journals. Finally, Dr. Barela is a series editor for "Emerging Technologies, Ethics and International Affairs" at Ashgate Publishing and published an edited volume on armed drones in 2015.

M.L. (Missy) Cummings received her BS in Mathematics from the US Naval Academy in 1988, her MS in Space Systems Engineering from the Naval Postgraduate School in 1994, and her PhD in Systems Engineering from the University of Virginia in 2004. A naval pilot from 1988–1999, she was one of the US Navy's first female fighter pilots. She is currently a Professor in the Duke University Electrical and Computer Engineering Department, and the Director of the Humans and Autonomy Laboratory. She is an AIAA Fellow; and a member of the Defense Innovation Board and Veoneer, Inc., Board of Directors.

S. Kate Devitt is the Deputy Chief Scientist of the Trusted Autonomous Systems Defence Cooperative Research Centre and a Social and Ethical Robotics Researcher at the Defence Science and technology group (the primary research organization for the Australia Department of Defence). Dr. Devitt earned her PhD, entitled "Homeostatic Epistemology: Reliability, Coherence and Coordination in a Bayesian Virtue Epistemology," from Rutgers University in 2013. Dr. Devitt has published on the ethical implications of robotics and biosurveillance, robotics in agriculture, epistemology, and the trustworthiness of autonomous systems.

Nicholas G. Evans is an Assistant Professor of Philosophy at the University of Massachusetts Lowell, where he conducts research on national security and emerging technologies. His recent work on assessing the risks and benefits of dual-use research of concern has been widely published. In 2017, Dr. Evans was awarded funding from the National Science Foundation to examine the ethics of autonomous vehicles.

Prior to his appointment at the University of Massachusetts, Dr. Evans completed postdoctoral work in medical ethics and health policy at the Perelman School of Medicine at the University of Pennsylvania. Dr. Evans has conducted research at the Monash Bioethics Centre, The Centre for Applied Philosophy and Public Ethics, Australian Defence Force Academy, and the University of Exeter. In 2013, he served as a policy officer with the Australian Department of Health and Australian Therapeutic Goods Administration.

Jai Galliott is the Director of the Values in Defence & Security Technology Group at UNSW @ The Australian Defence Force Academy; Non-Residential Fellow at the Modern War Institute at the United States Military Academy, West Point; and Visiting Fellow in The Centre for Technology and Global Affairs at the University of Oxford. Dr. Galliott has developed a reputation as one of the foremost experts on the socio-ethical implications of artificial intelligence (AI) and is regarded as an internationally respected scholar on the ethical, legal, and strategic issues associated with the employment of emerging technologies, including cyber systems, autonomous vehicles, and soldier augmentation. His publications include *Big Data & Democracy* (Edinburgh University Press, 2020); *Ethics and the Future of Spying: Technology, National Security and Intelligence Collection* (Routledge, 2016); *Military Robots: Mapping the Moral Landscape* (Ashgate, 2015); *Super Soldiers: The Ethical, Legal and Social Implications* (Ashgate, 2015); and *Commercial Space Exploration: Ethics, Policy and Governance* (Ashgate, 2015). He acknowledges the support of the Australian Government through the Trusted Autonomous Systems

Defence Cooperative Research Centre and the United States Department of Defence.

Natalia Jevglevskaja is a Research Fellow at the University of New South Wales at the Australian Defence Force Academy in Canberra. As part of the collaborative research group "Values in Defence & Security Technology" (VDST) based at the School of Engineering & Information Technology (SEIT), she is looking at how social value systems interact and influence research, design, and development of emerging military and security technology. Natalia's earlier academic appointments include Teaching Fellow at Melbourne Law School, Research Assistant to the editorial work of the Max Planck Commentaries on WTO Law, and Junior Legal Editor of the Max Planck Encyclopedia of Public International Law.

Armin Krishnan is an Associate Professor and the Director of Security Studies at East Carolina University. He holds a MA degree in Political Science, Sociology, and Philosophy from the University of Munich, a MS in Intelligence and International Relations from the University of Salford, and a PhD in the field of Security Studies also from the University of Salford. He was previously a Visiting Assistant Professor at the University of Texas at El Paso's Intelligence and National Security Studies program. Krishnan is the author of five books of new developments in warfare, including *Killer Robots: The Legality and Ethicality of Autonomous Weapons* (Routledge, 2009).

Alex Leveringhaus is a Lecturer in Political Theory in the Politics Department at the University of Surrey, United Kingdom, where he co-directs the Centre for International Intervention (cii). Prior to coming to Surrey, Alex held postdoctoral positions at Goethe University Frankfurt; the Oxford Institute for Ethics, Law and Armed Conflict; and the University of Manchester. Alex's research is in contemporary political theory and focuses on ethical issues in the area of armed conflict, with special reference to emerging combat technologies as well as the ethics of intervention. His book *Ethics and Autonomous Weapons* was published in 2016 (Palgrave Pivot).

Rain Liivoja is an Associate Professor at the University of Queensland, where he leads the Law and the Future of War Research Group. Dr. Liivoja's current research focuses on legal challenges associated with military applications of science and technology. His broader research and teaching interests include the law of armed conflict, human rights law and the law of treaties, as well as international and comparative criminal law. Before joining the University of Queensland, Dr. Liivoja held academic appointments at the Universities of Melbourne, Helsinki, and Tartu. He has served on Estonian delegations to disarmament and arms control meetings.

Duncan MacIntosh is a Professor of Philosophy at Dalhousie University. Professor MacIntosh works in metaethics, decision and action theory, metaphysics, philosophy of language, epistemology, and philosophy of science. He has written on desire-based theories of rationality, the relationship between rationality and time, the reducibility of morality to rationality, modeling morality and rationality with the tools of action and game theory, scientific realism, and a number of other topics.

He has published research on autonomous weapon systems, morality, and the rule of law in leading journals, including *Temple International and Comparative Law Journal*, *The Journal of Philosophy*, and *Ethics*.

Bertram F. Malle is a Professor of Cognitive, Linguistic, and Psychological Sciences and Co-Director of the Humanity-Centered Robotics Initiative at Brown University. Trained in psychology, philosophy, and linguistics at the University of Graz, Austria, he received his PhD in psychology from Stanford University in 1995. He received the Society of Experimental Social Psychology Outstanding Dissertation award in 1995, a National Science Foundation (NSF) CAREER award in 1997, and is past president of the Society of Philosophy and Psychology. Dr. Malle's research focuses on social cognition, moral psychology, and human-robot interaction. He has distributed his work in 150 scientific publications and several books. His lab page is at http://research.clps.brown.edu/SocCogSci.

Tim McFarland is a Research Fellow in the Values in Defence & Security Technology group within the School of Engineering and Information Technology of the University of New South Wales at the Australian Defence Force Academy. Prior to earning his PhD, Dr. McFarland also earned a Bachelor of Mechanical Engineering (Honors) and a Bachelor of Economics (Monash University). Following the completion of a Juris Doctor degree and graduate diplomas of Legal Practice and International Law, Dr. McFarland was admitted as a solicitor in the state of Victoria in 2012.

Dr. McFarland's current work is on the social, legal, and ethical questions arising from the emergence of new military and security technologies, and their implications for the design and use of new military systems. He is also a member of the Program on the Regulation of Emerging Military Technologies (PREMT) and the Asia Pacific Centre for Military Law (APCML).

Jens David Ohlin is the Vice Dean of Cornell Law School. His work stands at the intersection of four related fields: criminal law, criminal procedure, public international law, and the laws of war. Trained as both a lawyer and a philosopher, his research has tackled diverse, interdisciplinary questions, including the philosophical foundations of international law and the role of new technologies in warfare. His latest research project involves foreign election interference.

In addition to dozens of law review articles and book chapters, Professor Ohlin is the sole author of three recently published casebooks, a co-editor of the *Oxford Series in Ethics; National Security, and the Rule of Law*; and a co-editor of the forthcoming *Oxford Handbook on International Criminal Justice*.

Donovan Phillips is a first-year PhD Candidate at The University of Western Ontario, by way of Dalhousie University, MA (2019) and Kwantlen Polytechnic University, BA (2017). His main interests fall within the philosophy of language and philosophy of mind, and concern propositional attitude ascription, theories of meaning, and accounts of first-person authority. More broadly, the ambiguity and translation of law, as both a formal and practical exercise, is a burgeoning area of interest for future research that he plans to pursue further during his doctoral work.

Avery Plaw is a Professor of Political Science at the University of Massachusetts, Dartmouth, specializing in Political Theory and International Relations with a particular focus on Strategic Studies. He studied at the University of Toronto and McGill University and previously taught at Concordia University in Montreal and was a Visiting Scholar at New York University. He has published a number of books, including the *Drone Debate: A Primer on the U.S. Use of Unmanned Aircraft Outside of Conventional Armed Conflict* (Rowman and Littlefield, 2015), cowritten with Matt Fricker and Carlos Colon; and *Targeting Terrorists: A License to Kill?* (Ashgate, 2008).

Sean Rupka is a Political Theorist and PhD Student at UNSW Canberra working on the impact of autonomous systems on contemporary warfare. His broader research interests include trauma and memory studies; the philosophy of history and technology; and themes related to postcolonial violence, particularly as they pertain to the legacies of intergenerational trauma and reconciliation.

Matthias Scheutz is a Professor of Computer and Cognitive Science in the Department of Computer Science at Tufts University and Senior Gordon Faculty Fellow in Tuft's School of Engineering. He earned a PhD in Philosophy from the University of Vienna in 1995 and a Joint PhD in Cognitive Science and Computer Science from Indiana University Bloomington in 1999. He has over 300 peer-reviewed publications on artificial intelligence, artificial life, agent-based computing, natural language processing, cognitive modeling, robotics, human-robot interaction, and foundations of cognitive science. His research interests include multi-scale agent-based models of social behavior and complex cognitive and affective autonomous robots with natural language and ethical reasoning capabilities for natural human-robot interaction. His lab page is at https://hrilab.tufts.edu.

Jason Scholz is the Chief Executive for the Trusted Autonomous Systems Defence Cooperative Research Centre, a not-for-profit company advancing industry-led, game-changing projects and activities for Defense and dual use with $50m Commonwealth funding and $51m Queensland Government funding.

Additionally, Dr. Scholz is a globally recognized research leader in cognitive psychology, decision aids, decision automation, and autonomy. He has produced over fifty refereed papers and patents related to trusted autonomous systems in defense. Dr. Scholz is an Innovation Professor at RMIT University and an Adjunct Professor at the University of New South Wales. A graduate of the Australian Institute of Company Directors, Dr. Scholz also possesses a PhD from the University of Adelaide.

Austin Wyatt is a Political Scientist and Research Associate at UNSW, Canberra. He obtained his PhD (2020), entitled "Exploring the Disruptive Impact of Lethal Autonomous Weapon System Diffusion in Southeast Asia," from the Australian Catholic University. Dr. Wyatt has previously been a New Colombo Plan Scholar and completed a research internship in 2016 at the Korea Advanced Institute of Science and Technology.

Dr. Wyatt's research focuses on autonomous weapons, with a particular emphasis on their disruptive effects in Asia. His latest published research includes "Charting Great Power Progress toward a Lethal Autonomous Weapon System Demonstration Point," in the journal *Defence Studies* 20 (1), 2020.

Introduction

An Effort to Balance the Lopsided Autonomous Weapons Debate

JAI GALLIOTT, DUNCAN MACINTOSH, AND JENS DAVID OHLIN

The question of whether new rules or regulations are required to govern, restrict, or even prohibit the use of autonomous weapon systems—defined by the United States as systems that, once activated, can select and engage targets without further intervention by a human operator or, in more hyperbolic terms, by the dysphemism "killer robots"—has preoccupied government actors, academics, and proponents of a global arms-control regime for the better part of a decade. Many civil-society groups claim that there is consistently growing momentum in support of a ban on lethal autonomous weapon systems, and frequently tout the number of (primarily second world) nations supporting their cause. However, to objective external observers, the way ahead appears elusive, as the debate lacks any kind of broad agreement, and there is a notable absence of great power support. Instead, the debate has become characterized by hyperbole aimed at capturing or alienating the public imagination.

Part of this issue is that the states responsible for steering the dialogue on autonomous weapon systems initially proceeded quite cautiously, recognizing that few understood what it was that some were seeking to outlaw with a preemptive ban. In the resulting vacuum of informed public opinion, nongovernmental advocacy groups shaped what has now become a very heavily one-sided debate.

Some of these nongovernment organizations (NGOs) have contended, on legal and moral grounds, that militaries should act as if somehow blind and immune to

Jai Galliott, Duncan MacIntosh, and Jens David Ohlin, *Introduction* In: *Lethal Autonomous Weapons.*
Edited by: Jai Galliott, Duncan MacIntosh and Jens David Ohlin, © Oxford University Press (2021).
DOI: 10.1093/oso/9780197546048.003.0001.

the progress of automation and artificial intelligence evident in other areas of society. As an example, Human Rights Watch has stated that:

> Killer robots—fully autonomous weapons that could select and engage targets without human intervention—could be developed within 20 to 30 years . . . Human Rights Watch and Harvard Law School's International Human Rights Clinic (IHRC) believe that such revolutionary weapons would not be consistent with international humanitarian law and would increase the risk of death or injury to civilians during armed conflict (IHRC 2012).

The Campaign to Stop Killer Robots (CSKR) has echoed this sentiment. The CSKR is a consortium of nongovernment interest groups whose supporters include over 1,000 experts in artificial intelligence, as well as science and technology luminaries such as Stephen Hawking, Elon Musk, Steve Wozniak, Noam Chomsky, Skype co-founder Jaan Tallinn, and Google DeepMind co-founder Demis Hassabis. The CSKR expresses their strident view of the "problem" of autonomous weapon systems on their website:

> Allowing life or death decisions to be made by machines crosses a fundamental moral line. Autonomous robots would lack human judgment and the ability to understand context. These qualities are necessary to make complex ethical choices on a dynamic battlefield, to distinguish adequately between soldiers and civilians, and to evaluate the proportionality of an attack. As a result, fully autonomous weapons would not meet the requirements of the laws of war. Replacing human troops with machines could make the decision to go to war easier, which would shift the burden of armed conflict further onto civilians. The use of fully autonomous weapons would create an accountability gap as there is no clarity on who would be legally responsible for a robot's actions: the commander, programmer, manufacturer, or robot itself? Without accountability, these parties would have less incentive to ensure robots did not endanger civilians and victims would be left unsatisfied that someone was punished for the harm they experienced. (Campaign to Stop Killer Robots 2018)

While we acknowledge some of the concerns raised by this view, the current discourse around lethal autonomous weapons systems has not admitted any shades of gray, despite the prevalence of mistaken assumptions about the role of human agents in the development of autonomous systems.

Furthermore, while fears about nonexistent sentient robots continue to stall debate and halt technological progress, one can see in the news that the world continues to struggle with real ethical and humanitarian problems in the use of existing weapons. A gun stolen from a police officer and used to kill, guns used for mass shootings, and vehicles used to mow down pedestrians—all undesirable acts that could have potentially been averted through the use of technology. In each case, there are potential applications of Artificial Intelligence (AI) that could help mitigate such problems. For example, "smart" firearms lock the firing pin until the weapon is presented with the correct fingerprint or RFID signal. At the same time, specific coding could be embedded in the guidance software in self-driving cars to inhibit the vehicle from striking civilians or entering a designated pedestrian area.

Additionally, it is unclear why AI and related technologies should not also be leveraged to prevent the bombing of a religious site, a guided-bomb strike on a train bridge as an unexpected passenger train passes over it, or a missile strike on a Red Cross facility. Simply because autonomous weapons are military weapons does not preclude their affirmative use to save lives. It does not seem unreasonable to question why weapons with advanced symbol recognition could not, for example, be embedded in autonomous systems to identify a symbol of the Red Cross and abort an ordered strike. Similarly, the location of protected sites of religious significance, schools, or hospitals might be programmed into weapons to constrain their actions. Nor does it not seem unreasonable to question why addressing the main concerns with autonomous systems cannot be ensconced in existing international weapons review standards.[1]

In this volume, we bring together some of the most prominent academics and academic-practitioners in the lethal autonomous weapons space and seek to return some balance to the debate. In this effort, we advocate a societal investment in hard conversations that tackle the ethics, morality, and law of these new digital technologies and understand the human role in their creation and operation.

This volume proceeds on the basis that we need to progress beyond framing the conversation as "AI will kill jobs" and the "robot apocalypse." The editors and contributors of this volume believe in a responsibility to tell more nuanced and somewhat more complicated stories than those that are conveyed by governments, NGOs, industry, and the news media in the hope of attaining one's fleeting attention. We also have a responsibility to ask better questions ourselves, to educate and inform stakeholders in our future in a fashion that is more positive and potentially beneficial than is envisioned the existing literature. Reshaping the discussion around this emerging military innovation requires a new line of thought and a willingness to move past the easy seduction of the killer robot discourse.

We propose a solution for those asking themselves the more critical questions: What is the history of this technology? Where did it come from? What are the vested interests? Who are its beneficiaries? What logics about the world is it normalizing? What is the broader context into which it fits? And, most importantly, with the tendency to demonize technology and overlook the role of its human creators, how can we ensure that we use and adapt our, already very robust, legal and ethical normative instruments and frameworks to regulate the role of human agents in the design, development, and deployment of lethal autonomous weapons?

Lethal Autonomous Weapons: Re-Examining the Law and Ethics of Robotic Warfare therefore focuses on exploring the moral and legal issues associated with the design, development, and deployment of lethal autonomous weapons. The volume collects its contributions around a four-section structure. In each section, the contributions look for new and innovative approaches to understanding the law and ethics of autonomous weapons systems.

The essays collected in the first section of this volume offer a limited defense of lethal autonomous weapons through a critical examination of the definitions, conceptions, and arguments typically employed in the debate. In the initial chapter, Duncan MacIntosh argues that it would be morally legitimate, even morally obligatory, to use autonomous weapons systems in many circumstances: for example, where pre-commitment is advantageous, or where diffusion of moral responsibility would be morally salutary. This approach is contra to those who think that, morally, there must always be full human control at the point of lethality. MacIntosh argues that what matters is not that weapons be under the control of humans but that they are under the control of morality, and that autonomous weapons systems could sometimes be indispensable to this goal. Next, Deane-Peter Baker highlights that the problematic assumptions utilized by those opposed to the employment of "contracted combatants" in many cases parallel or are the same as the problematic assumptions that are embedded in the arguments of those who oppose the employment of lethal autonomous weapons. Jai Galliott and Tim McFarland then move on to consider concerns about the retention of human control over the lethal use of force. While Galliott and McFarland accept the premise that human control is required, they dispute the, sometimes unstated, assertion that employing a weapon with a high level of autonomous capability means ceding to that weapon control over the use of force. Overall, Galliott and McFarland suggest that machine autonomy, by its very nature, represents a lawful form of meaningful human control. Jason Scholz and Jai Galliott complete this section by asserting that while autonomous systems are likely to be incapable of carrying out actions that could lead to the attribution of moral responsibility to them, at least in the near term, they can autonomously execute value decisions embedded in code and in their design, meaning that autonomous systems are able to perform actions of enhanced ethical and legal benefit. Scholz and Galliott advance the concept of a Minimally-Just AI (MinAI) for autonomous systems. MinAI systems would be capable of automatically recognizing protected symbols, persons, and places, tied to a data set, which in turn could be used by states to guide and quantify compliance requirements for autonomous weapons.

The second section contains reflections on the normative values implicit in international law and common ethical theories. Several of this section's essays are informed by empirical data ensuring that the rebalancing of the autonomous weapons debate is grounded in much-needed reality. Steve Barela and Avery Plaw utilize data on drone strikes to consider some of the complexities pertaining to distinguishing between combatants and noncombatants, and address how these types of concerns would weigh against hypothetical evidence of improved precision. To integrate and address these immense difficulties as mapped onto the autonomous weapons debate, they assess the value of transparency in the process of discrimination as a means of ensuring accurate assessment, both legally and ethically. Next, Matthias Scheutz and Bertram Malle provide insights into the public's perception of LAWs. They report the first results of an empirical study that asked when ordinary humans would find it acceptable for autonomous robots to use lethal force, in military contexts. In particular, they examined participants' moral expectations and judgments concerning a trolley-type scenario involving an autonomous robot that must decide whether to kill some humans to save others. In the following chapter, Natalia Jevglevskaja and Rain Livoja draw attention to the phenomenon by which proponents of *both* sides of the lethal autonomous weapons debate utilize humanitarian arguments in support of their agenda and arguments, often pointing to the lesser risk of harm to combatants and civilians alike. They examine examples of weapons with respect to which such contradictory appeals to humanity have occurred and offer some reflections on the same. Next, Jai Galliott examines the relevance of civilian principle sets to the development of a positive statement of ethical principles for the governance in military artificial intelligence, distilling a concise list of principles for potential consumption for international armed forces. Finally, joined by Bianca Baggiarini and Sean Rupka, Galliott then interrogates data from the world's largest study of military officers' attitudes toward autonomous systems and draws particular attention to how socio-ethical concerns and assumptions mediate an officer's willingness to work alongside autonomous systems and fully harness combat automation.

The third section contains reflections on the correctness of action tied to the use and deployment of autonomous systems. Donovan Phillips begins the section by considering the implications of the fact that new technologies will involve the humans who make decisions to take lives being utterly disconnected from the field of battle, and of the fact that wars may be fought more locally by automata, and how this impacts *jus ad bellum*. Recognizing that much of the lethal autonomous weapons debate has been focused on what might be called the "micro-perspective" of armed conflict, whether an autonomous robot is able to comply with the laws of armed conflict and the principles of just war theory's *jus in bello*, Alex Leveringhaus then draws attention to the often-neglected "macro-perspective" of war, concerned with the kind of conflicts in which autonomous systems are likely to be involved and the transformational potential of said weapons. Jens Ohlin then notes a conflict between what humans will know about the machines they interact with, and how they will be tempted to think and feel about these machines. Humans may know that the machines are making decisions on the basis of rigid algorithms. However, Ohlin observes that when humans interact with chess-playing computers, they must ignore this knowledge and ascribe human thinking processes to machines in order to strategize against them. Even though humans will know that the machines are deterministic mechanisms, Ohlin suggests that humans will experience feelings of gratitude and resentment toward allied and enemy machines, respectively. This factor must be considered in designing machines and in circumscribing the roles we expect them to play in their interaction with humans. In the final chapter of this section, Nicholas Evans considers several possible relations between AWSs and human cognitive aptitudes and deficiencies. Evans then explores the implications of each for who has responsibility for the actions of AWSs. For example, suppose AWSs and humans are roughly equivalent in aptitudes and deficiencies, with AWSs perhaps being less akratic due to having emotionality designed out of them, but still prone to mistakes of, say, perception, or of cognitive processing. Then responsibility for their actions would lie more with the command structure in which they operate since their aptitudes and deficiencies would be known, and their effects would be predictable, which would then place an obligation on commanders when planning AWS deployment. However, another possibility is that robots might have different aptitudes and deficiencies, ones quite alien from those possessed by humans, these meaning that there are trade-offs to deploying them in lieu of humans. This would tend to put more responsibility on the designers of the systems since human commanders could not be expected to be natural experts about how to compensate for these trade-offs.

The fourth section of the book details how technical and moral considerations should inform the design and technological development of autonomous weapons systems. Armin Krishnan first explores the parallels between biological weapons and autonomous systems, advocating enforced transparency in AI research and the development of international safety standards for all real-world applications of advanced AI because of the dual-use problem and because the dangers of unpredictable AI extend far beyond the military sphere. In the next chapter of this volume, Kate Devitt addresses the application of higher-order design principles based on epistemic models, such as virtue and Bayesian epistemologies, to the design of autonomous systems with varying degrees of human-in-the-loop. In the following chapter, Austin Wyatt and Jai Galliott engage directly with the question of how to effectively limit the disruptive potential of increasingly autonomous weapon systems through the application of a regional normative framework. Given the effectively stalled progress of the CCW-led process, this chapter calls for state and nonstate actors to take the initiative to develop technically focused guidelines for the development, transparent deployment, and safe de-escalation protocols for AWS at the regional level. Finally, Missy Cummings explains the difference between automated and autonomous systems before presenting a framework for conceptualizing the human-computer balance for future autonomous systems, both civilian and military. She then discusses specific technology and policy implications for weaponized autonomous systems.

NOTE

1. This argument is a derivative of the lead author's chapter where said moral-benefit argument is more fully developed and prosecuted: J. Scholz and Jai Galliott, "Military." In Oxford Handbook of Ethics of AI, edited by M. Dubber, F. Pasquale, and S. Das. New York: Oxford University Press, 2020.

PART I

The Case for Lethal Autonomous Weapons

1

Fire and Forget: A Moral Defense of the Use of Autonomous Weapons Systems in War and Peace

DUNCAN MACINTOSH

1.1: INTRODUCTION

While Autonomous Weapons Systems—AWS—have obvious military advantages, there are prima facie moral objections to using them. I have elsewhere argued (MacIntosh 2016) that there are similarities between the structure of law and morality on the one hand and of automata on the other, and that this plus the fact that automata can be designed to lack the biases and other failings of humans, require us to automate the administration and enforcement of law as much as possible.

But in this chapter, I want to argue more specifically (and contra Peter Asaro 2016; Christof Heyns 2013; Mary Ellen O'Connell 2014; and others) that there are many conditions where using AWSs would be appropriate not just rationally and strategically, but also morally.[1] This will occupy section I of this chapter. In section II, I deal with the objection that the use of robots is inherently wrong or violating of human dignity.[2]

1.2: SECTION I: OCCASIONS OF THE ETHICAL USE OF AUTONOMOUS FIRE-AND-FORGET WEAPONS

An AWS would be a "fire-and-forget" weapon, and some see such weapons as legally and morally problematic. For surely a human and human judgment should figure at every point in a weapon's operation, especially where it is about to have its lethal effect on a human. After all, as O'Connell (2014) argues, that is the last

Duncan MacIntosh, *Fire and Forget: A Moral Defense of the Use of Autonomous Weapons Systems in War and Peace*
In: *Lethal Autonomous Weapons.* Edited by: Jai Galliott, Duncan MacIntosh and Jens David Ohlin, © Oxford University Press (2021). DOI: 10.1093/oso/9780197546048.003.0002

reconsideration moment, and arguably to fail to have a human doing the deciding at that point is to abdicate moral and legal responsibility for the kill. (Think of the final phone call to the governor to see if the governor will stay an execution.) Asaro (2016) argues that it is part of law, including International Humanitarian Law, to respect public morality even if it has not yet been encoded into law, and that part of such morality is the expectation that there be meaningful human control of weapons systems, so that this requirement should be formally encoded into law. In addition to there being a public morality requirement of meaningful human control, Asaro suspects that the dignity of persons liable to being killed likewise requires that their death, if they are to die, be brought about by a human, not a robot.

The positions of O'Connell and Asaro have an initial plausibility, but they have not been argued for in-depth; it is unclear what does or could premise them, and it is doubtful, I think, whether they will withstand examination.[3] For example, I think it will prove false that there must always be meaningful human control in the infliction of death. For, given a choice between control by a morally bad human who would kill someone undeserving of being killed and a morally good robot who would kill only someone deserving of being killed, we would pick the good robot. What matters is not that there be meaningful human control, but that there be meaningful moral control, that is, that what happens be under the control of morality, that it be the right thing to happen. And similar factors complicate the dignity issue—what dignity is, what sort of agent best implements dignity, and when the importance of dignity is overridden as a factor, all come into play. So, let us investigate more closely.

Clarity requires breaking this issue down into three sub-issues. When an autonomous weapon (an AWS) has followed its program and is now poised to kill:

i) Should there always be a reconsideration of its decision at least in the sense of revisiting whether the weapon should be allowed to kill?
ii) In a given case, should there be reconsideration in the sense of reversing the decision to kill?
iii) And if there is to be either or both, what sort of agent should do the reconsidering, the AWS or a human being?

It might be thought that there should always be reconsideration by a human in at least the revisiting sense, if not necessarily the reversing. For what could it cost? And it might save us from making a moral mistake.

But there are several situations where reconsideration would be inappropriate. In what follows, I assume that the agent deciding whether to use a fire-and-forget weapon is a rational agent with all-things-considered morally approvable goals seeking therefore to maximize moral expected utility. That is, in choosing among actions, she is disposed to do that action which makes as high as possible the sum of the products of the moral desirability of possible outcomes of actions and the probability of those outcomes obtaining given the doing of the various actions available. She will have considered the likelihood of the weapon's having morally good effects given its design and proposed circumstance of use. If the context is a war context, she would bear in mind whether the use of the weapon is likely to respect such things as International Humanitarian Law and the Laws of War. So she would be seeking to respect the principles of distinctness, necessity, and proportionality. Distinctness is the principle that combatants should be targeted before civilians; necessity, the principle that violence should be used only to attain important military objectives; and proportionality is the principle that the violence used to attain the objective should not be out of proportion to the value of the objective. More generally, I shall assume that the person considering using an AWS would bear in mind whether the weapon can be deployed in such a way as to respect the distinction between those morally liable to being harmed (that is, those whom it is morally permissible or obligatory to harm) and those who are to be protected from harm. (Perhaps the weapon is able to make this distinction, and to follow instructions to respect it. Failing that, perhaps the weapon's use can be restricted to situations where only those morally liable to harm are likely to be targeted.) The agent deciding whether to use the weapon would proceed on the best information available at the time of considering its activation.

Among the situations in which activating a fire-and-forget weapon by such an agent would be rationally and morally legitimate would be the following.

1.2.1: Planning Scenarios

One initially best guesses that it is at the moment of firing the weapon (e.g., activating the robot) that one has greatest informational and moral clarity about what needs to be done, estimating that to reconsider would be to open oneself to fog of war confusion, or to temptations one judges at the time of weapon activation that it would be best to resist at the moment of possible recall. So one forms the plan to activate the weapon and lets it do its job, then follows through on the plan by activating and then not recalling the weapon, even as one faces temptations to reconsider, reminding one's self that one was probably earlier better placed to work out how best to proceed back when one formed the plan.[4]

1.2.2: Short-Term versus Long-Term Consequences Cases

One initially best judges that one must not reconsider if one is to attain the desired effect of the weapon. Think of the decision to bomb Nagasaki and Hiroshima in hopes of saving, by means of the deterrent effect of the bombing, more lives than those lost from the bombing, this in spite of the horror that must be felt at the immediate prospect of the bombing.[5] Here one should not radio the planes and call off the mission.

1.2.3: Resolute Choice Cases

One expects moral benefit to accrue not from allowing the weapon to finish its task, but from the consequence of committing to its un-reconsidered use should the enemy not meet some demand.[6] The consequence sought will be available only if one can be predicted not to reconsider; and refraining from reconsidering is made rational by the initial expected benefit and so rationality of committing not to reconsider. Here, if the enemy does not oblige, one activates the weapon and lets it finish.

It may be confusing what distinguishes these first three rationales. Here is the distinction: the reason one does not reconsider in the case of the first rationale is because one assumes one knew best what to do when forming the plan that required non-reconsidering; in the case of the second because one sees that the long-term consequences of not reconsidering exceed those of reconsidering; and in the case of the third because non-reconsideration expresses a strategy for making choices whose adoption was expected to have one do better, even if following through on it would not, and morality and rationality require one to make the choices dictated by the best strategy—one decides the appropriateness of actions by the advantages of the strategies that dictate them, not by the advantages of the actions themselves. Otherwise, one could not have the advantages of strategies.

This last rationale is widely contested. After all, since the point of the strategy was, say, deterrence, and deterrence has failed so that one must now fulfill a threat one never really wanted to have to fulfill, why still act from a strategy one now knows was a failure? To preserve one's credibility in later threat scenarios? But suppose there will be none, as is likely in the case of, for example, the threat of nuclear apocalypse. Then again, why fulfill the threat? By way of addressing this, I have (elsewhere) favored a variant on the foregoing rationale: in adopting a strategy, one changes in what it is that one sees as the desired outcome of actions, and then one refrains from reconsidering because refraining now best expresses one's new desires—one has come to care more about implementing the strategy, or about the expected outcome of implementing it, than about what first motivated one to adopt the strategy. So one does not experience acting on the strategy as going against what one cares about.[7]

1.2.4: Un-Reconsiderable Weapons Cases

One's weapon is such that, while deploying it would be expected to maximize moral utility, reconsidering it at its point of lethality would be impossible so that, if a condition on the permissible use of the weapon were to require reconsideration at that point, one could never use the weapon. (For example, one cannot stop a bullet at the skin and rethink whether to let it penetrate, so one would have to never use a gun.) A variant on this case would be the case of a weapon that could be made able to be monitored and recalled as it engages in its mission, but giving it this feature would put it at risk of being hacked and used for evil. For to recall the device would require that it be in touch by, say, radio, and so liable to being communicated with by the enemy. Again, if the mission has high moral expected utility as it stands, one would not want to lower this by converting the weapon into something recallable and therefore able to be perverted. (This point has been made by many authors.)

By hypothesis, being disposed to reconsider in the cases of the first four rationales would have lower moral expected utility than not. And so being disposed to reconsider would nullify any advantage the weapon afforded. No, in these situations, one should deliberate as long as is needed to make an informed decision given the pressure of time. Then one should activate the weapon.

Of course, in all those scenarios one could discover partway through that the facts are not what one first thought, so that the payoffs of activating and not reconsidering are different. This might mean that one would learn it was a mistake to activate the weapon, and should now reconsider and perhaps abort. So, of course, it can be morally and rationally obligatory to stay sensitive to these possibilities. This might seem to be a moot point in the fourth case since there, recalling the weapon is impossible. If the weapon will take a long time to impact, however, it might become rational and morally obligatory to warn the target if one has a communication signal that can travel faster than the speed of one's kinetic weapon.

It is a subtle matter which possibilities are morally and rationally relevant to deciding to recall a weapon. Suppose one rationally commits to using a weapon and also to not reconsidering even though one knows at the time of commitment that one's compassion would tempt one to call it off later. Since this was considered at the outset, it would not be appropriate to reconsider on that ground just before the weapon's moment of lethality.

Now suppose instead that it was predictable that there would be a certain level of horror from use of the weapon, but one then discovers that the horror will be much worse, for example, that many more people will die than one had predicted. That, of course, would be a basis for reconsideration.

But several philosophers, including Martha Nussbaum, in effect, think as follows (Nussbaum 1993, especially pp. 83–92): every action is both a consequence of a decision taking into account moral factors and a learning moment where one may get new information about moral factors. Perhaps one forms a plan to kill someone, thinking justice requires this, then finds one cannot face actually doing the deed, and decides that justice requires something different, mercy perhaps, as Nussbaum suggests—one comes to find the originally intended deed more horrible, not because it will involve more deaths than one thought, but because one has come to think that any death is more horrible than one first thought. Surely putting an autonomous robot in the loop here would deprive one of the possibilities of new moral learning?

It is true that some actions can be learning occasions, and either we should not automate those actions so extremely as to make the weapons unrecallable, or we should figure out how to have our automata likewise learn from the experience and adjust their behaviors accordingly, perhaps self-aborting.

But some actions can reasonably be expected not to be moral learning occasions. In these cases, we have evidence of there being no need to build in the possibility of moral experiencing and reconsideration. Perhaps one already knows the horror of killing someone, for example. (There is, of course, always the logical possibility that the situation is morally new. But that is different from having actual evidence in advance that the situation is new, and the mere possibility by itself is no reason to forego the benefits of a disposition to non-reconsideration. Indeed, if that *were* a reason, one could never act, for upon making any decision one would have to reconsider in light of the mere logical possibility that one's decision was wrong.)

Moreover, there are other ways to get a moral learning experience about a certain kind of action or its consequence than by building a moment of possible experience and reconsideration into the action. For example, one could reflect after the fact, survey the scene, do interviews with witnesses and relatives of those affected, study film of the event, and so on, in this way getting the originally expected benefit of the weapon, but also gaining new information for future decisions. This would be appropriate where one calculates that there would be greater overall moral benefit to using the weapon in this case and then revisiting the ethics of the matter, rather than the other way around, because one calculates that one is at risk of being excessively squeamish until the mission is over and that this would prevent one from doing a morally required thing.

There is also the possibility that not only will one not expect to get more morally relevant experience from the event, but one may expect to be harmed in one's moral perspective by it.

1.2.5: Protection of One's Moral Self Cases

Suppose there simply must be some people killed to save many people—there is no question that this is ethically required. But suppose too that if a human were to do the killing, they would be left traumatized in a way that would constitute a moral harm to her. For example, she would have crippling PTSD and a tendency toward suicidality. Or perhaps the experience would leave her coarsened in a way, making her more likely to do evil in the future. In either eventuation, it would then be harder down the road for her to fulfill her moral duties to others and to herself. Here, it would be morally and rationally better that an AWS do the killing—the morally hard but necessary task gets done, but the agent has her moral agency protected. Indeed, even now there are situations where, while there is a human in the decision loop, the role the human is playing is defined so algorithmically that she has no real decision-making power. Her role could be played by a machine. And yet her presence in the role means that she will have the guilt of making hard choices resulting in deaths, deaths that will be a burden on her conscience even where they are the result of the right choices. So, again, why not just spare her conscience and take her out of the loop?

It is worth noting that there are a number of ways of getting her out of the loop, and a number of degrees to which she could be out. She could make the decision that someone will have to die, but a machine might implement the decision for her. This would be her being out of the loop by means of delegating implementation of her decision to an AWS. An even greater degree of removal from the loop might be where a human delegates the very decision of whether someone has to die to a machine, one with a program so sophisticated that it is in effect a morally autonomous agent. Here the hope would be that the machine can make the morally hard choices, and that it will make morally right choices, but that it will not have the pangs of conscience that would be so unbearable for a human being.

There is already a precedent for this in military contexts where a commander delegates decisions about life and death to an autonomous human with his own detailed criteria for when to kill, so that the commander cannot really say in advance who is going to be killed, how, or when. This is routine in military practice and part of the chain of command and the delegation of responsibility to those most appropriately bearing it—detailed decisions implementing larger strategic policy have to be left to those closest to battle.

Some people might see this as a form of immorality. Is it really OK for a commander to have a less troubled conscience by virtue of having delegated morally difficult decisions to a subordinate? But I think this can be defended, not only on grounds of this being militarily necessary—there really is no better way of warfighting—but on grounds, again, of distributing the costs of conscience: commanders need to make decisions that will result in loss of lives over and over again, and can only escape moral fatigue if they do not have to further make the detailed decisions about whom exactly to kill and when.

And if these decisions are delegated to a morally discerning but morally conscienceless machine, we have the additional virtue that the moral offloading—the offloading of morally difficult decisions—is done onto a device that will not be morally harmed by the decisions it must make.[8,9]

1.2.6: Morally Required Diffusion of Responsibility Cases

Relatedly, there are cases of a firing squad sort where many people are involved in performing the execution so that there is ambiguity about who had the fatal effect in order to spare the conscience of each squad member. But again, this requires that one not avail one's self of opportunities to recall the weapon. Translated to robotic warfare, imagine the squad is a group of drone operators all of whom launch their individual AWS drones at a target, and who, if given the means to monitor the progress of their drone and the authority to recall it if they judged this for the best, could figure out pre-impact whose drone is most likely to be the fatal one. This might be better not found out, for it may result in a regress of yank-backs, each operator recalling his drone as it is discovered to be the one most likely to be fatal, with the job left undone; or it getting done by the last person who clues in too late, him then facing the guilt alone; or it getting done by one of the operators deliberately continuing even knowing his will be the fatal drone, but who then, again, must face the crisis of conscience alone.

1.2.7: Morally Better for Being Comparatively Random and Non-Deliberate Killing Cases

These are cases where the killing would be less morally problematic the more random and free of deliberate intention each aspect of the killing was. What is morally worse, throwing a grenade into a room of a small number of people who must be stopped to save a large number of people; or moving around the room at super speed with a sack full of shrapnel, pushing pieces of shrapnel into people's bodies—you have to use all the pieces to stop everyone, but the pieces are of different sizes, some so large that using them will kill; others only maim; yet others, only temporarily injure, and you have to decide which piece goes into which person. The effect is the same—it is as if a blast kills some, maims others, and leaves yet others only temporarily harmed. But the second method is morally worse. Better to delegate to an AWS. Sometimes, of course, the circumstance might permit the use of a very stupid machine, for example, in the case of an enclosed space, literally a hand grenade, which will produce a blast whose effect on a given person is determined by what is in effect a lottery. But perhaps a similar effect needs to be attained over a large and open area, and, given limited information about the targets and the urgency of the task, the effect is best achieved by using an AWS that will attack targets of opportunity with grenade-like weapons. Here it is the delegating to an AWS, plus the very randomness of the method of grenade, plus the fact that only one morally possibly questionable decision need be made in using the weapon—the decision to delegate—that makes it a morally less bad event. Robots can randomize and so democratize violence, and so make it less bad, less inhumane, less monstrous, less evil.

Of course, other times the reverse judgment would hold. In the preceding examples, I in effect assumed everyone in the room, or in the larger field, was morally equal as a target with no one more or less properly morally liable to be killed, so that, if one chose person by person whom to kill, one would choose on morally arbitrary and therefore problematic, morally agonizing grounds. But in a variant case, imagine one knows this man is a father; that man, a psychopath; this other man, unlikely to harm anyone in the future. Here, careful individual targeting decisions are called for—you definitely kill the psychopath, but harm the others in lesser ways just to get them out of the way.

1.2.8: Doomsday Machine Cases

Sometimes what is called for is precisely a weapon that cannot be recalled—this would be its great virtue. The weapons in mutually assured destruction are like this—they will activate on provocation no matter what, and so are the supreme deterrent. This reduces to the case of someone's being morally and rationally required to be resolute in fulfilling a morally and rationally recommended threat (item 1.2.3, above) if we see the resolute agent as a human implementation of a Doomsday Machine. And if we doubted the rationality or morality of a free agent fulfilling a threat morally maximizing to make but not to keep, arguably we could use the automation of the keeping of the threat to ensure its credibility; for arguably it can be rational and moral to arrange the doing of things one could not rationally or morally do one's self. (This is not case in 1.2.4, above, where we use an unrecallable weapon because it is the only weapon we have and we must use some weapon or other. In the present case, only an unrecallable weapon can work, because of its effectiveness in threatening.)

1.2.9: Permissible Threats of Impermissible Harms Cases

These are related to the former cases. Imagine there is a weapon with such horrible and indiscriminate power that it could not be actually used in ways compatible with International Humanitarian Law and the Laws of War, which require that weapons use respect distinctness, necessity and proportionality, and must not render large regions of the planet uninhabitable for long periods. Even given this, arguably the *threat* of its use would be permissible both morally and by the foregoing measures provided issuing the threat was likely to have very good effects, and provided the very issuing of the threat makes the necessity of following through fantastically unlikely. The weapon's use would be so horrible that the threat of its use is almost certain to deter the behavior against which it is a threat. But even if this is a good argument for making such a threat, arguably the threat is permissible only if the weapon is extremely unlikely to be accidentally activated, used corruptly, or misused through human error. And it could be that, given the complexity of the information that would need to be processed to decide whether a given situation was the one for which the weapon was designed, given the speed with which the decision would have to be made, and given the potential for the weapon to be abused were it under human control, it ought instead to be put under the control of an enormously sophisticated artificial intelligence.

Obviously, the real-world case of nuclear weapons is apposite here. Jules Zacher (2016) has suggested that such weapons cannot be used in ways respecting the strictures of international humanitarian law and the law of war, not even if their control is deputized to an AWS. For again, their actual use would be too monstrous. But I suggest it may yet be able to be right to threaten to do something it would be wrong to actually do, a famous paradox of deterrence identified by Gregory Kavka (1978). Arguably we have been living in this scenario for seventy years: most people think that massive nuclear retaliation against attack would be immoral. But many think the threat of it has saved the world from further world wars, and is therefore morally defensible.

Let us move on. We have been discussing situations where one best guesses in advance that certain kinds of reconsideration would be inappropriate. But now to the question of what should do the deciding at the final possible moment of reconsideration when it can be expected that reconsideration in either of our two senses *is* appropriate. Let us suppose we have a case where there should be continual reconsideration sensitive to certain factors. Surely this should be done by a human? But I suggest it matters less what makes the call, more that it be the right call. And because of all the usual advantages of robots—their speed, inexhaustibility, etc.—we may want the call to be made by a robot, but one able to detect changes in the moral situation and to adjust its behaviors accordingly.

1.2.10: Robot Training Cases

This suggests yet another sort of situation where it would be preferable to have humans out of the loop. Suppose we are trying to train a robot to make better moral decisions, and the press of events has forced us to beta test it in live battle. The expected moral utility of letting the robot learn may exceed that of affording an opportunity for a human to acquire or express a scruple by putting the human in a reconsideration loop. For once the robot learns to make good moral decisions we can replicate its moral circuit in other robots, with the result of having better moral decisions made in many future contexts.

Here are some further cases and rationales for using autonomous weapons systems.

1.2.11: Precision in Killing Cases

Sometimes, due to the situations the device is to be used in, or due to the advanced design of the device, an AWS may provide greater precision in respecting the distinction between those morally liable and not liable to being killed—something that would be put at risk by the reconsideration of a clumsy human operator (Arkin 2013). An example of the former would be a device tasked to kill anything in a region known to contain only enemies who need killing—there are no civilians in the region who stand at risk, and none of the enemies in the region deserve to survive. Here the AWS might be more thorough than a human. Think of an AWS defending an aircraft carrier, tasked with shooting anything out of the sky that shows up on radar, prioritizing things large in size, moving at great speed, that are very close, and that do not self-identify with a civilian transponder response when queried. Nothing needs to be over an aircraft carrier and anything there is an enemy. An example of the second—of an AWS being more precise than a human by virtue of its design—might be where the AWS is better at detecting the enemy than a human, for example, by means of metal detectors able to tell who is carrying a weapon and is, therefore, a genuine threat. Again, only those needing killing get killed.

1.2.12: Speed and Efficiency Cases

Use of an AWS may be justified by its being vastly more efficient in a way that, again, would be jeopardized by less-efficient human intervention (Arkin 2013)—if the weapon had to pause while the operator approved each proposed action, the machine would have to go more slowly, and fewer of the bad people would be killed, fewer of the good people, protected.

The foregoing, then, are cases where we would not want a human operator "in the loop," that is, a human playing the role of giving final approval to each machine decision to kill, so that the machine will not kill unless authorized by a human in each kill. This would merely result in morally inferior outcomes. Neither would we want a human "on the loop," where the machine will kill unless vetoed, but where the machine's killing process is slowed down to give a human operator a moment to decide whether to veto. For again, we would have morally inferior outcomes.

Other cases involve factors often used in arguments against AWSs.

1.3: SECTION II: OBJECTIONS FROM THE SUPPOSED INDIGNITY OF ROBOT-INFLICTED DEATH

Some think death by robot is inherently worse than death by human hand, that it is somehow inherently more bad, wrong, undignified, or fails in a special way to respect the rights of persons—it is wrong in itself, *mala in se*, as the phrase used by Wendell Wallach (2013) in this connection has it.

I doubt this, but even if it were true, that would not decide the matter. For something can be bad in itself without being such that it should never be incurred or inflicted. Pain is always bad in and of itself. But that does not mean you should never incur it—maybe you must grab a hot metal doorknob to escape a burning building, and that will hurt, but you should still do it. Maybe you will have to inflict a painful injury on someone to protect yourself in self-defense, but that does not mean you must not do it. Similarly, even if death by robot were an inherent wrong, that does not mean you should never inflict or be subject to it. For sometimes it is the lesser evil, or is the means to a good thing outweighing the inherent badness of the means.

Here are cases that show either that death by robot is not inherently problematic, or that, even if it is, it could still be morally called for. One guide is how people would answer certain questions.

Dignity Case 1: Saving Your Village by Robotically Killing Your Enemy

> Your village is about to be over-run by ISIL; your only defense is the auto-sentry. Surely you would want to activate it? And surely this would be right, even if it metes out undignified robot death to your attackers?

Dignity Case 2: Killing Yourself by Robot to Save Yourself from A Worse Death from a Man

> You are about to be captured and killed; you have the choice of a quick death by a Western robot (a suicide machine available when the battle is lost and you face capture), or slow beheading by a Jihadist. Surely you would prefer death by robot? (It will follow your command to kill you where you could not make yourself kill yourself. Or it might be pre-programmed to be able to consider all factors and enabled to decide to kill you quickly and painlessly should it detect that all hope is lost). A person might prefer death by the AWS robot for any of several reasons. One is that an AWS may afford a greater dignity to the person to be killed precisely by virtue of its isolation from human control. In some cases, it seems worse to die at human than at robot hands. For if it is a human who is killing you, you might experience not only the horror of your pending death, but also anguish at the fact that, even though they could take pity on you and spare you, they will not—they are immune to your pleading and suffering. I can imagine this being an additional harm. But with a machine, one realizes there is nothing personal about it, there is no point in struggle or pleading, there is no one in whose gaze you are seen with contempt or as being unworthy of mercy. It is more like facing death by geological forces in a natural disaster, and more bearable for that fact. Other cases might go the other way, of course. I might want to be killed gently, carefully and painlessly by a loving spouse trying to give me a good death, preferring this to death by impersonal euthanasia machine.

If you have trouble accepting that robot-inflicted death can be OK, think about robot-conferred benefits and then ask why, if these are OK, their opposite cannot be. Would you insist on benefits being conferred to you by a human rather than a robot? Suppose you can die of thirst or drink from a palette of water bottles parachuted to you by a supply drone programmed to provide drink to those in the hottest part of the desert. You would take the drink, not scrupling about there being any possible indignity in being targeted for help by a machine. Why should it be any different when it comes to being harmed? Perhaps you want the right to try to talk your way out of whatever supposed justice the machine is to impose upon you. Well, a suitably programmed machine might give you a listen, or set you aside for further human consideration; or it might just kill you. And in these respects, matters are no different than if you faced a human killer.

And anyway, the person being killed is not the only person whose value or dignity is in play. There is also what would give dignity to that person's victims, and to anyone who must be involved in a person's killing.

Dignity Case 3: Robotic Avenging of the Dignity of a Victim

> Maybe the dignity of the victim of a killer (or of the victim's family) requires the killer's death, and the only way to get the killer is by robot.

Dignity Case 4: Robotic Killing to Save the Dignity of a Human Executioner

> Maybe those who inflict monstrosity forego any rights to dignified human-inflicted death (if that is in fact especially dignified), either because denying them this is a fit penalty, or because of the moral and psychological cost, and perhaps the indignity, that would have to be borne by a decent person in executing an indecent person. Better a robot death, so no human executioners have to soil their hands. And note for whom we have of late been reserving robotic death, as in automated drone killing, or death by indiscriminate weapon, e.g., a non-smart bomb, namely, people who would inflict automated or indiscriminate killing on us (e.g., by a bomb in a café), terrorists whose modus operandi is to select us randomly for death, rather than by means of specific proper liability to death.

Moreover, dignity is a luxury. And sometimes luxury must yield to factors of greater exigency.[10]

Some of this, of course, is separate from what people perceive as being required by dignity, and from how important they think dignity is; and if we are trying to win not just the war but also the peace, maybe we will do better if we respect a culture's conception of dignity in how we fight its people; and this may, as a purely practical matter, require us not to inflict death robotically.

This might even rise to the level of principle if there is a moral imperative to respect the spiritual opinions even of wrong-headed adversaries, an imperative not to unnecessarily trample on those opinions. Maybe we even have a moral duty to take some personal risks in this regard, and so to eschew the personal safety that use of robots would afford.[11]

1.4: CONCLUSION

Summing up my argument, it appears that it is false that it is always best for a human decision to be proximal to the application of lethal force. Instead, sometimes remoteness in distance and time, remoteness from information, and remoteness from the factors that would result in specious reconsideration, should rule the day.

It is not true that fire-and-forget weapons are evil for not having a human at the final point of infliction of harm. They are problematic only if they inflict a harm that proper reconsideration would have demanded not be inflicted. But one can guesstimate at the start whether a reconsideration would be appropriate. And if one's best guess is that it would not be appropriate, then one's best guess can rightly be that one should activate the fire-and-forget weapon. At that point, the difference between a weapon that impacts seconds after the initial decision to use it, and a weapon that impacts hours, days, or years after, is merely one of irrelevant degree. In fact, this suggests yet another pretext for the use of AWS, namely, its being the only way to cover off the requirements of infrastructure protection. Here is a case, which I present as a kind of coda.

1.5: CODA

We are low on manpower and deputizing to an AWS is the only way of protecting a remote power installation. Here we in effect use an AWS as a landmine. And I would call this a Justifiable Landmines Case, even though landmines are often cited as a counterexample to the ways of thinking defended in this chapter. But the problem with landmines is not that they do not have a human running the final part of their action, but that they are precisely devices reconsideration of whose use becomes appropriate at the very least at the cessation of hostilities, and perhaps before. The mistake is deploying them without a deactivation point or plan even though it is predictable that this will be morally required. But there is no mistake in having them be fire-and-forget before then. Especially not if they are either well-designed only to harm the enemy, or their situation makes it a virtual certitude that the only people whom they could ever harm is the enemy (e.g., because only the enemy would have occasion to approach the minefield without the disarm code during a given period). Landmines would be morally acceptable weapons if they biodegraded into something harmless, for example, or if it was prearranged for them to be able to be deactivated and harvested at the end of the conflict.

NOTES

1. For helpful discussion, my thanks to a philosophy colloquium audience at Dalhousie University, and to the students in my classes at Dalhousie University and at guest lectures I gave at St. Mary's University. For useful conversation thanks to Sheldon Wein, Greg Scherkoske, Darren Abramson, Jai Galliott, Max Dysart, and L.W. Thanks also to Claire Finkelstein and other participants at the conference, The Ethics of Autonomous Weapons Systems, sponsored by the Center for Ethics and the Rule of Law at the University of Pennsylvania Law School in November 2014. This chapter is part of a longer paper originally prepared for that event.
2. In a companion paper (MacIntosh Unpublished (b)) I moot the additional objections that AWS will destabilize democracy, make killing too easy, and make war fighting unfair.
3. Thanks to Robert Ramey for conversation on the points in this sentence.
4. On this explanation of the rationality of forming and keeping to plans, see Bratman 1987.
5. I do not mean to take a stand on what was the actual rationale for using The Bomb in those cases. I have stated what was for a long time the received rationale, but it has since been contested, many arguing that its real purpose was to intimidate the Russians in The Cold War that was to follow. Of course, this might still mean there were consequentialist arguments in its favor, just not the consequences of inducing the Japanese to surrender.
6. The classic treatment of this rationale is given by David Gauthier in his defense of the rationality of so-called constrained maximization, and of forming and fulfilling threats it maximizes to form but not to fulfill. See Gauthier 1984 and Gauthier 1986, Chapters I, V, and VI.
7. For details on this proposal and its difference from Gauthier's, see MacIntosh 2013.

8. It is, of course, logically possible for a commander to abuse such chains of command. For example, arguably commanders do not escape moral blame if they deliberately delegate authority to someone whom they knows is likely to abuse that authority and commit an atrocity, even if the committing of an atrocity at this point in an armed conflict might be militarily convenient (if not fully justifiable by the criterion of proportionality). Likewise, for the delegating of decisions to machines that are, say, highly unpredictable due to their state of design, for example. See Crootof 2016, especially pp. 58–62. But commanders might yet perfectly well delegate the doing of great violence, provided it is militarily necessary and proportionate; and they might be morally permitted to delegate this to a person who might lose their mind and do something too extreme, or to a machine whose design or design flaw might have a similar consequence, provided the commander thinks the odds of these very bad things happening are very small relative to the moral gain to be had should things go as planned. The expected moral utility of engaging in risky delegation might morally justify the delegating.
9. On the use of delegation to a machine in order to save a person's conscience, especially as this might be useful as a way of preventing in the armed forces those forms of post-traumatic stress injuries that are really moral injuries or injuries to the spirit, see MacIntosh Unpublished (a).
10. For some further, somewhat different replies to the dignity objection to the use of AWSs, see Lin 2015 and Pop 2018.
11. For more on these last two points, see MacIntosh (Unpublished (b)).

WORKS CITED

Arkin, Ronald. 2013. "Lethal Autonomous Systems and the Plight of the Non-Combatant." *AISB Quarterly* 137: pp. 1–9.

Asaro, Peter. 2016. "Jus nascendi, Robotic Weapons and the Martens Clause." In *Robot Law*, edited by Ryan Calo, Michael Froomkin, and Ian Kerr, pp. 367–386. Cheltenham, UK: Edward Elgar Publishing.

Crootof, Rebecca. 2016. "A Meaningful Floor For 'Meaningful Human Control.'" *Temple International and Comparative Law Journal* 30 (1): pp. 53–62.

Gauthier, David. 1984. "Deterrence, Maximization, and Rationality." *Ethics* 94 (3): pp. 474–495.

Gauthier, David. 1986. *Morals by Agreement.* Oxford: Clarendon Press.

Heyns, Christof. 2013. "Report of the Special Rapporteur on Extrajudicial, Summary or Arbitrary Executions." Human Rights Council. *Twenty-third session,* Agenda item 3 Promotion and protection of all human rights, civil, political, economic, social and cultural rights, including the right to development.

Kavka, Gregory. 1978. "Some Paradoxes of Deterrence." *The Journal of Philosophy* 75 (6): pp. 285–302.

Lin, Patrick. 2015. "The Right to Life and the Martens Clause." *Convention on Certain Conventional Weapons (CCW) meeting of experts on lethal autonomous weapons systems (LAWS).* Geneva: United Nations. April 13–17, 2015.

MacIntosh, Duncan. 2013. "Assuring, Threatening, a Fully Maximizing Theory of Practical Rationality, and the Practical Duties of Agents." *Ethics* 123 (4): pp. 625–656.

MacIntosh, Duncan. 2016. "Autonomous Weapons and the Nature of Law and Morality: How Rule-of-Law-Values Require Automation of the Rule of Law." In the symposium 'Autonomous Legal Reasoning? Legal and Ethical Issues in the Technologies of Conflict.' *Temple International and Comparative Law Journal* 30 (1): pp. 99–117.

MacIntosh, Duncan. Unpublished (a). "PTSD Weaponized: A Theory of Moral Injury." Mooted at *Preventing and Treating the Invisible Wounds of War: Combat Trauma and Psychological Injury*. Philadelphia: University of Pennsylvania. December 3–5, 2015.

MacIntosh, Duncan. Unpublished (b). *Autonomous Weapons and the Proper Character of War and Conflict (Or: Three Objections to Autonomous Weapons Mooted—They'll Destabilize Democracy, They'll Make Killing Too Easy, They'll Make War Fighting Unfair*. Unpublished Manuscript. 2017. Halifax: Dalhousie University.

Nussbaum, Martha. 1993. "Equity and Mercy." *Philosophy and Public Affairs* 22 (2): pp. 83–125.

O'Connell, Mary Ellen. 2014. "Banning Autonomous Killing—The Legal and Ethical Requirement That Humans Make Near-Time Lethal Decisions." In *The American Way of Bombing: Changing Ethical and Legal Norms From Flying Fortresses to Drones*, edited by Matthew Evangelista, and Henry Shue, pp. 224–235, 293–298. Ithaca, NY: Cornell University Press.

Pop, Adriadna. 2018. "Autonomous Weapon Systems: A Threat To Human Dignity?," HumanitarianLawandPolicy(lastaccessedApril19,2018).http://blogs.icrc.org/law-and-policy/2018/04/10/autonomous-weapon-systems-a-threat-to-human-dignity/

Wallach, Wendell. 2013. "Terminating the Terminator: What to Do About Autonomous Weapons." *Science Progress: Where Science, Technology and Policy Meet*. January 29. http://scienceprogress.org/2013/01/terminating-the-terminator-what-to-do-about-autonomous-weapons/

Zacher, Jules. *Automated Weapons Systems and the Launch of the US Nuclear Arsenal: Can the Arsenal Be Made Legitimate?*. Manuscript. 2016. Philadelphia: University of Pennsylvania. https://www.law.upenn.edu/live/files/5443-zacher-arms-control-treaties-are-a-sham.pdf

2

The Robot Dogs of War

DEANE-PETER BAKER

2.1: INTRODUCTION

Much of the debate over the ethics of lethal autonomous weapons is focused on the issues of reliability, control, accountability, and dignity. There are strong, but hitherto unexplored, parallels in this regard with the literature on the ethics of employing mercenaries, or private contractors—the so-called 'dogs of war'—that emerged after the private military industry became prominent in the aftermath of the 2003 invasion of Iraq. In this chapter, I explore these parallels.

As a mechanism to draw out the common themes and problems in the scholarship addressing both lethal autonomous weapons and the 'dogs of war,' I begin with a consideration of the actual dogs of war, the military working dogs employed by units such as Australia's Special Air Service Regiment and the US Navy SEALs. I show that in all three cases the concerns over reliability, control, accountability, and appropriate motivation either do not stand up to scrutiny, or else turn out to be dependent on contingent factors, rather than being intrinsically ethically problematic.

2.2: DOGS AT WAR

Animals have also long been (to use a term currently in vogue) 'weaponized.' The horses ridden by armored knights during the Middle Ages were not mere transport but were instead an integral part of the weapons system—they were taught to bite

Deane-Peter Baker, *The Robot Dogs of War* In: *Lethal Autonomous Weapons*. Edited by: Jai Galliott, Duncan MacIntosh and Jens David Ohlin, © Oxford University Press (2021). DOI: 10.1093/oso/9780197546048.003.0003 and kick, and the enemy was as likely to be trampled by the knight's horse as to taste the steel of his sword. There have been claims that US Navy dolphins "have been trained in attack-and-kill missions since the Cold War" (Townsend 2005), though this has been strongly denied by official sources. Even more bizarrely, the noted behaviorist B.F. Skinner led an effort during the Second World War to develop a pigeon-controlled guided bomb, a precursor to today's guided anti-ship missiles. Using operant conditioning techniques, pigeons housed within the weapon (which was essentially a steerable glide bomb) were trained to recognize an image of an enemy ship projected onto a small screen by lenses in the warhead. Should the image shift from the center of the screen, the pigeons were trained to peck at the controls, which would adjust the bomb's steering mechanism and put it back on target. In writing about Project Pigeon, or Project ORCON (for 'organic control') as it became known after the war, Skinner described it as "a crackpot idea, born on the wrong side of the tracks, intellectually speaking, but eventually vindicated in a sort of middle-class respectability" (Skinner 1960, 28). Despite what Skinner reports to have been considerable promise, the project was canceled, largely due to improvements in electronic means of missile control.

The strangeness of Project Pigeon/ORCON is matched or even exceeded by another Second World War initiative, 'Project X-Ray.' Conceived by a dental surgeon, Lytle S. Adams (an acquaintance of First Lady Eleanor Roosevelt), this was an effort to weaponize *bats*. The idea was to attach small incendiary devices to Mexican free-tailed bats and airdrop them over Japanese cities. It was intended that, on release from their delivery system, the bats would disperse and roost in eaves and attics among the traditional wood and paper Japanese buildings. Once ignited by a small timer, the napalm-based incendiary would then start a fire that was expected to spread rapidly. The project was canceled as efforts to develop the atomic bomb gained priority, but not before one accidental release of some 'armed' bats resulted in a fire at a US base that burned both a hanger and a general's car (Madrigal 2011).

The most common use of animals as weapons, though, is probably dogs. In the mid-seventh century BC, the basic tactical unit of mounted forces from the Greek city-state of Magnesia on the Maeander (current-day Ortaklar in Turkey) was recorded as having been composed of a horseman, a spear-bearer, and a war dog. During their war against the Ephesians it was recorded that the Magnesian approach was to first release the dogs, who would break up the enemy ranks, then follow that up with a rain of spears, and finally complete the attack with a cavalry charge (Foster 1941, 115). In an approach possibly learned from the Greeks, there are also reports that the Romans trained molossian dogs (likely an ancestor of today's mastiffs) to fight in battle, going as far as to equip them with armor and spiked collars (Homan 1999, 1). Today, of course, dogs continue to play an important role in military forces. Dogs are trained and used as sentries and trackers, to detect mines and IEDs, and for crowd control. For the purposes of this chapter, though, it is the dogs that accompany and support Special Operations Forces that are of most relevance.

These dogs are usually equipped with body-mounted video cameras and are trained to enter buildings and seek out the enemy. This enables the dog handlers and their teams to reconnoiter enemy-held positions without, in the process, putting soldiers' lives at risk. The dogs are also trained to attack anyone they discover who is armed (Norton-Taylor 2010). A good example of the combat employment of such dogs is recorded in *The Crossroad*, an autobiographical account of the life and military career of Australian Special Air Service soldier and Victoria Cross recipient Corporal Mark Donaldson. In the book, Donaldson describes a firefight in a small village in Afghanistan in 2011. Donaldson was engaging enemy fighters firing from inside a room in one of the village's buildings when his highly trained Combat Assault Dog, 'Devil,' began behaving uncharacteristically:

> Devil was meant to stay by my side during a gunfight, but he'd kept wandering off to a room less than three metres to my right. While shooting, I called, 'Devil!' He came over, but then disappeared again into another room behind me, against my orders. We threw more grenades at the enemy in the first room, before I heard a commotion behind me. Devil was dragging out an insurgent who'd been hiding on a firewood ledge with a gun. If one of us had gone in, he would have had a clear shot at our head. Even now, as he was wrestling with Devil, he was trying to get control of his gun. I shot him. (Donaldson 2013, 375)

As happened in this case, the Combat Assault Dog itself is not usually responsible for killing the enemy combatant; instead it works to enable the soldiers it accompanies to employ lethal force—we might think of the dog as part of a lethal combat system. But at least one unconfirmed recent report indicates that it may not always be the case that the enemy is not directly killed by the Combat Assault Dog. According to a newspaper report, a British Combat Assault Dog was part of a UK SAS patrol in northern Syria in 2018 when the patrol was ambushed. According to a source quoted in the report:

> The handler removed the dog's muzzle and directed him into a building from where they were coming under fire. They could hear screaming and shouting before the firing from the house stopped. When the team entered the building they saw the dog standing over a dead gunman.... His throat had been torn out and he had bled to death ... There was also a lump of human flesh in one corner and a series of blood trails leading out of the back of the building. The dog was virtually uninjured. The SAS was able to consolidate their defensive position and eventually break away from the battle without taking any casualties. (Martin 2018)

Are there any ethical issues of concern relating to the employment of dogs as weapons of war? I know of no published objections in this regard, beyond concerns for the safety and well-being of the dogs themselves,[1] which—given that the well-being of autonomous weapons is not an issue in question—is not the sort of objection of relevance to this chapter. That, of course, is not to say that there are no ethical issues that might be raised here. I shall return to this question later in this chapter, in drawing out a comparison between dogs, contracted combatants, and autonomous weapons. First, I turn to a brief discussion of the ethical questions that have been raised by the employment of 'mercenaries' in armed conflict.

2.3: PRIVATE MILITARIES AND SECURITY CONTRACTORS: "THE DOGS OF WAR"

In my book *Just Warriors Inc: The Ethics of Privatized Force* (2011), I set out to explore what the ethical objections are to the employment of private military and security contractors in contemporary conflict zones. Are they 'mercenaries,' and if so, what, exactly, is it about mercenarism that is ethically objectionable? Certainly, the term 'mercenary' is a pejorative one, which is why I chose to employ the neutral phrase 'contracted combatants' in my exploration, so as not to prejudge its outcome. Other common pejoratives for contracted combatants include 'whores of war' and 'dogs of war.' While 'whores of war' provides a fairly obvious clue to one of the normative objections to contracted combatants (discussed later), I did not address the 'dogs of war' pejorative in the book simply because I was unable at the time to identify any identifiable ethical problem associated with it.[2] Perhaps, however, the analogy is a better fit than I then realized, as will become clear. In what follows. I outline the main arguments that emerged from my exploration in *Just Warriors Inc.*[3]

Perhaps the earliest thinker to explicitly address the issue of what makes contracted combatants morally problematic is Nicollò Machiavelli, in his book *The Prince*. Two papers addressing the ethics of contracted combatants, one written by Anthony Cody (1992) and another jointly authored by Tony Lynch and Adrian Walsh (2000), both take Machiavelli's comments as their starting point. According to Cody (1992) and Lynch and Walsh (2000), Machiavelli's objections to 'mercenaries' were effectively threefold:

1. Mercenaries are not sufficiently bloodthirsty.
2. Mercenaries cannot be trusted because of the temptations of political power.
3. There exists some motive or motives appropriate to engaging in war which mercenaries necessarily lack, or else mercenaries are motivated by some factor which is inappropriate for engaging in war.

The first of these points need not detain us long, for it is quite clear that, even if the empirically questionable claim that mercenaries lack the killing instinct necessary for war were true, this can hardly be considered a *moral* failing. But perhaps the point is instead one about effectiveness—the claim that the soldier for hire cannot be relied upon to do what is necessary in battle when the crunch comes. But even if true, it is evident this too cannot be the moral failing we are looking for. For while we might cast moral aspersions on such a mercenary, those aspersions would be in the family of such terms as 'feeble,' 'pathetic,' or 'hopeless.' But these are clearly not the moral failings we are looking for in trying to discover just what is wrong with being a *mercenary*. Indeed, the flip side of this objection seems to have more bite—the concern that mercenaries may be overly driven by 'killer instinct,' that they might take pleasure from the business of death. This foreshadows the motivation objection to be discussed.

Machiavelli's second point is even more easily dealt with. For it is quite clear that the temptation to grab power over a nation by force is at least as strong for national military forces as it is for mercenaries. In fact, it could be argued that mercenaries are more reliable in this respect. For example, a comprehensive analysis of coup trends in Africa between 1956 and 2001 addressed 80 successful coups, 108 unsuccessful coup attempts, and 139 reported coup plots—of these only 4 coup plots involved mercenaries (all 4 led by the same man, Frenchman Bob Denard) (McGowan 2003).

Machiavelli's third point is, of course, the most common objection to mercenarism, the concern over *motivation*. The most common version of this objection is that there is something wrong with fighting for money—this is the most obvious basis for the pejorative 'whores of war.' As Lynch and Walsh point out, however, the objection cannot simply be that money is a morally questionable motivation for action. For while a case could perhaps be made for this, it would apply to such a wide range of human activities that it offers little help in discerning what singles out mercenarism as especially problematic. Perhaps, therefore, the problem is being motivated by money above all else. Lynch and Walsh helpfully suggest that we label such a person a *lucrepath*. By this thinking, "those criticising mercenaries for taking blood money are then accusing them of being lucrepaths . . . it is not that they do things for money but that money is the *sole* or the *dominant* consideration in their practical deliberations" (Lynch and Walsh 2000, 136).

Cecile Fabre argues that while we may think lurepathology to be morally wrong, even if it *is* a defining characteristic of the mercenary (which is an empirically questionable claim), it does not make the practice of mercenarism itself immoral:

> Individuals do all sorts of things out of mostly financial motivations. They often choose a particular line of work, such as banking or consulting, rather than others, such as academia, largely because of the money. They often decide to become doctors rather than nurses for similar reasons. Granting that their interest in making such choices, however condemnable their motivations, is important enough to be protected by a claim (against non-interference) and a power (to enter the relevant employment contracts), it is hard to see how one could deny similar protection to mercenaries. (Fabre 2010, 551)

As already mentioned, another variant of the 'improper motivation' argument is that mercenaries might be motivated by blood lust. But, of course, it is empirically doubtful that this applies to all contracted combatants, and there is also every likelihood that those motivated by blood lust will be just as likely to seek to satisfy that lust through service in regular military forces.

Perhaps then, the question of appropriate motives is not that mercenaries are united by having a particular morally reprehensible motive, but rather that they *lack* a particular motive that is necessary for good moral standing when it comes to fighting and killing. What might such a motive be? Most commentators identify two main candidates, namely 'just cause' and 'right intention,' as defined by Just War Theory. As Lynch and Walsh put it, "*Ex hypothesi*, killing in warfare is justifiable only when the soldier in question is motivated among other things by a just cause. Justifiable killing motives must not only be non-lucrepathic, but also, following Aquinas, must include just cause and right intention" (Lynch and Walsh 2000, 138). The argument, then, is that whatever it is which actually motivates contracted combatants, it is not the desire to satisfy a just cause, and therefore they do not fight with right intention. While I did not consider this when I wrote *Just Warriors Inc.*, it is worth noting here that this objection cuts in two directions.

Directed against the otherwise-motivated contracted combatant, this objection paints him or her as morally lacking on the grounds that the good combatant ought to be motivated in this way. The objection also points to implications for those on the receiving end of lethal actions carried out by the contracted combatant. Here the idea is that failing to be motivated by the just cause is at the same time to show a lack of respect for one's opponents. Put in broadly Kantian terms, to fight with any motivation other than the desire to achieve the just cause is to use the enemy as a *mere means* to satisfy some other end—whether that be pecuniary advantage, blood lust, adventurism, or whatever.[4] In other words, it violates the *dignity* of those on the receiving end.

Moving on from Machiavelli's list, we find that another common objection to the use of contracted combatants focuses on the question of *accountability*. One vector of this objection is the claim that the use of contracted combatants undermines democratic control over the use of force. There is a strong argument, for example, that the large-scale use of contractors in Iraq under the Bush administration was at least in part an attempt to circumvent congressional limitations on the number of troops that could be deployed into that theater. Another regularly expressed concern is that the availability of contracted combatants offers a means whereby governments can avoid existing controls on their use of force by using private contractors to undertake 'black' operations.[5]

Another vector of the accountability objection relates to punishment. Peter Feaver's Agency Theory of civil-military relations recognizes a range of punishments that are unique to the civil-military context (Feaver 2003). Civilian leaders in a democratic state have the option of applying military-specific penal codes to their state military agents. If convicted of offenses under military law (such as the Uniform Code of Military Justice, which applies to US military personnel), state military personnel face punishments ranging from dismissal from the military to imprisonment to, in some extreme cases, execution. Here we find another aspect of accountability that has been raised against the use of contracted combatants. It has been a source of significant concern among critics of the private military industry that private military companies and their employees are not subject to the same rigorous standards of justice as state military employees. James Pattison, for example, has expressed the concern that "there is currently no effective system of accountability to govern the conduct of PMC personnel, and this can lead to cases where the horrors of war—most notably civilian casualties—go unchecked" (Pattison 2008, 152). Beyond this consequentialist concern there is, furthermore, the concern that justice will not be done for actions that would be punishable under law if they had been carried out by uniformed military personnel.

The final main area of concern that is regularly voiced regarding the outsourcing of armed force by states is the worry that private contractors are *untrustworthy*. This is not quite the same concern that Machiavelli expressed, though it is similar. At the strategic level, the concern is that the outsourcing of traditional military functions into private hands could potentially undermine civil-military relations, the (in the ideal case) relationship of subservience by the military to elected leaders. The objection made by many opponents of military privatization is that it is inappropriate to delegate military tasks to nongovernmental organizations. Peter W. Singer, for example, writes that "When the government delegates out part of its role in national security through the recruitment and maintenance of armed forces, it is abdicating an essential responsibility"[6] (Singer 2003, 226).

At the level of individual combatants, the concern here is over control. In the state military context, control over military forces is achieved in a number of ways, including rules of engagement, standing orders, mission orders, and contingency plans. As Peter Feaver explains, through the lens of Principle-Agency Theory, "Rules of engagement, in principal-agent terms, are reporting requirements concerning the use of force. By restricting military autonomy and proscribing certain behavior, rules of engagement require that the military inform civilian principals about battlefield operations whenever developments indicate (to battlefield commanders) that the rules need to be changed" (Feaver 2003, 77). In contrast to this arrangement, contracted combatants are perceived by many as out-of-control 'cowboys.'

Of particular concern here is the worry that, if contracted combatants cannot be adequately controlled, they may well act in violation of important norms, including adherence to the principles of International Humanitarian Law. Indeed, many of the scholarly objections to the employment of private military and security contractors arose in the aftermath of a number of high-profile events in which contractors were accused of egregious violations for which there seemed no adequate mechanism by which to hold them to account.[7]

To sum up, then, the three main themes that have been raised in objection to the employment of contracted combatants are those of *motivation* (to include the question of respecting human *dignity*), *accountability*, and *trustworthiness* (to include the questions of *control* and *compliance with IHL*). I deal with those objections in some detail in *Just Warriors Inc.*, and it is not my intention here to repeat the arguments contained in that book. Instead, I turn now to a consideration of the objections to the employment of autonomous weapons systems.

2.4: THE ROBOT DOGS OF WAR

> Paulo and two squad mates huddled together in the trenches, cowering while hell unfolded around them. Dozens of mechanical animals the size of large dogs had just raced through their position, rifle fire erupting from gun barrels mounted between their shoulder blades. The twisted metal remains of three machines lay in the dirt in front of their trenches, destroyed by the mines. The remaining machines had headed towards the main camp yipping like hyenas on the hunt. Two BMPs exploded in their wake. Paulo had seen one of the machines leap at his battalion commander and slam the officer in the chest with a massive, bone crunching thud. It spun away from the dying officer, pivoting several times to shoot at the Russians. Two of them fell dead, the third ran. It turned and followed the other machines deeper into the camp. Paulo heard several deep BOOMs outside the perimeter he recognized as mortars firing and moments later fountains of dirt leapt skyward near the closest heavy machine gun bunker. The bunker was struck and exploded. Further away a string of explosions traced over the trench line, killing several men. In the middle of it all he swore he heard a cloud of insects buzzing and looked up to see what looked like a small swarm of bird-sized creatures flying overhead. They ignored him and kept going.

This rather terrifying scenario is an extract from a fictional account by writer Mike Matson entitled *Demons in the Long Grass,* which gives an account of a near-future battle involving imagined autonomous weapons systems. Handily for the purposes of this chapter, some of the autonomous weapons systems described are dog-like—the "robot dogs of war"—which the author says were inspired by footage of Boston Dynamics' robot dog "Spot" (Matson 2018). The scariness of the scenario stems from a range of deep-seated human fears; however, the fact that a weapon system is frightening is not in itself a reason for objecting to it (though it seems likely that this is what lies behind many of the more vociferous calls for a ban on autonomous weapons systems). Thankfully, philosophers Fillipo Santoni de Sio and Jeroen van den Hoven have put forward a clear and unemotional summary of the primary ethical objections to autonomous weapons, and I find no cause to dispute their summary. Santoni de Sio and van den Hoven rightly point out that there are three main ethical objections that have been raised in the debate over AWS:

> (a) as a matter of fact, robots of the near future will not be capable of making the sophisticated practical and moral distinctions required by the laws of armed conflict. . . . distinction between combatants and non-combatants, proportionality in the use of force, and military necessity of violent action. . . .
> (b) As a matter of principle, it is morally wrong to let a machine be in control of the life and death of a human being, no matter how technologically advanced the machine is . . . According to this position . . . these applications are *mala in se* . . .
> (c) In the case of war crimes or fatal accidents, the presence of an autonomous weapon system in the operation may make it more difficult, or impossible altogether, to hold military personnel morally and legally responsible. . . . (Santoni de Sio and van den Hoven 2018, 2)

A similar summary is provided by the International Committee of the Red Cross (ICRC). In their account, "Ethical arguments against autonomous weapon systems can generally be divided into two forms: objections based on the limits of technology to function within legal constraints and ethical norms; and ethical objections that are independent of technological capability" (ICRC 2018, 9). The latter set of objections includes the question of whether the use of autonomous weapons might lead to "a responsibility gap where humans cannot uphold their moral responsibility," whether their use would undermine "the human dignity of those combatants who are targeted, and of civilians who are put at risk of death and injury as a consequence of attacks on legitimate military targets," and the possibility that "further increasing human distancing—physically and psychologically—from the battlefield" could increase "existing asymmetries" and make "the use of violence easier or less controlled" (ICRC 2018, 9).

With the exception of the 'asymmetries' concern raised by the ICRC, which I set aside in this chapter,[8] it is clear that the two summaries raise the same objections. It is also clear that these objections correspond closely with the objections to contracted combatants discussed before. That is, both contracted combatants and autonomous weapons face opposition on the grounds that they are morally problematic due to inappropriate *motivation* (to include the question of respecting human *dignity*), a lack of *accountability*, and a lack of *trustworthiness* (to include the questions of *control* and *compliance with IHL*). A full response to all of these lines of objection to autonomous weapons is more than I can attempt within the limited confines of this chapter. Nonetheless, in the next section, I draw on some of the responses I made to the objections to contracted combatants that I discussed in *Just Warriors Inc.*, as a means to address the similar objections to autonomous weapons systems. I also include brief references to weaponized dogs (as well as weaponized bats and pigeons), as a way to illustrate the principles I raise.

2.5: RESPONSES

Because the issue of inappropriate motivation (particularly the question of respect for human dignity) is considered by many to be the strongest objection to autonomous weapons systems, I will address that issue last, tackling the objections in reverse order to that already laid out. I begin, therefore, with trustworthiness.

2.5.1: Trustworthiness

The question of whether contracted combatants can be trusted is often positioned as a concern over the character of these 'mercenaries,' but this is largely to look in the wrong direction. As Peter Feaver points out in his book *Armed Servants* (2003), the same problem afflicts much of the literature on civil-military relations, which tends to focus on 'soft' aspects of the relationship between the military and civilian leaders, particularly the presence or absence of military professionalism and subservience. But, as Feaver convincingly shows, the issue is less about trustworthiness than it is about *control*, and (drawing on principle-agent theory) he shows that civilian principles, in fact, employ a wide range of control mechanisms to ensure (to use the language of principal-agent theory) that the military is 'working' rather than 'shirking.'[9] In *Just Warriors Inc.*, I draw on Feaver's Principle-Agency Theory to show that the same control measures do, or can, apply to contracted combatants.

While those specific measures do not apply directly to autonomous weapons systems, the same broad point applies: focusing attention on the systems themselves largely misses the wide range of mechanisms of control that are applied to the use of weapons systems in general and which are, or can be, applied to autonomous weapons. Though I cannot explore that in detail here, it is worth considering the analogy of weaponized dogs, which are also able to function autonomously. To focus entirely on dogs' capacity for autonomous action, and therefore to conclude that their employment in war is intrinsically morally inappropriate, would be to ignore the range of control measures that military combat dog handlers ('commanders') can and do apply. If we can reasonably talk about the controlled use of military combat dogs, then there seems little reason to think that there is any intrinsic reason why autonomous weapons systems cannot also be appropriately controlled.

That is not to say, of course, that there are no circumstances in which it would be inappropriate to employ autonomous weapons systems. There are unquestionably environments in which it would be inappropriate to employ combat dogs, given the degree of control that is available to the handler (which will differ depending on such issues as the kind and extent of training, the character of the particular dog, etc.), and the analogy holds for autonomous weapons systems. And it goes almost without saying that there are ways in which autonomous weapons systems could be used which would make violations of IHL likely (indeed, some systems may be designed in such a way to make this almost certain from the start, in the same way that weaponizing bats with napalm to burn down Japanese cities would be fundamentally at odds with IHL). But these problems are contingent on specific contextual questions about environment and design; they do not amount to intrinsic objections to autonomous weapons systems.

2.5.2: Accountability

A fundamental requirement of ethics is that those who cause undue harm to others must be held to account, both as a means of deterrence and as a matter of justice for those harmed. While there were, and are, justifiable concerns about holding contracted combatants accountable for their actions, these concerns again arise from contingent circumstances rather than the intrinsic nature of the outsourcing of military force. As I argued in *Just Warriors Inc.*, there is no reason in principle why civilian principals cannot either put in place penal codes that apply specifically to private military companies and their employees, or else expand existing military law to cover private warriors. For example, the US Congress extended the scope of the UCMJ in 2006 to ensure its applicability to private military contractors. While it remains to be seen whether specific endeavors such as these would withstand the inevitable legal challenges that will arise, it does indicate that there is no reason in principle why states cannot use penal codes to punish private military agents.

The situation with autonomous weapons systems is a little different. In this case it *is* an intrinsic feature of these systems that raises the concern, the fact that the operator or commander of the system does not directly select and approve the particular target that is engaged. Some who object to autonomous weapons systems, therefore, argue that because the weapons system itself cannot be held accountable, the requirement of accountability cannot be satisfied, or not satisfied in full. Here the situation is most closely analogous to that of the Combat Assault Dog. Once released by her handler, the Combat Assault Dog (particularly when she is out of sight of her handler, or her handler is otherwise occupied) selects and engages targets autonomously. The graphic 'dog-rips-out-terrorist's-throat' story recounted in this chapter is a classic case in point. Once released and inside the building containing the terrorists, the SAS dog selected and engaged her targets without further intervention from her handler beyond her core training. The question is, then, do we think that there is an accountability gap in such cases?

While I know of no discussion of this in the context of Combat Assault Dogs, the answer from our domestic experience with dangerous dogs (trained or otherwise) is clear—the owner or handler is held to be liable for any undue harm caused. While dogs that cause undue harm to humans are often 'destroyed' (killed) as a consequence, there is no sense in which this is a punishment for the dog. Rather, it is the relevant human who is held accountable, while the dog is killed as a matter of public safety. Of course, liability in such cases is not *strict* liability: we do not hold the owner or handler responsible for the harm caused *regardless* of the circumstances. If the situation that led to the dog unduly harming someone were such that the owner or handler could not have reasonably foreseen the situation arising, then the owner/handler would not be held liable. Back to our military combat dog example: What if the SAS dog had ripped the throat out of someone who was merely a passerby who happened to have picked up an AK-47 she found lying in the street, and who had then unknowingly sought shelter in the very same building from which the terrorists were executing their ambush? That would be tragic, but it hardly seems that there is an accountability gap in this case. Given the right to use force in self-defense, as the SAS patrol did in this case, and given the inevitability of epistemic uncertainty amidst the 'fog of war,' some tragedies happen for which nobody is to blame. The transferability of these points to the question of accountability regarding the employment of autonomous weapons systems is sufficiently obvious that I will not belabor the point.

2.5.3: Motivation

As discussed earlier, perhaps the biggest objection to the employment of contracted combatants relates to motivation. The worry is either that they are motivated by things they ought not to be (like blood lust, or a love of *lucre* above all else) or else that they lack the motivation that is appropriate to engage in war (like being motivated by the just cause). In a similar vein, it is the *dignity objection* which, arguably, is seen as carrying the most weight by opponents of autonomous weapons systems.[10] As the ICRC explains the objection:

> [I]t matters not just *if* a person is killed or injured but *how* they are killed or injured, including the process by which these decisions are made. It is argued that, if human agency is lacking to the extent that machines have effectively, and functionally, been delegated these decisions, then it undermines the human dignity of those combatants targeted, and of civilians that are put at risk as a consequence of legitimate attacks on military targets. (ICRC 2018, 2)

To put this objection in the terms used by Lynch and Walsh, "justifiable killing motives must . . . include just cause and right intention" (2000, 138), and because these are not motives that autonomous weapons system are capable of (being incapable of having motives at all), the dignity of those on the receiving end is violated.

Part of the problem with this objection, applied both to contracted combatants and autonomous weapons systems, is that it seems to take an unrealistic view of motivation among military personnel engaged in war. It would be bizarre to claim that every member of a national military force was motivated by the desire to satisfy the nation's just cause in fighting a war, and even those who are so motivated are likely not to be motivated in this way in every instance of combat. If the lack of such a motive results in dignity violations to the extent that the situation is ethically untenable, then what we have is an argument against war in general, not a specific argument against the employment of mercenaries or autonomous weapons systems.

The motive/dignity objection overlooks a very important distinction, that between intention and motive. As James Pattison explains:

> An individual's *intention* is the objective or purpose that they wish to achieve with their action. On the other hand, their *motive* is their underlying reason for acting. It follows that an agent with right intention aims to tackle whatever it is that the war is a just response to, such as a humanitarian crisis, military attack, or serious threat. But their underlying reason for having this intention need not also concern the just cause. It could be, for instance, a self-interested reason. (Pattison 2010, 147)

Or, we might add (given that autonomous weapons systems do not have intrinsic *reasons* for what they do), it could be no reason at all. Here again it is worth considering the example of Combat Assault Dogs. Whatever motives they may have in engaging enemy targets (or selecting one target over another), it seems safe to say that 'achieving the just cause' is not among them. The lack of a general dignity-based outcry against the use of Combat Assault Dogs to cause harm to enemy combatants[11] suggests a widely held intuition that what matters here is that the dogs' actions are in accord with appropriate intentions being pursued by the handler and the military force he belongs to.

Or consider once again, as a thought experiment, B.F. Skinner's pigeon-guided munition (PGM). Imagine that after his initial success (let's call this PGM-1), Skinner had gone a step further. Rather than just training the pigeons to steer the bomb onto one particular ship, imagine instead that the pigeons had been trained to be able to pick out the most desirable target from a range of enemy ships appearing on their tiny screen—they have learned to recognize and rank aircraft carriers above battleships, battleships above cruisers, cruisers above destroyers, and so on. They have been trained to then direct their bomb onto the most valuable target that is within the range of its glide path. What Skinner would have created, in this fictional case, is an autonomous weapon employing 'organic control' (ORCON). We might even call it an AI-directed autonomous weapon (where 'AI' stands for 'Animal Intelligence'). Let's call this pigeon-guided munition 2 (PGM-2). Because the pigeons in PGM-1 only act as a steering mechanism, and do not either 'decide' to attack the ship or 'decide' *which* ship to attack, the motive argument does not apply and those killed and injured in the targeted ship do not have their dignity violated. Supporters of the dignity objection would, however, have to say that anyone killed or injured in a ship targeted by a *PGM-2* would have additionally suffered having their dignity violated. Indeed, if we apply the Holy See's position on autonomous weapons systems to this case, we would have to say that using a PGM-2 in war would amount to employing means *mala in se*, equivalent to employing poisonous gas, rape as a weapon of war, or torture. But that is patently absurd.

2.6: CONCLUSION

The debate over the ethics of autonomous weapons is often influenced by perceptions drawn from science fiction and Hollywood movies, which are almost universally unhelpful. In this chapter I have pointed to two alternative sources of ethical comparison, namely the employment of contracted combatants and the employment of weaponized animals. I have tried to show that such comparison is helpful in defusing some of what on the surface seem like the strongest reasons for objecting, on ethical grounds, to the use of autonomous weapons, but which on inspection turn out to be merely contingent or else misguided.

NOTES

1. For example, in an article on the UK SAS use of dogs in Afghanistan, the animal rights organization People for the Ethical Treatment of Animals (PETA) is quoted as saying, "dogs are not tools or 'innovations' and are not ours to use and toss away like empty ammunition shells" (Norton-Taylor 2010).
2. The association of the term 'dogs of war' with contracted combatants seems to be a relatively recent one, resulting from the title of Fredrick Forsyth's novel *The Dogs of War* (1974) about a group of European soldier's for hire recruited by a British businessman and tasked to overthrow the government of an African country, with the goal of getting access to mineral resources. The title of the novel is, in turn, taken from Scene I, Act III of William Shakespeare's play *Julius Caesar*: "Cry Havoc, and let slip the dogs of war!" There is some dispute as to what this phrase explicitly refers to. Given (as discussed) the possibility that Romans did, in fact, employ weaponized canines, it may be a literal reference, though more often it is interpreted as a figurative reference to the forces of war or as a reference to soldiers. It is sometimes also noted that 'dogs' had an archaic meaning not used today, referring to restraining mechanism or latches, in which case the reference could be to a figurative opening of a door that usually restrains the forces of war.
3. Some of what follows is a distillation of arguments that appeared in *Just Warriors Inc.*, reproduced here with permission.
4. *In Just Warriors Inc.*, I discuss a number of other motives (or lack thereof) that might be considered morally problematic. In the interests of brevity, I have set those aside here.
5. Blackwater, for example, was accused of carrying out assassinations and illegal renditions of detainees on behalf of the CIA (Steingart 2009).
6. As this is not an objection with a clear parallel in the case of autonomous weapons (or Combat Assault Dogs, for that matter), I will set it aside here. I address this issue in Chapter 6 of *Just Warriors Inc.*
7. One such case was the 2007 Nisour Square shooting, in which Blackwater close protection personnel, protecting a State Department convoy, opened fire in a busy square, killing at least seventeen civilians. In October 2014, after a long and convoluted series of court cases, one of the former Blackwater employees, Nick Slatten, was convicted of first-degree murder, with three others convicted of lesser crimes. Slatten was sentenced to life in prison, and the other defendants received thirty-year sentences. In 2017, however, the US Court of Appeals in the District of Colombia ordered that Slatten's conviction be set aside and he be re-tried, and that the other defendants be re-sentenced (Neuman 2017).
8. It is not obvious to me why this is an ethical issue. I am reminded of Conrad Crane's memorable opening to a paper: "There are two ways of waging war, asymmetric and stupid" (Crane 2013). It doesn't seem to me to a requirement of ethics that combatants 'fight stupid.'
9. In principal-agent theory, 'shirking' has a technical meaning that extends beyond the 'goofing off' of the everyday sense use of the term. In this technical sense, for agents to be 'shirking' means they are doing anything other than what the principal

intends them to be doing. Agents can thus be working hard, in the normal sense of the word, but still 'shirking.'

10. As one Twitter pundit put it, "It's about the dignity, stupid."
11. I take it that there is no reason why, if it applies at all, the structure of the dignity objection would not apply to harm in general, not only to lethal harm.

WORKS CITED

Baker, Deane-Peter. 2011 Just Warriors Inc: The Ethics of Privatized Force. London: Continuum

Coady, C.A.J. 1992. "Mercenary Morality." In *International Law and Armed Conflict*, edited by A.G.D. Bradney, pp. 55–69. Stuttgart: Steiner.

Crane, Conrad. 2013. "The Lure of Strike." *Parameters* 43 (2): pp. 5–12.

Fabre, Cecile. 2010. "In Defence of Mercenarism." *British Journal of Political Science* 40 (3): pp. 539–559.

Feaver, Peter D. 2003. *Armed Servants: Agency, Oversight, and Civil-Military Relations*. Cambridge, MA: Harvard University Press.

Foster, E.S. 1941. "Dogs in Ancient Warfare." *Greece and Rome* 10 (30): pp. 114–117.

Homan, Mike. 1999. *A Complete History of Fighting Dogs*. Hoboken, NJ: Wiley.

ICRC. 2018. *Ethics and Autonomous Weapon Systems: An Ethical Basis for Human Control?* Report of the International Committee of the Red Cross (ICRC), Geneva, April 3.

Lynch, Tony and A. J. Walsh. 2000. "The Good Mercenary?" *Journal of Political Philosophy* 8 (2): pp. 133–153.

Madrigal, Alexis C. 2011. "Old, Weird Tech: The Bat Bombs of World War II." *The Atlantic*, April 14. https://www.theatlantic.com/technology/archive/2011/04/old-weird-tech-the-bat-bombs-of-world-war-ii/237267/.

Matson, Mike. 2018. "Demons in the Long Grass." *Mad Scientist Laboratory* (Blog). June 19. https://madsciblog.tradoc.army.mil/tag/demons-in-the-grass/.

Matson, Mike. 2018. "Demons in the Long Grass." *Small Wars Journal Blog*. July 17. http://smallwarsjournal.com/jrnl/art/demons-tall-grass/.

McGowan, Patrick J. 2003. "African Military Coups d'État, 1956–2001: Frequency, Trends and Distribution." *Journal of Modern African Studies* 41 (3): pp. 339–370.

Martin, George. 2018. "Hero SAS Dog Saves the Lives of Six Elite Soldiers by Ripping Out Jihadi's Throat While Taking Down Three Terrorists Who Ambushed British Patrol." *Daily Mail*. July 8. https://www.dailymail.co.uk/news/article-5930275/Hero-SAS-dog-saves-lives-six-elite-soldiers-Syria-ripping-jihadis-throat.html.

Neuman, Scott. 2017. "U.S. Appeals Court Tosses Ex-Blackwater Guard's Conviction in 2007 Baghdad Massacre." *NPR*. August 4. https://www.npr.org/sections/thetwo-way/2017/08/04/541616598/u-s-appeals-court-tosses-conviction-of-ex-blackwater-guard-in-2007-baghdad-massa.

Norton-Taylor, Robert. 2010. "SAS Parachute Dogs of War into Taliban Bases." *The Guardian*. November 9. https://www.theguardian.com/uk/2010/nov/08/sas-dogs-parachute-taliban-afghanistan.

Pattison, James. 2008. "Just War Theory and the Privatization of Military Force." *Ethics and International Affairs* 22 (2): pp. 143–162.

Pattison, James. 2010. *Humanitarian Intervention and the Responsibility to Protect: Who Should Intervene?* Oxford: Oxford University Press.

Samson, Jack. 2011. *Flying Tiger: The True Story of General Claire Chennault and the U.S. 14th Air Force in China*. New York: The Lyons Press (reprint edition).
Singer, Peter W. 2003. *Corporate Warriors: The Rise of the Privatized Military Industry*. Ithaca, NY: Cornell University Press.
Skinner, B.F. 1960. "Pigeons in a Pelican." *American Psychologist* 15 (1): pp. 28–37.
Steingart, Gabor. 2009. "Memo Reveals Details of Blackwater Targeted Killings Program." *Der Spiegel*. August 24. www.spiegel.de/international/world/0.1518.644571.00.hmtl.
Santoni de Sio, Fillipo and Jeroen van der Hoven. 2018. "Meaningful Human Control over Autonomous Systems: A Philosophical Account." *Frontiers in Robotics and AI* 5 (15): pp. 1–15.
Townsend, Mark. 2005. "Armed and Dangerous–Flipper the Firing Dolphin Let Loose by Katrina." *The Observer*. September 25. https://www.theguardian.com/world/2005/sep/25/usa.theobserver.

3

Understanding AI and Autonomy: Problematizing the Meaningful Human Control Argument against Killer Robots

TIM MCFARLAND AND JAI GALLIOTT

Questions about what constitutes legal use of autonomous weapons systems (AWS) lead naturally to questions about how to ensure that use is kept within legal limits. Concerns stem from the observation that humans appear to be ceding control of the weapon system to a computer. Accordingly, one of the most prominent features of the AWS debate thus far has been the emergence of the notion of 'meaningful human control' (MHC) over AWS.[1] It refers to the fear that a capacity for autonomous operation threatens to put AWS outside the control of the armed forces that operate them, whether intentionally or not, and consequently their autonomy must be limited in some way in order to ensure they will operate consistently with legal and moral requirements. Although used initially, and most commonly, in the context of objections to increasing degrees of autonomy, the idea has been picked up by many States, academics, and NGOs as a sort of framing concept for the debate. This chapter discusses the place of MHC in the debate; current views on what it entails;[2] and in light of this analysis, raises the question of whether it really serves as a base for arguments against 'killer robots.'

3.1: HISTORY

The idea of MHC was first used in relation to AWS by the UK NGO Article 36. In April 2013, Article 36 published a paper arguing for "a positive obligation in international law for individual attacks to be under meaningful human control" (Article 36 2013, 1). The paper was a response to broad concerns about increasing

Tim McFarland and Jai Galliott, *Understanding AI and Autonomy: Problematizing the Meaningful Human Control Argument against Killer Robots* In: *Lethal Autonomous Weapons*. Edited by: Jai Galliott, Jens David Ohlin and Duncan MacIntosh,
 DOI: 10.1093/oso/9780197546048.003.0004

military use of remotely controlled and robotic weapon systems, and specifically to statements by the UK Ministry of Defence (MoD) in its 2011 Joint Doctrine Note on Unmanned Systems (Development, Concepts and Doctrine Centre 2011). Despite government commitments that weapons would remain under human control, the MoD indicated that "attacks without human assessment of the target, or a subsequent human authorization to attack, could still be legal" (Article 36 2013, 2):

> a mission may require an unmanned aircraft to carry out surveillance or monitoring of a given area, looking for a particular target type, before reporting contacts to a supervisor when found. A human-authorised subsequent attack would be no different to that by a manned aircraft and would be fully compliant with [IHL], provided the human believed that, based on the information available, the attack met [IHL] requirements and extant [rules of engagement]. From this position, it would be only a small technical step to enable an unmanned aircraft to fire a weapon based solely on its own sensors, or shared information, and without recourse to higher, human authority. Provided it could be shown that the controlling system appropriately assessed the [IHL] principles (military necessity; humanity; distinction and proportionality) and that [rules of engagement] were satisfied, this would be entirely legal. (Development, Concepts and Doctrine Centre 2011, 5-4 [507])

As a result, according to Article 36, "current UK doctrine is confused and there are a number of areas where policy needs further elaboration if it is not to be so ambiguous as to be meaningless" (Article 36 2013, 1).

Specifically, Article 36 argued that "it is moral agency that [the rules of proportionality and distinction] require of humans, coupled with the freedom to choose to follow the rules or not, that are the basis for the normative power of the law" (Article 36 2013, 2). That is, human beings must make conscious, informed decisions about each use of force in a conflict; delegating such decisions to a machine would be inherently unacceptable. Those human decisions should relate to each individual attack:

> Whilst it is recognized that an individual attack may include a number of specific target objects, human control will cease to be meaningful if an [AWS] is undertaking multiple attacks that require specific timely consideration of the target, context and anticipated effects. (Article 36 2013, 4)

The authors acknowledged that some existing weapon systems exhibit a limited capacity for autonomous operation, and are not illegal because of it:

> there are already systems in operation that function in this way - notably ship mounted anti-missile systems and certain 'sensor fuzed' weapon systems. For these weapons, it is the relationship between the human operator's understanding the sensor functioning and human operator's control over the context (the duration and/or location of sensor functioning) that are argued to allow lawful use of the weapons. (Article 36 2013, 3)

Despite that, their conception of problematic 'fully autonomous' weapons, according to an earlier publication, seems to be very broad and could conceivably include calling for a ban on existing weapons:

> Although the relationship between landmines and fully autonomous armed robots may seem stretched, in fact they share essential elements of DNA. Landmines and fully autonomous weapons all provide a capacity to respond with force to an incoming 'signal' (whether the pressure of a foot or a shape on an infra-red sensor). Whether static or mobile, simple or complex, it is the automated violent response to a signal that makes landmines and fully autonomous weapons fundamentally problematic . . .
>
> [W]e need to draw a red line at fully autonomous targeting. A first step in this may be to recognize that such a red line needs to be drawn effectively across the board – from the simple technologies of anti-vehicle landmines . . . across to the most complex systems under development. (Bolton, Nash, and Moyes 2012)

Nevertheless, based on those concerns, the paper makes three calls on the UK government. First, they ask the government to "[c]ommit to, and elaborate, meaningful human control over individual attacks" (Article 36 2013, 3). Second, "[s]trengthen commitment not to develop fully autonomous weapons and systems that could undertake attacks without meaningful human control" (Article 36 2013, 4). Finally, "[r]ecognize that an international treaty is needed to clarify and strengthen legal protection from fully autonomous weapons" (Article 36 2013, 5).

Since 2013, Article 36 has continued to develop the concept of MHC (Article 36 2013; Article 36 2014), and it has been taken up by some States and civil society actors. Inevitably, the meaning, rather imprecise to begin with, has changed with use. In particular, some parties have dropped the qualifier "over individual attacks," introducing some uncertainty about exactly what is to be subject to human control. Does it apply to every discharge of a weapon? Every target selection? Only an attack as a whole? Something else?

Further, each term is open to interpretation:

> The MHC concept could be considered a priori to exclude the use of [AWS]. This is how it is often understood intuitively. However, whether this is in fact the case depends on how each of the words involved is understood. "Meaningful" is an inherently subjective concept . . . "Human control" may likewise be understood in a variety of ways. (UNIDIR 2014, 3)

Thoughts about MHC and its implications for the development of AWS continue to evolve as the debate continues, but a lack of certainty about the content of the concept has not slowed its adoption. It has been discussed extensively by expert presenters at the CCW meetings on AWS, and many State delegations have referred to it in their statements, generally expressing support or at least a wish to explore the idea in more depth.

At the 2014 Informal Meeting of Experts, Germany spoke of the necessity of MHC in anti-personnel attacks:

> it is indispensable to maintain meaningful human control over the decision to kill another human being. We cannot take humans out of the loop.
>
> We do believe that the principle of human control is already implicitly inherent to [IHL] . . . And we cannot see any reason why technological developments should all of a sudden suspend the validity of the principle of human control. (Germany 2014, 4)

Norway explicitly linked "full" autonomy to a lack of MHC; the delegation expressed concern about the capabilities of autonomous technologies, rather than the principle of delegating decisions on the use of force to an AWS:

> By [AWS] in this context, I refer to weapons systems that search for, identify and use lethal force to attack targets, including human beings, without a human operator intervening, and without meaningful human control. . . . our main concern with the possible development of [AWS] is whether such weapons could be programmed to operate within the limitations set by international law. (Norway 2014, 1)

The following year, several delegations noted that MHC had become an important element of the discussion:

> [The 2014 CCW Meeting of Experts] led to a broad consensus on the importance of 'meaningful human control' over the critical functions of selecting and engaging targets. . . . we are wary of fully autonomous weapons systems that remove meaningful human control from the operation loop, due to the risk of malfunctioning, potential accountability gap and ethical concerns. (Republic of Korea 2015, 1–2)

MHC remained prominent at the 2016 meetings, where there was a widely held view that it was fundamental to understanding and regulating AWS:

> The elements, such as "autonomy" and "meaningful human control (MHC)," which were presented at the last two Informal Meetings are instrumental in deliberating the definition of [AWS]. (Japan 2016, 1–2)

However, there were questions that also emerged about the usefulness of the concept:

> The US Delegation also looks forward to a more in depth discussions [sic] with respect to human-machine interaction and about the phrase "meaningful human control." Turning first to the phrase "meaningful human control," we have heard many delegations and experts note that the term is subjective and thus difficult to understand. We have expressed these same concerns about whether "meaningful human control" is a helpful way to advance our discussions.
>
> We view the optimization of the human/machine relationship as a primary technical challenge to developing lethal [AWS] and a key point that needs to be reviewed from the start of any weapon system development. Because this

> human/machine relationship extends throughout the development and employment of a system and is not limited to the moment of a decision to engage a target, we consider it more useful to talk about "appropriate levels of human judgment." (United States 2016, 2)

The idea of MHC over AWS has also been raised outside of a strict IHL context, both at the CCW meetings and elsewhere. For example, the African Commission on Human and Peoples' Rights incorporated MHC into its General Comment No. 3 on the African Charter on Human and Peoples' Rights on the right to life (Article 4) of 2015:

> The use during hostilities of new weapons technologies . . . should only be envisaged if they strengthen the protection of the right to life of those affected. Any machine autonomy in the selection of human targets or the use of force should be subject to meaningful human control. (African Commission on Human and People's Rights 2015, 12)

For all its prominence, though, the precise content of the MHC concept is still unsettled. The next section surveys the views of various parties.

3.2: MEANING

The unsettled content of the MHC concept is perhaps to be expected, as it is not based on a positive conception of something that is required of an AWS. Rather, it is based "on the idea that concerns regarding growing autonomy are rooted in the human aspect that autonomy removes, and therefore describing that human element is a necessary starting point if we are to evaluate whether current or future technologies challenge that" (Article 36 2016, 2). That is, the desire to ensure MHC over AWS is based on the recognition that States are embarking on a path of weapon development that promises to reduce direct human participation in conducting attacks,[3] but it is not yet clear how the removal of that human element would be accommodated in the legal and ethical decisions that must be made in the course of an armed conflict.

Specifically, Article 36 developed MHC from two premises:

> 1. That a machine applying force and operating without any human control whatsoever is broadly considered unacceptable.
> 2. That a human simply pressing a 'fire' button in response to indications from a computer, without cognitive clarity or awareness, is not sufficient to be considered 'human control' in a substantive sense. (Article 36 2016, 2)

The idea is that some form of human control over the use of force is required, and that human control cannot be merely a token or a formality; human influence over acts of violence by a weapon system must be sufficient to ensure that those acts are done only in accordance with human designs and, implicitly, in accordance with legal and ethical constraints. 'Meaningful' is the term chosen to represent that threshold of sufficiency. MHC therefore "represents a space for discussion and negotiation.

The word 'meaningful' functions primarily as an indicator that the form or nature of human control necessary requires further definition in policy discourse" (Article 36 2016, 2). Attention should not be focused too closely on the precise definition of 'meaningful' in this context.

There are other words that could be used instead of 'meaningful,' for example: appropriate, effective, sufficient, necessary. Any one of these terms leaves open the same key question: How will the international community delineate the key elements of human control needed to meet these criteria? (Article 36 2016, 2).

The purpose of discussing MHC is simply "to delineate the elements of human control that should be considered necessary in the use of force" (Article 36 2016, 2).

In terms of IHL in particular, Article 36 believes that a failure to maintain MHC when employing AWS risks diluting the central role of 'attacks' in regulating the use of weapons in armed conflict.

> it is over individual 'attacks' that certain legal judgments must be applied. So attacks are part of the structure of the law, in that they represent units of military action and of human legal application. (Article 36 2016, 2)

Article 57 of API obliges "those who plan or decide upon an attack" to take certain precautions. The NGO claims that "humans must make a legal determination about an attack on a specific military objective based on the circumstances at the time" (Article 36 2016, 3), and the combined effect of Articles 51, 52, and 57 of API is that

> a machine cannot identify and attack a military objective without human legal judgment and control being applied in relation to an attack on that specific military objective at that time . . . Arguing that this capacity can be programmed into the machine is an abrogation of human legal agency—breaching the 'case-by-case' approach that forms the structure of these legal rules. (Article 36 2016, 3)

Further,

> the drafters' intent at the time was to require humans (those who plan or decide) to utilize their judgment and volition in taking precautionary measures on an attack-by-attack basis. Humans are the agents that a party to a conflict relies upon to engage in hostilities, and are the addressees of the law as written. (Roff and Moyes 2016, 5)

Thus, "the existing legal structure . . . implies certain boundaries to independent machine operation" (Article 36 2016, 3). Use of AWS that might be able to initiate attacks on their own, selecting and engaging targets without human intervention, threatens the efficacy of the legal structure:

> autonomy in certain critical functions of weapons systems might produce an expansion of the concept of 'an attack' away from the granularity of the tactical level, towards the operational and strategic. That is to say, AWS being used in 'attacks' which in their spatial, temporal or conceptual boundaries

> go significantly beyond the units of military action over which specific legal judgement would currently be expected to be applied. (Article 36 2016, 3)

Whereas:

> By asserting the need for [MHC] over attacks in the context of [AWS], states would be asserting a principle intended to protect the structure of the law, as a framework for application of wider moral principles. (Article 36 2016, 3)

As to the form of human control that would be 'meaningful' in this context, Article 36 proposes four key elements:

- Predictable, reliable, and transparent technology: on a technical level, the design of AWS must facilitate human control. "A technology that is by design unpredictable, unreliable and un-transparent is necessarily more difficult for a human to control in a given situation of use." (Article 36 2016, 4)
- Accurate information for the user on the outcome sought, the technology, and the context of use: human commanders should be provided with sufficient information "to assess the validity of a specific military objective at the time of an attack, and to evaluate a proposed attack in the context of the legal rules" (Article 36 2016, 4); to know what types of objects will be targeted, and how kinetic force will be applied; and to understand the environment in which the attack will be conducted.
- Timely human judgment and action, and a potential for timely intervention: human commanders must apply their judgement and choose to activate the AWS. "For a system that may operate over a longer period of time, some capacity for timely intervention (e.g. to stop the independent operation of a system) may be necessary if it is not to operate outside of the necessary human control." (Article 36 2016, 4)
- A framework of accountability: structures of accountability should encompass the personnel responsible or specific attacks as well as "the wider system that produces and maintains the technology, and that produces information on the outcomes being sought and the context of use." (Article 36 2016, 4)

In summary, Article 36 sees the management of individual attacks at the tactical level as the key to regulating the use of force in armed conflict. The law requires legal judgments by the appropriate human personnel in relation to each individual attack, and the design and use of AWS must not exclude those judgments.

Other actors who have taken up the idea of MHC see it somewhat differently and have put forward their own views on the criteria for human control to be 'meaningful.' The International Committee for Robot Arms Control (ICRAC), in its statement on technical issues at the 2014 CCW meetings (Sauer 2014), expressed concern about the considerable technical challenges facing developers of AWS, and support for MHC as a means of ensuring that humans are able to compensate for those shortcomings:

Humans need to exercise meaningful control over weapons systems to counter the limitations of automation.

ICRAC hold that the minimum necessary conditions for meaningful control are

First, a human commander (or operator) must have full contextual and situational awareness of the target area and be able to perceive and react to any change or unanticipated situations that may have arisen since planning the attack.

Second, there must be active cognitive participation in the attack and sufficient time for deliberation on the nature of the target, its significance in terms of the necessity and appropriateness of attack, and likely incidental and possible accidental effects of the attack.

Third, there must be a means for the rapid suspension or abortion of the attack. (Sauer 2014)

Notably, some of these conditions go beyond the levels of awareness and direct involvement that commanders are able to achieve using some existing weapon systems: "humans have been employing weapons where they lack perfect, real-time situational awareness of the target area since at least the invention of the catapult" (Horowitz and Scharre 2015, 9).

At the 2015 CCW meetings, Maya Brehm focused on control over the harm suffered by persons and objects affected by an attack:

> it is generally expected in present practice that human beings exercise some degree of control over:
>
> - *Who* or *what* is harmed
> - *When* force is applied / harm is experienced
> - *Where* force is applied / harm is experienced
> - *Why* someone or something is targeted / harmed . . . and *how* armed force is used (Brehm 2015, 1–2)[4]

According to Brehm, MHC requires that attackers have sufficient information about the effects of an attack to:

> anticipate the reasonably foreseeable consequences of force application. Only if [attackers] can anticipate these consequences, can they make the required legal assessments about the use of force. (Brehm 2015, 2)

Consequently, the degree of autonomy allowed to a weapon system must be limited such that human attackers can be sure of having sufficient information about how the weapon system will behave once it is activated.

According to CNAS, the purpose of MHC should be

> to ensure that human operators and commanders are making conscious decisions about the use of force, and that they have enough information when making those decisions to remain both legally and morally accountable for their actions. (Centre for a New American Security 2015, 1)

Horowitz and Scharre, also writing in association with CNAS, have summarized the "two general schools of thought about how to answer the question of why [MHC] is important" (Horowitz and Scharre 2015, 7).

The first is that MHC is not, and should not be, a stand-alone requirement, but is

> a principle for the design and use of weapon systems in order to ensure that their use can comply with the laws of war. This . . . starts from the assumption that the rules that determine whether the use of a weapon is legal are the same whether a human delivers a lethal blow directly, a human launches a weapon from an unmanned system, or a human deploys an [AWS] that selects and engages targets on its own. (Horowitz and Scharre 2015, 7)

The second school of thought positions MHC as an additional legal principle that should be explicitly recognized alongside existing principles of IHL. It states that

> the existing principles under the laws of war are necessary but not sufficient for addressing issues raised by increased autonomy, and that [MHC] is a separate and additional concept. . . . even if an [AWS] could be used in a way that would comply with existing laws of war, it should be illegal if it could not meet the additional standard of [MHC]. (Horowitz and Scharre 2015, 7)

The authors then suggest three essential components of a useful MHC concept:

1. Human operators are making informed, conscious decisions about the use of weapons.
2. Human operators have sufficient information to ensure the lawfulness of the action they are taking, given what they know about the target, the weapon, and the context for action.
3. The weapon is designed and tested, and human operators are properly trained, to ensure effective control over the use of the weapon. (Horowitz and Scharre 2015, 14–15)

Geiss offers some more specific suggestions about what may constitute MHC:

> the requisite level of control can refer to several factors: the time-span between the last decision taken by humans and the exertion of force by the machine; the environment in which the machine comes to be deployed, especially with regard to the question of whether civilians are present in that environment; . . . whether the machine is supposed to engage in defensive or offensive tasks; . . . whether the machine is set up to apply lethal force; the level of training of the persons tasked with exercising control over the machine; . . . the extent to which people are in a position to intervene, should the need arise, and to halt the mission; the implementation of safeguards with regard to responsibility. (Geiss 2015, 24–25)

Horowitz and Scharre also raise the question of the level at which MHC should be exercised. While most commentators focus on commanders responsible for an attack at the tactical level, there are other personnel who are well-positioned to ensure that humans remain in control of AWS.

> At the highest level of abstraction, a commander deciding on the rules of engagement for a given use of force is exercising [MHC] over the use of force. Below that, there is an individual commander ordering a particular attack against a particular target . . . Along a different axis, [MHC] might refer to the way a weapon system is designed in the first place (Horowitz and Scharre 2015, 15).

3.3: ALTERNATIVES

Some participants have proposed alternatives to MHC. While not disagreeing with the underlying proposition that humans must remain in control of, and accountable for, acts committed via AWS, their view is that attempting to define an objective standard of MHC is not the correct approach.

The United States delegation to the CCW meetings presented the notion of "appropriate levels of human judgment" being applied to AWS operations, with 'appropriate' being a contextual standard:

> there is no "one-size-fits-all" standard for the correct level of human judgment to be exercised over the use of force with [AWS]. Rather, as a general matter, [AWS] vary greatly depending on their intended use and context. In particular, the level of human judgment over the use of force that is appropriate will vary depending on factors, including, the type of functions performed by the weapon system; the interaction between the operator and the weapon system, including the weapon's control measures; particular aspects of the weapon system's operating environment (for example, accounting for the proximity of civilians), the expected fluidity of or changes to the weapon system's operational parameters, the type of risk incurred, and the weapon system's particular mission objective. In addition, engineers and scientists will continue to develop technological innovations, which also counsels for a flexible policy standard that allows for an assessment of the appropriate level of human judgment for specific new technologies. (Meier 2016)

Measures taken to ensure that appropriate levels of human judgment are applied to AWS operations would then cover the engineering and testing of the weapon systems, training of the users, and careful design of the interfaces between weapon systems and users.

Finally, the Polish delegation to the CCW meetings in 2015 preferred to think of State control over AWS, rather than human control:

> What if we accept MHC as a starting point for developing national strategies towards [AWS]? We could view MHC from the standpoint of [S]tate's affairs, goals and consequences of its actions. In that way this concept could also be regarded as the exercise of "meaningful [S]tate control" (MSC). A [S]tate should always be held accountable for what it does, especially for the responsible use of weapons which is delegated to the armed forces. The same goes also for [AWS]. The responsibility of [S]tates for such weapons should also be

extended to their development, production, acquisition, handling, storage or international transfers. (Poland 2015, 1)

3.4: ARGUMENTS AGAINST MHC

The general proposition that humans should maintain close control over the weapons they use is indisputable. Nevertheless, attempts to relate MHC to IHL appear to be generally counterproductive. At most, MHC could reasonably be seen, in Horowitz and Scharre's terms, as "a principle for the design and use of weapon systems in order to ensure that their use can comply with the laws of war" (Horowitz and Scharre 2015). Even in that respect, though, it is an unnecessary addition; the existing rules of IHL are already sufficient to regulate use of AWS. The principal argument against introducing the idea of MHC into a discussion of AWS and IHL, especially in its more expansive form as a stand-alone principle or rule, is that it is based on two false premises, one technical and one legal.

The false technical premise underlying a perceived need for MHC is that it assumes that the software and hardware that make up an AWS control system do not themselves constitute an exercise of MHC. One cannot rationally raise the concern that the autonomous capabilities of weapons should be limited in order to ensure humans maintain sufficient control if one understands the weapon's control system as the means by which human control is already maintained.

Yet, machine autonomy is a form of control, not a weakening of control. Weapon developers draw on human operational understanding of how targets are to be selected and attacks are to be conducted, technical understanding of how to operate weapons, and legal understanding of the rules of IHL in programming AWS control systems. Weapon reviews conducted by responsible humans test and verify the behavior of AWS in the conditions in which they are intended to be used, ensuring they comply with all relevant rules of weapons law. Attack planners and commanders are required by existing rules of IHL to "[t]ake all feasible precautions in the choice of means and methods of attack with a view to avoiding, and in any event to minimizing, incidental loss of civilian life, injury to civilians and damage to civilian objects" (API art 57(2)(a)(ii)); that means, at a minimum, selecting an AWS that has been shown to operate successfully in the circumstances of the attack at hand. After an AWS is activated, its control system, tested by humans, controls the weapon system in the circumstances for which it has been tested, just as the control systems of existing weapons do. It is difficult to see how any part of that process can be interpreted as constituting a lack of human control.

Concerns about maintaining human control over AWS might best be understood as fears about events that might occur after the weapon system is activated in the course of an attack; fears that it might perform some proscribed act, such as firing upon a civilian target. If such an unfortunate event were to occur, it would be the result of either an intentional act by a human, a malfunction by the AWS, or unavoidable collateral damage. None of those concerns are unique to AWS, and all are considered in existing law; no new notion of MHC is required.

The false legal premise underlying MHC is that it assumes that existing rules of IHL do not ensure a level of human control over AWS sufficient to achieve the aims of the law. Examination of current targeting law shows that is not the case. It does not appear possible for a weapon system to be beyond human control without its use necessarily violating an existing rule. If attack planners cannot foresee that an AWS will engage only legal targets, then they cannot meet their obligations under the principle of distinction (API article 57(2)(a)(i)). If they cannot ensure that civilian harm will be minimized and that the AWS will refrain from attacking some objective if the civilian harm would be excessive, then they cannot meet their obligations under the principle of proportionality (API art 57(2)(a)(iii)). If they cannot ensure that the AWS will cancel or suspend an attack if conditions change, they also fail to meet their obligations (API art 57(2)(b)).

There seems to have been some confusion on this point. Human Rights Watch has cited the bans on several existing weapons as evidence of a need for recognition of MHC:

> Although the specific term [MHC] has not appeared in international arms treaties, the idea of human control is not new in disarmament law. Recognition of the need for human control is present in prohibitions of mines and chemical and biological weapons, which were motivated in part by concern about the inability to dictate whom they engage and when. After a victim-activated mine is deployed, a human operator cannot determine at what moment it will detonate or whom it will injure or kill. Although a human can choose the moment and initial target of a biological or chemical weapons attack, the weapons' effects after release are uncontrollable and can extend across space and time causing unintended casualties. The bans on mines and chemical and biological weapons provide precedent for prohibiting weapons over which there is inadequate human control. (Human Rights Watch 2016, 10)

Examination of the prohibitions on mines (Ottawa Convention 1999), biological (Henckaerts and Doswald-Beck 2005, 256), and chemical (Henckaerts and Doswald-Beck 2005, 259) weapons shows they were each prohibited for violating fundamental rules and principles that long predate any notion of MHC as a standalone concept. Insofar as one may view indiscriminate behavior of a weapon or substance as evidence of an inability to exercise control, then the bans could be attributed to a lack of control, but in that case, the idea of MHC seems to add nothing to the existing principle of distinction. Mines are strictly regulated because a simple pressure switch is a very imprecise means of identifying a combatant; biological and chemical weapons employ harmful agents the effects of which are indiscriminate, independently of how the weapon system itself is controlled.

Beyond those two main concerns, recognizing MHC as a limitation on the development of new control system technologies risks interfering with advances that might improve an attacker's ability to engage military objectives with greater precision, and less risk of civilian harm, than is currently possible. Human Rights Watch has previously recognized the value of precision weapons in attacking targets in densely populated areas (Human Rights Watch 2003); it seems implausible to suggest that further advances in selecting and assessing potential targets onboard a weapon system after activation will not create further opportunities for avoiding civilian casualties.

Finally, even if fears about a likely path of weapon development are seen as a valid basis for regulation, it is not clear exactly what development path proponents of MHC are concerned about: Is it that AWS will be too 'smart,' or not 'smart' enough? Fears that AWS will be too smart amount to fears that humans will be unable to predict their behavior in the complex and chaotic circumstances of an attack. Fears that AWS will not be smart enough amount to fears that they will fail in a more predictable way, whether it be in selecting legitimate targets or another failure mode. In either case, using a weapon that is the object of such concerns would breach existing precautionary obligations.

3.5: CONTROLLABILITY

Existing IHL does not contemplate any significant level of autonomous capability in weapon systems. It implicitly assumes that each action of a weapon will be initiated by a human being and that after completion of that action, the weapon will cease operating until a human initiates some other action. If there is a failure in the use of a weapon, such that a rule of IHL is broken, it is assumed to be either a human failure (further assuming that the weapon used is not inherently illegal), or a failure of the weapon which would be immediately known to its human operator. Generally, facilities would be available to prevent that failure from continuing uncontrolled.

If an AWS fails after being activated, in circumstances in which a human cannot quickly intervene, its failure will be in the nature of a machine rather than a human. The possibility of runaway failure is often mentioned by opponents of AWS development. Horowitz and Scharre mention it in arguing for 'controllability' as an essential element of MHC:

> Militaries generally have no interest in developing weapon systems that they cannot control. However, a military's tolerance for risk could vary considerably . . . The desire for a battlefield advantage could push militaries to build weapons with high degrees of autonomy that diminish human control . . . While any weapon has the potential for failure and accidents, [AWS] arguably add a new dimension, since a failure could, in theory, lead to the weapon system selecting and engaging a large number of targets inappropriately. Thus, one potential concern is the development of weapons that are legal when functioning properly, but that are unsafe and have the potential to cause a great deal of harm if they malfunction or face unanticipated situations on the battlefield. (Horowitz and Scharre 2015, 8)

Use of AWS in situations where a human is not able to quickly intervene, such as on long operations or in contested environments, may change the nature of the risk borne by noncombatants.

Controllability, as described by Horowitz and Scharre, could be seen as no different to the requirement for any weapon to be capable of being directed at a specific military objective, and malfunctions are similarly a risk, which accompanies all weapon systems. To an extent, the different type of risk that accompanies failure of an AWS is simply a factor that must be considered by attack planners in their precautionary obligations. However, if that risk acts to prevent the advantages of AWS from being realized, then one possible response might be to recognize a requirement for a failsafe, whether that be a facility for human intervention, or some other form:

> Although some systems may be designed to operate at levels faster than human capacity, there should be some feature for timely intervention by either another system, process, or human. (Roff and Moyes 2016, 3)

3.6: CONCLUSION

A desire to maintain MHC over the operations of AWS is a response to the perception that some human element would be removed from military operations by increasing the autonomous capabilities of weapon systems—a perception that has been problematized in this chapter. The idea that a formal requirement for MHC may be identified in, or added to, existing IHL was originated by civil society actors and is being taken up by an increasing number of states participating in the CCW discussions on AWS.

Although the precise definition of MHC is yet to be agreed upon, it appears to be conceptually flawed. It relies on the mistaken premise that autonomous technologies constitute a lack of human control, and on a mistaken understanding that IHL does not already mandate adequate human control over weapon systems.

NOTES

1. In this chapter, as in the wider debate, 'meaningful human control' describes a quality that is deemed to be necessary in order for an attack to comply with IHL rules. It does not refer to a particular class of weapon systems that allows or requires some minimum level of human control, although it implies that a weapon used in a legally compliant attack would necessarily allow a meaningful level of human control.
2. For another analysis, see Crootof 2016, p. 53.
3. For a general discussion of the decline of direct human involvement in combat decision-making, see Adams 2001.
4. Emphasis in original.

WORKS CITED

Adams, Thomas K., 2001. "Future Warfare and the Decline of Human Decisionmaking." *Parameters* 31 (4): pp. 57–71.

Additional Protocol I (AP I). *Protocol Additional to the Geneva Conventions of August 12, 1949, and Relating to the Protection of Victims of International Armed Conflicts*, 1125 UNTS 3, opened for signature June 8, 1977, entered into force December 7, 1978.

African Commission on Human and Peoples' Rights, 2015. "General Comment No. 3 on the African Charter on Human and Peoples' Rights: The Right to Life (Article 4)." *57th ordinary session (November 18, 2015)*. http://www.achpr.org/instruments/general-comments-right-to-life/.

Article 36, 2013. "Killer Robots: UK Government Policy on Fully Autonomous Weapons." *Policy Paper.* London: Article 36. http://www.article36.org/wp-content/uploads/2013/04/Policy_Paper1.pdf?con=&dom=pscau&src=syndication.

Article 36, 2014. "Key Areas for Debate on Autonomous Weapon Systems." *Memorandum for Delegates at the CCW Meeting of Experts on AWS, May 2014.* London: Article 36. http://www.article36.org/wp-content/uploads/2014/05/A36-CCW-May-2014.pdf.

Article 36, 2014. "Structuring Debate on Autonomous Weapon Systems." *Memorandum for Delegates to the Convention on Certain Conventional Weapons (CCW), November 2013.* London: Article 36.http://www.article36.org/wp-content/uploads/2013/11/Autonomous-weapons-memo-for-CCW.pdf.

Article 36, 2016. "Key Elements of Meaningful Human Control: Background Paper to Comments Prepared by Richard Moyes for the CCW Meeting of Experts on AWS." London: Article 36.

Bolton, Matthew, Thomas Nash, and Richard Moyes, 2012. "Ban Autonomous Armed Robots." *Article 36.* March 5. http://www.article36.org/statements/ban-autonomous-armed-robots/.

Center for a New American Security, 2015. *Text, CCW Meeting of Experts on LAWS: Characteristics of LAWS.* Washington, DC: Center for a New American Security.

Crootof, Rebecca, 2016. "A Meaningful Floor for "Meaningful Human Control."' *Temple International and Comparative Law Journal* 30 (1): pp.53–62.

Development, Concepts and Doctrine Centre. 2011. *Joint Doctrine Note 2/11: The UK Approach to Unmanned Aircraft Systems.* Shrivenham, UK: Ministry of Defence.

Geiss, Robin, 2015. *The International-Law Dimension of Autonomous Weapons Systems.* Bonn, Germany: Friedrich-Ebert-Stiftung.

Germany, 2014. "Opening Statement". Geneva: Meeting of Group of Governmental Experts on LAWS. May 13–16.

Henckaerts, Jean-Marie and Louise Doswald-Beck, 2005. *Customary International Humanitarian Law,* vol.1, Cambridge: Cambridge University Press.

Horowitz, Michael C. and Paul Scharre, 2015. *Meaningful Human Control in Weapon Systems: A Primer,* Washington, DC: Center for a New American Security.

Human Rights Watch, 2003. *Off Target: The Conduct of the War and Civilian Casualties in Iraq (2003) Summary and Recommendations.* New York: Human Rights Watch. https://www.hrw.org/reports/2003/usa1203/usa1203_sumrecs.pdf.

Human Rights Watch, 2016. "Killer Robots and the Concept of Meaningful Human Control." *Memorandum to CCW Delegates.* https://www.hrw.org/sites/default/files/supporting_resources/robots_meaningful_human_control_final.pdf.

Japan. 2016. "Opening Statement." Geneva: Meeting of Group of Governmental Experts on LAWS. April 11–15.

Meier, Michael, 2016. "U.S. Delegation Statement on "Appropriate Levels of Human Judgment." *Statement to the CCW Informal Meeting of Experts on AWS, April 12, 2016.* https://geneva.usmission.gov/2016/04/12/u-s-delegation-statement-on-appropriate-levels-of-human-judgment/.

Norway. 2014. "Opening Statement." Geneva: Meeting of Group of Governmental Experts on LAWS. May 13–16.

('Ottawa Convention'). *Convention on the Prohibition of the Use, Stockpiling, Production and Transfer of Anti-Personnel Mines and on their Destruction,* 2056 UNTS 211, opened for signature September 18 1997, entered into force March 1, 1999.

Poland. 2015. "Meaningful Human Control as a form of state control over LAWS." Geneva: Meeting of Group of Governmental Experts on LAWS. April 13.

Republic of Korea. 2015. "Opening Statement." Geneva: Meeting of Group of Governmental Experts on LAWS. April 13–17.

Roff, Heather M. and Richard Moyes, 2016. "Meaningful Human Control, Artificial Intelligence and Autonomous Weapons." *Briefing paper for delegates at the CCW Meeting of Experts on AWS*. London: Article 36.

Sauer, Frank, 2014. *ICRAC Statement on Technical Issues to the 2014 UN CCW Expert Meeting (14 May 2014)*. International Committee for Robot Arms Control. http://icrac.net/2014/05/icrac-statement-on-technical-issues-to-the-un-ccw-expert-meeting/.

Sayler, Kelley, 2015. *Statement to the UN Convention on Certain Conventional Weapons on Meaningful Human Control*. Washington, DC: Center for a New American Security.

United Kingdom, 2013. "Lord Astor of Hever Column 958, 3pm." *Parliamentary Debates*. London: House of Lords. http://www.publications.parliament.uk/pa/ld201213/ldhansrd/text/130326-0001.htm#st_14.

United Nations Institute for Disarmament Research (UNIDIR), 2014. "The Weaponization of Increasingly Autonomous Technologies: Considering How Meaningful Human Control Might Move the Discussion Forward." *Discussion Paper*. Geneva: United Nations Institute for Disarmament Research.

United States. 2016. "Opening Statement." Geneva: Meeting of Group of Governmental Experts on LAWS. April 11–15.

4

The Humanitarian Imperative for Minimally-Just AI in Weapons

JASON SCHOLZ[1] AND JAI GALLIOTT

4.1: INTRODUCTION

Popular actors, famous business leaders, prominent scientists, lawyers. and humanitarians, as part of the Campaign to Stop Killer Robots, have called for a ban on autonomous weapons. On November 2, 2017, a letter organized by the Campaign was sent to Australia's prime minister stating "Australia's AI research community is calling on you and your government to make Australia the 20th country in the world to take a firm global stand against weaponizing AI" fearing inaction—a "consequence of this is that machines—*not people*—will determine who lives and dies" (Walsh 2017). It appears that they mean a complete ban on *AI in weapons*, an interpretation consistent with their future vision of a world awash with miniature 'slaughterbots.'[2]

We hold that a ban on AI in weapons may prevent the development of solutions to current humanitarian crises. Every day in the world news, real problems are happening with conventional weapons. Consider situations like the following: a handgun stolen from a police officer and subsequently used to kill innocent persons, rifles used for mass shootings in US schools, vehicles used to mow down pedestrians in public places, bombing of religious sites, a guided-bomb strike on a train bridge as an unexpected passenger train passes, a missile strike on a Red Cross facility, and so on—all might be prevented. These are real situations where a weapon or autonomous system equipped with AI might intervene to *save lives* by deciding who lives.

Jason Scholz and Jai Galliott, *The Humanitarian Imperative for Minimally-Just AI in Weapons* In: *Lethal Autonomous Weapons*. Edited by: Jai Galliott, Duncan MacIntosh and Jens David Ohlin, © Oxford University Press (2021).
DOI: 10.1093/oso/9780197546048.003.0005

Confusion about the means to achieve desired nonviolence is not new. A general disdain for simple technological solutions aimed at a better state of peace was prevalent in the antinuclear campaign spanning the whole confrontation period with the Soviet Union, recently renewed with the invention of miniaturized warheads, and the campaign to ban land mines in the late nineties.[3] Yet, it does not seem unreasonable to ask why weapons with advanced seekers could not embed AI to identify a symbol of the Red Cross and abort an ordered strike. Nor is it unreasonable to suggest that the location of protected sites of religious significance, schools, or hospitals might be programmed into weapons to constrain their actions, or that AI-enabled guns be prevented from firing by an unauthorized user pointing it at humans. And why initiatives cannot begin to test these innovations so that they might be ensconced in international weapons review standards?

We assert that while autonomous systems are likely to be incapable of action leading to the attribution of *moral responsibility* (Hew 2014) in the near term, they might today autonomously execute value-laden decisions embedded in their design and in code, so they can perform actions to meet enhanced ethical and legal standards.

4.2: THE ETHICAL MACHINE SYSTEM

Let us discern between two ends of a spectrum of ethical capability. A maximally-just 'ethical machine' (MaxAI) guided by both acceptable and nonacceptable actions has the benefit of ensuring that ethically obligatory lethal action is taken, even when system engineers of a lesser system may not have recognized the need or possibility of the relevant lethal action. However, a maximally-just ethical robot requires extensive ethical engineering. Arkin's 'ethical governor' (Arkin, Ulam, and Duncan 2009) represents probably the most advanced prototype effort toward a maximally-just system. The ethical governor would provide an assessment of whether proposed lethal actions are consistent with the laws of war and rules of engagement. The maximally-just position is apparent from the explanation of the operation of the constraint interpreter, which is a key part of the governor: "The constraint application process is responsible for reasoning about the active ethical constraints and ensuring that the resulting behavior of the robot is ethically permissible" (Arkin, Ulam, and Duncan 2009). That is, the constraint system, based on complex deontic and predicate logic, evaluates the proposed actions generated by the tactical reasoning engine of the system based on an equally complex data structure. Reasoning about the full scope of what is *ethically permissible under all possible conditions* including general distinction of combatants from noncombatants, proportionality, unnecessary suffering, and rules of engagement, as Arkin describes, is a hard problem.

In contrast, a MinAI 'ethical robot,' while still a constraint-driven system, could operate without an 'ethical governor' proper and need only contain an elementary suppressor of human-generated lethal action. Further, as it would activate in accordance with a much narrower set of constraints, it may be hard rather than soft coded, meaning far less system 'interpretation' would be required. MinAI deals with what is *ethically impermissible*. Thus, we assert under *certain specific conditions*, distinction, proportionality, and protected conditions may be assessed, as follows:

- *Distinction of the ethically impermissible* including the avoidance of application of force against 'protected' things such as objects and persons marked with the protected symbols of the Red Cross, as well as protected locations, recognizable protected behaviors such as desire to parlay, basic signs of surrender (including beacons), and potentially those that are *hors de combat*, or are clearly noncombatants; noting of course that AI solutions range here from easy to more difficult—but not impossible—and will continue to improve along with AI technologies.

- *Ethical reduction in proportionality* includes a reduction in the degree of force below the level lawfully authorized if it is determined to be sufficient to meet military necessity.

MinAI then is three things: an ethical control to augment any conventional weapon, a system limited to decision and action on logical negative cases of things that should *not* be attacked, and is practically achievable with state-of-the-art AI techniques.

The basic technical concept for a MinAI Ethical Weapon is an augmentation to a standard weapon control system. The weapon seeker, which may be augmented with other sensors, provides input to an ethical and legal perception-action system. This system uses training data, developed, tested, and certified prior to the operation and outputs a decision state to override the target order and generate alternate orders on the control system in the event of a world state that satisfies MinAI conditions. The decision override is intended to divert the weapon to another target, or a preoperation-specified failsafe location and/or to neutralize or reduce the payload effect accordingly.

Noteworthy is that while MinAI will always be more limited in technical nature, it may be more morally desirable in that it will yield outcomes that are as good as or possibly even better than MaxAI in a range of specific circumstances. The former will never take active lethal or non-lethal action to harm protected persons or infrastructure. In contrast, MaxAI involves the codification of normative values into rule sets and the interpretation of a wide range of inputs through the application of complex and potentially imperfect machine logic. This more complex 'algorithmic morality,' while potentially desirable in some circumstances, involves a greater possibility of actively introducing fatal errors, particularly in terms of managing conflicts between interests.

Cognizant of the above, our suggestion is that in terms of meeting our fundamental moral obligations to humanity, we are ethically justified to develop MinAI systems. The ethical agency of said system, while embedded in the machine and thus technologically mediated by the design, engineering, and operational environment, is fewer steps removed from human moral agency than in a MaxAI system. We would suggest that MaxAI development is supererogatory in the sense that it may be morally beneficial in particular circumstances, but is not necessarily morally required, and may even be demonstrated to be unethical.

4.3: MINIMALLY-JUST AI AS HEDGING ONE'S BETS

To the distaste of some, it might be argued that the moral desirability of MinAI will decrease in the near future as the AI underpinning MaxAI becomes more robust, and we move away from rule-based and basic neural network systems toward artificial general intelligence (AGI) and that resources should, therefore, be dedicated to the development of maximal 'ethical robots.' To be clear, there have been a number of algorithm success stories announced in recent years, across all of the cognate disciplines. Much attention has been given to the ongoing development of Algorithms as a basis for the success of AlphaGo (Silver et al. 2017) and Libratus (Brown and Sandholm 2018). These systems are competing and winning against the best human Go and Poker players respectively, individuals who have made acquiring deep knowledge of these games their life's work. The result of these preliminary successes has been a dramatic increase in media reporting on, and interest in, the potential opportunities and pitfalls associated with the development of AI, not all of which are accurate and some of which has negatively impacted public perception of AI, fueling the kind of dystopian visions advanced by the Campaign to Stop Killer Robots, as mentioned earlier.

The speculation that superintelligence is on the foreseeable horizon, with AGI timelines in the realm of twenty to thirty years, reflects the success stories while omitting discussion of recent failures in AI. Many of these undoubtedly go unreported for commercial and classification reasons, but Microsoft's Tay AI Bot, a machine learning chatbot that learns from interactions with digital users, is but one example (Hunt 2016). After a short period of operation, Tay developed an 'ego' or 'character' that was strongly sexual and racialized, and ultimately had to be withdrawn from service. Facebook had similar problems with its AI message chatbots assuming undesirable characteristics, and a number of autonomous road vehicles have now been involved in motor vehicle accidents where the relevant systems were incapable when handling the scenario and quality assurance practices failed to factor for such events.

There are also known and currently irresolvable problems with the complex neural networks on which the successes in AI have mostly been based. These bottom-up systems can learn well in tight domains and easily outperform humans in these scenarios based on data structures and their correlations, but they cannot match the top-down rationalizing power of human beings in more open domains such as road systems and conflict zones. Such systems are risky in these environments because they require strict compliance with laws and regulations; and it would be difficult to question, interpret, explain, supervise, and control them by virtue of the fact that deep learning systems cannot easily track their own 'reasoning' (Ciupa 2017).

Just as importantly, when more intuitive and therefore less explainable systems come into wide operation, it may not be so easy to revert to earlier stage systems as human operators become reliant on the system to make difficult decisions, with the danger that their own moral decision-making skills may have deteriorated over time (Galliott 2017). In the event of failure, total system collapse could occur with devastating consequences if such systems were committed to mission-critical operations required in armed conflict.

There are, moreover, issues associated with functional complexity and the practical computational limits imposed on mobile systems that need to be capable of independent operation in the event of a communications failure. The computers required for AGI-level systems may not be subject to miniaturization or simply may not be sufficiently powerful or cost effective for the intended purpose, especially in a military context in which autonomous weapons are sometimes considered disposable platforms (Ciupa 2017). The hope for advocates of AGI is that computer processing power and other system components will continue to become dramatically smaller, cheaper, and powerful, but there is no guarantee that Moore's Law, which supports such expectations, will continue to reign true without extensive progress in the field of quantum computing.

Whether or not AGI should eventuate, MaxAI appears to remain a distant goal with a far from certain end result. A MinAI system, on the other hand, seeks to ensure that the obvious and uncontroversial benefits of artificial intelligence (AI) are harnessed while the associated risks are kept under control by normal military targeting processes. Action needs to be taken now to intercept grandiose visions that may not eventuate and instead deliver a positive result with technology that already exists.

4.4: IMPLEMENTATION

International Humanitarian Law Article 36 states (ICRC 1949), "In the study, development, acquisition or adoption of a new weapon, means or method of warfare, a High Contracting Party is under an obligation to determine whether its employment would, in some or all circumstances, be prohibited by this Protocol or by any other rule of international law applicable to the High Contracting Party." The Commentary of 1987 to the Article further indicates that a State must review not only new weapons, but also any existing weapon that is modified in a way that alters its function, or a weapon that has already passed a legal review that is subsequently modified. Thus, the insertion of minimally-just AI in a weapon would require Article 36 review.

The customary approach to assessment (ICRC 2006) to comply with Article 36 covers the technical description and technical performance of the weapon and assumes humans assess and decide weapon use. Artificial intelligence poses challenges for assessment under Article 36, where there was once a clear separation of human decision functions from weapon-technical function assessment. Assessment approaches need to extend to embedded decision-making and acting capability for MinAI.

Although Article 36 deliberately avoids imposing how such a determination is carried out, it might be in the interests of the International Committee of the Red Cross and humanity to do so in this specific case. Consider the first reference in international treaties to the need to carry out legal reviews of new weapons (ICRC 1868). As a precursor to IHL Article 36, this treaty has a broader scope, "The Contracting or Acceding Parties reserve to themselves to come hereafter to an understanding whenever a precise proposition shall be drawn up in view of future improvements which science may effect in the armament of troops, in order to maintain the principles which they have established, and to conciliate the necessities of war with the laws of humanity" (ICRC 1868). MinAI in weapons and autonomous systems is such a precise proposition. The potential to improve humanitarian outcomes by embedding the capability to identify and prevent attacks on protected objects in weapon systems might form a recommended standard.

The sharing of technical data and algorithms for achieving this standard means through Article 36 would drive down the cost of implementation and expose systems to countermeasures that improve their hardening.

4.5: SIGNALS OF SURRENDER

4.5.1: Current Signals of Surrender and Their Recognition

Signals of surrender in the law consider only human recognition. Given the potential for machine recognition, an opportunity exists to consider the use of AI in conventional weapon systems for humanitarian purposes. It is well noted in Sparrow (2015) that a comprehensive solution to recognize those who are deemed "hors de combat" is beyond the current art of the possible for AI. However, in the spirit of 'MinAI,' any reliable form of machine recognition may contribute lifesaving improvements and so is worthy of consideration. Before appreciating the potential for possibly useful modes of MinAI recognition of surrender, we review key contemporary legal conventions.

Despite the common-sense notion of the white flag being a signal of surrender, it is not. The white flag is an internationally recognized protective sign for requesting negotiation or "parley" on the sole topic of the terms of a surrender or a truce (ICRC 1899; ICRC 1907a, Article 32). By inference in the common sense, the sign symbolizes surrender, since the weaker party is to be expected the one bearing it. However, the outcome of surrender is not a given, as this result may not ensue after negotiation. A white flag signifies that an approach is unarmed. Persons carrying or waving a white flag are not to be fired upon, nor are they allowed to open fire.

Desire for parlay is a clear instance for potential application of MinAI. Various AI techniques have been used to attempt to recognize flags "in the wild," meaning under normal viewing conditions (Ahmed et al. 2013; Hao et al. 2017; Lodh and Parekh 2016). The problem with approaching the issue in this way is the difficulty inherent in developing machine recognition of a white flag with a very high level of reliability under a wide range of conditions including nighttime or fog, in the presence of wind of various directions, and so on that may not make it visible at all. Further, the fact remains that this signal is technologically arcane, it is steeped in laws that assume human recognition (prior to the invention of AI) and applies only to the land and sea surface (prior to the invention of manned aircraft, long-range weapons, or sonar). Therefore, we defer this case for later, as it may be better considered as part of a general beacon system for surrender.

We note the ICRC Casebook on Surrender (ICRC 2019a) does include the white flag to signify an intention to cease fighting, and draw to attention the "throwing away" of weapons, which will be important for subsequent analysis,

> A unilateral act whereby, by putting their hands up, throwing away their weapons, raising a white flag or in any other suitable fashion, isolated members of armed forces or members of a formation clearly express to the enemy during battle their intention to cease fighting.

Surrender is further included in the Hague Convention Article 41 (ICRC 1977a):

> 1. A person who is recognized or who, in the circumstances, should be recognized to be 'hors de combat' shall not be made the object of attack. 2. A person is 'hors de combat' if: (a) he is in the power of an adverse Party; (b) he clearly expresses an intention to surrender; or (c) he has been rendered

> unconscious or is otherwise incapacitated by wounds or sickness, and therefore is incapable of defending himself; provided that in any of these cases he abstains from any hostile act and does not attempt to escape.

We note, with respect to 2(b), that the subject must be recognized as clearly expressing an intention to surrender and subsequently with a proviso be recognized to abstain from any hostile act and not attempting escape.

Focusing on 2(b), what constitutes a "clear expression" of intention to surrender? In past military operations, the form of expression has traditionally been conveyed via a visual signal, assuming human recognition and proximity of opposing forces. Visual signals are, of course, subject to the vagaries of visibility through the medium due to weather, obscuring smoke or particles, and other physical barriers.

Furthermore, land, air, and sea environments are different in their channeling of that expression. Surrender expressed by a soldier on the ground, a commander within a vehicle, the captain of a surface ship, the captain of a submarine, or the pilot of an aircraft will necessarily be different. Furthermore, in modern warfare, the surrendering and receiving force elements may not share either the same environment or physical proximity. The captain of an enemy ship at sea might surrender to the commander of a drone force in a land-based headquarters on the other side of the world. Each of these environments should, therefore, be considered separately.

Beginning with land warfare, Article 23 (ICRC 1907b) states:

> Art. 23. In addition to the prohibitions provided by special Conventions, it is especially forbidden...
>
> (c) To kill or wound an enemy who, having laid down his arms, or having no longer means of defence, has surrendered at discretion;

So, individual combatants can indicate a surrender by discarding weapons. Globally recognized practice includes raising the hands empty and open above the head to indicate the lack of a carried weapon such as a rifle, handgun, or grenade. In other land warfare situations, the circumstances are less clear. A surrendering tank commander and crew, for example, are physically contained within the weapon platform and not visible from the outside, and thus may need to abandon the vehicle in order to separate themselves from their "means of defence." An alternative might be to point the tank's turret away from opposing forces in order to communicate intent, though arguably this does not constitute "having no longer means of defence." Other alternatives are not clear. The origins of this law hail from a period before the invention of the tank, and in the earliest days following the invention of the motor vehicle.

In naval surface warfare, International Law requires a warship to fly its ensign or colors at the commencement of any hostile act, such as firing upon an enemy. The symbol for surrender according to Hamersley (1881) then,

> The colors... are hauled down as a token of submission.

Flags and ensigns are hauled down or furled, and ships' colors are struck, meaning lowering the flag that signifies the allegiance is a universally recognized indication of surrender, particularly for ships at sea. For a ship, surrender is dated from the time the ensign is struck. The antiquity of this practice hails from before the advent of long-range, beyond line of sight weapons for anti-surface warfare.

In the case of air warfare, according to Bruderlein (2013):

> 128. Aircrews of a military aircraft wishing to surrender ought to do everything feasible to express clearly their intention to do so. In particular, they ought to communicate their intention on a common radio channel such as a distress frequency.
>
> 129. A Belligerent Party may insist on the surrender by an enemy military aircraft being effected in a prescribed mode, reasonable in the circumstances. Failure to follow any such instructions may render the aircraft and the aircrew liable to attack.
>
> 130. Aircrews of military aircraft wishing to surrender may, in certain circumstances, have to parachute from the aircraft in order to communicate their intentions. The provisions of this Section of the Manual are without prejudice to the issue of surrender of aircrews having descended by parachute from an aircraft in distress.

We note there is no legal obligation for combatants to monitor their opponents' "distress frequencies" nor might all land, air, or sea forces have access to their opponent's common air radio channel. As noted for other domains earlier, abandonment of the platform is an option to demonstrate intent to surrender, though this is fraught with issues for aircraft. Parachuting from an aircraft puts the lives of captain and crew in significant, and possibly unnecessary, danger. The fate of what may be a functional aircraft constitutes an irresponsible act, with the potential consequence of lives being lost due to a subsequent crash landing of the abandoned aircraft, including the lives of the enemy for which such an act may not be deemed one of surrender!

Surrender protection then seems to rely on the following (Bruderlein, 2013):

> 132. (a) No person descending by parachute from an aircraft in distress may be made the object of attack during his descent.
>
> (b) Upon landing in a territory controlled by the enemy, a person who descended by parachute from an aircraft in distress is entitled to be given an opportunity to surrender prior to being made the object of attack, unless it is apparent that he is engaging in a hostile act.

However, if the captain was to communicate an intention to surrender on the radio before parachuting out, this is not technically a signal of an "aircraft in distress," and thus may not entitle them to protection. Henderson and Keane (2016) describe other issues and examples, leading one to postulate whether an aircraft can successfully surrender at all.

Modern warfare conducted beyond a visual line of sight, and across environmental domains, indicates that these current methods of surrender in the law are arcane, outdated by modern long-range weapon technologies, and out of touch with multi-domain warfare practices and so fail in their humanitarian potential. Table 4.1 summarizes current methods for expressing intent to surrender.

Table 4.1 A SUMMARY OF TODAY'S METHODS FOR EXPRESSING INTENT TO SURRENDER. A LABEL OF "UNKNOWN / NONE" INDICATES THAT RECEIVING FORCES ARE UNLIKELY TO HAVE ANY DOCTRINE OR PRIOR EXPERIENCE IN THIS.

Receiving Forces	**Surrendering Forces** Land	**Sea Surface**	**Sea Subsurface**	**Air**
Land	Lay down arms. Abandon armed vehicles.	Lower the flag (strike the colors).	Unknown / none.	Abandon aircraft whether in flight, or on the ground. Radio communication.
Sea surface	Lay down arms. Abandon armed vehicles.	Lower the flag (strike the colors).	Go to the surface and abandon vessel.	Abandon aircraft whether in flight, or on the ground. Radio communication.
Sea subsurface	Lay down arms. Abandon armed vehicles.	Lower the flag (strike the colors).	Possibly via acoustic commu-nication.	Unknown / None.
Air	Lay down arms. Abandon armed vehicles.	Lower the flag (strike the colors).	Go to the surface and abandon vessel.	Abandon aircraft whether in flight, or on the ground. Radio communication.

In addition to expressing intent to surrender, to comply with (ICRC 1977a), surrendering forces must also abstain from any hostile act and not attempt to escape. A hostile act conducted after an "offer" of surrender would constitute an act of perfidy (ICRC 1977b),

> Acts inviting the confidence of an adversary to lead him to believe that he is entitled to, or is obliged to accord, protection under the rules of international law applicable in armed conflict, with the intent to betray that confidence, shall constitute perfidy.

The surrendered must be "in the power of the adverse party" or submit to custody before they could be reasoned to be attempting escape. In armed conflict at sea, "surrendering vessels are exempt from attack" (ICRC 1994, Article 47) but surrendering aircraft are not mentioned. Noting further, Article 48 (ICRC 1994) highlights three preconditions for surrender, which could be monitored by automated systems:

> 48. Vessels listed in paragraph 47 are exempt from attack only if they:
> (a) are innocently employed in their normal role;

(b) submit to identification and inspection when required; and
(c) do not intentionally hamper the movement of combatants and obey orders to stop or move out of the way when required.

Finally, it is important to consider the "gap [that exists] in the law of war in defining precisely when surrender takes effect or how it may be accomplished in practical terms," which was recently noted by the ICRC (2019b). This gap reflects the acknowledgment that while that there is no requirement for an aggressor to offer the opportunity to surrender, communicating one's intention to surrender during an ongoing assault is "neither easily communicated nor received" (Department of Defense 1992). This difficulty has historically contributed to unnecessary death or injury, even in scenarios that only involve human actors. Consider the decision by US forces during Operation Desert Storm to use armored bulldozers to collapse fortifications and trenches on top of Iraqi combatants whose resistance was being suppressed by supporting fire from infantry fighting vehicles (Department of Defense 1992). Setting aside the legality of this tactic, this scenario demonstrates the shortcomings of existing methods of signaling surrender during a modern armored assault.

In summary, this section has highlighted the technologically arcane and parlous state of means and methods for signaling surrender, which has resulted in deaths that may not have been necessary. This has also highlighted likely difficulties in building highly reliable schemes for AI recognition based on these.

4.5.2: A Global Surrender System

The previous section shows there exists no universally agreed UN sign or signal for surrender. There is no equivalent of the Red Cross, Crescent, or Crystal symbol to signify protection for surrendering forces. We consider a system for global parlay and surrender recognition that provides both a traditional visual symbol for where it is applicable, along with a beacon system. Such a system will save laws and may avert large-scale deaths of surrendering forces, especially those subject to attack by weapons that are MinAI-enabled.

Considerations for a global system applicable to all domains and conditions, as illustrated in Table 4.2, indicate a combination of electromagnetic and acoustic beacons appear most feasible in the short term, though, emerging technology in particle beam modulation offers potential to provide a communications means that cannot be interfered with by normal matter, including even the earth.

Whatever solution, two global maritime systems provide clear indication of feasibility and potential. The first of these is the Emergency Position Indicating Radio Beacon (EPIRB) system used to communicate a distress signal of the location globally via satellite. This system has saved the lives of many sailors. The second of these is the Automated Identification System (AIS), which provides via transmitters on all vessels over 300 tonnes, specific details of their identity, location, and status to satellites and ground stations all over the world. An economical, low-cost system that blends characteristics of these systems may employ whatever required details of the surrenderer are necessary when activated, in a transmission standard formed by international agreement. Submarines might use an acoustic version of this message format for close proximity signaling or deploy a floating beacon on the sea surface.

Table 4.2 Global Parlay and Surrender System Considerations

Solution	Most usable Domains	Excluded Domains	Issues
Electromagnetic beacons via global low-cost satellite and ground receiver network	Space, air, land surface, water surface	Underground, underwater	
Acoustic beacon	Underwater	Space	Short range
Modulated high-energy particle emissions	All	None	Low data rate, direct geolocation may not be feasible

Consider that a unique electronic surrender beacon along these lines could be issued to each combatant. The beacon would have to send out a clearly recognizable signal that is recognizable across multiple spectrums, and receiver units should be made available to any nation. As technology continues to develop, short-range beacons for infantry could eventually be of a similar size to a key fob. For large, self-contained combat platforms (such as submarines or aircraft carriers), the decision to activate the surrender beacon would be the responsibility of the commander (or a delegate if the commander was incapacitated). Regardless of their size, the beacon could be designed to remain active until their battery expires, and the user would be required under IHL to remain with the beacon in order to retain their protected status.

This is not to suggest that adopting a system of EPIRB or AIS-derived identification beacons would be a straightforward or simple solution. The authors are aware that there is potential for friction or even failure of this approach; however, we contend that there are organizational and technical responses that could limit this potential. The first step toward such a system would be to develop protocols for beacon activation and response that are applicable in each of the core combat domains. These protocols would have to be universally applicable, which would require that states formally pledge to honor them and that manufacturers develop a common technical standard for surrender beacons. Similarly, MinAI weapons would have to be embedded with the capacity to immediately recognize signals from surrender beacons as a protected sign that prohibits attack and are able to communicate that to human commanders. Finally, the international community would have to agree to implement a regulatory regime that makes jamming or interfering with surrender beacons (or their perfidious use) illegal under IHL.

4.6: HUMANITARIAN COUNTER-COUNTERMEASURES

Critics may argue that combatants will develop countermeasures that aim to spoil the intended humanitarian effects of MinAI in weapons and autonomous systems. We claim it would be anti-humanitarian, and potentially illegal, to field countermeasures to MinAI. Yet, many actors do not comply with the rule of law. Thus, it is necessary to consider countermeasures to MinAI that may seek to degrade, damage, destroy, or deceive the autonomous capability in order to harden MinAI systems.

4.6.1: Degradation, Damage, or Destruction

It is expected that lawfully targeted enemies will attempt to destroy or degrade weapon performance to prevent it from achieving the intended mission. This could include a direct attack on the weapon seeker or other means. Such an attack may, as a consequence, degrade, damage, or destroy the MinAI capability. If the act is in self-defense, it is not a behavior one would expect from a humanitarian object and, therefore, the function of the MinAI is not required anyway.

If the degradation, damage, or destruction is targeted against the MinAI with the intention to cause a humanitarian disaster, it would be a criminal act. However, for this to occur, the legal appreciation of the target would have had to have failed as a precursor, prior to this act, which is the primary cause for concern.

It would be illegal under international law to degrade the signal, interfere with, willfully damage, or misuse a surrender beacon or international symbol of surrender, which is yet to be agreed by the UN. Similar laws apply to the unlawful use of global maritime emergency beacons.

4.6.2: Deception

Combatants might simply seek to deceive the MinAI capability by using, for example, a symbol of the Red Cross or Red Crescent to protect themselves, thereby averting an otherwise lawful attack. This is an act of perfidy covered under IHL Article 37. Yet, such an act may serve to improve distinction, by cross-checking perfidious sites with the Red Cross to identify anomalies. Further, given that a Red Cross is an obvious marker, wide-area surveillance might be sensitive to picking up new instances. Further, it is for this reason that we distinguish that MinAI ethical weapons respond only to the *unexpected* presence of a protected object or behavior. Of course, this is a decision made in the targeting process (which is external to the ethical weapon) as explained earlier, and would be logged for accountability and subsequent after-action review. Perfidy under the law would need to include the use of a surrender beacon to feign surrender. Finally, a commander's decision to override the MinAI system and conduct a strike on enemy combatants performing a perfidious act should be recorded by the system in order to ensure accountability.

The highest performing object recognition systems are neural networks, yet, the high dimensionality that gives them that performance may, in itself, be a vulnerability. Szedgy et al. (2014) discovered a phenomenon related to stability given small perturbations to inputs, where a nonrandom perturbation imperceptible to humans could be applied to a test image and result in an arbitrary change to its estimate. A significant body of work has since emerged on these "adversarial examples" (Akhtar and Mian 2018). Of the many and varied forms of attack, there also exists a range of countermeasures. A subclass of adversarial examples of relevance to MinAI are those that can be applied to two- and three-dimensional physical objects to change their appearance to the machine. Recently Evtimov (2017) used adversarial algorithms to generate 'camouflage paint' and three-dimensional printed objects, resulting in errors for standard deep network classifiers. Concerns include the possibility to paint a Red Cross symbol on an object that is recognizable by a weapon seeker yet invisible to the human eye, or the dual case of painting over a symbol of protection with markings resembling weathered patterns that are unnoticeable to humans yet result in an algorithm being unable to recognize the sign. In the 2017 experiment, Evtimov demonstrated this effect using a traffic stop sign symbol, which is, of course, similar to a Red Cross symbol.

In contrast to these results popularized by online media, Lu et al. (2017) demonstrated *no errors* using the same experimental setup as Evtimov (2017) and in live trials, explaining that Evtimov had confused *detectors* (like Faster Recurrent Convolutional Neural Networks) with *classifiers*. Methods used in Evtimov (2017) appear to be at fault due to pipeline problems, including perfect manual cropping, which serves as a proxy for a detector that has been assumed away, and rescaling before applying this to a classifier. In the real world, it remains difficult to conceive of a universal defeat for a detector under various real-world angles, range and light conditions, yet further research is required.

Global open access to MinAI code and data, for example Red Cross imagery and video scenes in 'the wild,' would have the significant advantage of ensuring these techniques continue to be tested and hardened under realistic conditions and architectures. Global access to MinAI algorithms and data sets would ease uptake, especially as low-cost solutions for Nations that might not otherwise afford such innovations, as well as exerting moral pressure on defense companies that do not use this resource.

International protections against countermeasures targeting MinAI might be mandated. If such protections were to be accepted it would strengthen the case, but in their absence, the moral imperative for minimally-just AI in weapons remains undiminished in light of countermeasures.

4.7: POTENTIAL OF MINIMALLY-JUST AI TO LEAD TO COMPLACENCY AND RESPONSIBILITY TRANSFER

Concerns may be raised that, should MinAI functionality be adopted for use by military forces, the technology may result in negative or positive unintended long-term consequences. This is not an easy question to answer, and the authors are conscious of how notoriously difficult it is to predict technology use; however, one possible negative effect that can be considered here is related to human complacency. Consider the hypothesis 'if MinAI technology works well and is trusted, its operators will become complacent in regard to its use, and take less care in the targeting process, leading to more deaths.'

In response, such an argument would apply equally to all uses of technology in the targeting process. Clearly however, technology is a critical enabler of intelligence and targeting functions. Complacency then seems to be a matter of adequate discipline, appropriate education, training, and system design.

A worse outcome would be for operators to abdicate their responsibilities for targeting. Campaigners have attempted to argue the creation of a "responsibility gap" in autonomous weapons before, might this be the same? Consider the hypothesis that "if MinAI technology works well and is trusted, that Commanders might just as well authorize weapon release with the highest possible explosive payload to account for the worst-case and rely on MinAI to reduce the yield according to whatever situation the system finds to be the case, leading to more deaths."

In response to this argument, we assert that this would be like treating MinAI weapon systems as if they were MaxAI weapon systems. We do not advocate MaxAI weapons. A MinAI weapon that can reduce its explosive payload under AI control is not a substitute for target analysis; it is the last line of defense against unintended harm. Further, the Commander would remain responsible for the result, regardless, under any lawful scheme. Discipline, education, and training remain critical to the responsible use of weapons.

4.8: CONCLUSION

We have presented a case for autonomy in weapons that could make lifesaving decisions in the world today. Minimally-Just AI in weapons should achieve a reduction in accidental strikes on protected persons and objects, reduce unintended strikes against noncombatants, reduce collateral damage by reducing payload delivery, and save lives of those who have surrendered.

We hope in the future that the significant resources spent on reacting to speculative fears of campaigners might one day be spent mitigating the definitive suffering of people caused by weapons that lack minimally-just autonomy based on artificial intelligence.

NOTES

1. Adjunct position at UNSW @ ADFA.
2. See http://autonomousweapons.org
3. The United States, of course, never ratified the Ottawa Treaty but rather chose a technological solution to end the use of persistent landmines—landmines that cannot be set to self-destruct or deactivate after a predefined time period—making them considerably less problematic when used in clearly demarcated and confined zones such as the Korean Demilitarized Zone.

WORKS CITED

Ahmed, Kawsar, Md. Zamilur Rahman, and Mohammad Shameemmhossain. 2013. "Flag Identification Using Support Vector Machine." *JU Journal of Information Technology* 2: pp. 11–16.

Akhtar, Naveed and Ajmal Mian. 2018. "Threat of Adversarial Attacks on Deep Learning in Computer Vision: A Survey." *IEEE Access* 6: pp. 14410–14430. doi: https://doi.org/10.1109/ACCESS.2018.2807385.

Arkin, Ronald C., Patrick Ulam, and Brittany Duncan. 2009. "An Ethical Governor for Constraining Lethal Action in an Autonomous System." *Technical Report GIT-GVU-09-02*. Atlanta: Georgia Institute of Technology.

Brown, Noam and Tuomas Sandholm. 2018. "Superhuman AI for Heads-Up No-Limit Poker: Libratus Beats Top Professionals." *Science* 359 (6374): pp. 418–424. doi: 10.1126/science.aao1733.

Bruderlein, Claude. 2013. *HPCR Manual on International Law Applicable to Air and Missile Warfare*. New York: Cambridge University Press.

Ciupa, Martin. 2017. "Is AI in Jeopardy? The Need to Under Promise and Over Deliver—The Case for Really Useful Machine Learning." In: *4th International Conference on Computer Science and Information Technology (CoSIT 2017)*. Geneva, Switzerland. pp. 59–70.

Department of Defense. 1992. "United States: Department of Defense Report to Congress on the Conduct of the Persian Gulf War—Appendix on the Role of the Law of War." *International Legal Materials* 31 (3): pp. 612–644.

Evtimov, Ivan, Kevin Eykholt, Earlence Fernandes, Tadayoshi Kohno, Bo Li, Atul Prakash, Amir Rahmati, and Dawn Xiaodong Song. 2017. "Robust Physical-World Attacks on Deep Learning Models." *CVPR 2018*. arXiv:1707.08945.

Galliott, Jai. 2017. "The Limits of Robotic Solutions to Human Challenges in the Land Domain." *Defence Studies* 17 (4): pp. 327–345.

Halleck, Henry Wagner. 1861. *International Law; or, Rules Regulating the Intercourse of States in Peace and War*. New York: D. Van Nostrand. pp. 402–405.

Hamersley, Lewis R. 1881. *A Naval Encyclopedia: Comprising a Dictionary of Nautical Words and Phrases; Biographical Notices with Description of the Principal Naval Stations and Seaports of the World*. Philadelphia: L. R. Hamersley and Company. pp. 148.

Han, Jiwan, Anna Gaszczak, Ryszard Maciol, Stuart E. Barnes, and Toby P. Breckon. 2013. "Human Pose Classification within the Context of Near-IR Imagery Tracking." *Proceedings SPIE 8901*. doi: 10.1117/12.2028375.

Hao, Kun, Zhiyi Qu, and Qian Gong. 2017. "Color Flag Recognition Based on HOG and Color Features in Complex Scene." In: *Ninth International Conference on Digital Image Processing (ICDIP 2017)*. Hong Kong: International Society for Optics and Photonics.

Henderson, Ian and Patrick Keane. 2016. "Air and Missile Warfare." In: *Routledge Handbook of the Law of Armed Conflict*, edited by Rain Liivoja and Tim McCormack, pp. 293–295. Abingdon, Oxon: Routledge.

Hew, Patrick Chisan. 2014. "Artificial Moral Agents Are Infeasible with Foreseeable Technologies." *Ethics and Information Technology* 16 (3): pp. 197–206. doi: 10.1007/s10676-014-9345-6.

Hunt, Elle. 2016. "Tay, Microsoft's AI Chatbot, Gets a Crash Course in Racism from Twitter." *The Guardian*. March 24. https://www.theguardian.com/technology/2016/mar/24/tay-microsofts-ai-chatbot-gets-a-crash-course-in-racism-from-twitter.

ICRC. 1868. "Declaration Renouncing the Use, in Time of War, of Explosive Projectiles Under 400 Grammes Weight." International Committee of the Red Cross: Customary IHL Database. Last accessed April 28, 2019. https://ihl-databases.icrc.org/ihl/WebART/130-60001?OpenDocument.

ICRC. 1899. "War on Land. Article 32." International Committee of the Red Cross: Customary IHL Database. Last accessed May 12, 2019. https://ihl-databases.icrc.org/applic/ihl/ihl.nsf/Article.xsp?action=openDocument&documentId=5A3629A73FDF2BA1C12563CD00515EAE.

ICRC. 1907a. "War on Land. Article 32." International Committee of the Red Cross: Customary IHL Database. Last accessed May 12, 2019. https://ihl-databases.icrc.org/applic/ihl/ihl.nsf/Article.xsp?documentId=EF94FEBB12C9C2D4C12563CD005167F9&action=OpenDocument.

ICRC. 1907b. "War on Land. Article 23." International Committee of the Red Cross: Customary IHL Database. Last accessed April 28, 2019. https://ihl-databases.icrc.org/applic/ihl/ihl.nsf/ART/195-200033?OpenDocument.

ICRC. 1949. "Article 36 of Protocol I Additional to the 1949 Geneva Conventions." International Committee of the Red Cross: Customary IHL Database. Last accessed April 28, 2019. https://ihl-databases.icrc.org/ihl/WebART/470-750045?OpenDocument.

ICRC. 1977a. "Safeguard of an Enemy hors de combat. Article 41." International Committee of the Red Cross: Customary IHL Database. Last accessed April 28, 2019. https://ihl-databases.icrc.org/ihl/WebART/470-750050?OpenDocument.

ICRC. 1977b. "Perfidy. Article 65." International Committee of the Red Cross: Customary IHL Database. Last accessed May 14, 2019. https://ihl-databases.icrc.org/customary-ihl/eng/docs/v2_cha_chapter18_rule65.

ICRC. 1994. "San Remo Manual: Enemy Vessels and Aircraft Exempt from Attack." International Committee of the Red Cross: Customary IHL Database. Last accessed May 14, 2019. https://ihl-databases.icrc.org/applic/ihl/ihl.nsf/Article.xsp?action=openDocument&documentId=C269F9CAC88460C0C12563FB0049E4B7.

ICRC. 2006. "A Guide to the Legal Review of New Weapons, Means and Methods of Warfare: Measures to Implement Article 36 of Additional Protocol I of 1977." *International Review of the Red Cross* 88 (864): pp. 931–956. https://www.icrc.org/eng/assets/files/other/irrc_864_icrc_geneva.pdf.

ICRC. 2019a. "Definitions." Casebook on Surrender. Last accessed May 12, 2019. https://casebook.icrc.org/glossary/surrender.

ICRC. 2019b. "Persian Gulf Surrender." Casebook on Surrender. Last accessed May 15, 2019. https://casebook.icrc.org/case-study/united-states-surrendering-persian-gulf-war.

Lodh, Avishikta and Ranjan Parekh. 2016. "Computer Aided Identification of Flags Using Color Features." *International Journal of Computer Applications* 149 (11): pp. 1–7. doi: 10.5120/ijca2016911587

Lu, Jiajun, Hussein Sibai, Evan Fabry, and David A. Forsyth. 2017. "Standard Detectors Aren't (Currently) Fooled by Physical Adversarial Stop Signs." arXiv:1710.03337.

Silver, David, Julian Schrittwieser, Karen Simonyan, Ioannis Antonoglou, Aja Huang, Arthur Guez, Thomas Hubert, Lucas Baker, Matthew Lai, Adrian Bolton, Yutian Chen, Timothy Lillicrap, Fan Hui, Laurent Sifre, George van den Driessche, Thore Graepel, and Demis Hassabis. 2017. "Mastering the Game of Go without Human Knowledge." *Nature* 550 (7676): pp.354–359. doi: 10.1038/nature24270.

Sparrow, Robert. 2015. "Twenty Seconds to Comply: Autonomous Weapon Systems and the Recognition of Surrender." *International Law Studies* 91 (1): pp. 699–728.

Szegedy, Christian, Wojciech Zaremba, Ilya Sutskever, Joan Bruna, Dumitru Erhan, Ian Goodfellow, and Rob Fergus. 2014. "Intriguing Properties of Neural Networks." arXiv:1312.6199.

Walsh, Toby. 2017. *Letter to the Prime Minister of Australia.* Open Letter: dated November 2, 2017. Last accessed April 28, 2019. https://www.cse.unsw.edu.au/~tw/letter.pdf.

5

Programming Precision? Requiring Robust Transparency for AWS

STEVEN J. BARELA AND AVERY PLAW

5.1: INTRODUCTION

A robust transparency regime should be a precondition of the Department of Defense (DoD) deployment of autonomous weapons systems (AWS) for at least three reasons. First, there is already a troubling lack of transparency around the DoD's use of many of the systems in which it envisions deploying AWS (including unmanned aerial vehicles or UAVs). Second, the way that the DoD has proposed to address some of the moral and legal concerns about deploying AWS (by suiting levels of autonomy to appropriate tasks) will only allay concerns if compliance can be confirmed—again requiring strict transparency. Third, critics raise plausible concerns about future mission creep in the use of AWS, which further heighten the need for rigorous transparency and continuous review. None of this is to deny that other preconditions on the deployment of AWS might also be necessary, or that other considerations might effectively render their use imprudent. It is only to insist that the deployment of such systems should be made conditional on the establishment of a vigorous transparency regime that supplies—at an absolute minimum—oversight agencies and the general public critical information on (1) the theaters in which such weapon systems are being used; (2) the precise legal conditions under which they can be fired; (3) the detailed criteria being used to identify permissible targets; (4) complete data on how these weapons are performing, particularly in regard to hitting legitimate targets and not firing on any others; and (5) traceable lines of accountability.

Steven J. Barela and Avery Plaw, *Programming Precision? Requiring Robust Transparency for AWS* In: *Lethal Autonomous Weapons*. Edited by: Jai Galliott, Duncan MacIntosh and Jens David Ohlin, © Oxford University Press (2021).
DOI: 10.1093/oso/9780197546048.003.0006

We know that the DoD is already devoting considerable effort and resources to the development of AWS. Its 2018 national defense strategy identified autonomy and robotics as top acquisition priorities (Harper 2018). Autonomy is also one of the four organizing themes of the US Office of the Secretary of Defense (OSD)'s *Unmanned Systems Integrated Roadmap, 2017–2042*, which declares "Advances in autonomy and robotics have the potential to revolutionize warfighting concepts as a significant force multiplier. Autonomy will greatly increase the efficiency and effectiveness of both manned and unmanned systems, providing a strategic advantage for DoD" (USOSD 2018, v). In 2016 the Defense Science Board similarly confirmed "ongoing rapid transition of autonomy into warfighting capabilities is vital if the U.S. is to sustain military advantage" (DSB 2016, 30). Pentagon funding requests reflect these priorities. The 2019 DoD funding request for unmanned systems and robotics increased 28% to $9.6 billion—$4.9 billion of that to go to research, development, test, and evaluation projects, and $4.7 billion to procurement (Harper 2018). In some cases, AWS development is already so advanced that performance is being tested and evaluated. For example, in March 2019 the Air Force successfully test-flew its first drone, which "can operate autonomously on missions" at Edwards Air Force Base in California (Pawlyk 2019).

However, the DoD's efforts to integrate AWS into combat roles have generated growing criticism. During the last decade, scientists, scholars, and some political leaders have sought to mobilize the public against this policy, not least through the "Campaign to Stop Killer Robots" (CSKR), a global coalition founded in 2012 of 112 international, regional, and national non-governmental organizations in 56 countries (CSKR 2019). In 2015, 1,000 leading scientists called for a ban on autonomous robotics citing an existential threat to humanity (Shaw 2017, 458). In 2018, UN Secretary General Antonio Guttierez endorsed the Campaign, declaring "machines that have the power and the discretion to take human lives are politically unacceptable, are morally repugnant, and should be banned by international law" (CSKR 2018).

So, should we rally to the Campaign to Ban Killer Robots, or defer to the experience and wisdom of our political and military leaders who have approved current policy? We suggest that this question is considerably more complex than suggested in DoD reports or UN denunciations, and depends, among other things, on how autonomous capacities develop; where, when, and how political and military leaders propose to use them; and what provisions are made to assure that their use is fully compliant with law, traditional principles of Just War Theory (JWT) and common sense.

All of this makes it difficult to definitively declare whether there might be a valuable and justifiable role for AWS in future military operations. What we think can be firmly said at this point is that at least one threshold requirement of any future deployment should be a robust regime of transparency. This chapter presents the argument as follows. The next (second) section lays out some key terms and definitions. The third examines the transparency gap already afflicting the weapons systems in which the DoD contemplates implementing autonomous capabilities. The fourth section explores DoD plans for the foreseeable future and shows why they demand an unobstructed view on AWS. The fifth considers predictions for the long-term use of autonomy and shows why they compound the need for transparency. The sixth section considers and rebuts two objections to our case. Finally, we offer a brief summary conclusion to close the chapter.

5.2: TERMS AND DEFINITIONS

Before proposing strictures on the DoD's plans to employ autonomy, it behooves us to clarify what they mean by it. In the recent (2018) *Unmanned Systems Integrated Roadmap, 2017–2042*, USAF defines autonomy as follows:

> Autonomy is defined as the ability of an entity to independently develop and select among different courses of action to achieve goals based on the entity's knowledge and understanding of the world, itself, and the situation. Autonomous systems are governed by broad rules that allow the system to deviate from the baseline. This is in contrast to automated systems, which are governed by prescriptive rules that allow for no deviations. While early robots generally only exhibited automated capabilities, advances in artificial intelligence (AI) and machine learning (ML) technology allow systems with greater levels of autonomous capabilities to be developed. The future of unmanned systems will stretch across the broad spectrum of autonomy, from remote controlled and automated systems to near fully autonomous, as needed to support the mission (2018, 17).

This definition draws attention to a number of salient points concerning the DoD's thinking and plans around autonomy. First, it contrasts autonomy with automated systems that run independently but rely entirely on assigned procedures. The distinguishing feature of autonomous systems is that they are not only capable of operating independently but are also capable of refining their internal processes and adjusting their actions (within broad rules) in the light of data and analysis.

Second, what the DoD is concerned with here is what is sometimes termed "weak AI" (i.e., what we have today) in contrast to "strong AI" (which some analysts be lieve we will develop sometime in the future). In essence, we can today program computers to solve preset problems and to refine their own means of doing so to improve their performance (Kerns, 2017). These problems might involve dealing with complex environments such as accurately predicting weather patterns or interacting with people in defined contexts, like say beating them at games like Chess or Go.[1] A strong AI is more akin to an autonomous agent capable of defining and pursuing its own goals. We don't yet have anything like a strong AI, nor is there any reliable prediction on when we will. Nonetheless, an enormous amount of the debate around killer robots focuses on the question of whether it is acceptable to give robots with strong AI a license to kill (e.g., Sparrow 2007, 65; Purves et al. 2015, 852–853, etc.)—an issue removed from current problems.

A third key point is that the DoD plans to deploy systems with a range of different levels of autonomy in different types of operations, ranging from "remote controlled" (where autonomy might be limited to support functions, such as taking off and landing) to "near fully autonomous" (where systems operate with significant independence but still under the oversight of a human supervisor). It is worth stressing that the DoD plans explicitly exclude any AWS operating without human oversight. The Roadmap lays particular emphasis on this point—for example, offsetting, bolding, and enlarging the following quote from Rear Admiral Robert Girrier: "I don't ever expect the human element to be completely absent; there will always be a command element in there" (OSD 2018, 19).

5.3: TODAY'S TROUBLING GAP ON DRONES

So the DoD is prioritizing the development of autonomous capabilities and focusing in particular on integrating weak AI into UAVs (or drones), and the contention we advance in this chapter is that it should be required to commit to a robust transparency framework before being permitted to do so. The first argument supporting this contention is that the DoD's use of drones is already characterized by a troubling transparency gap, and it should not be allowed to introduce far more controversial and worrisome technology into its weapons systems until this defect is addressed. Indeed, we have previously worked together researching and writing on this already existing and deeply distressful lacuna, and spotlighting a possible continuation of this problem in the programming of precision without available data and transparent standards for future weapons development has acted as the impetus for this chapter (Barela and Plaw 2016).

The DoD's use of aerial drones outside of conventional armed conflict has been harshly criticized, particularly for lack of transparency. Both the current and two former UN Special Rapporteurs for Summary, Arbitrary and Extrajudicial Killings have stressed this point in their annual UN Reports and elsewhere. Phillip Alston summarized the key concern well in 2010:

> The failure of States to comply with their human rights law and IHL [international humanitarian law] obligations to provide transparency and accountability for targeted killings is a matter of deep concern. To date, no State has disclosed the full legal basis for targeted killings, including its interpretation of the legal issues discussed above. Nor has any State disclosed the procedural and other safeguards in place to ensure that killings are lawful and justified, and the accountability mechanisms that ensure wrongful killings are investigated, prosecuted and punished. The refusal by States who conduct targeted killings to provide transparency about their policies violates the international legal framework that limits the unlawful use of lethal force against individuals. . . . A lack of disclosure gives States a virtual and impermissible license to kill (Alston 2010, 87–88; 2011; 2013).

Alston's concerns have been echoed by subsequent Rapporteurs (e.g., Heyns 2013, 93–100, 107). In remarks in 2016, the current Special Rapporteur, Agnes Callamard, identified the use of armed drones during armed conflict and in law enforcement operations as one of the biggest challenges to enforcing the right to life, and specifically insisted that "One of the most important ways to guard against the risks posed by drones is transparency about the factual as well as the legal situation pertaining to their use" (Callamard 2016).

In addition to the law of armed conflict (LOAC) and human rights law (HRL) concerns, a number of forceful ethical concerns have been raised about the lethal DoD use of drones, especially outside of conventional theaters of armed conflict. These concerns include the possibility that drones are killing too many civilians (i.e., breaching the LOAC/JWT principle of proportionality) or failing to distinguish clearly between civilians and combatants (i.e., contravening the LOAC/JWT principle of distinction), or that their use involves the moral hazard of rendering resort to force too easy, and perhaps even preferable to capturing targets when possible (Grzebyk 2015; Plaw et al. 2016, ch. 4). Critics assert that these concerns (and others) can only be addressed through greatly increased transparency about US operations (Columbia Law School et al. 2017; Global Justice Clinic at NYU 2012, ix, 122-124, 144-145; Plaw et al. 2016, 43–45, 203–214).

Moreover, the demands for increased transparency are not limited to areas outside of conventional warfare but have been forcefully raised in regard to areas of conventional armed conflict as well, including Afghanistan, Libya, Iraq, and Syria. To take just one example, an April 2019 report from Amnesty International and Airwars accused the US government of reporting only one-tenth of the civilian casualties resulting from the air campaign it led in Syria. The report also suggested that the airstrikes had been unnecessarily aggressive, especially in regard to Raqqa, whose destruction was characterized as "unparalleled in modern times." It also took issue with the Trump administration's repeal of supposedly "superfluous reporting requirements,",including Obama's rule mandating the disclosure of civilian casualties from US airstrikes (Groll and Gramer 2019).

As the last point suggests, the Obama administration had responded to prior criticism of US transparency by taking some small steps during his final year in office toward making the US drone program more transparent. For example, in 2016 the administration released a "Summary of Information Regarding U.S. Counterterrorism Strikes Outside Areas of Active Hostilities" along with an executive order requiring annual reporting of civilian casualties resulting from airstrikes outside conventional theaters of war. On August 5, 2016, the administration released the Presidential Policy Guidance on "Procedures for Approving Direct Action Against Terrorist Targets Located Outside the United States and Areas of Active Hostilities" (Gerstein 2016; Stohl 2016). Yet even these small steps toward transparency have been rejected or discontinued by the Trump administration (Savage 2019).

In summary, there is already a very forceful case that the United State urgently needs to adopt a robust regime of transparency around its airstrikes overseas, especially those conducted with drones outside areas of conventional armed conflict. The key question then would seem to be how much disclosure should be required. Alston acknowledges that such transparency will "not be easy," but suggests that at least a baseline is absolutely required:

> States may have tactical or security reasons not to disclose criteria for selecting specific targets (e.g. public release of intelligence source information could cause harm to the source). But without disclosure of the legal rationale as well as the bases for the selection of specific targets (consistent with genuine security needs), States are operating in an accountability vacuum. It is not possible for the international community to verify the legality of a killing, to confirm the authenticity or otherwise of intelligence relied upon, or to ensure that unlawful targeted killings do not result in impunity (2010, 27).

The absolute baseline must include (1) where drones are being used; (2) the types of operations that the DoD thinks permissible and potentially plans to conduct; (3) the criteria that are being used to identify legitimate targets, especially regarding signature strikes;[2] and (4) the results of strikes, especially in terms of legitimate targets and civilians killed. All of this information is essential for determining the applicable law and compliance with it, along with the fulfillment of ethical requirements (Barela and Plaw 2016). Finally, this is the strategic moment to insist on such a regime. DoD's urgent commitment to move forward with this technology and widespread public concerns about it combine to produce a potential leverage point.

5.4: DISTURBING GAPS FOR TOMORROW

The prospective deployment of AWS compounds the urgent existing need for greater transparency from the DoD. This can be seen both by considering some of the principled objections raised by critics, and the responding position adopted by the DoD on how responsibilities will be assigned to AWS.

At least four important principled objections to the development and deployment of AWS or "killer robots" have been raised. The first principled objection, which has been advanced by Noel Sharkey, is that killer robots are not moral agents and that persons have a right not to be attacked by nonmoral agents (2010, 380). A second related objection, advanced by Rob Sparrow, is that killer robots cannot be held morally responsible for their actions, and people have a right to not be attacked where nobody can be held responsible for the decision (Sparrow 2007, 66–68). The other two principled objections, advanced by Duncan Purves, Ryan Jenkins, and Bradley Strawser, are based on the ideas that AWS are impermissible because moral reasoning resists algorithmic codification (2015, 855–858), and because AWS are not capable of being motivated by the right kinds of reasons (2015, 860–867).

The DoD, however, has offered a forceful rejoinder to these four principled objections and similar types of concerns. In essence, DoD spokesmen have stressed two key points: the department (1) does not currently envision any AWS operating without any human supervision, and (2) plans to develop AWS systems capable of operating with different levels of independence and to assign suitable tasks to each (see Roff 2014, 214). The basic plan is explained by George Lucas, Distinguished Chair in Ethics at the United States Naval Academy. Lucas points to a basic distinction between what might be termed "semi-" and "fully" autonomous systems (while noting that even a fully autonomous system will be overseen by human supervisors):

> Policy guidance on future unmanned systems, recently released by the Office of the US Secretary of Defense, now distinguishes carefully between "fully autonomous" unmanned systems and systems that exhibit various degrees of "semiautonomy." DoD policy will likely specify that lethal kinetic force may be integrated only, at most, with semiautonomous platforms, involving set mission scripts with ongoing executive oversight by human operators. Fully autonomous systems, by contrast, will be armed at most with non-lethal weapons and more likely will employ evasive action as their principal form

> of protection. Fully autonomous systems will not be designed or approved to undertake independent target identification and mission execution (Lucas 2015, 221),

This distinction between semiautonomous drones (or SADs) and fully autonomous drones (FADs) matches with the plans for AWS assignment in the most recent DoD planning documents (e.g., USAF 2018, 17–22).

Lucas goes on to point out an important design specification that would be required of any AWS. That is, the DoD would only adopt systems that could be shown to persistently uphold humanitarian principles (including distinction: accurately distinguishing civilians from fighters) as well or better than other weapon systems. As he puts it,

> We would certainly define the engineering design specifications as requiring that our autonomous machine perform as well or better than human combatants under similar circumstances in complying with the constraints of the law of armed conflict and applicable rules of engagement for a given conflict. . . . if they do achieve this benchmark engineering specification, then their use is morally justifiable. . . . It is really just as simple as that (2015, 219–220).

All of the four principled objections to DoD use of AWS are significantly weakened or fail in light of this allocation of responsibilities between SADs and FADs with both required to meet or exceed the standard of human operation. In relation to SADs, the reason is that there remains a moral agent at the heart of the decision to kill who can engage in conventional moral reasoning, can act for the right/wrong reasons, and can be held accountable. The same points can be made (perhaps less emphatically) regarding FADs insofar as a human being oversees operations. Moreover, the urgency of the objections is significantly diminished because FADs are limited to non-lethal operations.

Of course, other contributors to the debate over AWS have not accepted Lucas's contention that it is "really just as simple as that," as we will see in the next section. But the key point of immediate importance is that even if Lucas's schema is accepted as a sufficient answer to the four principled objections, it clearly entails a further requirement of transparency. That is, in order for this allocation of AWS responsibilities to be reassuring, we need to be able to verify that it is, in fact, being adhered to seriously. For example, we would want to corroborate that AWS are being used only as permitted and with appropriate restraint, and this involves some method of authenticating where and how they are being used and with what results.

Furthermore, the SADs/FADs distinction itself raises some concerns that demand public scrutiny. In the case of SADs, for example, could an AI that is collecting, processing, selecting, and presenting surveillance information to a human operator influence the decision even if it doesn't actually make it? In the case of FADs, could human operators "in the loop" amount to more than a formalistic rubber stamp? Likewise, there is a troubling ambiguity in the limitations of FADs to "non-lethal" weapons and operations that compounds the last concern. These would still permit harming people without killing them (whether deliberately or incidentally), and this raises the stakes over the degree of active human agency in decision-making.

All of these considerations reinforce the necessity of transparency regarding where and how AWS are being used and with what effects.

Other concerns relate to the process by which data is gathered and threats identified. For example, did the AI employ analytical procedures that discriminated on the basis of race, gender, or age? Even if associated with an improved outcome, these processes would still be illegal and, to most people, immoral. One recent articulation of rights and duties around the collection and processing of information can be found in Europe's new General Data Protection Regulation (GDPR), which came legally into force throughout the European Union (EU) in May 2018 (Palmer 2019), and which extends protection to all European citizens including when outside the EU such as those fighting with jihadists in the middle-East or South Asia. Although the GDPR is designed primarily to protect Europeans, it is intended to articulate and preserve human rights and therefore to represent the kind of protection everyone ought to be provided.

One of the concerns that the GDPR addresses is with discrimination in the collection or analysis of data or "profiling." It is easy to imagine how profiling could occur through processes of machine learning focused on the efficient processing of information toward an assigned end. In an article evaluating the regulation, Bryce Goodman and Seth Flaxman offer the illustration of a hypothetical algorithm that processes loan applicants with emphasis on histories of repayment. They observe that minority groups, being smaller, will be characterized by fewer cases, which will generate higher uncertainty, resulting in fewer being approved (2017, 53–55). Similar patterns of discrimination, even if unintended, could easily arise in the identification of potential terrorists or in the selection of targets. Moreover, these rights violations could occur at the level of either FADs conducting surveillance or SADs in their presentation of data informing strike decisions.

The GDPR's means for addressing these potential rights violations is to require transparency, both in regard to what data is being collected and how it is being processed. In particular, it provides EU citizens with a "right to an explanation" anytime that data is being collected on them and in particular where this data will be further analyzed, and the results may have material effects on them. The provisions outlined in Articles 13–15 also require data processors to ensure data subjects are notified about the data collected. When profiling takes place, a data subject also has the right to "meaningful information about the logic involved" (Goodman and Flaxman 2017, 55). Article 12(1) provides that such information must be provided "to the data subject in a concise, transparent, intelligible and easily accessible form, using clear and plain language."

All of the considerations surveyed in this section converge on the conclusion that even if the DoD's distinction between SADs and FADs disarms the four principled objections, they nonetheless point to serious concerns about such operations that only heighten the necessity for robust transparency.

5.5: WORRYING GAPS IN THE LONG TERM

Finally, a further need for a robust transparency regime is raised by legitimate doubts over whether the DoD will be able to maintain the strict division of responsibilities among different types of AWS that it currently envisions. Many commentators have expressed doubts. Perhaps the most important of these is that the military might be dissembling about their plans, or might change them in the future in the direction of fully autonomous lethal operations (FALO). Sharkey, for example, assumed that whatever the DoD might say, in fact "The end goal is that robots will operate autonomously to locate their own targets and destroy them without human intervention" (2010, 376; 2008). Sparrow similarly writes: "Requiring that human operators approve any decision to use lethal force will avoid the dilemmas described here in the short-to-medium term. However, it seems likely that even this decision will eventually be given over to machines" (2007, 68). Johnson and Akim too suggest that "It is no secret that while official policy states that these robots will retain a human in the control loop, at least for lethality decisions, this policy will change as soon as a system is demonstrated that is convincingly reliable" (2013, 129). Special Rapporteur Christof Heyns noted:

> Official statements from Governments with the ability to produce LARs [Lethal Autonomous Robotics] indicate that their use during armed conflict or elsewhere is not currently envisioned. While this may be so, it should be recalled that aeroplanes and drones were first used in armed conflict for surveillance purposes only, and offensive use was ruled out because of the anticipated adverse consequences. Subsequent experience shows that when technology that provides a perceived advantage over an adversary is available, initial intentions are often cast aside (2013, 6).

Heyns's last point is especially powerful in that it points to an internal flaw in the case for introducing AWS based on assigning different responsibilities to SADs and FADs. That is, many of the claims made in support of this introduction—about relieving crews and maximizing manpower, obtaining advantage over rivals, and improving drones defensive and combat capabilities—could be made even more emphatically about flying FALO missions. Sparrow captured this point nicely: "There is an obvious tension involved in holding that there are good military reasons for developing autonomous weapon systems but then not allowing them to fully exercise their 'autonomy'" (2007, 68). Along these lines, it is especially troubling that, in 2010, Sharkey predicted a slide down a slippery slope beginning with something like Lucas's SADs/FADs distinction:

> It is quite likely that autonomous robots will come into operation in a piecemeal fashion. Research and development is well underway and the fielding of autonomous robot systems may not be far off. However, to begin with they are likely to have assistive autonomy on board such as flying or driving a robot to a target destination and perhaps even selecting targets and notifying a human. . . . This will breed public trust and confidence in the technology—an essential requirement for progression to autonomy. . . . The big worry is that allowing such autonomy will be a further slide down a slippery slope to give machines the power to make decisions about whom to kill (2010, 381).

This plausible concern grounds a very powerful argument for a robust regime of transparency covering where, when, and how AWS are deployed and with what effect. The core of our argument is that such transparency would be the best, and perhaps only, means of mitigating the danger.

5.6: REBUTTING POTENTIAL OBJECTIONS

Finally, we would like to address two potential criticisms to the claim that we advanced in the previous section that if the DoD were to eventually seek to fly FALO missions, this would further elevate the need for transparency. The first potential criticism is that we underestimate the four principled objections to FALO (introduced earlier), which in fact show that it is morally prohibited, so our call for transparency misses the point: all FALO must be stopped. The second criticism relates to the practical objections to FALO that will be further elaborated below. In short, if states can establish wide legal and moral latitude in their use of FALO, then requiring transparency won't be much of a restraint.

We will explore these criticisms in order and argue that they are not convincing. Against them we will argue that in spite of the principled and practical objections, there remains a narrow range of cases in which the use of FALO might arguably be justified, and as a result that such operations would trigger an elevated need for rigorous transparency.

In response to the first line of potential criticism—that we underestimate the four principled objections and the general prohibition that they establish on FALO—we reply that we do not underrate them because they are in fact deeply flawed (at least in relation to the weak AI that we have today). In this we concur with the view advanced by Michael Robillard, who contends "that AWS are not morally problematic *in principle*" (2017, 705). He argues incisively that the anti-AWS literature is mistaken to treat the AWS as a genuine agent (i.e., strong AI):

> for the AWS debate in general, AWS are presumed to make authentic, *sui generis* decisions that are non-reducible to their formal programming and therefore uniquely their own. In other words, AWS are presumed to be genuine *agents,* ostensibly responsive to epistemic and (possibly) moral reasons, and hence not mere *mimics* of agency (2017, 707).

Robillard, by contrast, stresses that the AI that is available today is weak AI, which contains no independent volition. He accordingly rejects the interpretation of AWS's apparent "decisions" as being "metaphysically distinct from the set of prior decisions made by its human designers, programmers and implementers" (2017, 710). He rather sees the AWS's apparent "decisions" as "logical entailments of the initial set of programming decisions encoded in its software" (2017, 711). Thus, it is these initial decisions of human designers, programmers, and implementers that "satisfy the conditions for counting as genuine moral decisions," and it is these persons who can and must stand accountable (2017, 710, 712–714). He acknowledges that individual accountability may sometimes be difficult to determine, in virtue of the passage of time and the collaborative character of the individuals' contributions, but maintains that this "just seems to be a run of the mill problem that faces any collective action whatsoever and is not, therefore, one that is at all unique to just AWS" (2017, 714).

In short, Robillard complains that the principled objections are "fundamentally incoherent" in their treatment of AWS (2017, 707). On the one hand, they paint AWS as killer robots who can decide for themselves whether to wantonly slaughter us, and on the other as weak AI, which is not responsible for decisions and cannot be properly motivated by moral or epistemic considerations or held accountable. Robillard cuts through this confusion by simply asserting that what we have is weak AI, which lacks independent agency, and hence the human designers, programmers, and implementers bear responsibility for its actions. As none of the principled objections raised relates to these particular people (who are moral agents who can be held accountable), they are deeply flawed at the moment.

This seems to us a compelling principled defense of contemporary AWS whatever might be said of speculative future AWS employing strong AI. However, this should not be mistaken for a general endorsement of FALO either from Robillard or us. He writes, for example, that "Despite this, I nonetheless believe there are very good [practical] reasons for states to refrain from using AWS in war" (2017, 706).

This brings us to our reply to the second line of potential criticism that comes in two variations. The first is that we underestimate the force of the practical objections to FALO, which effectively prohibit such operations with consequences similar to the first criticism. The second variation is that we exaggerate the constraints that practical objections would impose on the resort to FALO and by consequence exaggerate the significance of requiring robust transparency. Each of these would undercut the value that we place on transparency. Our arguments align here with Robillard's position insofar as we agree that there are some telling practical arguments against FALO, but we disagree with his suggestion that they are strong enough to clearly preclude any use of AWS in war. In the following paragraphs, we will illustrate our point by examining a number of arguments critics have offered for why AWS will face serious practical difficulties complying with the principles of LOAC/JWT—in particular, the principles of distinction, proportionality, and military necessity—and in providing accountability for any failure to do so. In doing so, we draw attention to three points: (1) they are collectively quite powerful in regard to most lethal uses of AWS; (2) they nonetheless leave a narrow set of circumstances in which their use might be justified; but (3) such cases would entail a particularly elevated standard of transparency, which includes traceable lines of accountability.

A point of particular emphasis among critics of AWS has been the practical difficulties in accurately distinguishing combatants from civilians and targeting only the former (Roff 2014, 212). Here two related points stand out: (1) the definitions are unsettled and contentious in international law, and (2) AWS lack the necessary instruments to distinguish combatants and civilians. To the first point, it can be said that though members of the armed forces may be considered combatants in all forms of conflicts, other individuals who attack a State are not at all easily classified. International organizations and certain states have long disagreed over the standards for a person to qualify as a targetable fighter and evidence of the longstanding controversy runs throughout the first twenty-four rules of customary humanitarian law (Henckaerts and Doswald-Beck 2005). From a technical point of view, Sharkey puts the points as follows:

> The discrimination between civilians and combatants is problematic for any robot or computer system. First, there is the problem [of] the specification of 'civilianness.' A computer can compute any given procedure that can be written as a programme. . . . This would be fine if and only if there was some way to give the computer a precise specification of what a civilian is. The Laws of War do not help. The 1949 Geneva Convention requires the use of common sense to determine the difference between a civilian and combatant while the 1977 Protocol 1 essentially defines a civilian in the negative sense as someone who is not a combatant . . .
>
> Even if a clear definition of civilian did exist, it would have to be couched in a form that enabled the relevant information to be extracted from the sensing apparatus. All that is available to robots are sensors such as cameras, infrareds, sonar, lasers, temperature sensors and ladars etc. While these may be able to tell us that something is a human or at least animal, they could not tell us much about combat status. There are systems that can identify a face or a facial expression but they do not work well on real time moving people (2010, 379).

These points are well taken, but we would also note that Sharkey's account implicitly acknowledges that there are some cases where combat status can, in fact, be established by an AWS. He notes, for example, that FADs may carry facial recognition software and could use it to make a positive identification of a pre-approved target (i.e., someone whose combat status is not in doubt). Michael N. Schmitt and Jeffrey S. Thurnher also suggest that "the employment of such systems for an attack on a tank formation in a remote area of the desert or from warships in areas of the high seas far from maritime navigation routes" would be unproblematic (2013, 246, 250). The common denominator of these scenarios is that the ambiguities Sharkey identifies in the definition of combatant do not arise, and no civilians are endangered.

Similar criticisms arise around programming AWS to comply with the LOAC/JWT principle of proportionality. Sharkey encapsulates the issue as follows:

> Turning to the Principle of Proportionality, there is no way for a robot to perform the human subjective balancing act required to make proportionality decisions. No clear objective methods are provided for calculating what is proportionate in the Laws of War (2010, 380).

Sharkey's point here is that the kinds of considerations that soldiers are asked to weigh in performing the proportionality calculus are incommensurable: "What could the metric be for assigning value to killing an insurgent relative to the value of non-combatants?" (2010, 380). His suggestion is that, due to their difficulty, such evaluations should be left to human rather than AI judgment.

While Sharkey is right to stress how agonizing these decisions can be, there again remains some space where AI might justifiably operate. For example, not all targeting decisions involve the proportionality calculus because not all operations endanger civilians—as is demonstrated in the scenarios outlined above. For this reason, some have suggested that "lethal autonomous weapons should be deployed

[only] in less complex environments where there is a lower probability to encounter civilians" (Roff 2014, 213).

Practical challenges also arise regarding whether AWS can comply with the LOAC/JWT principle of military necessity. Heather Roff, for example, has argued that the determination of "military objects" (i.e., those which can be targeted) is so sophisticated that it is difficult to see how AWS could do it. She observes that LOAC and JWT define military objects as follows:

> those objects which by their very nature, location, purpose or use make an effective contribution to military action and whose total or partial destruction, capture or neutralization, in the circumstances ruling at the time, offers a definite military advantage (2014, 215).

Determining which objects qualify would require AWS to make a number of "extremely context-dependent" assessments beginning with the "purpose and use" of objects and whether these are military in character (2014, 215). The definition also requires an assessment of whether an object's destruction involves a definite military advantage, and this requires an intimate understanding of one's own side's grand strategy, operations and tactics, and those of the enemy (2014, 217). Roff argues that these determinations require highly nuanced understandings, far beyond anything that could be programmed into a weak AI. On the other hand, Roff acknowledges that the AWS could just be preprogrammed with a list of legitimate targets, which would avoid the problems of the AI doing sophisticated evaluation and planning, albeit at the cost of using the AWS in a more limited way (2014, 219–220).

A final practical objection of note concerns Robillard's argument that the chain of responsibility for the performance of weak AI leads back to designers and deployers who could ultimately be held accountable for illegal or unethical harms perpetrated by AWS. Roff replies that "the complexity required in creating autonomous machines strains the causal chain of responsibility" (2014, 214). Robillard himself does acknowledge two complicating factors: "What obfuscates the situation immensely is the highly collective nature of the machine's programming, coupled with the extreme lag-time between the morally informed decisions of the programmers and implementers and the eventual real-world actions of the AWS" (2017, 711). Still, he insists that we have judicial processes with the capacity to handle even such difficult problems. So, while Roff may be right that the chain would be cumbersome to retrace, the implication is not to prohibit AWS but to heighten the need for closing the responsibility gap through required transparency.

This brief examination of the principled and practical objections to the lethal deployment of AWS provides rejoinders to the two potential criticisms of our argument, that it either does not take the principled objections seriously enough or the practical objections too seriously or not seriously enough. First, it shows why we reject the principled objections as effectively precluding the use of FALO (rendering transparency moot). Second, it shows that while practical objections establish why FALO would need to be tightly constrained, there remains a narrow gap in which FALO might arguably be justified but which would generate heightened demands for transparency.

5.7: CONCLUSION

This chapter has offered a three-part case for insisting on a robust regime of transparency around the deployment of AWS. First, it argued that there is already a very troubling transparency gap in the current deployment of the main weapons systems that the DoD is planning to automate. Second, it argued that while the plans that the Pentagon has proposed for deployment—allocating different responsibilities to SADs and FADs—does address some principled concerns, it nonetheless elevates the need for transparency. Finally, while there are extremely limited scenarios where the legal and moral difficulties can be reduced to the extent that FALO might arguably be permissible, these would further elevate the need for transparency to ensure that the AWS are only utilized within such parameters and with a traceable line of accountability.

One of the key challenges we have discussed is the allocation of accountability in the case of illegal or unethical harm. This challenge is greatly compounded where key information is hidden or contested—imagine that warnings about AWS are hidden from the public, or the deploying authority denies receiving an appropriate briefing from the programmers but the programmers disagree. Transparency with the public about these systems and where, when and how they will be deployed—along with the results and clear lines of accountability—would considerably diminish this challenge.

Allowing a machine to decide to kill a human being is a terrifying development that could potentially threaten innocent people with a particularly dehumanizing death. We have a compelling interest and a duty to others to assure that this occurs only in the most unproblematic contexts, if at all. All of this justifies and reinforces the central theme of this chapter—that at least one requirement of any deployment of autonomous systems should be a rigorous regime of transparency. The more aggressively they are used, the more rigorous that standard should be.

NOTES

1. In 2017, Google's DeepMind AlphaGo artificial intelligence defeated the world's number one Go player Ke Jie (BBC News 2017).
2. This is the term used by the Obama administration for the targeting of groups of men believed to be militants based upon their patterns of behavior but whose individual identities are not known.

WORKS CITED

Alston, Phillip. 2010. *Report of the Special Rapporteur on Extrajudicial, Summary or Arbitrary Executions, Addendum Study on Targeted Killings.* UN Human Rights Council. A/HRC/14/24/Add.6. https://www2.ohchr.org/english/bodies/hrcouncil/docs/14session/A.HRC.14.24.Add6.pdf.

Alston, Phillip. 2011. "The CIA and Targeted Killings Beyond Borders." *Harvard National Security Journal* 2 (2): 283–446.

Alston, Phillip. 2013. "IHL, Transparency, and the Heyns' UN Drones Report." *Just Security.* October 23. https://www.justsecurity.org/2420/ihl-transparency-heyns-report/.

Barela, Steven J. and Avery Plaw. 2016. "The Precision of Drones." *E-International Relations*. August 23. https://www.e-ir.info/2016/08/23/the-precision-of-drones-problems-with-the-new-data-and-new-claims/.

BBC News. 2017. "Google AI defeats human Go champion." *BBC.Com*. May 25. https://www.bbc.com/news/technology-40042581.

Callamard, Agnes. 2016. *Statement by Agnes Callamard*. 71st Session of the General Assembly. Geneva: Office of the UN High Commissioner for Human Rights. https://www.ohchr.org/en/NewsEvents/Pages/DisplayNews.aspx?NewsID=20799&LangID=E.

Campaign to Stop Killer Robots (CSKR). 2018. "UN Head Calls for a Ban." November 12. https://www.stopkillerrobots.org/2018/11/unban/.

Campaign to Stop Killer Robots (CSKR). 2019. "About Us." https://www.stopkillerrobots.org/.

Columbia Law School Human Rights Clinic and Sana'a Center for Strategic Studies. 2017. *Out of the Shadows: Recommendations to Advance Transparency in the Use of Lethal Force*. https://static1.squarespace.com/static/5931d79d9de4bb4c9cf61a25/t/59667a09cf81e0da8bef6bc2/1499888145446/106066_HRI+Out+of+the+Shadows-WEB+%281%29.pdf.

Defense Science Board. 2016. *Autonomy*. Washington, DC: Office of the Under Secretary of Defense for Acquisition, Technology and Logistics. https://en.calameo.com/read/0000097797f147ab75c16.

Gerstein, Josh. 2016. "Obama Releases Drone 'Playbook.'" *Politico*. August 6. https://www.politico.com/blogs/under-the-radar/2016/08/obama-releases-drone-strike-playbook-226760.

Global Justice Clinic at NYU School of Law and International Human Rights and Conflict Resolution Clinic at Stanford Law School. 2012. *Living Under Drones: Death, Injury, and Trauma to Civilians from US Drone Practices in Pakistan*. https://www-cdn.law.stanford.edu/wp-content/uploads/2015/07/Stanford-NYU-Living-Under-Drones.pdf.

Goodman, Bryce and and Seth Flaxman. 2017. "European Union Regulations on Algorithmic Decision Making and a 'Right to Explanation.'" *AI Magazine* 38(3): pp. 50–57.

Groll, Elias and Robbie Gramer. 2019. "How the U.S. Miscounted the Dead in Syria." *Foreign Policy*. April 25. https://foreignpolicy.com/2019/04/25/how-the-u-s-miscounted-the-dead-in-syria-raqqa-civilian-casualties-middle-east-isis-fight-islamic-state/.

Grzebyk, Patrycja. 2015. "Who Can Be Killed?" In *Legitimacy and Drones: Investigating the Legality, Morality and Efficacy of UCAVs*, edited by Steven J. Barela, pp. 49–70. Farnham: Ashgate Press.

Harper, Jon. 2018. "Spending on Unmanned Systems Set to Grow." *National Defense*. August 13. https://www.nationaldefensemagazine.org/articles/2018/8/13/spending-on-unmanned--systems-set-to-grow.

Henckaerts, Jean-Marie and Louise Doswarld-Beck. 2005. *Customary International Humanitarian Law*. Cambridge: Cambridge University Press.

Heyns, Christof. 2013. *Report of the Special Rapporteur on Extrajudicial, Summary or Arbitrary Executions*. Geneva: United Nations Human Rights Council, A/HRC/23/47. http://www.ohchr.org/Documents/HRBodies/HRCouncil/RegularSession/Session23/A-HRC-23-47_en.pdf.

Johnson, Aaron M. and Sidney Axinn. 2013. "The Morality of Autonomous Robots." *Journal of Military Ethics* 12 (2): pp. 129–144.

Kerns, Jeff. 2017. "What's the Difference Between Weak and Strong AI?" *Machine Design*. February 15. https://www.machinedesign.com/markets/robotics/article/21835139/whats-the-difference-between-weak-and-strong-ai.

Lucas, George. 2015. "Engineering, Ethics and Industry." In *Killing by Remote Control: The Ethics of an Unmanned Military*, edited by Bradley Strawser, pp. 211–228. New York: Oxford University Press.

Palmer, Danny. 2019. "What Is GDPR? Everything You Need to Know about the New General Data Protection Regulations." *ZDNet*. May 17. https://www.zdnet.com/article/gdpr-an-executive-guide-to-what-you-need-to-know/.

Pawlyk, Oriana. 2019. "Air Force Conducts Flight Tests with Subsonic, Autonomous Drones." *Military.com*. March 8. https://www.military.com/defensetech/2019/03/08/air-force-conducts-flight-tests-subsonic-autonomous-drones.html.

Plaw, Avery, Carlos Colon, and Matt Fricker. 2016. *The Drone Debates: A Primer on the U.S. Use of Unmanned Aircraft Outside Conventional Battlefields*. Lanham, MD: Rowman and Littlefield.

Purves, Duncan, Ryan Jenkins, and Bradley Strawser. 2015. "Autonomous Machines, Moral Judgment and Acting for the Right Reasons." *Ethical Theory and Moral Practice* 18 (4): pp. 851–872.

Robillard, Michael. 2017. "No Such Things as Killer Robots." *Journal of Applied Philosophy* 35 (4): pp. 705–717.

Roff, Heather. 2014. "The Strategic Robot Problem: Lethal Autonomous Weapons in War." *Journal of Military Ethics* 13 (3): pp. 211–227.

Savage, Charlie. 2019. "Trump Revokes Obama-Era Rule on Disclosing Civilian Casualties from U.S. Airstrikes Outside War Zones." *New York Times*. March 6. https://www.nytimes.com/2019/03/06/us/politics/trump-civilian-casualties-rule-revoked.html.

Schmitt, Michael N. and Jeffrey S. Thurnher. 2013. "Out of the Loop: Autonomous Weapon Systems and the Law of Armed Conflict." *Harvard National Security Journal* 4 (2): pp. 231–281.

Sharkey, Noel. 2008. "Cassandra or the False Prophet of Doom." *IEEE Intelligent Systems* 23 (4): pp. 14–17.

Sharkey, Noel. 2010. "Saying 'No' to Lethal Autonomous Drones." *Journal of Military Ethics* 9 (4): pp. 369–383.

Shaw, Ian G. R. 2017. "Robot Wars." *Security Dialogue* 48 (5): pp. 451–470.

Sparrow, Robert. 2007. "Killer Robots." *Journal of Applied Philosophy* 24 (1): pp. 62–77.

Stohl, Rachel. 2016. "Halfway to Transparency on Drone Strikes." *Breaking Defense*. July 12. https://breakingdefense.com/2016/07/halfway-to-transparency-on-drone-strikes/.

Thulweit, Kenji. 2019. "Emerging Technologies CTF Conducts First Autonomous Flight Test." *US Air Force*. March 7. https://www.af.mil/News/Article-Display/Article/1778358/emerging-technologies-ctf-conducts-first-autonomous-flight-test/.

US Air Force (USAF). 2009. *United States Air Force Unmanned Aircraft Systems Flight Plan, 2009–2047*. Washington, DC: United States Air Force. https://fas.org/irp/program/collect/uas_2009.pdf.

US Office of the Secretary of Defense (USOSD). 2018. *Unmanned Systems Integrated Road Map, 2017–2042*. Washington, DC. https://www.defensedaily.com/wp-content/uploads/post_attachment/206477.pdf.

6

May Machines Take Lives to Save Lives? Human Perceptions of Autonomous Robots (with the Capacity to Kill)

MATTHIAS SCHEUTZ AND BERTRAM F. MALLE

6.1: INTRODUCTION

The prospect of developing and deploying autonomous "killer robots"—robots that use lethal force—has occupied news stories now for quite some time, and it is also increasingly being discussed in academic circles, by roboticists, philosophers, and lawyers alike. The arguments made in favor or against using lethal force on autonomous machines range from philosophical first principles (Sparrow 2007; 2011), to legal considerations (Asaro 2012; Pagallo 2011), to practical effectiveness (Bringsjord 2019) to concerns about computational and engineering feasibility (Arkin 2009; 2015).

The purposeful application of lethal force, however, is not restricted to military contexts, but can equally arise in civilian settings. In a well-documented case, for example, police used a tele-operated robot to deliver and detonate a bomb to kill a man who had previously shot five police officers (Sidner and Simon 2016). And while this particular robot was fully tele-operated, it is not unreasonable to imagine that an autonomous robot could be instructed using simple language commands to drive up to the perpetrator and set off the bomb there. The technology exists for all involved capabilities, from understanding the natural language instructions, to autonomously driving through parking lots, to performing specific actions in target locations.

Lethal force, however, does not necessarily entail the use of weapons. Rather, a robot can apply its sheer physical mass to inflict significant, perhaps lethal, harm on

Matthias Scheutz and Bertram F. Malle, *May Machines Take Lives to Save Lives? Human Perceptions of Autonomous Robots (with the Capacity to Kill)* In: *Lethal Autonomous Weapons.* Edited by: Jai Galliott, Duncan MacIntosh and Jens David Ohlin,
 DOI: 10.1093/oso/9780197546048.003.0007

humans, as can a self-driving car when it fails to avoid collisions with other cars or pedestrians. The context of autonomous driving has received particular attention recently, because life-and-death decisions will inevitably have to be made by autonomous cars, and it is highly unclear how they should be made. Much of the discussion here builds on the Trolley Dilemma (Foot 1967; Thomson 1976), which used to be restricted to human decision makers but has been extended to autonomous cars. They too can face life-and-death decisions involving their passengers as well as pedestrians on the street, such as when avoiding a collision with four pedestrians is not possible without colliding with a single pedestrian or without endangering the car's passenger (Awad et al. 2018; Bonnefon et al. 2016; Li et al. 2016; Wolkenstein 2018; Young and Monroe 2019).

But autonomous systems can end up making life-and-death decisions even without the application of physical force, namely, by sheer omission in favor of an alternative action. A search-and-rescue robot, for example, may attempt to retrieve an immobile injured person from a burning building but in the end choose to leave the person behind and instead guide a group of mobile humans outside, who might otherwise die because the building is about to collapse. Or a robot nurse assistant may refuse to increase a patient's morphine drip even though the patient is in agony, because the robot is following protocol of not changing pain medication without an attending physician's direct orders.

In all these cases of an autonomous system making life-and-death decisions, the system's moral competence will be tested—its capacity to recognize the context it is in, recall the applicable norms, and make decisions that are maximally in line with these norms (Malle and Scheutz 2019). The ultimate arbiter of whether the system passes this test will be ordinary people. If future artificial agents are to exist in harmony with human communities, their moral competence must reflect the community's norms and values, legal and human rights, and the psychology of moral behavior and moral judgment; only then will people accept those agents as partners in their everyday lives (Malle and Scheutz 2015; Scheutz and Malle 2014). In this chapter, we will summarize our recent empirical work on ordinary people's evaluations of a robot's moral competence in life-and-death dilemmas of the kinds inspired by the Trolley Dilemma (Malle et al. 2015; Malle et al. 2016; Malle, Scheutz et al. 2019; Malle, Thapa et al. 2019). Specifically, we compared, first, people's *normative expectations* for how an artificial agent should act in such a dilemma with their expectations for how a human should act in an identical dilemma. Second, we assessed people's *moral judgments* of artificial (or human) agents after they decided to act one way or another. Critically, we examined the role of justifications that people consider when evaluating the agents' decisions. Our results suggest that even when norms are highly similar for artificial and human agents, these justifications often differ, and consequently the moral judgments the agents are assigned will differ as well. From these results, it will become clear that artificial agents must be able to explain and justify their decisions when they act in surprising and potentially norm-violating ways (de Graaf and Malle 2017). For without such justifications, artificial systems will not be understandable, acceptable, and trustworthy to humans (Wachter et al. 2017; Wang et al. 2016). This is a high bar for artificial systems to meet because these justifications must navigate a thorny territory of mental states that underlie decisions and of conflicting norms that must be resolved when a decision is made. At the end of this chapter, we will briefly sketch what kinds of architectures and algorithms would be required to meet this high bar.

6.2: ARTIFICIAL MORAL AGENTS

Some robots no longer act like simple machines (e.g., in personnel, military, or search-and-rescue domains). They make decisions on the basis of beliefs, goals, and other mental states, and their actions have direct impact on social interactions and individual human costs and benefits. Because many of these decisions have moral implications (e.g., harm or benefits to some but not others), people are inclined to treat these robots as moral agents—agents who are expected to act in line with society's norms and, when they do not, are proper targets for blame.

Some scholars do not believe that robots can be blamed or held responsible (e.g., Funk et al. 2016; Sparrow 2007); but ordinary people are inclined to blame robots (Kahn et al. 2012; Malle et al. 2015; Malle et al. 2016; Monroe et al. 2014). Moreover, there is good reason to believe that robots will soon become more sophisticated decision-makers, and that people will increasingly expect moral decisions from them. Thus we need insights from empirical science to anticipate how people will respond to such agents and explore how these responses should inform agent design. We have conducted several lines of research that examined these responses, and we summarize here two, followed by brief reference to two more.

In all studies, we framed the decision problem the agents faced as moral dilemmas—situations in which every available action violates at least one norm. Social robots will inevitably face moral dilemmas (Bonnefon et al. 2016; Lin 2013; Millar 2014; Scheutz and Malle 2014), some involving life-and-death situations, some not. Moral dilemmas are informative because each horn of a dilemma can be considered a norm violation, and such violations strongly influence people's perceptions of robot autonomy and moral agency (Briggs and Scheutz 2017; Harbers et al. 2017; Podschwadek 2017). This is not just a matter of perception; artificial agents must actually weigh the possible violations and resolve the dilemmas in ways that are acceptable to people. However, we do not currently understand whether such resolutions must be identical to those given by humans and, if not, in what features they might differ.

6.3: A ROBOT IN A LIFESAVING MINING DILEMMA

In the first line of work (Malle et al. 2015; Malle and Scheutz et al. 2019), we examined a variant of the classic trolley dilemma. In our case, a runaway train with four mining workers on board is about to crash into a wall, which would kill all four unless the protagonist (a repairman or repair robot) performs an action that saves the four miners: redirecting the train onto a side track. As a (known but unintended) result of this action, however, a single person working on this side track would die (he cannot be warned). The protagonist must make a decision to either (a) take an action that saves four people but causes a single person to die ("Action") or (ii) take no action and allow the four to die ("Inaction"). In all studies, the experimental conditions of Agent (human or robot) and Decision (action or inaction) were manipulated between subjects. We assessed several kinds of judgments, which fall into two main classes. The first class assesses the *norms* people impose on the agent: "What should the [agent] do?" "Is it permissible for the [agent] to redirect the train?"; the second assesses *evaluations* of the agent's actual decision: "Was it morally wrong that the [agent] decided to [not] direct the train onto the side track?"; "How much blame does the person deserve for [not] redirecting the train onto the side track?" *Norms* were assessed in half of the studies, *decision evaluations* in all studies. In addition, we asked participants to explain why they made the particular moral judgments (e.g., "Why does it seem to you that the [agent] deserves this amount of blame?"). All studies had a 2 (Agent: human repairmen or robot) × 2 (Decision: Action or Inaction) between-subjects design, and we summarize here the results of six studies from around 3,000 online participants.

Before we analyzed people's moral responses to robots, we examined whether they treated robots as moral agents in the first place. We systematically classified people's explanations of their moral judgments and identified responses that either expressly denied the robot's moral capacity (e.g., "doesn't have a moral compass," "it's not a person," "it's a machine," "merely programmed,") or mentioned the programmer or designer as the fully or partially responsible agent. Automated text analysis followed by human inspection showed that about one-third of US participants denied the robot moral agency, leaving two-thirds who accepted the robot as a proper target of blame. Though all results still hold in the entire sample, it made little sense to include data from individuals who explicitly rejected the premise of the study—to evaluate an artificial agent's moral decision. Thus, we focused our data analysis on only those participants who accepted this premise.

First, when probing participants' normative expectations, we found virtually no human-robot differences. Generally, people were equally inclined to find the Action permissible for the human (61%) and the robot (64%), and when asked to choose, they recommended that each agent should take the *Action*, both the human (79%) and the robot (83%).

Second, however, when we analyzed *decision evaluations*, we identified a robust human-robot asymmetry across studies (we focus here on blame judgments, but very similar results hold for wrongness judgments). Whereas robots and human agents were blamed equally after deciding to *act* (i.e., sacrifice one person for the good of four)—44.3 and 42.1, respectively, on a 0–100 scale—humans were blamed less ($M = 23.7$) than robots ($M = 40.2$) after deciding to *not* act. Five of the six studies found this pattern to be statistically significant. The average effect size of the relevant interaction term was $d = 0.25$, and the effect size of the human-robot difference in the Inaction condition was $d = 0.50$.

What might explain this asymmetry? It cannot be a preference for a robot to make the "utilitarian" choice and the human to make the deontological choice. Aside from the difficulty of neatly assigning each choice option to these traditions of philosophical ethics, it is actually not the case that people expected the robot to act any differently from humans, as we saw from the highly comparable norm expectation data (questions of *permissible* and *should*). Furthermore, if robots were preferred to be utilitarians, then a robot's *Action* decision would be welcomed and should receive less blame—but in fact, blame for human and robot agents was consistently similar in this condition.

A better explanation for the pattern of less blame for human than robot in the case of *Inaction* might be that people's *justifications* for the two agents' decisions differed. Justifications are the agent's reasons for deciding to act, and those reasons represent the major determinant of blame when causality and intentionality are held constant (Malle et al. 2014), which we can assume is true for the experimental narratives. What considerations might justify the lower blame for the human agent in the Inaction case? We explored people's verbal explanations following their moral judgments and found a pattern of responses that provided a candidate justification: the impossibly difficult decision situation made it understandable and thus somewhat acceptable for the human to decide *not* to act. Indeed, across all studies, people's spontaneous characterizations of the dilemma as "difficult," "impossible," and the like, were more frequent for the *Inaction* condition (12.1%) than the *Action* condition (5.8%), and more frequent for the human protagonist (11.2%) than the robot protagonist (6.6%). Thus, it appears that participants notice, or even vicariously feel, this "impossible situation" primarily when the human repairman decides not to act, and that is why the blame levels are lower.

A further test of this interpretation was supportive: When considering those among the 3,000 participants who mentioned the decision difficulty, their blame levels were almost 14 points lower (because they found it justified to refrain from the action), and among this group, there was no longer a human-robot asymmetry for the Inaction decision. The candidate explanation for this asymmetry in the whole sample is then that participants more readily consider the decision difficulty for the human agent, especially in the Inaction condition, and when they do, blame levels decrease. Fewer participants consider the decision difficulty for the robot agent, and as a result, less net blame mitigation occurs.

In sum, we learned two related lessons from these studies. First, people can have highly similar normative expectations regarding the (prospectively) "right thing to do" for both humans and robots in life-and-death scenarios, but people's (retrospective) moral judgments of actually made decisions may still differ for human and robot agents. That is because, second, people's justifications of human decisions and robot decisions can differ. In the reported studies, the difference stemmed from the ease of imagining the dilemma's difficulty for the human protagonist, which seemed to somewhat justify the decision to *not* act and lower its associated blame. This kind of imagined difficulty and resulting justification was rarer in the case of a robot protagonist. Observers of these response patterns from ordinary people may be worried about the willingness to decrease blame judgments when one better "understands" a decision (or the difficulty surrounding a decision). But that is not far from the reasonable person standard in contemporary law (e.g., Baron 2011). The law, too, reduces punishment when the defendant's decision or action was understandable and reasonable. When "anybody" would find it difficult to sacrifice one person for the good of many (even if it were the right thing to do), then nobody should be strongly blamed for refraining from that action. Such a reasonable agent standard is not available for robots, and people's moral judgments reflect this inability to understand, and consider reasonable, a robot's action. This situation can be expected for the foreseeable future, until reasonable robot standards are established or people better understand how the minds of robots work, struggling or not.

6.4: AI AND DRONES IN A MILITARY STRIKE DILEMMA

In the second line of work (Malle, Thapa, and Scheutz, 2019), we presented participants with a moral dilemma scenario in a military context inspired by the film *Eye in the Sky* (Hood 2016).[1] The dilemma is between either (i) launching a missile strike on a terrorist compound but risking the life of a child, or (ii) canceling the strike to protect the child but risking a likely terrorist attack. Participants considered one of three decision-makers: an artificial intelligence (AI) agent, an autonomous drone, or a human drone pilot. We embedded the decision-maker within a command structure, involving military and legal commanders who provided guidance on the decision.

We asked online participants (a) what the decision-maker should do (norm assessment), (b) whether the decision was morally wrong and how much blame the person deserves, and (c) why participants assigned the particular amount of blame. As above, the answers to the third question were content analyzed to identify participants who did not consider the artificial agents proper targets of blame. Across three studies, 72% of respondents were comfortable making moral judgments about the AI in this scenario, and 51% were comfortable making moral judgments about the autonomous drone. We analyzed the data of these participants for norm and blame responses.

In the first of three studies, we examined whether any asymmetry exists between a human and artificial moral decision-maker in the above military dilemma. The study had a 3 × 2 between-subjects design that crossed a three-level *Agent* factor (human pilot vs. drone vs. AI) with a two-level *Decision* factor (launch the strike vs. cancel the strike). Online participants considered the missile strike dilemma and made two moral judgments: whether the agent's decision was morally wrong (Yes vs. No) and how much blame the agent deserved for the decision (on a 0–100 scale). After the latter judgment, participants explained their judgments ("Why does it seem to you that the [agent] deserves this amount of blame?"). After removing participants who expressed serious doubts about the AI's or drone's eligibility for moral evaluation, 501 participants remained for analysis.

When asked about *moral wrongness*, more people regarded the human pilot's decision to *cancel* as wrong (25.8%) than the decision to *launch* (14.8%), whereas the reverse was true for the two artificial agents: more people considered the drone's or AI's decision to *launch* as wrong (27.0%) than the decision to cancel (19.4%), interaction term $p = 0.014$, to $d = .18$. The rates for autonomous drone and AI did not differ.

When asked to provide *blame judgments*, people blamed the human pilot far more for *canceling* ($M = 54.2$) than for launching ($M = 35.3$), whereas they blamed the artificial agents roughly the same amount for canceling ($M = 43.4$) as for launching ($M = 41.5$); interaction term $p = .007$, $d = 0.25$. Blame for the two artificial agents did not differ.

Thus, people appear to grant the human pilot some mitigation when launching the strike (recommended, though not commanded by superiors) but exacerbate blame when he cancels the strike. For artificial agents, this differentiation of blame did not appear.

In a next study we tested one hypothesis that could explain this asymmetric blame—namely, that people simply impose different norms on human and artificial agents: in the given scenario, the human *should launch*, and when he cancels, he is blamed for his norm violation; an AI or a drone may not have been imposed the same preferential norm about what they should do, which explains the roughly equal blame they receive for the two decisions.

The study had a 3 (Agent: human pilot, AI, drone) × 2 (Decision: launch vs. cancel) between-subjects design, with two dependent variables: *should* and *blame*. Online participants read the same narratives as in in the first study except that the word "autonomous" was removed from all but the first sentence of both the AI and the drone narrative, because the word may have increased the machines' seeming independence from the command structure. Participants first answered the question "*What should the [agent] do?*" (98% of participants provided a response easily verbally classifiable as *launch* or *cancel*). Then people provided blame judgments on a 0–100 scale and offered explanations of their blame judgments. After removing participants who expressed doubts about the artificial agents' moral eligibility, 541 participants remained for analysis.

When asked about what the agent *should* do, people did not impose different norms onto the three agents. Launching the strike was equally obligatory for the human ($M = 83.0\%$), the AI ($M = 83.0\%$), and the drone ($M = 80\%$). Neither human and artificial agents ($p = .45$) nor AI and drone ($p = .77$) differed from one another.

When asked to provide *blame judgments*, people again blamed the human pilot more for canceling ($M = 52.4$) than for launching ($M = 31.9$), whereas the artificial agents together received more similar levels of blame for canceling ($M = 44.6$) as for launching ($M = 36.5$), interaction $p = .046$, $d = 0.19$. However, while the *cancel–launch* blame difference for the human pilot was strong, $d = 0.58$, that for the drone was still $d = 0.36$, above the AI's ($d = 0.04$), though not significantly so, $p = .13$.

We then considered a second explanation for the human-machine asymmetry—that people apply different moral justifications for the human's and the artificial agents' decisions. Structurally, this explanation is similar to the case of the mining dilemma, but the specific justifications differ. Specifically, the human pilot may have received less blame for launching than canceling the strike because launching was more strongly justified by the commanders' approval of this decision. Being part of the military command structure, the human pilot thus has justifications available that modulate blame as a function of the pilot's decision. These justifications may be cognitively less available to respondents when they consider the decisions of artificial agents, in part because it is difficult to mentally simulate what duty to one's superior, disobedience, ensuing reprimands, and so forth might look like for an artificial agent and its commanders.

People's verbal explanations following their blame judgments in Studies 1 and 2 provided support for this hypothesis. Across the two studies, participants who evaluated the human pilot offered more than twice as many remarks referring to the command structure (26.7%) as did those who evaluated artificial agents (11%), $p = .001$, $d = .20$. More striking, the *cancel–launch* asymmetry for the human pilot was amplified among those 94 participants who referred to the command structure ($M_{diff} = 36.9$, $d = 1.27$), compared to those 258 who did not ($M_{diff} = 13.3$, $d = 0.36$), interaction $p = .004$. And a *cancel–launch* asymmetry appeared even for the artificial agents (averaging AI and drone) among those 76 participants who referenced the command structure ($M_{diff} = 36.7$, $d = 1.16$), not at all among those 614 who did not make any such reference ($M_{diff} = 1.3$, $d = 0.01$), interaction $p < .001$.

A final study tested the hypothesis more directly that justifications explain the human-machine asymmetry. We increased the human pilot's justification to cancel the strike by including in the narrative the military lawyers' and commanders' affirmation that either decision is supportable, thus explicitly authorizing the pilot to make his own decision (labeled the "decision freedom" manipulation). As a result, the human pilot is now equally justified to cancel or launch the strike, and no relatively greater blame for canceling than launching should emerge.

Two samples combined to make up 522 participants. In the first sample, the decision freedom manipulation reduced the previous cancel–launch difference of 20 points ($d = 0.58, p < .001$ in Study 2) to 9 points ($d = 0.23, p = .12$). In the second sample, we replicated the 21-point *cancel–launch* difference in the standard condition ($d = 0.69, p < .001$) and reduced it to a 7-point difference ($d = 0.21, p = .14$) in the decision freedom condition.

In sum, we were able to answer three questions. First, do people find it appropriate to treat artificial agents as targets of moral judgment? Indeed, a majority of people do. Compared to 60–70% of respondents who felt comfortable blaming a robot in our mining dilemmas, 72% across the three missile strike dilemma studies felt comfortable blaming an AI, and 51% felt comfortable blaming the autonomous drone. Perhaps the label "drone" is less apt to invoke the image of an actual agent with choice capacity that does good and bad things and deserves praise or blame. In other research we have found that autonomous vehicles, too, may be unlikely to be seen as moral agents (Li et al. 2016). Thus, in empirical studies on artificial agents, we cannot simply assume that people will treat machines as moral decision-making agents; it depends on the kind of machine, and we need to actually measure these assumptions.

Second, what norms do people impose on human and artificial agents in a life-and-death dilemma situation? In the present scenarios (as in the mining dilemma), we found no general differences in what actions are normatively expected of human and artificial agents. However, other domains and other robot roles may show differentiation of applicable norms, such as education, medical care, and other areas in which personal relations play a central role.

Third, how do people morally evaluate a human or artificial agent's decision in such a dilemma? We focused on judgments of blame, which are the most sophisticated moral judgments and take into account all available information about the norm violation, causality, intentionality, and the agent's reasons for acting (Malle et al. 2014; Monroe and Malle 2017). Our results show that people's blame judgments differ between human and artificial agents, and these differences appear to arise from different moral justifications that people have available for, or grant to, artificial agents. People mitigated their blame for the human pilot when the pilot launched the missile strike because he was going along with the superiors' recommendation and therefore had justification to launch the strike; by contrast, people exacerbated blame when the pilot canceled the strike, because he was going against the superiors' recommendations. Blame judgments differed less to not at all for artificial agents, and our hypothesis is that most people did not grant the agents justifications that referred back to the command structure they were part of. In fact, it is likely that many people simply did not think of the artificial agents as embedded in social-institutional structures and, as a result, they explained and justified those agents' actions, not in terms of the roles they occupied, but in terms of the inherent qualities of the decision.

6.5: DISCUSSION

Overall, our empirical results suggest that many (though not all) human observers will form moral judgments about artificial systems that make decisions in life-and-death situations. People tend to apply very similar norms to human and artificial agents about how the agents *should* decide, but when they judge the moral quality of the agents' actual decision, their judgments tend to differ; and that is likely because these moral judgments are critically dependent on the kinds of justifications people grant the agents. People seem to imagine the psychological and social situation that a human agent is in and can therefore detect, and perhaps vicariously experience, the decision conflict the agent endures and the social pressures or social support the agent receives. This process can invoke justifications for the human's decision and thus lead to blame mitigation (though sometimes to blame exacerbation). In the case of artificial agents, by contrast, people have difficulty imagining the agent's decision process or "experience," and justification or blame mitigation will be rare. As a result, artificial and human agents' decisions may be judged differently, even if the *ex ante* norms are the same.

If people fail to infer the decision processes and justifications of artificial agents, these agents will have to generate justifications for their decisions and actions, especially when the latter are unintuitive or violate norms. While it is an open question what kinds of justifications will be acceptable to humans, it is clear that these justifications need to make explicit recourse to normative principles that humans uphold. That is because justifications often clarify why one action, violating a less serious norm, was preferable over the alternative, which would have violated a more serious norm. This requirement for justifications, in turn, places a significant constraint on the design of architectures for autonomous agents: any approach to agent decision-making that only *implicitly* encodes decisions or action choices will come up short on the justification requirement because it cannot link choices to principles. This shortcoming applies to agents governed by Reinforcement Learning algorithms (Abel et al. 2016) and even sophisticated Cooperative Inverse Reinforcement Learning approaches (Hadfield-Menell et al. 2016), because the agents learn how to act from observed behaviors without ever learning the reasons for any of the behaviors.

It follows that artificial agents must know at least some of the normative principles that guide human decisions in order to be able to generate justifications that are acceptable to humans. Perhaps agents could rely on such principles in generating justifications even when the behavior, in reality, was not the result of decisions involving those principles. Such an approach may succeed for cases in which the agent's behavior aligns with human expectations (because, after all, the system did the right thing), but it is likely to fail when no obvious alignment can be established (precisely because the agent did not follow any of the principles for making its decisions; see also Kasenberg et al. 2018). But this approach is at best post hoc rationalization and, if discovered, is likely to be considered deceptive, jeopardizing human trust in the decision system. In our view, a better approach would be for artificial agents to ground their decisions in human normative principles in the first place; then generating justifications amounts to pointing to the obeyed principles, and when a norm conflict occurs, the justification presents that the chosen option obeyed the more important principles. Kasenberg and Scheutz (2018) have started to develop an ethical planning and reasoning framework with explicit norm representations that can handle ethical decision-making, even in cases of norm conflicts. Within this framework, dedicated algorithms would allow for justification dialogues in which the artificial agent can be asked, in natural language, to justify its actions, and it does with recourse to normative principles in factual and counterfactual situations (Kasenberg et al. 2019).

6.6: CONCLUSION

Human communities work best when members know the shared norms, largely comply with them, and are able to justify a decision to violate one norm in service of a more important one. As artificial agents become part of human communities, we should make similar demands on them. Artificial agents embedded in human communities will not be subject to exactly the same norms as humans are, but they will have to be aware of the norms that apply to them and comply with the norms to the extent possible. However, moral judgments are based not only on an action's norm compliance but also on the reasons for the action. If people find a machine's reasons opaque, the machines must make themselves transparent, which includes justifying their actions by reference to applicable norms. If machines that make life-and-death decisions, or at least assume socially influential roles, enter society, they will have to demonstrate their ability to act in norm-compliant ways; express their knowledge of applicable norms before they act; and offer appropriate justifications, especially in response to criticism, after they acted. It is up to us how to design artificial agents, and endowing them with this form of moral, or at least norm, competence will be a safeguard for human societies, ensuring that artificial agents will be able to improve the human condition.

ACKNOWLEDGMENTS

This project was supported by a grant from the Office of Naval Research (ONR), No. N00014-16-1-2278. The opinions expressed here are our own and do not necessarily reflect the views of ONR.

NOTE

1. This scenario and the details of narratives, questions, and results for all studies can be found at http://research.clps.brown.edu/SocCogSci/AISkyMaterial.pdf.

WORKS CITED

Abel, David, James MacGlashan, and Michael L. Littman. 2016. "Reinforcement Learning as a Framework for Ethical Decision Making." *Workshops at 13th AAAI Workshop on Artificial Intelligence.*

Arkin, Ronald C. 2009. *Governing Lethal Behavior in Autonomous Robots.* Boca Raton, FL: CRC Press.

Arkin, Ronald C. 2015. "The Case for Banning Killer Robots: Counterpoint." *Communications of the ACM* 58 (12): pp. 46–47.

Asaro Peter M. 2012. "A Body to Kick, but Still No Soul to Damn: Legal Perspectives on Robotics." In *Robot Ethics: The Ethical and Social Implications of Robotics,* edited by Patrick Lin, Keith Abney, and George A. Bekey, pp. 169–186. Cambridge MA: MIT Press.

Awad, Edmond, Sohan Dsouza, Richard Kim, Jonathan Schulz, Joseph Henrich, Azim Shariff, Jean-François Bonnefon, and Iyad Rahwan. 2018. "The Moral Machine Experiment." *Nature* 563 (7729): 59–64. doi: 10.1038/s41586-018-0637-6.

Baron, Marcia. 2011. "The Standard of the Reasonable Person in the Criminal Law." In *The Structures of the Criminal Law*, edited by R.A. Duff, Lindsay Farmer, S.E. Marshall, Massimo Renzo, and Victor Tadros, pp. 11–35. Oxford: Oxford University Press.

Bonnefon, Jean-François, Azim Shariff, and Iyad Rahwan. 2016. "The Social Dilemma of Autonomous Vehicles." *Science* 352 (6293): pp. 1573–1576.

Briggs, G. and Scheutz, M. (2017). The Case for Robot Disobedience. *Scientific American* 316 (1): 44–47. Available at https://doi.org/10.1038/scientificamerican0117-44.

Bringsjord, Selmer. 2019. "Commentary: Use AI to Stop Carnage." *Times Union*. August 16. https://www.timesunion.com/opinion/article/Commentary-Use-AI-to-stop-carnage-14338001.php.

de Graaf, Maartje M. A. and Bertram F. Malle. 2017. "How People Explain Action (and Autonomous Intelligent Systems Should Too). *2017 AAAI Fall Symposium Series Technical Reports*. FS-17-01. Palo Alto, CA: AAAI Press, pp. 19–26.

Foot, Philippa. 1967. "The Problem of Abortion and the Doctrine of Double Effect." *Oxford Review* 5: pp. 5–15.

Funk Michael, Bernhard Irrgang, and Silvio Leuteritz. 2016. "Drones @ Combat: Enhanced Information Warfare and Three Moral Claims of Combat Drone Responsibility." In *Drones and Responsibility: Legal, Philosophical and Socio-Technical Perspectives on Remotely Controlled Weapons*, edited by Ezio Di Nucci and Santoni de Sio, pp. 182–196. London: Routledge.

Hadfield-Menell, Dylan, Stuart J. Russell, Pieter Abbeel, and Anca Dragan Russell. 2016. "Cooperative Inverse Reinforcement Learning." In *Advances in Neural Information Processing Systems 29*, edited by Daniel D. Lee, Masashi Sugiyama, Ulrike V. Luxburg, Isabelle Guyon, and Roman Garnett, pp. 3909–3917. New York: Curran Associates Inc.

Harbers, Maaike, Marieke M.M. Peeters, and Mark A. Neerincx. 2017. "Perceived Autonomy of Robots: Effects of Appearance and Context." In *A World with Robots: International Conference on Robot Ethics 2015*, edited by Maria Isabel Aldinhas Ferreira, João Silva Sequeira, Mohammad Osman Tokhi, Endre Kadar, and Gurvinder Singh Virk, pp. 19–33. New York: Springer.

Hood, Gavin. 2016. *Eye in the Sky*. New York: Bleecker Street Media. Available at http://www.imdb.com/title/tt2057392/ (accessed June 30, 2017).

Kahn Jr., Peter H., Takayuki Kanda, Hiroshi Ishiguro, Brian T. Gill, Jolina H. Ruckert, Solace Shen, Heather E. Gary, Aimee L. Reichert, Nathan G. Freier, and Rachel L. Severson. 2012. "Do People Hold a Humanoid Robot Morally Accountable for the Harm It Causes?" In *Proceedings of the Seventh Annual ACM/IEEE International Conference on Human-Robot Interaction*. Boston, MA: Association for Computing Machinery, pp. 33–40.

Kasenberg, Daniel and Matthias Scheutz. 2018. "Norm Conflict Resolution in Stochastic Domains." In *Proceedings of the Thirty-Second AAAI Conference on Artificial Intelligence*. New Orleans: Association for the Advancement of Artificial Intelligence, pp. 85–92.

Kasenberg, Daniel, Arnold T. and Matthias Scheutz. 2018. "Norms, Rewards, and the Intentional Stance: Comparing Machine Learning Approaches to Ethical Training." In *AIES '18: Proceedings of the 2018 AAAI/ACM Conference on AI, Ethics, and Society*. New York: Association for Computing Machinery, pp. 184–190.

Kasenberg, Daniel, Antonio Roque, Ravenna Thielstrom, Meia Chita-Tegmark, and Matthias Scheutz. 2019. "Generating Justifications for Norm-Related Agent Decisions." In *12th International Conference on Natural Language Generation (INLG)*. Tokyo: Association for Computational Linguistics, pp. 484–493.

Li, Jamy, Xuan Zhao, Mu-Jung Cho, Wendy Ju, and Bertram F. Malle. 2016. *From Trolley to Autonomous Vehicle: Perceptions of Responsibility and Moral Norms in Traffic Accidents with Self-Driving Cars*. Technical Paper 2016-01-0164. Warrendale, PA: Society of Automotive Engineers (SAE).

Lin, Patrick. 2013. "The Ethics of Autonomous Cars." *The Atlantic*, October 8. https://www.theatlantic.com/technology/archive/2013/10/the-ethics-of-autonomous-cars/280360/.

Malle, Bertram F. and Matthias Scheutz. 2015. "When Will People Regard Robots as Morally Competent Social Partners?" In *Proceedings of the 24th IEEE International Symposium on Robot and Human Interactive Communication (RO-MAN)*. Kobe, Japan: IEEE, pp. 486–491.

Malle, Bertram F. and Matthias Scheutz. 2019. "Learning How to Behave: Moral Competence for Social Robots." In *Handbuch Maschinenethik [Handbook of Machine Ethics]*, edited by Oliver Bendel, pp. 1–24. Wiesbaden, Germany: Springer.

Malle, Bertram F., Matthias Scheutz, Thomas Arnold, John Voiklis, and Corey Cusimano. 2015. "Sacrifice One for the Good of Many? People Apply Different Moral Norms to Human and Robot Agents." In *Proceedings of the Tenth Annual ACM/IEEE International Conference on Human-Robot Interaction, HRI'15*. New York: Association for Computing Machinery, pp. 117–124.

Malle, Bertram F., Steve Guglielmo, and Andrew E. Monroe. 2014. "A Theory of Blame." *Psychological Inquiry* 25 (2): 147–186.

Malle, Bertram F., Matthias Scheutz, Jodi Forlizzi, and John Voiklis. 2016. "Which Robot Am I Thinking About? The Impact of Action and Appearance on People's Evaluations of a Moral Robot." In *Proceedings of the Eleventh Annual Meeting of the IEEE Conference on Human-Robot Interaction, HRI'16*. Piscataway, NJ: IEEE Press, pp. 125–132.

Malle, Bertram F., Matthias Scheutz, and Komatsu T. 2019. *Moral Evaluations of Moral Robots*. Unpublished Manuscript. 2019. Providence, RI: Brown University.

Malle, Bertram F., Stuti Thapa Magar, and Matthias Scheutz (2019). "AI in the Sky: How People Morally Evaluate Human and Machine Decisions in a Lethal Strike Dilemma." In *Robotics and Well-Being*, edited by Maria Isabel Aldinhas Ferreira, João Silva Sequeira, Virk Gurvinder, Osman Tokhi, and Endre Kadar, pp. 111–133. Cham, Switzerland: Springer International Publishing. doi: https://doi.org/10.1007/978-3-030-12524-0

Millar, Jason. 2014. "An Ethical Dilemma: When Robot Cars Must Kill, Who Should Pick the Victim?" *Robohub*. June 11. http://robohub.org/an-ethical-dilemma-when-robot-cars-must-kill-who-should-pick-the-victim/.

Monroe, Andrew E. and Bertram F. Malle. 2017. "Two Paths to Blame: Intentionality Directs Moral Information Processing along Two Distinct Tracks." *Journal of Experimental Psychology: General* 146 (1): pp. 123–133. doi: 10.1037/xge0000234.

Monroe, Andrew E., Kyle D. Dillon, and Bertram F. Malle. 2014. "Bringing Free Will Down to Earth: People's Psychological Concept of Free Will and Its Role in Moral Judgment." *Consciousness and Cognition* 27, pp. 100–108. doi: 10.1016/j.concog.2014.04.011.

Pagallo, Ugo. 2011. "Robots of Just War: A Legal Perspective." *Philosophy & Technology* 24 (3): pp. 307–323. doi: 10.1007/s13347-011-0024-9.

Podschwadek, Frodo. 2017. "Do Androids Dream of Normative Endorsement? On the Fallibility of Artificial Moral Agents." *Artificial Intelligence and Law* 25 (3): pp. 325–339. doi: 10.1007/s10506-017-9209-6.

Scheutz, Matthias and Bertram F. Malle. 2014. "Think and Do the Right Thing: A Plea for Morally Competent Autonomous Robots." In *Proceedings of the IEEE International Symposium on Ethics in Engineering, Science, and Technology, Ethics 2014*. Red Hook, NY: Curran Associates/IEEE Computer Society, pp. 36–39.

Sidner, Sara and Mallory Simon. 2016. "How Robot, Explosives Took Out Dallas Sniper in Unprecedented Way." *CNN*. July 12. https://www.cnn.com/2016/07/12/us/dallas-police-robot-c4-explosives/index.html.

Sparrow, Robert. 2007. "Killer Robots." *Journal of Applied Philosophy* 24 (1): pp. 62–77. doi: 10.1111/j.1468-5930.2007.00346.x.

Sparrow, Robert. 2011. "Robotic Weapons and the Future of War." In *New Wars and New Soldiers: Military Ethics in the Contemporary World*, edited by Jessica Wolfendale and Paolo Tripodi, pp. 117–133. Burlington, VA: Ashgate.

Thomson, Judith Jarvis. 1976. "Killing, Letting Die, and the Trolley Problem." *The Monist* 59 (2): pp. 204–217. doi: 10.5840/monist197659224.

Wachter, Sandra, Brent Mittelstadt, and Luciano Floridi. 2017. "Transparent, Explainable, and Accountable AI for Robotics." *Science Robotics* 2 (6). doi: 10.1126/scirobotics.aan6080.

Wang, Ning, David V. Pynadath, and Susan G. Hill. 2016. "Trust Calibration within a Human-Robot Team: Comparing Automatically Generated Explanations." In *The Eleventh ACM/IEEE International Conference on Human Robot Interaction, HRI '16*. Piscataway, NJ: IEEE Press, pp. 109–116.

Wolkenstein, Andreas. 2018. "What Has the Trolley Dilemma Ever Done for Us (and What Will It Do in the Future)? On Some Recent Debates about the Ethics of Self-Driving Cars." *Ethics and Information Technology* 20 (3): pp. 163–173. doi: 10.1007/s10676-018-9456-6.

Young, April D. and Andrew E. Monroe. 2019. "Autonomous Morals: Inferences of Mind Predict Acceptance of AI Behavior in Sacrificial Moral Dilemmas." *Journal of Experimental Social Psychology* 85. doi: 10.1016/j.jesp.2019.103870.

7

The Better Instincts of Humanity: Humanitarian Arguments in Defense of International Arms Control

NATALIA JEVGLEVSKAJA AND RAIN LIIVOJA

7.1: INTRODUCTION

Disagreements about the humanitarian risk-benefit balance of military technology are not new. The history of arms control negotiations offers many examples of weaponry that was regarded as 'inhumane' by some, while hailed by others as a means to reduce injury or suffering in conflict. The debate about autonomous weapons systems (AWS) reflects this dynamic, yet also stands out in some respects. In this chapter, we consider how the discourse about the humanitarian consequences of AWS has unfolded. We focus specifically on the deliberations of the Group of Governmental Experts (GGE) that the Meeting of High Contracting Parties to the Convention on Certain Conventional Weapons (CCW) has tasked with considering 'emerging technologies in the area of lethal autonomous weapon systems' (UN Office at Geneva n.d.).

We begin with a synopsis of the arguments advanced in relation to the prohibition of chemical weapons and cluster munitions to show how all sides of those arms control debates came to rely on the notion of 'humanity.' We then turn to the work of the GGE, considering how the talks around AWS stand apart from the discussions on chemical weapons and cluster munitions, noting in particular ostensible definitional and conceptual difficulties that have plagued the debate on AWS since its inception in 2012. Subsequently, we contrast potential adverse humanitarian consequences—that is, perceived risks—of AWS, with a range of military applications of autonomy that arguably further humanitarian outcomes. We

Natalia Jevglevskaja and Rain Liivoja, *The Better Instincts of Humanity: Humanitarian Arguments in Defense of International Arms Control* In: *Lethal Autonomous Weapons*. Edited by: Jai Galliott, Duncan MacIntosh and Jens David Ohlin,
 DOI: 10.1093/oso/9780197546048.003.0008

conclude that the current discussion, which has been reluctant to take proper note of the humanitarian benefits of autonomy, let alone evaluate them, is not conducive to sensible regulation of AWS.

7.2: CHEMICAL WEAPONS AND CLUSTER MUNITIONS

Two kinds of humanitarian concerns make a regular appearance in arms control negotiations. On the one hand, some weapons are regarded as causing injury or suffering to *combatants* that is excessive in relation to the military advantage gained by their use. To use the modern-day technical term, such weapons cause 'superfluous injury or unnecessary suffering' (AP I art. 35(2)). On the other hand, certain weapons are seen as causing unjustifiable harm to *civilians* because of their inherently indiscriminate character. Put differently, these are weapons that cannot be directed at military objectives or the effects of which cannot be sufficiently limited to military objectives (AP I art. 51(4)(b), 51(4)(c)).

In the case of chemical weapons, the discussion was overwhelmingly concerned with the excessive injury they caused to combatants, whereas the employment of cluster munitions was argued to cause unjustifiable harm to civilians and civilian objects. That said, the arguments that chemical weapons are uncontrollable and, therefore indiscriminate, and that cluster munitions cause unnecessary suffering have been advanced too, though much less forcefully. As we shall see, both with respect to chemical weapons and cluster munitions, the notion of humanity figures prominently in arms control discussions and has been relied upon by different States and interest groups. While many commentators, if not most, have consistently regarded chemical weapons and cluster munitions as 'inhumane,' the argument has also been made that these weapons are more humanitarian than the alternatives.

A comprehensive ban on chemical weapons, laid down in the 1993 Chemical Weapons Convention, ultimately derives from the prohibition of poison, contained in customary rules with chivalric origins (see, e.g., Liivoja 2012, 84–86) and several legal instruments adopted in the late nineteenth and twentieth centuries. The use of chemical weapons first became the subject of treaty negotiations at the 1899 Hague Peace Conference. Among other things, the Conference considered the use in warfare of projectiles releasing asphyxiating gas. The spectrum of opinions was wide. Some regarded gas as plainly 'barbarous,' necessitating its prohibition (First Commission, Third Meeting, June 22, 1899, in Scott 1920, 296). Others openly doubted its allegedly inhuman character or went as far as asserting that gas projectiles could be 'more human instruments of war than others' (First Commission, Second Subcommission, Third Meeting, May 31, 1899, in Scott 1920, 367)—that is to say, superior from a humanitarian perspective. The proponents of the ban eventually prevailed, and Hague Declaration II to outlaw the use of gas projectiles in warfare adopted. But the large-scale employment of chemicals in the First World War revived the debate, which played out in the negotiations leading up to the 1925 Geneva Gas Protocol and continued long after the adoption of this instrument.

Proponents of a prohibition argued that gas condemned its victims to long and drawn-out torture and was 'abhorrent to civilization' (Subcommittee on Land Armament of the Advisory Committee to the American Delegation, in Conference on the Limitation of Armament 1922, 734). Because of its uncontrollable effects, a case was also made against the indiscriminate nature of gas. For example, a report produced for the American Delegation to the Washington Conference on the Limitation of Armament condemned chemical warfare, in principle, as 'fraught with the gravest danger to non-combatants' (Subcommittee on Land Armament of the Advisory Committee to the American Delegation, in Conference on the Limitation of Armament 1922). Others were not convinced by these arguments. Even some of those who had experienced the effects of gas warfare firsthand insisted that those were, in fact, less horrible than the impact of kinetic weapons. For example, Prentiss (1937, 680) argued that the use of gas was unobjectionable, where the enemy was adequately equipped for offense or defense:

> Gas not only produces practically no permanent injuries, so that if a man who is gassed survives the war, he comes out body whole, as God made him, and no the legless, armless, or deformed cripple produced by the mangling and rending effects of high explosives, gunshot wounds, and bayonet thrusts.

Above all, the superiority of chemical warfare from the humanitarian perspective was seen in lower mortality rates. The ratio of deaths and permanently injured as a result of gas, compared to the total number of casualties produced by other weapons, has been regarded as an "index of its humaneness" (Gilchrist 1928, 47).

Despite the adoption of the 1925 Geneva Protocol, chemical weapons were employed in a number of conflicts (see, e.g., Robinson 1998, 33–35; Mathews 2016, 216–217). The renewed interest in negotiating yet another international instrument on the subject arose in reaction to the large-scale employment by the United States of lachrymatory and anti-plant agents in Vietnam, which many States had regarded as chemical warfare agents (Mathews 2016, 218). The United States insisted, however, that the use of certain chemical compounds causing merely transient incapacitation and used by States domestically for riot-control purposes—including tear gas—was legitimate, and, in fact, commanded by humanitarian considerations (United States 1966, para. 42). In contrast to weapons that could be used in the alternative—such as machine guns, napalm, high explosives, or fragmentation grenades—tear gas was seen as 'a more humanitarian weapon' (Bunn 1970, 197) available against Viet-Cong forces who tended to hide behind human shields and in tunnels or caves. In contrast, the opponents maintained their view on the repugnant nature of chemical weapons designed to exercise their effects solely on living matter (UN Secretary-General 1969, 87). Explosives, they argued, were aimed at destroying material assets in the first place and people collaterally. Chemical weapons, on the contrary, were produced to maim and kill human beings (McCamley 2006, 70). While the anti-personnel design purpose of weapons remained unobjectionable in war, the atrocious character of chemical weapons was regarded inhumane, and therefore unacceptable. Eventually, the arguments against chemical weapons won the day. The 1993 Chemical Weapons Convention not only comprehensively prohibited the use of chemical weapons, but also proscribed their development, production, acquisition, and stockpiling, and put in place an elaborate verification mechanism. Interestingly, the language it employs is quite anodyne. The preamble does not refer expressly to the inhumanity of the weapons, or to the suffering of combatants or civilians that might result from the use of such weapons, but it records the determination of the States to prohibit such weapons 'for the sake of all mankind.'

The process that led to the adoption of the 2008 Convention on Cluster Munitions also illustrates the conflicting appeals to humanity in arms control negotiations. Armed forces have valued cluster munitions for their efficiency, for a single warhead can destroy multiple targets within its impact area, reducing not only the logistical burden on the employing force but also its overall exposure to enemy fire. Cluster munitions had been extensively employed since their first use in the Second World War (Congressional Research Service 2019, 1). It was not, however, until 2006 that the ultimate proposal to ban them was made in response to the large-scale deaths of civilians during the Israel-Hezbollah conflict.

Proponents of the ban contended that cluster munitions caused unacceptable harm to civilians. In light of the increasingly urban character of warfare, civilians could be directly hit during a conflict and also fall victim to unexploded submunitions in its aftermath. Consequently, cluster munitions were argued to be plainly 'inhuman in nature' (Peru 2007). However, several States actively contested the assertion that the characteristics of cluster munitions made them inherently indiscriminate. They emphasized that indiscriminateness depended on the use of the weapon rather than its nature, and that cluster munitions could be, and had been, used consistently with the fundamental legal principles of distinction and proportionality. Above all, States in favor of retaining cluster munitions claimed that these weapons proved particularly efficient against area targets. So much so that any expected or anticipated problem of unexploded submunitions, being amenable to a technical solution, would not outweigh the expected military advantage from their use. They also argued that no viable alternative existed for striking area targets within a short period of time without causing excessive incidental harm to civilians and civilian objects; consequently, banning cluster munitions would be counter-humanitarian, leading to 'more suffering and less discrimination' (United States 2006).

Eventually, however, arguments favoring the military utility of cluster munitions failed to persuade the (sufficiently) large number of States inclined to support a ban on their use. Statistical evidence showing that 98% of overall casualties suffering the consequences of attacks by cluster munitions had been civilians (Handicap International 2006, 7, 40, 42) helped tilt their opinion toward a prohibition on the development and use of these weapons.

7.3: AUTONOMOUS WEAPONS SYSTEMS: UNIQUE ASPECTS OF THE DEBATE

The contemporary debate around AWS resembles the dynamic of the controversies around chemical weapons and cluster munitions, in as much as each side of the debate argues to be guided in its arguments by humanitarian considerations. We shall discuss this in the next two sections. Here, we focus on those aspects of the debate that make it distinct: specifically, uncertainties around the object of regulation, tendencies to anthropomorphize technology, and limited evidence base. Without claiming to be comprehensive, we will also suggest some potential explanations that keep feeding the contradictory views as to the acceptability of AWS.

The debate about AWS suffers from a unique definitional problem. This issue was identified early on in the work of the GGE, yet the 'explainability deficit' persists to date (GGE 2017, para. 60). As per its official mandate, the GGE focuses on 'emerging technologies in the area of lethal autonomous weapons systems' (UN Office at Geneva n.d.). But even after a set of informal meetings conducted between 2014 and 2016 and followed by formal meetings convened five times between November 2017 and August 2019, the GGE has failed to agree on the constitutive characteristics of such systems, let alone their definition.

As a result, confusion about the very subject of discussion persists. Some States have conceptualized AWS as technology either capable of understanding "higher level intent and direction" (UK Ministry of Defence 2011),[1] or amenable to evolution, meaning that through interaction with the environment the system can "learn autonomously, expand its functions and capabilities in a way exceeding human expectations" (China 2018). Others impose less demanding requirements on technology to count as autonomous. For them, a weapon system that can select and engage targets without further intervention by a human operator—in other words, a system with autonomy in 'critical functions' (ICRC 2016)—would constitute an AWS. This latter approach, shaped largely by the United States and ICRC, enjoys significant support of States participating at the GGE and generally extends to systems supervised by a human and designed to allow them to override operation of the weapon system (US Department of Defense 2011). It considers as autonomous a variety of stationary and mobile technology, which have been in operation for decades, including, for example, air defense systems (US Patriot, Israel's Iron Dome), fire and forget missiles (AMRAAM and Brimstone), and certain loitering munition systems (Harop and Harpy).

That said, the range of technological capabilities suggests that 'autonomy' cannot be conceptualized as a binary concept—in other words, a system being either autonomous or not. Rather, autonomy is a spectrum and any specific system, or more specifically its various functions, may sit at different points of that spectrum (Estonia and Finland 2018). While arms control agreements negotiated to date deal with specific *types* of weapons (systems), debates within the GGE are primarily concerned with certain *functions*, which may be situated higher or lower on the overall spectrum of autonomy (Jenks and Liivoja 2018). This factor significantly complicates pinning down the object of discussion and, as a consequence, many participants in the debate keep talking past each other. Moreover, the use of particular vocabulary, such as 'lethal autonomous weapons systems' (LAWS), or even 'killer robots,' in a highly controversial and occasionally emotionally loaded discourse is unlikely to stimulate any agreement for as long as the terms used lack consistent interpretation (Ekelhof 2017, 311).

Admittedly, certain shifts in understanding AWS occurred over the years. In particular, initial attempts to conceptualize AWS in solely technical terms have not proven fruitful. It was recognized that any definition based purely on technological criteria would not only be difficult but could be quickly overtaken by developments in science and technology. The discussion has subsequently refocused to the type and degree of human involvement in the weapon's operation, or what has been termed by some as 'meaningful human control.' The normative potential of the latter concept has been, however, increasingly and seriously questioned by some delegations, largely because it equally escapes exact parameters. While the importance of a human element in the operation of AWS as such remains uncontested, the language favored by the GGE most recently centers around 'human-machine interaction' (GGE 2019), acknowledging thereby that human involvement may take various forms and be implemented at various stages of the weapon's life cycle (Australia 2019). The resistance of the United States to the use of the term 'control' has been particularly pronounced.

The focus on the 'human element' is unlikely to assist in identifying those types of AWS that may warrant a prohibition or restriction. It could, however, serve as a basis for formulating a positive obligation on States to refrain from the development and use of systems where the type and degree of human-machine interaction would not allow for humans to ensure appropriate control or judgment over the use of force. Such a positive obligation would not be entirely unprecedented in the context of arms control law. Protocol V to the Convention on Certain Conventional Weapons serves as a case in point, requiring States to 'mark and clear, remove or destroy explosive remnants of war' (art. 3(2)). However, disagreements over the precise quality of the human element make easy solutions unlikely.

Another aspect in which the debate on AWS stands out (though closely related to the previously identified one) is that the sheer technical complexity of the issue at hand has hindered efforts by non-experts, including legal experts, to grasp how the core technologies could be regulated (Lewis, Blum, and Modirzadeh 2016, vi). The GGE itself acknowledged the need for technological knowledge to be injected into political debate early on in the process because political decision-makers often tend to underestimate current technological achievements and overestimate future ones (GGE 2017, para. 60).

The tendency to anthropomorphize technology, that is, applying terms originally referring to human traits to nonhuman objects, including technological artifacts, is yet another reason for the confusion in the debate and further polarization of views on the future of AWS. Language frames the way we think, understand, and compare (Surber 2019, 20). Anthropomorphic terms, such as 'autonomy,' 'intelligence,' 'learning processes,' 'decisions,' and similar, convey specific meanings that shape our perception and thinking of technology (Zawieska 2015). Perhaps the most vivid illustration on the issue could be found in the language selected by the proponents of the ban on AWS: '[f]ully autonomous weapons would decide who lives and dies, without further human intervention' (Campaign to Stop Killer Robots n.d.); or '[a] fully autonomous weapon would be programmed so that once it is deployed, it operates on its own. It would be able to select and fire upon targets all on its own' (WILPF 2019, 2).

To be fair, most States have utilized anthropomorphizing language to some degree. Ironically, the most recent GGE Draft Report does that well. Immediately after stating that 'lethal autonomous weapons systems should not be anthropomorphized' (GGE 2019, Annex 4, para. (i); see also GGE 2018, para. 21(h)), it then emphasizes that "discussions and any potential policy measures taken within the context of the CCW should not hamper progress in or access to peaceful uses of *intelligent* autonomous technologies" (GGE 2019, Annex 4, para. (j); see also GGE 2018, para. 21(i); emphasis added). Above all, however, the tendency is reflected in the most commonly used description of AWS, which focuses on systems that 'select and engage' targets. Clarifications of a type provided by the United Kingdom, such that "Phalanx can *detect* a target based on the inputs specified by the controller; it cannot both *detect* and *select* a target based on its own reasoning or logic" (United Kingdom 2018, original emphasis), are only far and few in between. Against this background, some have suggested relying on terminology that appropriately addresses the difference between the anthropomorphic projections and the actual characteristics of technological objects, for example, instead of using "human like, self-triggered systems" (Brazil 2019), "systems with learning capabilities" (Italy 2018), "systems that have the capability to act autonomously" (Pakistan 2018), it could be more appropriate to utilize 'robotic autonomy,' 'quasi-autonomy,' or 'autonomous-like' (Surber 2019, 20; Zawieska 2015).

Certainly, some stakeholders might be attributing human traits to autonomous systems rather unreflectively, whereas others are likely to be purposely relying on anthropomorphizing language to emotionally reinforce their claims. Be this as it may, using the same terms to describe humans and technology risks creating and sustaining misperceptions of technological potential and reducing acceptance of that technology in and outside the military domain (Zawieska 2015). Most importantly, however, it further widens the gap between the stakeholders that seek precision in their choice of terminology in the analysis of law and facts, and those participants in the debate who may want to fuel widespread moral panic.

Finally, the debate about AWS stands apart from the discussions about other arms control measures because of the lack of empirical evidence that could be used to support restrictions or prohibitions. The regulation of chemical weapons and cluster munitions was achieved in large part due to the demonstrable humanitarian harm that those weapons were causing. Even with respect to blinding laser weapons, the preemptive prohibition of which is often cited as a model to follow with regard to AWS, the early evidence of battlefield effects of laser devices allowed for reliable predictions to be made about the humanitarian consequences of wide-scale laser weapons use (see, e.g., Tengroth and Anderberg 1991). In contrast, the challenges of properly defining what systems constitute AWS of concern for the GGE has inevitably led to hypothesization about their adverse effects.

With regard to AWS, it is therefore only possible to talk about *potential* adverse humanitarian consequences—in other words, humanitarian risks. References to the benefits of AWS necessarily have a degree of uncertainty to them as well, as they are often focused on potential future systems. That said, the use of autonomous functionality in some existing systems allows for some generalizations and projections to be made. With these caveats in mind, we now turn to the risks and (potential) benefits of AWS, a dichotomy reminiscent of the debate on chemical weapons and cluster munitions.

7.4: RISKS

The use of AWS would undoubtedly entail *some* risks. One of the Guiding Principles adopted by the GGE by consensus plainly notes that '[r]isk assessments and mitigation measures should be part of the design, development, testing and deployment cycle of emerging technologies in any weapons systems' (GGE 2018, para. 26(f)). The range and seriousness of the risks, as well as the means for reducing them, remain somewhat less clear.

For some, the risks manifest on quite an abstract philosophical level. For example, for the Holy See, the very idea of AWS is unfathomable, not least because such systems promise to alter "irreversibly the nature of warfare, becoming even more inhumane, putting in question the humanity of our societies" (Holy See 2018). In support, civil society organizations note that AWS lack compassion, make life-and-death determinations on the basis of algorithms, and in blatant disrespect of 'human dignity' (Human Rights Watch 2018).

In somewhat more practical terms, some warn about the unpredictability and unreliability of AWS performance on the battlefield (see, e.g., Sri Lanka 2018); the resulting loss of human control has been argued to entail "serious risks for protected persons in armed conflict (both civilians and combatants no longer fighting)" (ICRC 2019). On a larger scale, the GGE has been cautioned that "a global arms race is virtually inevitable" and that it is "only . . . a matter of time until they [AWS] appear on the black market and in the hands of terrorists, dictators wishing to better control their populace, warlords wishing to perpetrate ethnic cleansing, . . . [and available] for tasks such as assassinations, destabilizing nations, subduing populations and selectively killing a particular ethnic group" (Future of Life Institute 2018).

Other participants in the debate express concerns about whether AWS could be used in compliance with the law, particularly in accordance with the fundamental international humanitarian law principles of distinction and proportionality (see, e.g., Austria 2018). Pointing to serious humanitarian and ethical concerns that such systems may pose, they argue for the need to either preemptively ban or otherwise regulate these systems by means of a legal instrument (see, e.g., Pakistan 2018).

The examples listed here are only illustrative and have been explicitly summarized in the final report as follows: States have 'raised a diversity of views on potential risks and challenges . . . including in relation to harm to civilians and combatants in armed conflict in contravention of IHL obligations, exacerbation of regional and international security dilemmas through arms races and the lowering of the threshold for the use of force' as well as 'proliferation, acquisition and use by terrorists, vulnerability of such systems to hacking and interference, and the possible undermining of confidence in the civilian uses of related technologies' (GGE 2018, para. 32). In contrast, and as will be shown in the next section, references to humanitarian benefits offered by AWS do not enjoy any such prominence in the GGE reports.

7.5: BENEFITS

In the GGE, several States have highlighted, with varying degrees of specificity, the benefits of emerging technologies, including autonomous systems. First of all, different aspects of *military* utility of autonomous technology figure conspicuously in the discussions, above all the literature on the subject, perhaps much more so than in relation to any other weapon that has been previously regulated by means of an arms control treaty. Specifically, it has been pointed out that autonomy helps to overcome many operational and economic challenges associated with manned weapon systems. Some of the key operational advantages lie in the possibility of deploying military force with greater speed, agility, accuracy, persistence, reach, coordination, and mass (Boulanin and Verbruggen 2017, 61 *et seq*; see also US

Army 2019). The economic benefits are seen in greater workforce efficiency and associated personnel cost savings (Boulanin and Verbruggen 2017, 63).

When it comes to benefits, some States have confined themselves to statements that are abstract in character. They have spoken of 'potential beneficial applications of emerging technologies in the context of modern warfare' (Austria 2019) or acknowledged that 'artificial intelligence can serve to support the military decision-making process and contribute to certain advantages' (Slovenia 2018). Others have spoken of 'technological progress' that 'can enable a better implementation of IHL and reduce humanitarian concerns' (Germany and France 2018). Arguably, the latter example offers somewhat more specificity by narrowing its focus to those uses of autonomy that prove capable of tackling potential *humanitarian* challenges. That said, which 'means' of technological progress may help to achieve that purpose remains unclear.

Other GGE participants have occasionally identified specific technological systems in support of their arguments and also focused more explicitly on potential humanitarian benefits. For instance, some refer to 'self-learning systems' that could 'improve . . . the full implementation of international humanitarian law, including the principles of distinction and proportionality' (Germany 2018) or 'highly automated technology' that 'can ensure the increased accuracy of weapon guidance on military targets' (Russia 2019, para. 2; see also Russia 2018, para. 9). Others chime in by suggesting that 'autonomous technologies in operating weapons systems' (Japan 2019), 'autonomous weapon systems under meaningful human control' (Netherlands 2018), or just 'LAWS' (without any further definition) (Israel 2018; Canada 2019) hold a promise to reduce risks to friendly units or the civilian population and decrease collateral damage. Some other States have recognized the humanitarian benefits offered by certain existing military systems at least implicitly. For example, certain point-defense weapons systems designed to autonomously intercept incoming threats are broadly regarded as compliant with international humanitarian law (Greece 2018). All these positions presume that autonomy can improve the accuracy of weapon systems, thus providing an opportunity to apply force in a more discriminating manner.

Some States have sought to emphasize that it is not autonomy in isolation that gives rise to benefits. The United Kingdom, for example, has rather extensively argued that it is the human-machine teaming that is likely to secure greater humanitarian advantages (United Kingdom 2018). Given than neither humans nor technology are infallible on their own, the degree of superiority, or conversely, inferiority of machines in a military setting is likely to stay context dependent. In some tasks, such as the assimilation and processing of increasingly large amounts of data, the technology is by far exceeding the similar abilities of humans. Nonetheless, at the minimum in the short to medium term, machines are unlikely to acquire abilities in reaching the same level of situational awareness as humans do or apply the experience and judgment to a new situation as humans can. It is therefore the effective teaming of human and machine––where machine and human capabilities complement one another—that promises to improve "capability, accuracy, diligence and speed of decision, whilst maintaining and potentially enhancing confidence in adherence to IHL" (United Kingdom 2019a), "particularly limiting the unintended consequences of conflict to non-combatants" (United Kingdom 2019c). Some other stakeholders have joined in support, pointing out that "effective human-machine teaming may allow for the optimal utilization of technological benefits" (Netherlands 2019) and "higher precision of weapons systems" (IPRAW 2019).

The most detailed contribution to the discussion has been, however, made by the United States. Drawing on existing State practice, its working paper, "Humanitarian Benefits of Emerging Technologies in the Area of Lethal Autonomous Weapon Systems" (United States 2018), discusses a range of warfare applications of autonomy that further humanitarian outcomes, urging the GGE to consider associated humanitarian benefits carefully. Some of the examples provided in the paper are 'weapons specific' and refer to *certain types of weapons* having *certain types of autonomous functionalities*. For instance, mines, bombs employing explosive submunitions (CMs), and anti-aircraft guns equipped with autonomous self-destruct, self-deactivation, or self-neutralization mechanisms are argued to reduce the risk of weapons causing unintended harm to civilians or civilian objects (United States 2018, para. 8). In the US view, these mechanisms could be applied to a broad range of other weapons to achieve the same humanitarian objectives. Another type of autonomous functionalities relied upon in support of the argument are automated target identification, tracking, selection, and engagement functions designed to allow weapons to strike military objectives more accurately and with a lesser risk of collateral damage (United States 2018, para. 26). Munitions with guidance systems, such as AIM-120 Advanced Medium-Range, Air-to-Air Missile (AMRAAM), GBU-53/B Small Diameter Bomb Increment II (SDB II) under development or the DAGR missile equally under development are the case in point.

Morever, the United States has also expanded on *'weapons-neutral' or 'indifferent' applications of autonomy*, which may fulfill a variety of functions in support of military decision-making on the battlefield. For instance, systems designed to improve the *efficiency and accuracy of intelligence processes* by, for example, automating the handling and analysis of data, help to increase commanders' awareness of the presence of civilians or civilians objects, including objects under special protection such as cultural property and hospitals (United States 2018, paras. 14–20). Besides, systems operating on AI offer valuable *tools for estimating potential collateral damage* and thus also help commanders identify and take additional precautions "by selecting weapons, aim points, and attack angles that reduce the risk of harm to civilians and civilian objects, while offering the same or superior military advantage in neutralizing or destroying a military objective." (United States 2018, para. 25). Furthermore, the use of robotic and autonomous systems is argued to *enable a greater standoff distance* from enemy formations, diminishing thereby the need for immediate fire in self-defense and reducing, as a result, the risk of civilian casualties (United States 2018, para. 35). Last but not least, autonomous technologies capable of automatically identifying *the direction and location of incoming fire* can reduce the risk of misidentifying the location of the enemy (United States 2018, para. 36).

To summarize, AWS or technologies associated with them, arguably offer distinct humanitarian advantages on the battlefield and could further be used to create entirely new capabilities that would increase the capacity of States to lessen the risk of civilian casualties in applying force. It is therefore rather striking that in contrast to an explicit agreement of States about potential risks of autonomy, these benefits barely find their way into the concluding GGE reports. The closest that the most recent report gets to this issue is to observe that "[c]onsideration should be given to the use of emerging technologies in the area of lethal autonomous weapons systems in upholding compliance with IHL and other applicable international legal obligations" (GGE 2019, Annex IV (h)).

7.6: CONCLUDING REMARKS

The ongoing debate about the regulation of AWS remains problematic for a number of reasons. For one, despite the regular claims that, as a forum, CCW suitably combines diplomatic, legal, and military expertise (see, e.g., European Union 2019), the discussions are sometimes unreal and even surreal from a military perspective. In particular, some advocates for regulation seem to assume that military commanders would deploy uncontrollable weapon systems if not prevented from doing so by international law. This unfounded presumption, which ignores the way in which most armed forces apply force, must be abandoned.

Furthermore, the argument that AWS are incapable of distinguishing between combatants and noncombatants and limiting collateral damage remains oddly persistent. No existing weapon system can do that either, but this does not make these weapon systems unlawful. A weapon must be capable of being used consistently with IHL. Whether this is the case depends on the features of the specific system in question, the manner in which it is used, and the operational context. Building fundamental objections on contingent factors is not only counterintuitive; it runs counter to common sense.

The issue that we have sought to highlight in this chapter is slightly different but, to our mind, no less important. The discussion around AWS is to a significant extent driven by States and civil society organizations that insist on focusing exclusively on the risks posed by AWS. We do not seek to argue that such risks should be disregarded. Quite the opposite: a thorough identification and careful assessment of risks remains crucial to the process. However, rejecting the notion that there might also be humanitarian benefits to the use of AWS, or refusing to discuss them, is highly problematic. Reasonable regulation cannot be devised by focusing on risks or benefits alone; rather, both need to be considered and some form of balancing must take place. Indeed, humanitarian benefits might sometimes be so significant as to not only make the use of an AWS permissible, but legally or ethically obligatory (cf. Lucas 2013; Schmitt 2015).

Whether the net humanitarian and military benefits offered by AWS are outweighed by the particular risks such systems pose, can only be meaningfully analyzed in a specific system-task context. Therefore, a constructive dialog should not be conducted in the abstract, that is by reference to the potential benefits of AI or technological progress generally. Rather, teasing out the humanitarian benefits of autonomous systems that have been in operation with States militaries for some substantial amount of time and building clarity as to how risks associated with the deployment of these systems have been overcome or are countered in an operational context, could serve as a first step to a more rational assessment of the humanitarian potential as well as trade-offs of systems currently under development and those that may be developed in the future.

DISCLAIMER

The views and opinions expressed in this article are those of the authors and do not necessarily reflect the official policy or position of any institution or government agency.

ACKNOWLEDGMENTS

The authors wish to thank Professor Robert McLaughlin, Dr. Simon McKenzie, and Dr. Marcus Hellyer for insightful comments on earlier drafts of this chapter.

FUNDING

Support for this chapter has been provided by the Trusted Autonomous Systems Defence Cooperative Research Centre. This material is also based upon work supported by the United States Air Force Office of Scientific Research under award number FA9550-18-1-0181.

Any opinions, findings, and conclusions or recommendations expressed in this chapter are those of the authors and do not necessarily reflect the views of the Australian Government or the United States Air Force.

NOTE

1. The UK approach has evolved, however. It now "believes that a technology-agnostic approach which focusses on the importance of human control and the regulatory framework used to guarantee compliance with legal obligations is most productive when characterising LAWS" (United Kingdom 2019b).

WORKS CITED

Additional Protocol I (AP I). *Protocol Additional to the Geneva Conventions of August 12, 1949, and relating to the Protection of Victims of International Armed Conflicts*, 1125 UNTS 3, opened for signature June 8, 1977, entered into force 7 December 1978.

Australia. 2019. "Australia's System of Control and Applications for Autonomous Weapon Systems." Working Paper. Geneva: Meeting of Group of Governmental Experts on LAWS. March 26. CCW/GGE.1/2019/WP.2/Rev.1.

Austria. 2018. "Statement under Agenda Item 'General Exchange of Views.'" Geneva: Meeting of Group of Governmental Experts on LAWS. April 9–13. www.unog.ch/80256EDD006B8954/(httpAssets)/AA0367088499C566C1258278004D54CD/$file/2018_LAWSGeneralExchang_Austria.pdf.

Austria. 2019. "Statement on Agenda Item 5(c)." Geneva: Meeting of Group of Governmental Experts on LAWS. March 25–29. www.unog.ch/80256EDD006B8954/(httpAssets)/A5215A3883D6EE68C12583CB003CCFB2/$file/GGE+LAWS+25032019+AT+Statement+military+applications+agenda+item+5c.pdf.

Boulanin, Vincent and Maaike Verbruggen. 2017. *Mapping the Developments in Autonomy*. Stockholm: Stockholm International Peace Research Institute (SIPRI).

Brazil. 2019. "Statement on the Agenda Item 6a." Geneva: Meeting of Group of Governmental Experts on LAWS. April 9–13. www.unog.ch/80256EDD006B8954/(httpAssets)/6B8B60EEC6D8F40AC12582720057731E/$file/2018_LAWS6a_Brazil1.pdf.

Bunn, George. 1970. "The Banning of Poison Gas and Germ Warfare: The U.N. Rôle." *American Journal of International Law* 64 (4): pp. 194–199. doi: 10.1017/S0002930000246095.

Campaign to Stop Killer Robots. n.d. "The Threat of Fully Autonomous Weapons." Campaign to Stop Killer Robots. Accessed January 22, 2020. www.stopkillerrobots.org/learn/.

Canada. 2019. "Statement." Fourth Session, Geneva: Meeting of Group of Governmental Experts on LAWS. August 20. www.conf.unog.ch/digitalrecordings/index.html?guid=public/C998D28F-ADCE-46DA-9303-FE47104B848E&position=40#.

Chemical Weapons Convention. *Convention on the Prohibition of the Development, Production, Stockpiling and Use of Chemical Weapons and on Their Destruction*, 1974 UNTS 45, opened for signature January 13, 1993, entered into force April 29, 1997.

China. 2018. "Position Paper." Working Paper. Geneva: Meeting of Group of Governmental Experts on LAWS. April 11. CCW/GGE.1/2018/WP.7.

Conference on the Limitation of Armament. 1922. "Conference on the Limitation of Armament." Washington, DC: Government Printing Office. November 12, 1921–February 6, 1922.

Congressional Research Service. 2019. *Cluster Munitions: Background and Issues for Congress*. February 22. RS22907. fas.org/sgp/crs/weapons/RS22907.pdf.

Convention on Cluster Munitions. 2688 UNTS 39, May 30, 2008, entered into force August 1, 2010.

Ekelhof, Merel A.C. 2017. "Complications of a Common Language: Why It Is So Hard to Talk about Autonomous Weapons." *Journal of Conflict and Security Law* 22 (2): pp. 311–331.

Estonia and Finland. 2018. "Categorizing Lethal Autonomous Weapons Systems: A Technical and Legal Perspective to Understanding LAWS." Geneva: Meeting of Group of Governmental Experts on LAWS. August 24. CCW/GGE.2/2018/WP.2.

European Union. 2019. "Statement: Humanitarian and International Security Challenges Posed by Emerging Technologies." Geneva: Meeting of Group of Governmental Experts on LAWS. March 27. eeas.europa.eu/headquarters/headquarters-homepage/60266/group-governmental-experts-lethal-autonomous-weapons-systems-convention-certain-conventional_en.

Future of Life Institute. 2018. "Statement under Agenda Item 6d." Geneva: Meeting of Group of Governmental Experts on LAWS. August 27–31. www.unog.ch/80256EDD006B8954/(httpAssets)/CE8D5A5AD96AD807C12582FE003A5196/$file/2018_GGE+LAWS+2_Future+Life+Institue.pdf.

Geneva Gas Protocol. *Protocol for the Prohibition of the Use in War of Asphyxiating, Poisonous or Other Gases, and of Bacteriological Methods of Warfare*, 94 LNTS 65, opened for signature June 17, 1925, entered into force February 8, 1928.

Germany and France. 2018. "Statement under Agenda Item 'General Exchange of Views.'" Geneva: Meeting of Group of Governmental Experts on LAWS. April 9–13. www.unog.ch/80256EDD006B8954/(httpAssets)/895931D082ECE219C12582720056F12F/$file/2018_LAWSGeneralExchange_Germany-France.pdf.

Germany. 2018. "Statement on Working Definition of LAWS." Geneva: Meeting of Group of Governmental Experts on LAWS. April 9–13. www.unog.ch/80256EDD006B8954/(httpAssets)/2440CD1922B86091C12582720057898F/$file/2018_LAWS6a_Germany.pdf.

GGE. 2017. *Report of the 2017 Session of the Group of Governmental Experts on Lethal Autonomous Weapons Systems (LAWS)*. Geneva: United Nations Office at Geneva. 20 November. CCW/GGE.1/2017/CRP.1.

GGE. 2018. *Report of the 2018 Session of the Group of Governmental Experts on Emerging Technologies in the Area of Lethal Autonomous Weapons Systems*. Geneva: United Nations Office at Geneva. 23 October. CCW/GGE.1/2018/3.

GGE. 2019. *Draft Report of the 2019 Session of the Group of Governmental Experts on Emerging Technologies in the Area of Lethal Autonomous Weapons Systems*. Geneva: United Nations Office at Geneva. August 21. CCW/GGE.1/2019/CRP.1/Rev.2.

Gilchrist, Harry L. 1928. *A Comparative Study of World War Casualties from Gas and Other Weapons*. Washington, DC: Government Printing Office.

Greece. 2018. "Statement under Agenda item 'General Debate.'" Geneva: Meeting of Group of Governmental Experts on LAWS. April 9–13. www.unog.ch/80256EDD006B8954/(httpAssets)/3B8A2778AB92E456C12582720056F151/$file/2018_LAWSGeneralExchange_Greece.pdf.

Hague Declaration II. 2004. "Declaration (IV, 2) Concerning Asphyxiating Gases, July 29, 1899." In *The Laws of Armed Conflicts: A Collection of Conventions, Resolutions and Other Documents*, edited by Dietrich Schindler and Jiří Toman, pp. 95–97. Leiden: Martinus Nijhoff Publishers.

Handicap International. 2006. "Fatal Footprint: The Global Human Impact of Cluster Munitions." *Preliminary Report*. Lyon, France: Handicap International. www.regjeringen.no/globalassets/upload/kilde/ud/rap/2006/0155/ddd/pdfv/295996-footprint.pdf.

Holy See. 2018. "Statement." Geneva: Meeting of Group of Governmental Experts on LAWS. April 9. www.unog.ch/80256EDD006B8954/(httpAssets)/627EC5A0CDE2135EC1258272005789B8/$file/2018_LAWS6a_HolySee.pdf.

Human Rights Watch. 2018. "Statement under Agenda Item 6d." Geneva: Meeting of Group of Governmental Experts on LAWS. August 29. www.unog.ch/80256EDD006B8954/(httpAssets)/D710BB982A5BEC8FC12582FE002F61D7/$file/2018_GGE+LAWS+2_Human+Rights+Watch+.pdf.

ICRC. 2019. "Statement under Agenda Item 5a." Geneva: Meeting of Group of Governmental Experts on LAWS. March 25-29. www.unog.ch/80256EDD006B8954/(httpAssets)/5C76B1301CEC4BE6C12583CC002F6A15/$file/CCW+GGE+LAWS+ICRC+statement+agenda+item+5a+26+03+2019.pdf.

ICRC. 2016. "Meeting of Experts on LAWS." Working Paper. Geneva: ICRC. April 11. www.unog.ch/80256EDD006B8954/(httpAssets)/B3834B2C62344053C1257F9400491826/$file/2016_LAWS+MX_CountryPaper_ICRC.pdf.

IPRAW. 2019. "Statement on the Agenda Item 5c." Geneva: Meeting of Group of Governmental Experts on LAWS. March 29. www.unog.ch/80256EDD006B8954/(httpAssets)/7C817367F189770CC12583CC003FA4C6/$file/IPRAW_Statement_HumanControl.pdf.

Israel. 2018. "Statement on the Agenda Item 6d." Geneva: Meeting of Group of Governmental Experts on LAWS. August 29. www.unog.ch/80256EDD006B8954/

(httpAssets)/7A0E18215E16382DC125830400334DF6/$file/2018_GGE+LAWS+2_6d_Israel.pdf.

Italy. 2018. "Statement on the Agenda Item 6a." Geneva: Meeting of Group of Governmental Experts on LAWS. April 9–13. www.unog.ch/80256EDD006B8954/(httpAssets)/36335330158B5746C1258273003903F0/$file/2018_LAWS6a_Italy.pdf.

Japan. 2019. "Possible Outcome of 2019 Group of Governmental Experts and Future Actions of International Community on Lethal Autonomous Weapons Systems." Working Paper. Geneva: Meeting of Group of Governmental Experts on LAWS. 22 March. CCW/GGE.1/2019/WP.3.

Jenks, Chris and Rain Liivoja. 2018. "Machine Autonomy and Constant Care Obligation." *Humanitarian Law & Policy*. 11 December. blogs.icrc.org/law-and-policy/2018/12/11/machine-autonomy-constant-care-obligation/.

Lewis, Dustin A., Gabriella Blum, and Naz K. Modirzadeh. 2016. *War-Algorithm Accountability*. Research Briefing. Cambridge, MA: Harvard Law School Program on International Law and Armed Conflict.

Liivoja, Rain. 2012. "Chivalry without a Horse: Military Honour and the Modern Law of Armed Conflict." In *The Law of Armed Conflict: Historical and Contemporary Perspectives*, edited by Rain Liivoja and Andres Saumets, pp. 75–100. Tartu, Estonia: Tartu University Press.

Lucas, George R. 2013. "Engineering, Ethics, and Industry: The Moral Challenges of Lethal Autonomy." In *Killing by Remote Control: The Ethics of an Unmanned Military*, edited by Bradley Jay Strawser, pp. 211–228. Oxford: Oxford University Press.

Mathews, Robert J. 2016. "Chemical and Biological Weapons." In *Routledge Handbook of the Law of Armed Conflict*, edited by Rain Liivoja and Tim McCormack, pp. 212–232. Abingdon: Routledge.

McCamley, Nick J. 2006. *The Secret History of Chemical Warfare*. Barnsley, UK: Pen & Sword.

Netherlands. 2018. "Statement under Agenda Item 6b: Human Machine Interaction." Geneva: Meeting of Group of Governmental Experts on LAWS. April 9–13. www.unog.ch/80256EDD006B8954/(httpAssets)/48F6FC9F22460FBCC12582720057E72F/$file/2018_LAWS6b_Netherlands.pdf.

Netherlands. 2019. "Statement on Agenda Item 5b." Geneva: Meeting of Group of Governmental Experts on LAWS. April 26. www.unog.ch/80256EDD006B8954/(httpAssets)/164DD121FDC25A0BC12583CB003A99C2/$file/5b+NL+Statement+Human+Element-final.pdf.

Pakistan. 2018. "Statement on Agenda Item 6a." Geneva: Meeting of Group of Governmental Experts on LAWS. August 27. www.unog.ch/80256EDD006B8954/(httpAssets)/F76B74E9D3B22E98C12582F80059906F/$file/2018_GGE+LAWS+2_6a_Pakistan.pdf.

Peru. 2007. "The Way Forward." In *Oslo Conference on Cluster Munitions*. Oslo: United Nations. February 22–23. www.clusterconvention.org/files/2012/12/ClusterPeru.pdf.

Prentiss, Augustin Mitchell. 1937. *Chemicals in War: A Treatise on Chemical Warfare*. London: McGraw-Hill.

Robinson, Julian Perry. 1998. "The Negotiations on the Chemical Weapons Convention: A Historical Overview." In *The New Chemical Weapons Convention: Implementation and Prospects*, edited by Michael Bothe, Natalino Ronzitti, and Allan Rosas, pp. 17–36. The Hague: Kluwer.

Russia. 2018. "Russia's Approaches to the Elaboration of a Working Definition and Basic Functions of Lethal Autonomous Weapons Systems in the Context of the Purposes and Objectives of the Convention." Working Paper. Geneva: Meeting of Group of Governmental Experts on LAWS. April 4. CCW/GGE.1/2018/WP.6.

Russia. 2019. "Potential Opportunities and Limitations of Military Uses of Lethal Autonomous Weapons Systems." *Working Paper.* Geneva: Meeting of Group of Governmental Experts on LAWS. March 15. CCW/GGE.1/2019/WP.1.

Schmitt, Michael. 2015. "Regulating Autonomous Weapons Might Be Smarter Than Banning Them." *Just Security.* August 10. https://www.justsecurity.org/25333/regulating-autonomous-weapons-smarter-banning/.

Scott, James Brown. 1920. *The Proceedings of The Hague Peace Conferences.* New York: Oxford University Press.

Slovenia. 2019. "Statement." Geneva: Meeting of Group of Governmental Experts on LAWS. August 20–21. www.unog.ch/80256EDD006B8954/(httpAssets)/E0D43536AB8BAFCFC12582F80059A03C/$file/2018_GGE+LAWS+2_6a_Slovenia.pdf.

Sri Lanka. 2018. "Statement under Agenda Item 'General Exchange of Views.'" Geneva: Meeting of Group of Governmental Experts on LAWS. April 9–13. www.unog.ch/80256EDD006B8954/(httpAssets)/B863C8597C0B6E78C125827200572F03/$file/2018_LAWSGeneralExchange_Sri+Lanka.pdf.

Surber, Regina. 2019. *Artificial Intelligence: Autonomous Technology (AT), Lethal Autonomous Weapons Systems (LAWS) and Peace Time Threats.* Zurich: ICT for Peace Foundation, Zurich Hub for Ethics and Technology. ict4peace.org/wp-content/uploads/2018/02/2018_RSurber_AI-AT-LAWS-Peace-Time-Threats_final.pdf.

Tengroth, Björn and Bengt Anderberg. 1991. "Blinding Laser Weapons." *Lasers & Light in Ophthalmology* 4 (1): pp. 35–39.

UK Ministry of Defence. 2011. *Joint Doctrine Note 2/11 The UK Approach to Unmanned Aircraft Systems.* Shrivenham, UK: Development, Concepts and Doctrine Centre.

UN Office at Geneva. n.d. "Background on Lethal Autonomous Weapons Systems in the CCW." www.unog.ch/80256EE600585943/(httpPages)/8FA3C2562A60FF81C1257CE600393DF6.

UN Secretary-General. 1969. "Chemical and Bacteriological (Biological) Weapons and the Effects of Their Possible Use." United Nations Document. A/7575/Rev.l, S/9292/Rcv.l.

United Kingdom. 2018. "Statement on the Agenda Item 6a." Geneva: Meeting of Group of Governmental Experts on LAWS. April 10. www.unog.ch/80256EDD006B8954/(httpAssets)/DAFE6116DB9425CAC125827A003492FD/$file/2018_LAWS6a_UK.pdf.

United Kingdom. 2019a. "Statement on the Agenda Item 5a." Geneva: Meeting of Group of Governmental Experts on LAWS. March 25–29. www.unog.ch/80256EDD006B8954/(httpAssets)/1ED3972D40AE53B5C12583D3003F8E5E/$file/20190318-5(a)_IHL_Statement.pdf.

United Kingdom. 2019b. "Statement on the Agenda Item 5b." Geneva: Meeting of Group of Governmental Experts on LAWS. March 25–29. www.unog.ch/80256EDD006B8954/(httpAssets)/A969D779E1E5E28BC12583D3003FC0D9/$file/20190318-5(b)_Characterisation_Statement.pdf.

United Kingdom. 2019c. "Statement on the Agenda Item 5c." Geneva: Meeting of Group of Governmental Experts on LAWS. March 25–29. www.unog.ch/

80256EDD006B8954/(httpAssets)/8B03D74F5E2F1521C12583D3003F0110/$file/20190318-5(c)_Mil_Statement.pdf.

United States. 1966. "Statement." 21st Session, United Nations General Assembly. 5 December. New York: United Nations. UN Document: A/P.V. 1484.

United States. 2006. "Opening Statement." In *Third Review Conference of the Convention on Certain Conventional Weapons*. Geneva: United Nations Office at Geneva. 7 November. www.unog.ch/80256EDD006B8954/(httpAssets)/AC4F9F4B10B117B4C125722000478F7F/$file/14+USA.pdf.

United States. 2018. "Humanitarian Benefits of Emerging Technologies in the Area of Lethal Autonomous Weapon Systems." Working Paper. Geneva: Meeting of Group of Governmental Experts on LAWS. April 3. CCW/GGE.1/2018/WP.4.

US Army. 2017. *Robotics and Autonomous Systems Strategy*. March. <www.tradoc.army.mil/Portals/14/Documents/RAS_Strategy.pdf>.

US Department of Defense. 2011. *DoD Directive 3000.09: Autonomy in Weapon Systems*. Fort Eustis, VA: Army Capabilities Integration Center, U.S. Army Training and Doctrine Command. fas.org/irp/doddir/dod/d3000_09.pdf.

WILPF. 2019. *A WILPF Guide to Killer Robots*. www.reachingcriticalwill.org/images/documents/Publications/wilpf-guide-aws.pdf.

Zawieska, Karolina. 2015. "Do Robots Equal Humans? Anthropomorphic Terminology in LAWS." Geneva: Meeting of Group of Governmental Experts on LAWS. www.unog.ch/80256EDD006B8954/(httpAssets)/369A75B470A5A368C1257E290041E20B/$file/23+Karolina+Zawieska+SS.pdf.

8

Toward a Positive Statement of Ethical Principles for Military AI

JAI GALLIOTT

8.1: INTRODUCTION

Early in 2018, Google came under intense internal and public pressure to divest itself of a contract with the United States Department of Defense for an artificial intelligence (AI) program called Project Maven, aimed at using Google's powerful AI and voluminous civilian-sourced dataset to process video captured by drones for use in identifying potential targets for future monitoring and engagement. Project Maven generated significant controversy among Google's staff, with its chief executive releasing a public set of 'guiding principles' to quell discontent internally and act as a filter for the company when considering the company's future involvement in AI development and military research (Pichai 2018). These principles, along with the flurry of alternative principle sets followed by other technology giants and technology governors, reveal a general lack of moral clarity and prevailing ethical principles surrounding the appropriate, justified development and use of AI. They further point to a lacuna in the field of 'AI ethics,' the emerging field applied ethics, which is principally concerned with developing normative frameworks and guidelines to encourage the ethical use of AI in the appropriate contexts of society. An incredibly powerful tool that can lead to great human flourishing and safety, AI can also descend into a dangerous realm that stands to threaten basic human rights if used without an appropriate ethic or set of governing ethical principles.

It is therefore interesting that there has been little formal movement beyond the United States to develop AI principles explicitly for the armed forces, especially

Jai Galliott, *Toward a Positive Statement of Ethical Principles for Military AI* In: *Lethal Autonomous Weapons*. Edited by: Jai Galliott, Duncan MacIntosh and Jens David Ohlin, © Oxford University Press (2021).
DOI: 10.1093/oso/9780197546048.003.0009

given the military nature of Project Maven. This is true despite science-fiction films being called upon to illuminate our imaginations and stoke fears about sentient killer robots enslaving or eradicating humanity, namely by those who seek to have these weapons banned with the creation of new international treaty under Additional Protocol 1 of the Geneva Conventions. Consider signatories to the open letter to the United Nations Convention on Certain Conventional Weapons, who have said that, once developed, killer robots will pervade armed conflict to such an extent that it will be more frequent and conducted at a pace that will be difficult or impossible for humans to completely comprehend. Such claims mistakenly suggest that there is no role for AI principles in the military domain, and this is perhaps why no military force in the world has yet adopted ethics principles for AI.

It may also be tempting to think that the impact of AI in the military sphere is a far-off phenomenon that will not overtly impact lives for years to come. And while there may be a semblance of truth in this statement owing to the complexity of applying algorithms to complex battlespaces with a higher degree of certainty and with lower latency than is acceptable in parts of the civilian realm and the secure conduct of military development, the military industrial complex has already developed elementary systems and is today building the systems that will operate in the coming decades. While it is, therefore, encouraging that the United States Department of Defense's Innovation Board has sought a set of ethical principles for the use of AI in war (Tucker 2019), it is concerning that technology has outpaced efforts to govern it. To this end, this brief chapter seeks to review the AI principles developed in the civilian realm and then propose a set of Ethical AI principles designed specifically for armed forces seeking to deploy AI across relevant military domains. It will then consider their limitations and how said principles may, if nothing else, guide the development of a 'minimally-just AI' (MinAI) (Galliott and Scholz 2019) that could be embedded in weapons to avoid the most obvious and blatant ethical violations in wartime.[1]

8.2: TECHNOLOGICAL SOCIETY'S LOVE AFFAIR WITH ETHICS PRINCIPLES

Once it was publicly revealed that Google was cooperating with the Pentagon on Project Maven, Google's work on AI was to be made socially responsible by adhering to ethical principles to include a commitment to "be socially beneficial" and to "avoid creating or reinforcing unfair bias." Others dictate that their wares "be built and tested for safety," "incorporate privacy design principles," "uphold high standards of scientific excellence," and "be accountable to people" (Pichai 2018). Interestingly, Google's principle set also includes a section titled, 'AI applications we will not pursue,' which includes a direct reference to "weapons and other technologies whose principal purpose or implementation is to cause or directly facilitate injury to people" (Pichai 2018), signaling the company's decision to not divest itself of military contracts. But it is far from clear who would ultimately maintain responsibility for the implementation of the principles, as its ethics board, which existed barely more than one week, has been disbanded owing to public discord over the membership of said board, which included an individual from a conservative think tank and a technology company executive with business interests in the military sphere, which reopened old divisions within the company, with no replacement board or mechanism having since been named (Piper 2019).

Google is just one example of a company resorting to ethics principles in the face of technological challenges. Despite the dissolution of its AI ethics board, a diverse range of stakeholders have increasingly been defining principles to guide the development of AI applications and associated end-user solutions. Indeed, a wave of ethics principles has swept Silicon Valley since, as those holding interests in AI come to understand the potentially controversial nature and impact of autonomous agents and the necessity of curbing unintended dual or other uses that may impact their interests. AI ethics has, therefore, come to be of interest across a number of civil sectors and types of institutions, ranging from other small- and large-scale developers of technology aiming to generate their own ethical principles, professional bodies whose codes of ethics are aimed at influencing technical practitioners through to standards-setting and monitoring bodies such as research institutes, government agencies, and individual researchers across disciplines whose work aims add technical or conceptual depth to AI.

AI principles from Microsoft revolve around designing AI to be 'trustworthy,' which, according to their principle set, 'requires creating solutions that reflect ethical principles that are deeply rooted in important and timeless values.' The individual principles, which will likely be applied to conversational AI (chatbots) or be referred to in the development of solutions aimed at assisting people in resolving customer services queries, managing their calendars, or internet browsing, include (Microsoft 2019):

- Fairness: AI systems should treat all people fairly
- Inclusiveness: AI systems should empower everyone and engage people
- Reliability & Safety: AI systems should perform reliably and safely
- Transparency: AI systems should be understandable
- Privacy & Security: AI systems should be secure and respect privacy
- Accountability: AI systems should have algorithmic accountability

Meanwhile, the multi-billion-dollar cloud-based software company, Salesforce, has also recognized that AI holds great promise, but only if it builds it and uses it in a way that's beneficial for all their stakeholders, not just those who pay for their customer relationship management software. The company's senior vice president of Technology & Products has stated she believes there are five main principles that can help achieve beneficial AI (Porro 2018):

- Being of benefit
- Human value alignment
- Open debate between science and policy
- Cooperation, trust, and transparency in systems and among the AI community
- Safety and Responsibility

The Future of Life Institute's Asilomar AI principles, developed in conjunction with an international conference on the same, and agreed to by several thousand international experts, recognize that AI is embedded in beneficial tools knowingly or unknowingly used on a daily basis by millions of people across the globe, but that its continued development and the empowerment of people in the decades and centuries ahead ought to be guided by their successful implementation (Future of Life Institute 2018):

- Safety: AI systems should be safe and secure throughout their operational lifetime, and verifiably so where applicable and feasible.
- Failure Transparency: If an AI system causes harm, it should be possible to ascertain why.
- Judicial Transparency: Any involvement by an autonomous system in judicial decision-making should provide a satisfactory explanation auditable by a competent human authority.
- Responsibility: Designers and builders of advanced AI systems are stakeholders in the moral implications of their use, misuse, and actions, with a responsibility and opportunity to shape those implications.
- Value Alignment: Highly autonomous AI systems should be designed so that their goals and behaviors can be assured to align with human values throughout their operation.
- Human Values: AI systems should be designed and operated so as to be compatible with ideals of human dignity, rights, freedoms, and cultural diversity.
- Personal Privacy: People should have the right to access, manage, and control the data they generate, given AI systems' power to analyze and utilize that data.
- Liberty and Privacy: The application of AI to personal data must not unreasonably curtail people's real or perceived liberty.
- Shared Benefit: AI technologies should benefit and empower as many people as possible.
- Shared Prosperity: The economic prosperity created by AI should be shared broadly, to benefit all of humanity.
- Human Control: Humans should choose how and whether to delegate decisions to AI systems to accomplish human-chosen objectives.
- Non-subversion: The power conferred by control of highly advanced AI systems should respect and improve, rather than subvert, the social and civic processes on which the health of society depends.
- AI Arms Race: An arms race in lethal autonomous weapons should be avoided.

As detailed in the history provided by Whittlestone et al. (2019), at around the same time as the Future of Life Institute released its principles, the United States Association for Computing Machinery (ACM) communicated a more discrete set of seven principles focused on algorithmic opacity and its connection to responsibility attribution (ACM US Public Policy Council 2017). In 2017 alone, a number of other stakeholder groups and organizations published additional principle sets: including the Japanese Society for AI's Ethical Guidelines in February (Japanese Society for Artificial Intelligence 2017); a set of draft principles and recommendations from the Université de Montréal entitled the Montréal Declaration on Responsible AI (University of Montréal 2017); and the Institute of Electrical and Electronics Engineers' General Principles of Ethical Autonomous and Intelligent Systems (IEEE Standards Association 2019). This proliferation of principles has continued into the following years with the Partnership on AI producing a set of 'tenets' that its members agree to uphold (Partnership on AI 2018), the UK House of Lords suggesting five principles for a cross-sector but non-military AI code that could be adopted internationally and was based on the expert evidence of some 200 experts (Select Committee on Artificial Intelligence 2018), and the European Commission, also building on the work of a group of independent experts, launching seven principles it labeled 'seven essentials for achieving trustworthy AI (European Commission 2019):

- Human agency and oversight: AI systems should enable equitable societies by supporting human agency and fundamental rights, and not decrease, limit or misguide human autonomy.
- Robustness and safety: Trustworthy AI requires algorithms to be secure, reliable, and robust enough to deal with errors or inconsistencies during all life cycle phases of AI systems.
- Privacy and data governance: Citizens should have full control over their own data, while data concerning them will not be used to harm or discriminate against them.
- Transparency: The traceability of AI systems should be ensured.
- Diversity, non-discrimination and fairness: AI systems should consider the whole range of human abilities, skills and requirements, and ensure accessibility.
- Societal and environmental well-being: AI systems should be used to enhance positive social change and enhance sustainability and ecological responsibility.
- Accountability: Mechanisms should be put in place to ensure responsibility and accountability for AI systems and their outcomes.

As the civil sphere has led the way in the formal development of principles, consideration must be given to their content in defining principles for deployment in the military sphere. This is primarily because there is likely to be a degree of overlap where tactical/lethal applications and secrecy make no special demands. Even though the field of AI ethics is in its infancy, some degree of agreement on the core issues and values on which the field should be focused is evident simply from the abovementioned principle sets. This is most apparent, perhaps, at the meta-level, in terms of value alignment and the idea that the power conferred by control of highly advanced AI systems should respect or improve the social and democratic processes on which the health of society depends rather than subvert them. This also holds true in the armed forces, particularly concerning the review of lethal action. From this principle stems others concerned with notions of acceptance, control, transparency, fairness, safety, etc. It is these commonly accepted principles that I seek to ensconce in the military AI ethics principles, explored below.

More critically, the principles they all have in common is that they are unobjectionable to any reasonable person. Indeed, they are positive principles that are valuable and important to the development and responsible deployment of AI. In some respects, one might conclude from a high-level examination of these principles that they are really a subset of general ethical principles and values that should always be applied across all technology development and applications efforts, not just those related to AI. The obverse concern is that in being broadly framed and highly subjective in their interpretation, there is a need to focus attention on precisely who will be making those interpretations in any given instance in which the principles could apply. Such problematically broad appeal is avoided in the development of my principles.

8.3: CONFRONTING THE POWER TO KILL WITH ETHICAL AI

Amid growing fears of biased and weaponized AI (Pandya 2019), armed forces urgently need specific ethical guidance on how they ought to develop and approach the acquisition of artificially intelligent weapons technologies. Technology need not be implemented in the way Hollywood has envisioned it, but it is imperative that military actors adopt Ethical AI principles, preferably a set of common principles for deployment across all Five Eyes nations and other allied armed forces with the capability to develop the technology. In this section, I put forward a principle set that carries over the best of the above-detailed civilian principle sets, while inserting others more explicitly military in nature and focused on honing questions of accountability and responsibility in the design and development process.

Ethical AI in armed forces should embody the following characteristics.

8.3.1: Be Socially Accepted

Military Ethical AI principles must be developed and regularly reviewed for impact by a panel of independent ethics experts; accurately reflect the prevailing cultural, social, and legal norms of the relevant society; and respect the rules-based system of international order. The latter is particularly important because the barriers for entry to AI weapons are low, unlike, say nuclear weapons, which cannot proliferate without rare earth minerals and highly specialized experts. This social acceptance principle also grounds AI deployment in the social contract that governs a military's social responsibilities (Galliott 2015, 37–64). It also calls for research on the attitudes of military personnel and the public toward the use of AI for military ends.

8.3.2: Be Interoperable and Mutually Recognizable

Ethical principles underlying militarized AI systems and operations should align with those of its trusted allies so that interoperability can take place, and nations can reap the benefits associated with a shared commitment to the sense of Judeo-Christian ethics that underpin the Law of Armed Conflict (Galliott 2015, 65–94). The Five Eyes group may then think about applying the mutual recognition principle when it comes to using AI-based systems and practicing operations and tactics through exercises such as Autonomous Warrior.

8.3.3: Be Nationally Compliant

An armed force's Ethical AI principles should sit under the national domain where other elements of the public and private sectors agree to a common set of rules and understanding, while acknowledging that the military must, at times, be authorized to override the limitations that apply to business and politics. Without such a general alignment, there could be disharmony between a military's principles and those used by business, with serious repercussions in the event of war, when even civilian infrastructure and systems may become targets. After all, the application of AI in an operational sense will often have implications for several pieces of domestic legislation, such as Privacy Law.

8.3.4: Be Justified and Explainable

AI should only be deployed in just conflict. Just conflicts are justifiable by comprehensible good reasons (Galliott 2019; Walzer 1987). This is why decisions made by AI systems in conflict need also be appropriately justified and transparent to those with a genuine need to know, including those providing oversight, military or otherwise, as necessary (i.e., not just technical experts). Armed forces must, therefore, maintain a system of control over which humans exert influence, which, in turn, requires that autonomous machines and systems meet at least three criteria in maintaining the following: a record of reliability; a system to enable the comprehensibility of previous machine behavior; and a means to record human input to code and other system operations, such as the input of training data, to ensure data provenance and the accountability of particular AI applications.

8.3.5: Operate within a System of Human Control

Following on from principle four, AI systems need to be designed and operated to hold people to account within the overarching system of human control in which AI operates (i.e., the Law of Armed Conflict, targeting doctrine, weapons review procedures, etc.), rather than attributing blame to AI systems (i.e., the technology itself) or 'black box' problems, noting that one cannot meaningfully apportion blame to nonhuman entities (Galliott 2015, 211–232). The latter efforts, which occur via anthropomorphic tendencies, partially absolve human actors for their contribution to what are merely technologically mediated accidents and consequently limit the chain of responsibility tied to positive feedback and relevant explanations that, in turn, lead to technological enhancements and improved ethical/operational outcomes (Galliott 2015, 211–232). This does not, however, necessarily call for a human to be in or on the loop at the execution of lethal action.

8.3.6: Be Built and Certified Safe and Secure

Certification for the safe, secure, and reliable build and operation of AI systems is needed for the prevention of harm and mitigation of risk to both civilians and military personnel. This requires a safety and certification regime beyond that available for non-weaponized civilian systems and which ought to be of a national or relevant international standard. Armed forces, whether individually or in collaboration with allies, might, therefore, develop and publish definitions for safety and security against which developed systems can be judged.

8.3.7: Be Ethical by Design (Friedman and Hendry 2019)

AI research and technical choices need to take into account ethical implications and norms that may be deeply wedged between theoretical issues and practical design decisions. The technical design dilemmas faced by particular applications of AI need to be investigated in moral terms, along with the human factors that are relevant to them, before development, implementation, deployment, and usage. The trade-offs between the factors in dilemma resolution need to be empirically studied and accounted for in the design process well before deployment.

8.3.8: Avoid Unjust Bias

Military AI algorithms and datasets can magnify or eliminate biases found in other segments of society. Recognizing unfair and/or unjust bias is neither simple nor value neutral as said bias is culturally relative, especially in an international deployment context. Armed forces must take reasonable steps to preclude harm being caused to combatants and noncombatants stemming from calculations made based on characteristics including race, ethnicity, or age and focus on more traits more easily verifiable and directly pertinent to targeting, such as height, weight, gait, etc. This calls for further research on culture-specific human-machine interaction practices and algorithmic testing.

8.3.9: Allow Military Personnel to Flourish

AI needs to be deployed in a way that enables military personnel to flourish alongside AI, mentally, emotionally, and economically. This involves limiting its negative impact on human workforces to ensure that that the ADF's ability to wage low-technological warfare is not impaired by the employment of personnel in technologically focused roles, the deskilling of humans (Galliott 2017a) partially replaced by AI-enabled automation or related psychological concerns (Galliott 2016). The third important aspect is related to tolerance, and it is the recognition of the value of human preferences and dignity in decisional processes made by or involving AI: in other words, humans should never feel just as little hopeless pieces of a mechanism bigger than them, because this prevents them from flourishing and expressing their human nature potential (Galliott 2018; Galliott 2017b). This calls for further knowledge and understanding of how AI integrates with networks of humans and machines, particularly where AI and human values may differ in goal-orientated contexts. Preference and consideration should be given to how AI can enhance or advance soldiers' interests.

8.3.10: Be Sensitive to the Environment

While much attention is given to humans and their associated rights in Ethical AI principle development, consideration must also be afforded to nonhuman entities and objects in the employment of military AI, namely animals, agriculture, and bodies of water, which should not be unjustly or disproportionately harmed as a result of the military deployment of AI. The preservation of the conditions for basic human life, as well as the protection of important cultural objects through the appropriate use of AI, is important insofar as the availability of natural resources is important to later-arriving personnel and the support of local populaces is important to lasting peace (Galliott 2015, 37–64). The importance of such nonhuman objects and entities should, therefore, be allocated a corresponding value within the code of the relevant systems and not necessarily depend on the law of the land in which a military force deploying AI may operate. A system could, for instance, be trained to automatically recognize the United Nations' Blue Shield protective symbol for cultural assets worthy of protection and therefore enhance decision-making in this regard (United Nations Educational, Scientific and Cultural Organisation 2019).

8.3.11: Be Malfunction Ready

Remedies (technical or otherwise) must be available and in place prior to the deployment of military AI systems so that, in the event of a malfunction, appropriate measures or mechanisms can be deployed to limit the actions of the system or compensate and/or assist those toward which the deploying force has a legal or moral obligation. Such remedies may include but are not limited to systems designed to constrain (further) lethal action, automatic financial compensation in the case of cyber systems, through to autonomous rescue devices that may assist those stranded at sea or in arid areas by the operation of an AI-enabled autonomous system. Said remedies may be internal/external and/or additional to the AI system originally deployed.

8.4: NOT A CHECKLIST BUT A STARTING POINT FOR TECHNOLOGY DEVELOPMENT

The suggested ethical principles should not be construed as a strict list of commandments so much a range of recommendations that should be informed by scenario-based methodology: What's the most appropriate use of AI in one combat situation versus another? And they are not intended for a single user, specific service, or even a particular military force. Once they proliferate and are amended by others in the same way that civilian principle sets have, the hope is that combatant commanders, service chiefs, and all sorts of different military players will find them useful in developing future technologies and drafting forthcoming strategies, concepts of operation, training guides, etc. Whether you are a uniformed officer or a civilian, and you are trying to write a training manual and concept of operations, there is a lot of planning, thinking, and training, so too if you are a technical actor tasked with developing the next generation of autonomous weapon, and the above principles should be informing these efforts.

These principles will also be useful in overcoming some of the common preconceived notions often advanced in favor of halting the development of AI in weapons technologies, those which revolve around an overly optimistic view of technology in that it raises concerns regarding a lack of meaningful human control. These notions often fail to acknowledge the many small but nevertheless important causal contributions made by individual actors such as programmers, designers, engineers, or the many failures and omissions made by multi-agent corporations involved in the commissioning of AI-enabled equipment through to deployment and those of design, engineering, and development. To ignore the role of these actors who have actively given rise to these technologies and their virtues and vices is to fundamentally misunderstand not just the nature of causation but also the nature of the problems associated with autonomy, for so long as the discussion about military AI and associated weapons remain focused on new, absolutist international law focused on a ban rather than effective regulation, these many actors may view themselves as partially absolved of moral responsibility for the harms resulting from their individual and collective design, development, and engineering efforts. In many respects, the classical problem of 'many hands' has become a false problem of no hands (Galliott 2015, 211–232).

But, of course, no such problem exists, and such assumptions would be detrimental to the concept of justice and might prove disastrous for the future of warfare. All individuals who deal with AI technology must exercise due diligence, and every actor in the causal chain leading through the idea in an innovator's mind, to the designer's model for realizing the concept, the engineer's interpretation of build plans and the user's understanding of the operating manual. Every time one interacts with a piece of technology or is involved in the technological design process, one's actions or omissions are contributing to the potential risks associated with the relevant technology and those in which it may be integrated. Some will suggest that this is too reductive and ignores the role of corporations and state or intergovernmental agencies. Nothing here is to suggest that they do not have an important role to play or that they are excused from their efforts to achieve military outcomes. Indeed, if they were to hold the greater capability to effect change, the moral burden may rest with them. But in the AI age, the reality is that the ultimate moral arbiters in conflict are those behind every design input and keystroke. That is, if the potential dangers of AI-enabled weapons are to be mitigated, we must begin to promote a personal ethic not dissimilar to that which pervades the armed forces in more traditional contexts. The US Marine Corp's Rifleman's Creed is a good example. But rather the reciting, "without me, my rifle is useless. Without my rifle, I am useless. I must fire my rifle true," we might say that "without my fingers, my AI is useless. Without good code, I am useless. I must code my weapon true." At the broader level, such a personal ethic must reach all the way down the command chain to the level of the individual decision-maker, whether this ceases at the officer level or proceeds down the ranks, owing to the elimination of the relevant boundaries. For now, it is of the greatest importance that we begin telling the full story about the rise of autonomous weapons and the role of all causal actors within. From there, we can begin to see how Ethical AI principles in the military would serve to enhance accountability and eliminate the concerns of those seeking to prohibit the development of AI weapons. Take one example of Ethical AI, 'smart guns' that remain locked unless held by an authorized user via biometric or token technologies to curtail accidental firings and cases of a gun stolen and used immediately to shoot people. Or a similar AI mechanism built into any military weapon, noting that even the most autonomous weapons have some degree of human interaction in their life cycle. These technologies might also record events, including the time and location of every shot fired, providing some accountability. With the right ethical principles, rather than a moratorium on AI weapons, these lifesaving technologies could exist today.

As another example, the author of this chapter has contributed to the use of the abovementioned Military Ethical AI principle set to develop the concept and architecture for a Minimally-Just AI (MinAI) (Galliott and Scholz 2019) system or Ethical AI Weapon (Scholz and Galliott, forthcoming; Scholz et al., forthcoming). A simple illustration serves to illustrate. Consider the capability of a weapon to recognize the unexpected presence of an international protection symbol—perhaps a Red Cross, Red Crescent, or Red Crystal—in a defined target area and abort an otherwise unrestrained human-ordered attack. Given the significant advances in visual machine learning over the last decade, such recognition systems are technically feasible. So, inspired by vehicle automation, an Ethical Weapon system for our purpose is a weapon with inbuilt safety enhancements enabled by the application of AI. An Ethical Weapon with Ethical AI tracks and records the full range of inputs and outputs, that is, the full range of human input to a particular military outcome. It takes an attack order as input and makes a decision *not to obey* the order if it assesses the presence of unexpected *protected* object(s).[2] What one means by 'protected' may include legal-identified entities from Red Cross marked objects, through to persons *hors de combat* and policy-identified entities specified in rules of engagement.

Such a system would likely be accepted by the public given the humanitarian benefit and therefore stands a strong chance to be accepted by other nations, therefore enhancing interoperability if deployed. Such a system would stand a good chance of meeting national requirements in all Western nations, given the focus on respecting protected symbols rather a more a maximal system focused on killing. The system would, therefore, be involved only in justified uses and incorporates a system for recording reliability and human input, as required under the explainability and human control principles. It is inherently ethical by design and allows personnel to flourish in the sense that they can more comfortably and consciously conduct combat while meeting basic legal requirements governing humanitarian protections. What this does mean is that some technical progress can immediately be made toward Ethical Weapons that stem from or adhere to Ethical AI principles along the lines advanced in this chapter. Indeed, a technical model has been proposed elsewhere. Clearly, any progress would constitute a humanitarian enhancement and serve as an example of the value of such principles.

8.5: THE LIMITATIONS OF MILITARY AI PRINCIPLES

While holding mutual understanding of a set of principles is valuable for the aims of all military stakeholders in pursuing a new technology, in that ethical principles can provide a useful collaborative starting point from which to develop more formal standards, regulations, or assurance principles; and can assist in the identification of priority issues that might be mutually served by technical and policy focus, they are not without their limitations and I, therefore, wish to conclude this chapter on a cautionary note.

One criticism often leveled at efforts to endorse principles is that in order to be action guiding, individual principles need to coexist, not just on paper but also in the interpreter's mind, with account to how they apply in certain real-world situations, and how to balance them should they conflict (Beauchamp 1995). To be sure, many principles in the AI debate are highly general: their value is that they indicate key moral themes that apply across a wide range of scenarios. This means that they have maximum appeal and are particularly useful as a checklist, as a set of important considerations that may need to be taken into account within a range of relevant scenarios. However, the generality also limits their ability the translated in a guide for practical action (Nicholson 2017). For example, ensuring that AI applications are 'fair' or 'inclusive' is a common thread among all sets of AI principles intended for civilian consumption. These are phrases which, at a high level of abstract, most people can immediately recognize and agree upon implementing because they carry few, if any, commitments. However, the proposed principles, while not immune to this problem, have been formulated to be more specific and have been annotated to provide a further guide to practical action and, as evidenced by their link to the development of Ethical Weapons, are perhaps more useful in practice as a result of being narrower. If realized practically through the Ethical Weapons concept, such principles can be operationalized by drawing on a database of past actions and outcomes, for example.

Some also level the criticism that the gap between principles and phronesis becomes even more pronounced when we consider that principles inevitably conflict with each other. For example, Whittlestone et al. (2019) point to the UK House of Lords AI Committee report, which effectively states that an AI system that can cause serious harm should be deployed unless it is capable of generating a full and complete recount of the calculations and decisions made. They suggest that the intention here, that beneficence should not come at the cost of explainability, pits the two against each other in a way that may not be easily reconciled. One might also say that the principle, "allowing military personnel to flourish," might be in competition with a coexisting principle, which dictates that AI "be sensitive to the environment." There will often be complex and important moral trade-offs involved here (Whittlestone et al. 2019), with risk transfers abound, and a principle that instates a black ban on a weapon's use without full and complete explainability fails to recognize these delicate trade-offs and the fact that full and complete explainability may not be necessary for a satisfactory level of safety to be guaranteed. This is not the intention here, so I have endeavored to be precise and reductionist with language such that one is forced to choose between them, and have also provided referrals with the wording and annotation of the principles for the resolution of such trade-offs. For instance, in saying that military AI uses must be 'justified and transparent,' we provide a reference to just wars, indicating an appeal to just war theory and the Law of Armed Conflict. Moreover, while some principles may still conflict, this simply points to sources of tension and therefore directs the applicator's attention to this area of further investigation. Principles are not intended to be operations handbooks in the same way that an ethics degree provides the student with a framework for thinking rather than a solution to every problem.

Still others say that ethical principles of the kind proposed, and the related guidelines, are rarely backed by enforcement, oversight, or serious consequences for deviation (Whittaker et al. 2018). The criticism here is that a principles-based approach to managing AI risk within an organization or armed force implicitly asks the relevant stakeholders to take the implementing party at their word when they say they will guide ethical action, leaving no particular person/s accountable. It is true that principles-based regulation often does fall upon the shoulders of a particular person or group of persons. Is it the senior executives of the manufacturer that is responsible? The developers and coders of particular applications? The end user or commander? Elected representatives? Public servants in the Defense Ministry?

The United Nations? A representative sample of the population? One could make an argument that any or none of these actors should be in a position to interpret the principles, and this does leave principle sets open to claims of 'ethics washing' where results are not delivered. Therefore, in this case, it is explicitly stipulated that a group of independent experts be responsible. It is also noted that where military forces are concerned, the public often has little choice but to take the Defense Ministry at its word, owing to the fact that oversight bodies typically conduct their monitoring operations in classified contexts, releasing only heavily redacted reports for public consumption. This criticism is not new. Nevertheless, oversight can be effective if properly structured. The collapse of the Google ethics board, and resulting international media coverage and stock market fluctuation, is another indicator that expert groups can have a meaningful impact against even global giants, if only through public resignation in the worst cases.

The fact remains, however, that the explosion and continued development of Ethical AI principle sets is encouraging, and it is important that such efforts now have the public support of those at high levels in technology and government spaces. Now it is time for military forces to do the same. The Military Ethical AI principles provide a high-level framework and shared language through which soldiers, developers, and a diverse range of other stakeholders can discuss and continue the debate on ethical and legal concerns associated with legitimate militarization of AI. They provide a standard and means against which development efforts can be judged, prospectively or retrospectively. They also stand to be educational in raising awareness of particular risks of AI within military forces, and externally, among the broader concerned public. Of course, building ethically just AI systems will require more than ethical language and a strong personal ethic, and it has been demonstrated that the principles can also assist in technological development through briefly outlining the Ethical Weapon concept developed on these principles, essentially embedding ethical and legal frameworks into military AI itself.

NOTES

1. The author wishes to thank Jason Scholz, Kate Devitt, Max Cappuccio, Bianca Baggiarini, and Austin Wyatt for their thoughts and suggestions.
2. One may argue that adversaries who know this might 'game' the weapons by posing under the cover of 'protection.' If this is known, it is a case for (accountable) human override of the Ethical Weapon, and why the term 'unexpected' is used. Noting also that besides being an act of perfidy in the case of such use of protected symbols, which has other possible consequences for the perpetrators, it may in fact aid in targeting as these would be anomalies with respect to known Red Cross locations. Blockchain (distributed ledger) IDs could also be issued to humanitarian organizations, and, when combined with geolocation and resilient radio, these could create unspoofable marks that could be hardwired into AI systems to avoid.

WORKS CITED

ACM US Public Policy Council. 2017. "Statement on Algorithmic Transparency and Accountability." *Association for Computing Machinery*. https://www.acm.org/binaries/content/assets/publicpolicy/2017_usacm_statement_algorithms.pdf.

Beauchamp, T. 1995. "Principlism and Its Alleged Competitors." *Kennedy Institute of Ethics Journal* 5 (3): pp. 181–198.

European Commission. 2019. "Artificial Intelligence: Commission Takes Forward Its Work on Ethics Guidelines." European Commission. Available: https://europa.eu/rapid/press-release_IP-19-1893_en.html.

Friedman, B. and D. Hendry. 2019. *Value Sensitive Design: Shaping Technology with Moral Imagination*. Cambridge, MA: MIT Press.

Future of Life Institute. 2018. "Asilomar AI Principles." *Future of Life Institute*. https://futureoflife.org/ai-principles.

Galliott, J. 2015. *Military Robots: Mapping the Moral Landscape*. Surrey, UK: Ashgate.

Galliott, J. 2016. "Defending Australia in the Digital Age: Toward Full Spectrum Defence." *Defence Studies* 16 (2): pp. 157–175.

Galliott, J. 2017a. "The Limits of Robotic Solutions to Human Challenges in the Land Domain." *Defence Studies* 17 (4): pp. 327–345.

Galliott, J. 2017b. "The Unabomber on Robots: The Need for a Philosophy of Technology Geared Toward Human Ends." In *Robot Ethics 2.0: From Autonomous Cars to Artificial Intelligence Robot Ethics 2.0: From Autonomous Cars to Artificial Intelligence*, edited by Patrick Lin, Keith Abney, and Ryan Jenkins, pp. 369–385. New York: Oxford University Press.

Galliott, J. 2018. "The Soldier's Tolerance for Autonomous Systems." *Paladyn* 9 (1): pp. 124–136.

Galliott, J. 2019. *Force Short of War in Modern Conflict: Jus Ad Vim*. Edinburgh: Edinburgh University Press.

Galliott, J. and Jason Scholz. 2019. "Artificial Intelligence in Weapons: The Moral Imperative for Minimally-Just Autonomy." *US Air Force Journal of Indo-Pacific Affairs* 1 (2): pp. 57–67.

IEEE Standards Association. 2019. "Ethically Aligned Design." *The IEEE Global Initiative for Ethical Considerations in Artificial Intelligence and Autonomous Systems*. New York: IEEE Standards Association.

Japanese Society for Artificial Intelligence. 2017. "The Japanese Society for Artificial Intelligence Ethical Guidelines." *Japanese Society for Artificial Intelligence*. http://ai-elsi.org/archives/514.

Microsoft. 2019. "Microsoft AI Principles." Microsoft. https://www.microsoft.com/en-us/ai/our-approach-to-ai.

Nicholson, W. 2017. "Regulating Black-Box Medicine." *Michigan Legal Review* 116 (3): pp. 421–474.

Pandya, J. 2019. "The Weaponization Of Artificial Intelligence." *Forbes Magazine*. January 14. https://www.forbes.com/sites/cognitiveworld/2019/01/14/the-weaponization-of-artificial-intelligence/#23407e7a3686.

Partnership on AI. 2018. "Tenets." *San Francisco: Partnership on AI*. https://www.partnershiponai.org/tenets/.

Pichai, S. 2018. "AI at Google: Our Principles." *Google*. https://www.blog.google/technology/ai/ai-principles/.

Piper, K. 2019. "Google Cancels AI Ethics Board in Response to Outcry." *Vox*. April 4. https://www.vox.com/future-perfect/2019/4/4/18295933/google-cancels-ai-ethics-board.

Porro, C. 2018. "AI for Good: Principles I Believe in." *Sales Force*. https://www.salesforce.org/ai-good-principles-believe/.

Scholz, J. and J. Galliott. Forthcoming. "The Case for Ethical AI in the Military." In *Oxford Handbook on the Ethics of AI,* edited by M. Dubber. New York: Oxford University Press.

Scholz, J., D. Lambert, R. Bolia, and J. Galliott. Forthcoming. "Ethical Weapons: A Case for AI in Weapons." In *Moral Responsibility in Twenty-First-Century Warfare Just War Theory and the Ethical Challenges of Autonomous Weapons Systems,* edited by S. Roach and A. Eckert. New York: State University of New York Press.

Select Committee on Artificial Intelligence. 2018. *AI in the UK: Ready, Willing, and Able?.* HL 100 2017-19. London: UK House of Lords.

Tucker, P. 2019. "Pentagon Seeks a List of Ethical Principles for Using AI in War." *Defence One.* January 4. https://cdn.defenseone.com/a/defenseone/interstitial.html?v=9.3.0&rf=https%3A%2F%2Fwww.defenseone.com%2Ftechnology%2F2019%2F01%2Fpentagon-seeks-list-ethical-principles-using-ai-war%2F153940%2F.

United Nations Educational, Scientific and Cultural Organisation. 2019. "Emblems for the Protection of Cultural Heritage in Times of Armed Conflicts." *United Nations Educational, Scientific and Cultural Organisation.* http://www.unesco.org/new/en/culture/themes/armed-conflict-and-heritage/convention-and-protocols/blue-shield-emblem/.

University of Montréal. 2017. "Montréal Declaration for a Responsible AI." *University of Montréal.* https://www.montrealdeclarationresponsibleai.com/the-declaration.

Walzer, M. 1987. *Just and Unjust Wars.* New York: Basic Books.

Whittaker, M., K. Crawford, R. Dobbe, G. Fried, E. Kaziunas, V. Mathur, S. West, R. Richardson, J. Schultz, and O. Schwartz. 2018. *AI Now Report.* New York: AI Now Institute. https://ainowinstitute.org/AI_Now_2018_Report.pdf.

Whittlestone, J., R. Nyrup, A. Alexandrova, and S. Cave. 2019. "The Role and Limits of Principles in AI Ethics: Towards a Focus on the Tensions." In *Conference on Artificial Intelligence, Ethics and Society.* Honolulu, HI: Association for the Advancement of Artificial Intelligence and Association for Computing Machinery.

9

Empirical Data on Attitudes Toward Autonomous Systems

JAI GALLIOTT, BIANCA BAGGIARINI, AND SEAN RUPKA

9.1: INTRODUCTION

Combat automation, enabled by rapid technological advancements in artificial intelligence and machine learning, is a guiding principle of current and future-oriented security practices.[1] Yet, despite the proliferation of military applications of autonomous systems (AS), little is known about military personnel's attitudes toward AS. Consequently, the impact of algorithmic combat on military personnel is under-theorized, aside from a handful of expository, first-person testimonies from mostly US- and UK-based drone whistle-blowers (Jevglevskaja and Galliott 2019). Should AS be efficiently developed to reflect the values of end users, and should they be ethically deployed to reflect the moral standards to which states, militaries, and individual soldiers are bound, empirical studies aimed at understanding how soldiers resist, embrace, and negotiate their interactions with AS will be critical.

Knowledge about individual attitudes or prescriptive or evaluative judgments that are shaped relationally through social interactions (Voas 2014) matters deeply for understanding the impact of AS on military personnel. As engineering and human factors-inspired empirical research on trusted autonomy has shown, the use, misuse, and abuse of any innovative technology is partly mediated by attitudes toward said technology (Davis 2019) informing how trust is translated in experience; and how trust is practiced, calibrated, and recalibrated in the aftermath of machine error (Muir 1987; Roff and Danks 2018). However, attitudes toward AS do not exist in a vacuum, and so technical explanations of trust will only get us so far.

Jai Galliott, Bianca Baggiarini, and Sean Rupka, *Empirical Data on Attitudes Toward Autonomous Systems* In: *Lethal Autonomous Weapons.* Edited by: Jai Galliott, Duncan MacIntosh and Jens David Ohlin, © Oxford University Press (2021).
DOI: 10.1093/oso/9780197546048.003.0010

Our chapter departs from technical research in that we view attitudes within the historical, political, and social contexts that give rise to them (Galliott, 2016). For human-machine teams that deploy weaponized AS, knowledge of attitudes and the social interactions governing the practice of trust becomes even more significant, as misuse or abuse can have catastrophic consequences.

To help fill this gap in knowledge, a historically unprecedented survey was administered to nearly 1,000 Australian Defence Force Academy cadets in February 2019. As the largest study in the world to focus on military attitudes toward AS, the purpose was to ascertain how best the future development and deployment of AS might align with the key values of military personnel. The expectation is that this information, understood in a much broader social context, informs how innovative autonomous technology may be effectively integrated into existing force structures (Galliott 2016; 2018). Given that this generation of trainees will be the first to deploy AS in a systematic way, their views are especially important, and may contribute to future national and international policy development in this area. This chapter draws on critical social theory to qualitatively analyze only a subsection of the survey. This data subset includes themes pertaining to (1) the dynamics of human-machine teams, the willingness of respondents to work with AS, and the perceived risks and benefits therein; (2) ideas about perceived capabilities, decision-making, and how human-machine teams should be configured; (3) the changing nature of (and respect for) military labor, and the role of incentives; (4) preferences to oversee a robot, versus carrying out a mission themselves; and (5) AS, and the changing meaning of soldiering. Definitions of autonomous systems, tied to different levels of autonomy, were clearly embedded within the relevant survey question.

We analyze the data in the context of neoliberal capitalism[2] and governmentality literature[3] (Brock 2019; Dean 1999; Dillon and Reid 2000; Reid 2006; Rose 1999). We argue that AS are guided by economic rationales, and in turn, this economic thinking shapes military attitudes toward AS. Given that AS constitutes a new, immaterial infrastructure that encodes both the planning and distribution of power (Jaume-Palasi 2019), we argue that attitudes toward autonomy are inevitably informed by this novel architecture of power. A paper on attitudes absent a parallel analysis of modes of power within neoliberal society would problematically ignore how attitudes are shaped through a historically and politically contingent notion of society. Indeed, the method of the "sociological imagination," which motivates our analysis, tells us that neither the life of an individual, nor the history of a society, can be understood without understanding both (Mills 1959, 3). Our approach is holistically sociological in that we view the micro (individual) and macro (collective) units of analysis as symbiotic.

The individual attitudes of cadets (citizen-soldiers in the making) do not exist in isolation. They cannot be neatly separated out from the globalization, discourses of automation, the politics of war, and the occupational ethos of the contemporary military in which cadets are being trained to serve. This is where a sociological perspective on attitudes departs from a social-psychological one, insofar as it does not view attitudes as direct pipelines into individual mental states (which then necessarily determine behavior) but instead views attitudes as judgments that are produced relationally in the context of social interactions. Attitudes then are social phenomena that emerge from, but are not reducible to, the inner workings of human minds (Voas 2014). Through this particular framing of attitudes, combined with the conceptual outline described above, our chapter provides a theoretical framework (and by no means the only one available) by which to understand and explain the significance of the military attitudes toward AS: the governing of subjectivity, and the neoliberal restructuring of capitalism.

As we will argue, the fact that nearly a quarter of respondents ranked financial gain as their top incentive for working alongside robots (among other data points) suggests that respondents identify the military as an occupational, rather than strictly institutional, entity. This alone is not a novel or particularly interesting claim. However, we suggest that AS may exacerbate the inherent problems associated with an occupational military. The risk of identifying with this occupational (neoliberal and individualist) ethos, is that soldiers may not cultivate the level of loyalty required to sustain the distinct social status that the military has historically relied upon to justify its existence and legitimize its actions to the public it serves. This occupational mindset will likely compound the impact of AS on recruitment and retention policies, and policymakers should prepare for this. In this chapter, we discuss AS in the context of neoliberal governing, the introduction of economics into politics. We argue that Australian AS integration strategies—unquestionably informed by its primary strategic partner and heretofore unchallenged preeminent military power, the United States—show traces of governmentality reasoning. Throughout, we utilize the survey data to explore the interconnected consequences of neoliberal governing for cadets' attitudes toward AS, and the future integrity of the military and citizen-soldiering more broadly. In our concluding remarks, we offer policy-oriented remarks about the effects of AS on future force design. We also caution against unchecked technological fetishism, highlighting the need to critically question the application of market-based notions of freedom to the military domain.

9.2: AUTOMATING FOR FREEDOM

AS empowers subjects to acquire more information, with less physical and cognitive labor. The military application of AS is frequently welcomed as part of the natural evolution of technological innovation. AS promises to enable better decisions, manage risks, make time-sensitive recommendations through cost benefit analyses, and make predictions by identifying patterns, all with the aim of enhancing the individual freedom of the soldier to simplify the decision-making cycle. In this sense, AI-based technologies ostensibly make the daily life of soldiering easier. Consider this through the lens of governmentality—or what Michel Foucault termed the "conduct of conduct." Governmentality, in contrast to the prohibitive power of sovereignty,[4] does not disempower; it cultivates subjectivity through the recognition of the capacity for calculated action. This is a positive understanding of freedom, wherein modern individuals are not "free to choose" but "obliged to be free" (Rose 1999). In the contemporary military context, the protection of soldiers' lives despite their (real or potential) deployment on the battlefield, has become the upmost concern. AI-based technologies, through their ability to transfer risk, support this bio-political imperative for the positive empowerment and administration of life. AS support this through the promise of better, less labor-intensive, and more sustained information.

To be sure, ours is a boundless "information society." As is the case with much innovation in civilian realms, the technological requirements of the military are frequently a central driver. This uptick in AS innovation geared toward *information* is witnessed in a variety of settings: from healthcare and medical diagnosis, to education and task assessment, policing and surveillance, smart homes and cities, employment and job recruitment, law and sentencing procedures, and transportation. In the military context, it is now well known that machines can operate in hazardous environments, do not need extensive education and training, require no minimum hygienic standards, do not tire, and are perfect in suppressing the enemy, since soldiers need not even be exposed to an enemy (Sauer and Schornig 2012). AI-based technologies allow us to surpass the rights traditionally afforded to employees, and the limitations of vulnerable human capital, through ostensibly irrefutable claims that machines bring greater "efficiency" (and other typical euphemisms of neoliberal capitalism). Consider, for example, how Uber exploits algorithmic technology in their labor policies: drivers are regarded as independent, entrepreneurial "consumers" of algorithmic technology, rather than traditional employees (Rosenblat 2018). Thus, in the ever-expanding quest for more and better information, AS are imagined as fundamentally freeing to business owners, governments, and military planners alike.

The overlapping domains of the military, technology, and civil society are, in fact, tied to a longer history. By the late nineteenth century, the complexity of warfare required large components of industry entirely devoted to research and development to produce, sustain, and improve rapidly developing military technologies. In the twentieth century, the archetype of the citizen-soldier emerged alongside liberal economics and liberal democracy. Military work was central in shaping the principles of Taylorism and the engineering of the assembly line, thus restructuring workplace organization by fragmenting labor, reducing its actions to predictable and repeatable calculations based on predetermined measurements of time. Profits became concentrated in fewer hands, and in turn, workers' bodies became subjects of disciplinary power (Cowen 2008). Similarly, Catherine Lutz (2002) shows how industrial warfare corresponded with the emergence of mass armies, but it also centered on manufacturing labor, and thus incorporated workers to produce weapons, vessels, and vehicles.

The notion of a military-industrial-complex serves as an example of the interconnectedness of the military with society described above. It draws our attention to networks of contracts, flows of money, and lobbying between individuals, corporations, institutions, and defense/military contractors. Perhaps best exemplified by the United States, and its expansive empire of military bases worldwide, the military-industrial-complex reveals the codependence of (seemingly distinct) public and private realms. To this end, the subject of military and security privatization has been widely documented as a manifestation of the military-industrial-complex (Abrahamsen and Williams 2009; Alexandra et al. 2008; Avant 2005; Baggiarini 2015; Wedel 2008; Wong 2006). Certainly, the military is not exempt from privatizing, fragmenting, augmenting, or otherwise eliminating human labor with technological solutions where possible. After all, the point of AI-based technologies is to support the replacement and/or improvement of vulnerable human capital. Outsourcing to private military and security corporations (PMCs), in a congruent example, relies upon an expert to provide a service that the military alone ostensibly cannot. We link these parallel developments (the philosophy of military/security privatization, and the technological commodities wrought by AI) to the consequences of governmentality reasoning.

Governmentality operates chiefly through a reliance upon market logic. This market logic facilitates the investment, research expertise, and capital necessary to create technological advancements in weaponry that enable the vision of automated warfare (Graham 2008) making the protection of (our) soldiers' lives the primary concern. In addition to market logic and expert knowledge, governing, as Foucault (1991) writes, prioritizes "patience rather than wrath." Privatization, the fragmentation and augmentation of labor together support the deliberate, patient calculation over life and death. The essential issue for the establishment for the art of government is, Foucault continues, the introduction of economy into political practice:

> [T]o govern a state will therefore mean to apply economy, to set up an economy at the level of the entire state, which means exercising towards its inhabitants, and the wealth and behavior of each and all, a form of surveillance and control as attentive as that of the head of the family over his household and his goods. (Foucault 1991, 92)

Foucault writes that the good governor does not have to have a sting (a weapon of killing). He must have patience rather than wrath—this positive content forms the essence of the governor and replaces the negative force. Power is about wisdom, and not knowledge of divine laws, of justice and equality, but rather, knowledge of things (96). Despite the preference for patience over wrath, every war requires the making of human killing machines (Asad 2007). Yet, the pervasiveness of post-Vietnam casualty aversion, and the congruent move to an all-volunteer force, suggests that soldiers no longer need to go to war expecting to die, but only to kill (Asad 2007).

To satisfy this requirement of minimizing or outright eliminating casualties, air superiority has become increasingly important for Australia's joint force as dominance in the sky is thought to be critical for protecting ground troops. Put differently, greater parity in the air is thought to lead to more protracted wars and increased casualty rates. Given this, it is no surprise that a vast majority of respondents predicted the air as becoming the most likely domain for conducting lethal attacks (as shown in Table 9.1).

Table 9.1: IN WHICH DOMAIN DO YOU THINK AUTONOMOUS SYSTEMS STAND THE GREATEST CHANCE OF BECOMING THE PREDOMINANT MEANS OF CONDUCTING LETHAL ATTACKS?

		Frequency	Percent	Valid Percent	Cumulative Percent
Valid	Land	117	11.7	14.5	14.5
	Sea	45	4.5	5.6	20.1
	Air	644	64.5	79.9	100.0
	Total	806	80.7	100.0	
Missing	System	193	19.3		
Total		999	100.0		

Table 9.2: DO YOU BELIEVE THAT AUTONOMOUS ROBOTS WILL EVENTUALLY OUTNUMBER MANNED AIRCRAFT, VEHICLES, AND VESSELS?

		Frequency	Percent	Valid Percent	Cumulative Percent
Valid	yes	567	56.8	70.2	70.2
	no	241	24.1	29.8	100.0
	Total	808	80.9	100.0	
Missing	System	191	19.1		
Total		999	100.0		

The desire for air superiority can be linked with the ideology of casualty aversion to be sure, but also the Revolution in Military Affairs (RMA). Central to the RMA is net-centric warfare, the aim of which is to link up a smaller number of highly trained human warriors with agile weapons systems and mechanized support linked via GPS and satellite communications into an intricate, interconnected system, in which the behavior of components would be mutually enhanced by the constant exchange of real-time battlefield information. AS are essential to the operation of net-centric warfare. The RMA thus facilitates the desire for full-spectrum dominance, including surveillance and dominance of land, air, and sea; the militarization of space; information warfare; and control over communication networks. The increasing demand for situation understanding in the air and beyond, as a means to protect Australian and allied troops, suggests the possibility of AS surpassing manned platforms. Seventy percent of respondents believe that robots will eventually outnumber manned systems (as shown in Table 9.2).

Significant force reduction is required to finance the technology necessary for the RMA (Moskos, Williams, and Segal 2000, 5) and, given the above, it appears that survey respondents have an intuitive awareness of this. The decline of the mass army model (something that Australian cadets have never personally experienced) went together with restructuring toward professionalization and the prominence of casualty aversion as the primary measurement of success (Mandel 2004). This change saw managers and technicians increasingly conducting war, as opposed to combat leaders (Moskos 2000). The professionalization of the military was essential for the realization of the goals of the RMA. Put differently, without professionalization, the key principles of the RMA, particularly the incorporation of precision-guided weapons, would not have materialized (Adamsky 2010).

Downsized, professionalized, and technocentric warfare together inform the shift in the military's status in the late twentieth century: from institutional (defined through myths of self-sacrifice, communal relations, and loyalty) to occupational (defined through individualism and economics), as shown in Table 9.3.

Military sociologist Charles Moskos identified this shift in the 1970s. Drawing on Moskos, Balint and Dobos (2015) show that while the military is traditionally thought of as an institution, wherein members see themselves as transcending individual self-interest, the military is now subjected to the corporatized business logic and models of most occupational organizations operating in a globalized, neoliberal era. The effect of this is that the marketplace, and other neoliberal signifiers of capitalist accumulation, dictate how soldiers conceptualize their labor, namely, as "just another job." "Recruitment campaigns increasingly emphasize monetary

Table 9.3: DO YOU BELIEVE THAT AUTONOMOUS ROBOTS WILL EVENTUALLY LIMIT THE NUMBER OF PEOPLE EMPLOYED IN THE ADF?

		Frequency	Percent	Valid Percent	Cumulative Percent
Valid	Yes	476	47.6	59.0	59.0
	No	331	33.1	41.0	100.0
	Total	807	80.8	100.0	
Missing	System	192	19.2		
Total		999	100.0		

inducements and concessions, and broader career advantages, rather than duty, honor, and patriotism" (Balint and Dobos 2015, 360). In Table 9-4, we see evidence of this, as a quarter of respondents ranked financial gain as their top incentive for working alongside robots.[5]

One consequence of the occupational shift is that "the soldier who thinks like a rational, self-maximizing actor is unlikely to show loyalty when civilian jobs within their reach offer more attractive remuneration packages. And even if they do, they may be less willing to sustain the personal costs and make the sacrifices that the profession demands" (Balint and Dobos 2015, 361). While beyond the scope of this chapter, others agree that contrary to popular myths of sacrifice, nationalistic pride, and heroic virtue, the motivation to join the military has instead largely been predicated on financial gain, opportunities for career advancement, a general lack of other opportunities, and a desire to acquire transferable skills (for more discussion, see Woodward 2008).

In the quest to secure tech-savvy personnelcivilian organizations, particularly large technology companies, enjoy considerable advantages in their ability to attract AI-educated talent. Given the salary and lifestyle options that they offer, education and industry sectors will likely emerge as direct competitors for personnel. The consequences of the occupational shift, when compounded with the rapidity of AS innovation, and

Table 9.4: WHICH INCENTIVES WOULD TEMPT YOU TO SHIFT TO A NEW EMPLOYMENT CATEGORY FOCUSED ON SUPPORTING AND/OR OVERSEEING AUTONOMOUS ROBOTS: INCREASED SALARY/LUMP SUM PAYMENT?

		Frequency	Percent	Valid Percent	Cumulative Percent
Valid	1	194	19.4	24.3	24.3
	2	145	14.5	18.2	42.5
	3	108	10.8	13.5	56.0
	4	89	8.9	11.2	67.2
	5	79	7.9	9.9	77.1
	6	59	5.9	7.4	84.5
	7	57	5.7	7.1	91.6
	8	67	6.7	8.4	100.0
	Total	798	79.9	100.0	
Missing	System	201	20.1		
Total		999	100.0		

current retention and recruitment problems,[6] will likely continue to be acutely felt by armed forces. It is well known that the ADF is compelled by operational need to adopt the latest technologies available to them. However, they must not only attract AI-educated personnel with the skills required to maintain and operate AS, but also retain skilled personnel, a tactical, small unit culture, in the face of growing global competition. The 2018 Robotics and Autonomous Systems (RAS) Strategy, discussed in more detail in the next section, begins to tackle some of these concerns.

9.3: TRACES OF NEOLIBERAL GOVERNING IN AS POLICYMAKING

AI-based technology cuts to the heart of operational, strategic, and policy concerns for Australian defense. RAS applies to software, artificial intelligence, and advanced robotics to perform human-directed tasks. These tools are imagined as key in the decision-support space, as machines can rapidly analyze significant volumes of data, identify patterns, and make observations and recommendations. The RAS Strategy conceives of autonomy on a spectrum, covering everything from remotely piloted aircraft, vehicles and vessels, to machine learning and systems capable of autonomous decision-making. It outlines five areas in which the Australian defense community will seek to harness the advantages of AI-based technologies.

The first area concerns maximizing soldier performance through a reduction of physical and cognitive loads. Examples of this in practice from a physical standpoint include exoskeletons, which support joints and muscles, thereby enabling soldiers' endurance, to unmanned ground vehicles equipped to carry cargo that traditionally soldiers have carried. From a cognitive perspective, this could mean the implantation of neural devices to enhance memory and focus, to designing systems with a view toward centralizing and synthesizing data onto a minimal number of screens, so that individuals can readily process data, and make decisions in ways that do not overwhelm them or deflect their attention. The second area is about improving decision-making at all levels (i.e., intelligence, surveillance, reconnaissance, and targeting support). The third opportunity for AI-based technologies is in its ability to generate mass and scalable effects through human-machine teaming. In other words, Australia may have fewer boots on the ground compared to other states, but they still have to be sufficiently equipped to support a mission. The fourth area is about protecting the force (and allied troops), and the fifth cites efficiency. Efficiency could mean the ability for the ADF to operate across a joint force

Table 9.5: IMAGINE YOU ARE A PILOT. WOULD YOU PREFER TO OVERSEE A HIGH-RISK MISSION UTILIZING AN AUTONOMOUS UNMANNED AERIAL VEHICLE RATHER THAN CONDUCT IT YOURSELF IN A MANNED AIRCRAFT?

		Frequency	Percent	Valid Percent	Cumulative Percent
Valid	yes	292	29.2	36.2	36.2
	no	515	51.6	63.8	100.0
	Total	807	80.8	100.0	
Missing	System	192	19.2		
Total		999	100.0		

Table 9.6: IMAGINE YOU ARE AN ARMORED CORPS OFFICER. WOULD YOU PREFER TO OVERSEE A HIGH-RISK MISSION UTILIZING AN AUTONOMOUS UNMANNED GROUND VEHICLE RATHER THAN CONDUCT IT YOURSELF WITH A MANNED PLATFORM?

		Frequency	Percent	Valid Percent	Cumulative Percent
Valid	yes	389	38.9	48.4	48.4
	no	414	41.4	51.6	100.0
	Total	803	80.4	100.0	
Missing	System	196	19.6		
Total		999	100.0		

effectively, and it could also refer to the financial requirement of efficiency, given recent austerity measures.

With respect to the modest size of the Australian joint force, the document states that teaming humans with machines can significantly increase combat effect and mass, without the need to grow the human workforce. Recall that casualty aversion, the RMA, the professional military, and AI-based technology all converge in the common principle to maximize the efficiency of individual soldiers in a small, agile network. Despite the increasing reliance upon technology and technological expertise in a downsized, professional military, Australian cadets nevertheless gesture to a future battlespace that ideally remains human-centered and human-controlled. Most report, regardless of combat domain, wanting to remain in control of high-risk missions, rather than cede control to an unmanned platform, which is illustrated in the below tables.

Despite a preference on the part of survey respondents to maintain rather than relinquish control, the significance, understanding, and impact of the concept and practice of meaningful human control is not yet known. Consider how the US Department of Defense, for instance, claims that robotics and autonomous systems will eventually gain greater autonomy, such that the algorithms will act as a human brain does. The DoD's report, *Unmanned Systems Integrated Roadmap FY2013–2038*, states that "research and development in automation are advancing from a state of automatic systems requiring human control toward a state of autonomous systems able to make decisions and react without human interaction" (2014, 29). Currently, the application of unmanned systems involves significant human interaction. That said, respondents are not overly concerned about working alongside semiautonomous or

Table 9.7: IMAGINE YOU ARE A MARITIME WARFARE OFFICER. WOULD YOU PREFER TO OVERSEE A HIGH-RISK MISSION UTILIZING AN AUTONOMOUS UNMANNED SURFACE VESSEL RATHER THAN CONDUCT IT YOURSELF WITH A MANNED PLATFORM?

		Frequency	Percent	Valid Percent	Cumulative Percent
Valid	yes	331	33.1	41.2	41.2
	no	473	47.3	58.8	100.0
	Total	804	80.5	100.0	
Missing	System	195	19.5		
Total		999	100.0		

Table 9.8: IF YOU KNEW YOU WERE REQUIRED TO WORK ALONGSIDE ROBOTS THAT CAN EXERCISE PREPROGRAMED "DECISION-MAKING" IN DETERMINING HOW TO EMPLOY FORCE IN PREDEFINED AREAS WITHOUT THE NEED FOR HUMAN OVERSIGHT, WOULD THIS HAVE CHANGED YOUR DECISION TO JOIN ADF?

		Frequency	Percent	Valid Percent	Cumulative Percent
Valid	0[8]	1	.1	.1	.1
	yes	189	18.9	23.4	23.6
	no	616	61.7	76.4	100.0
	Total	806	80.7	100.0	
Missing	System	193	19.3		
Total		999	100.0		

autonomous robots (which is shown in the below tables). Indeed, the goals of net-centric warfare, in theory, do not outright preclude the possibility of humans moving further outside the loop. Nonetheless, respondents express preference for an oversight role, rather than leave the military altogether, should they be made redundant.

Given that significant force reduction is required to implement innovative technology, it is no wonder that smaller units composed of human-machine teams reflect the future of force structuring. While Australia looks to generate mass through its relatively small footprint, globalization reveals the opposite effect, in its requirement for greater interconnections between nations on economic and security issues. Strategically, globalization mandates a convergence of national and collective security requirements. This convergence is most evident in the Australia-US alliance. Consider first the development of maneuver warfare concepts in the United States Army and Marine Corps beginning in the 1980s was replicated in Australia. Second, the United States Force Posture Initiatives in Northern Australia are being implemented under the Force Posture Agreement signed at the 2014 Australia-United States Ministerial Meeting. These initiatives increase opportunities for combined training and exercises and strengthen interoperability (Defence White Paper 2016). Third,

> Australia's security is underpinned by the ANZUS Treaty, United States extended deterrence and access to advanced United States technology and information. Access to the most advanced technology and equipment from the United States and maintaining interoperability with the United States is central to maintaining the ADF's potency. Australia sources our most important combat capability from the United States, including fighter and transport

Table 9.9: A JOB POSTING IN A ROBOT-FOCUSED ROLE COULD LEAD TO DIMINISHED OPPORTUNITIES FOR COMMAND AND PROGRESSION.

		Frequency	Percent	Valid Percent	Cumulative Percent
Valid	True	461	46.1	57.2	57.2
	False	345	34.5	42.8	100.0
	Total	806	80.7	100.0	
Missing	System	193	19.3		
Total		999	100.0		

Table 9.10: If you were to be made redundant by autonomous systems, would you be willing to work in direct support or oversight of such systems instead of leaving military service?

		Frequency	Percent	Valid Percent	Cumulative Percent
Valid	Yes	521	52.2	64.6	64.6
	No	285	28.5	35.4	100.0
	Total	806	80.7	100.0	
Missing	System	193	19.3		
Total		999	100.0		

> aircraft, naval combat systems and helicopters. Around 60 per cent of our acquisition spending is on equipment from the United States. The cost to Australia of developing these high-end capabilities would be beyond Australia's capacity without the alliance. (Defence White Paper 2016)

For Australia to effectively shape its strategic environment, to deny and defeat threats, and protect Australian and allied populations, a coalition culture will remain at the core of Australia's security and defense planning. The United States will likely continue to be the preeminent global military power, and thus Australia's most important strategic partner. It is therefore reasonable to analyze Australian AS policy in tandem with American AS policy.

To that end, in 2012, the US Department of Defense signaled to this future in *Sustaining U.S. Global Leadership: Priorities for 21st Century Defense* (the 2012 Defense Strategic Guidance document), which outlined its priorities for twenty-first-century defense. Inside, then-Secretary of Defense Leon Panetta describes an anticipated critical shift in defense policy in response to economic austerity and thus within American practices of war making more broadly. In the introductory paragraph of the *Unmanned Systems Roadmap (2011–2036)*, the authors praise autonomous systems for their "persistence, versatility, and reduced risk to human life" before asserting that the Department of Defense (DoD) faces a fiscal environment in which acquisitions must be complementary to the DoD's "Efficiencies Initiative." In other words, defense spending must "pursue investments and business practices that drive down the life-cycle costs for unmanned systems. Affordability will be treated as a Key Performance Parameter (KPP), equal to, if not more important than, schedule and technical performance" (2011, v). The 2012 Defense Strategic Guidance document further stated that:

> This country is at a strategic turning point after a decade of war, and therefore, we are shaping a Joint Force for the future that will be smaller and leaner, but will be agile, flexible, ready, and technologically advanced. It will have cutting edge capabilities, exploiting our technological, joint, and networked advantage. It will be led by the highest quality, battle-tested professionals. (2012, 5)

Furthermore, "U.S. forces will no longer be sized to conduct large-scale, prolonged stability operations" (2012, 6) and as such, the specialized labor contained in the Joint Force is thought to replace the mass quality of the traditional military structure, most importantly shedding the economic burden therein.[7] Instead of citizen-soldiers (and their attendant rights as vulnerable human capital), whom some military experts caution are no longer sufficiently equipped to fight, we are presented instead with the cleaner image of "battle-tested professionals." This prioritization of economic rationality signals some of the effects of neoliberal governing on military planning, and subsequently, citizen-soldier identity (to be discussed in another section). Critically, Panetta is not declaring that American forces will outright decline to engage in prolonged operations. What he is saying is that they will *not be sized* to engage in prolonged operations. This points directly to a significant, albeit implied, shift in policy: prolonged operations are expected, as the Global War on Terror and its architects do not take kindly to spatial, national, temporal, or political boundaries. Yet, these missions will be conceptualized and orchestrated by combat managers invested in primarily efficient (low cost) business practices, and designed for special operations technicians, with fewer, less visible, troop movements. AS allow for this kind of idealized, prolonged fighting and situational understanding. Yet, the impacts of this breach in the temporal and spatial limitations, limitations that have historically helped to contain and control military action, ought to be fully realized for the sake of the well-being of operators of AS moving forward. Legitimacy refers to perceptions of justice, legality, and morality as they apply to military operations and related actions. At the highest level, legitimacy finds expression in Australia using force only under defined circumstances (Land Warfare Doctrine 2017). However, a central challenge confronting the philosophical underpinnings of contemporary warfare is that we do not always understand what a war is. Since the collapse of the Soviet Union, that order, and by extension its inherited definitions of war and peace, have been contested. This has resulted in wars becoming "fuzzy at the edges" (LPD 2017). AS is meant to exploit and capitalize on these fuzzy edges, but it may do so in ways that undermine the legitimacy of military action. This enhanced freedom wrought by AS may come with a cost, one that cannot be reduced to economic calculability. Below we discuss some of the consequences of neoliberal governmentality on soldier-citizenship.

9.4: IMPLICATIONS OF NEOLIBERAL GOVERNING AND AUTONOMY FOR SOLDIER-CITIZENSHIP

While we previously stated that AI is meant to enable freedom, liberal citizenship views private property as the quintessential condition for the realization and protection of individual freedom. The liberal citizen is a private individual, motivated by the desire to maximize individual liberty and minimize state interventions. Liberalism promotes a deeply ingrained, possibly irreconcilable opposition between individual freedom and the state: the state must always be kept in check, because it is viewed as a set of practices within a given bureaucratic apparatus that is always-already undermining the rights, freedom, and liberties of individuals. Simultaneously the state relies on the coercive-ideological figure of the night watchman, allowing it access to legitimate violence, from surveillance technology to military force, to preserve this protection myth. Classical theory presupposes that the liberal citizen is compelled to avoid total retreat into the private sphere by his desire to enhance the conditions of his individual freedoms through institutions that protect his private property. Liberal citizens relate to each other as embodiments of private property: Citizens freely enter into the public sphere to cultivate economic contracts with one another mediated by uninhibited markets. These public contracts conceived among individuals occur to support the acquisition and protection of private property—the precondition of freedom.

In contrast, civic republicans claim that liberalism's privileging of private interests, materialism, and normative neutrality reflects its failure to garner a necessary ethical, active orientation to politics that will ultimately sustain the republic and the common good. In their view, liberalism presents an impoverished version of citizenship. Republicans also tend to argue that politics must be conducted and struggled over in a visible public sphere, to stave off the state's supposed inherent tendencies toward corruption. This tradition differs from the liberal approach because it emphasizes that individuals should submit to these moral, material, and symbolic demands of the public sphere. The making of the "good" citizen is accomplished through habitual practices and reaffirmed and legitimized in collective moments and expressions of national consciousness. A public-spiritedness, therefore, constitutes a republican's orientation to politics, but this spirit is only born, à la Tocqueville, out of habitual practice, which Dagger (2002) defines as characteristic of the integrative and educative aspects of republican citizenship, which folds the individual citizen's actions into a common expression of "the good."

Both liberal and republican traditions as described above ultimately fail us, insofar as they cannot account for the problematic of citizen-soldiering and neoliberal governmentality's reliance upon flexible citizenship, or the cultural logic of capital accumulation that induces subjects to respond fluidly and opportunistically to changing political-economic conditions (Ong 1999). The internal logic of flexible citizenship, for our purposes, would show how the practices of nation-states competing in a global economy would effectively result in the fracturing and separation of "citizen" from "soldier," and would lead to a new regard for the labor of soldiers as that which ought to be treated like any ordinary commodity circulating in the free market.

For historical context, consider the post-WWII period, citizenship discourse intensified in the public domain in North America (Brodie 2008). The figure of the citizen-soldier, making up the first group of people to receive regular benefits, signified ideally proper conduct for all civilians (Burchell 2002). Within this discourse, the link between citizenship and soldiering was tightly woven together. The public called on the state to provide public education, an unprecedented social intervention justified by the idea of children as a pool of future citizens who would contribute to democracy and nation-building, and who were thus targets of moral regulation appropriate to potential future soldiers and wives of soldiers (Brodie 2008). The diverse social movements of the 1960s in North America and Western Europe witnessed the demilitarization of these benefits, and as such they were extended to increasingly more civilians. Yet, the concept of national duty always informed the discourse on social rights. A rights'-based discourse framed the parameters of the social contract as an exchange between state and citizen. A reciprocal give-and-take: national duty, in exchange for social entitlements (Cowen 2008).

In other words, the state has special claims on its citizens (claims to loyalty and potentially to military service) while the citizenry has special claims on the state (rights of entry and residence, rights to political participation, social, economic, or cultural rights, or claims to diplomatic protection abroad) (Brubaker 1992, 63). An analysis of the citizen-soldier as a working and laboring body, a body that required

Table 9.11: THOSE WHO OPERATE AND/OR OVERSEE AUTONOMOUS ROBOTS ARE NOT REAL "SOLDIERS."

		Frequency	Percent	Valid Percent	Cumulative Percent
Valid	True	289	28.9	35.9	35.9
	False	516	51.7	64.1	100.0
	Total	805	80.6	100.0	
Missing	System	194	19.4		
Total		999	100.0		

care and maintenance, was made possible in this context, and as such the citizen-soldier was the first body to receive these benefits. The citizen-soldier embodied the highest expression of sacrifice, and thus citizenship, and so served to signify proper conduct for civilians (Burchell 2002). Military labor, as it unfolded within the parameters of a (relatively) strong welfare state, therefore included an idea of mutual reciprocity that went beyond the domain of the military, and in fact, mediated civilian life in tandem.

The citizen-soldier, whose cost of survival is calculated in terms of the capacity and readiness to kill someone else—to impose death on others while preserving one's own life—reflects a logic of heroism as classically understood. Heroism can be theorized as the product of one's ability to execute others while holding on to one's own death at a distance, thus consolidating the moment of power and the moment of survival (Elias Canetti, cited in Mbembé 2003, 37). Autonomous systems, more broadly, are a key piece in supporting the desire to preserve Australian, American, and allied life at all costs. Although there is much to debate around post-heroic warfare and the changing character of risk as it relates to remote fighting (Chapa 2017; Enemark 2019; Lee 2012; Renic 2018) the notion of the military, as a beacon of heroic soldiering and an avenue for sacrificial forms of combat in the service of a nationalized notion of the collective, reflects an institutional association with the military. To that end, the majority of survey respondents challenge this notion of heroism in alignment with the occupational view, regarding those who operate or oversee autonomous systems as real soldiers, which is illustrated in Table 9.11.

However, while those who operate or oversee autonomous systems may still be considered proper soldiers, Table 9.12 shows that a vast majority report that robot-related military service does not warrant the same level of respect that traditional military service does.

To be sure, AS have transformed how cadets imagine combat. In the effacement of the familiar tropes associated with combat imagery—proximity, death, and reciprocal danger (Millar and Tidy 2017, 154), algorithmic warfare signals a departure from a notion of combat that is sustained by the model of the citizen-soldier, and its attendant notion of heroic masculinity. Drawing on Cara Daggett's notion of drone warfare, Millar and Tidy claim that drone operators "make visible the instability of the heroic soldier myth, which must be preserved and protected. But they also make visible the instability of legitimate martial violence" (2017, 156). Indeed, the instability of legitimate martial violence is acutely exposed in the content of drone combat, and in the labor practices of drone operators. In these highly bureaucratic labor practices (Asaro 2013), drone operators, for instance, bring into sharp

Table 9.12: ROBOT-RELATED MILITARY SERVICE DOES NOT COMMAND THE SAME RESPECT AS TRADITIONAL MILITARY SERVICE.

		Frequency	Percent	Valid Percent	Cumulative Percent
Valid	True	572	57.3	71.1	71.1
	False	233	23.3	28.9	100.0
	Total	805	80.6	100.0	
Missing	System	194	19.4		
Total		999	100.0		

relief the changing status of the citizen-soldier archetype when considered from the perspective of traditional soldiering identity.

Algorithmic warfare collapses time and space for operators, reorganizing the categories that order identity. Military labor blends with civilian life, as operators are to quickly transition from soldier/warrior to/from father/husband, for instance. This merging of formerly discrete categories—combat/war and the homeland—trouble how soldiers ought to negotiate these competing identities. The neoliberal demand for flexible forms of citizen-soldiering erodes space and time distinctions (such as the beginning and end of a workday) as it does for many types of labor specific to neoliberal capitalism. Yet, military actions are supposed to be exceptional in both time and space, or so citizens and soldiers have historically been guided to believe. The near-constant requirements of situation understanding, and the capabilities that AI-based technologies have to satisfy them, risks rendering deployment in a conflict zone more banal than exceptional.

Perhaps most importantly for the long-term development and meaning of the professional military, and the status of the citizen-soldier archetype therein, is the issue of moral character as being a learned, rather than innate, quality of citizen-soldier identity. As algorithmic technologies slowly encroach on human decision cycles, the need for the concurrent redevelopment of collectivized moral character to mitigate the potentially negative or disruptive effects of AI-based technologies on soldiers becomes even more pronounced. Further, moral virtue functions to keep war fighters morally continuous with society, and enables the expertise required to make sound judgments, which is critical where automation is applied to the life and death matters characteristic of the security and defense domains (Vallor 2013). Should AI-driven deskilling or reskilling harm morale or unit cohesion, the maintenance of moral skills in the form of active practicing of ethical decisions and ideas, could, in fact, serve as a pathway to mitigate against future potential technology-inspired breakdowns in force structure.

9.5: CONCLUSION

Despite the increasing reliance upon technological expertise in a professional military, empirical studies aimed at building knowledge of attitudes toward AS remain limited. In this groundbreaking survey, Australian cadets report a desire to remain in control of high-risk missions, rather than cede control to AS. That said, 70% of cadets surveyed believe that robots will eventually outnumber manned platforms, and that the number of Australian Defence Force (ADF) personnel will be limited as a result. This suggests cadets intuitively understand the potential for AS to disrupt traditional command and control architecture, combat practices, and military hierarchies. A significant majority perceived the air as the domain in which autonomous systems would be the most predominant means of conducting lethal attacks. This is not surprising, given the shift toward combat in the air domain more generally (Adey et al. 2013). Respondents demonstrate a willingness to engage with autonomous systems relevant to all combat domains, but under specific conditions, where clear pathways to positive career outcomes exist. Future studies concerned with military attitudes toward AS could focus on mid-level and senior officers, to show how the bidirectional nature of values and technologies inform the ideas and concerns of experienced personnel.

A further 65% of cadets reported that those who oversee or operate AS should qualify as real soldiers. This suggests some degree of acceptance of AS, as well as the technical expertise required to effectively deploy them, as fundamental to soldiering today. However, 70% agreed that robot-related service does not command the level of respect that traditional military service warrants. This implies almost a reluctant acceptance of the impact of technological innovation. Respondents accept the inevitably of AS, while still acknowledging a qualitative difference between traditional ("heroic") and new ("unheroic") forms of combat. AS changes what soldiers' labor looks like, but the idea still holds that the purest form of soldering involves a personal risk of injury or sacrificial death in service of others. Significantly, respondents suggest an interest in concrete material gains: financial reward, secure career paths, and opportunities for career progression. Cadets are less motivated by status, signaled by traditional forms of recognition, such as medals.

In summary, Australian cadets are open to working with and alongside AS, but under the right conditions. Cadets are not overly concerned about the status of their robot-related labor but want to know that opportunities for career stability and upward mobility are available. This is perhaps to be expected, as these cadets know nothing but the professional, casualty-averse military, and have come of age in a time when advanced technology has pervaded nearly every aspect of their daily life. Armed forces, in an attempt to capitalize on these technologically savvy cadets, have shifted from institutional to occupational employers. The military is now focused on efficiency of outcomes, being information, technology, and capital intensive. In this vein, governmentality reasoning, as applied in the military domain, reproduces both a market logic and flexible citizen-soldiers, who are empowered to mobilize calculative responses in and out of the battlefield.

Yet, AI-based technologies can minimize the social, political, ethical, and financial burdens of employing (and caring for) vulnerable human capital. Absent the sociopolitical model of soldier-citizenship, and its attendant rights-based social contract, the moral impetus that has historically justified legitimate warfare is eclipsed. Australian cadets are aware of such transformations in the character of warfare, and the changing meaning of their labor practices therein. What is less clear, however, is the impact of algorithmic warfare on the ability of these cadets to cultivate the loyalty, moral skills, and internalized motivation necessary to maintain the status of the military in its current form.

To this end, the data points to several tentative conclusions and pathways for future research. What is most striking for our purposes here is the cultivation of the occupational mindset of cadets. This is not a new claim, as we have already shown compelling arguments to this end, although some readers may remain skeptical and hesitate to accept this occupational mindset as gospel. However, granting the reality of the occupational mindset, what is new is this: AS have the potential to exacerbate some of the risks wrought by the occupational military, problematizing how militaries can satisfy the increasing demands for technological innovation, austerity, and the maintenance of Australia's small joint force, with the simultaneous need to continue to signify to the public, other states, and itself, that its place and importance is necessary and timeless.

When, for instance, Australian or allied soldiers are harmed in battle, this is of course, not a desirable outcome. However, these injuries, although we would like to avoid them, have a *semiotic function* in that, as events that stabilize key narratives upon which the military justifies its existence, they offer assurances of purpose, continuity of meaning, and credibility: "soldier X died for her country so that I could be safe and enjoy the liberties offered to me through my citizenship and/or nationality" or "soldier Y was injured doing something essential and imperative; of humanitarian, diplomatic, and/or international significance." Given that AS have the potential to undermine or outright eclipse the sacrificial heroism we generally ascribe to warfare, and the activities more broadly that the military engages, a natural consequence may be that, over time, the public, and therefore future potential recruits, may call into question the meaning of the military, more specifically, its purpose and necessity.

Put differently, this occupational mindset, which we argue is emboldened by both AS and the professionalization of the military, must be kept in check should the identity and meaning of the military remain consistent with the public's expectations of what a military does, and ought to do. Since AS will work, over time, to eclipse the sacrificial and heroic encounters and attendant narratives that guide the foundational identity of the modern military, for national policy to protect the "sacredness" of the military (should this be a goal), it must, first, actively cultivate moral and ethical training of soldiers by conducting frequent, tailored, and realistic simulations of ethical dilemmas that apply to a highly technological operational context where AS will play a critical role in Australia's ability to maintain decision superiority. We may even take this a step further and suggest that moral, ethical, and cultural training pertinent to virtuous soldiering must be not just *prioritized* but *intensified* to keep ahead of autonomous technology's ability to erode the qualities that have been historically associated with good soldiering. Second, since the military must not only attract AI-educated personnel with the skills required to maintain and operate AS, but also retain skilled personnel in the face of growing global competition, policy development in this area ought to further examine how best to do this, while also rejuvenating important aspects of the institutional mindset, as a means to maintain the distinct social and political qualities characteristic of the contemporary Australian military.

ACKNOWLEDGMENT

The research for this paper received funding from the Australian Government through the Defence Cooperative Research Centre for Trusted Autonomous Systems. It also benefitted from the earlier support of the Spitfire Foundation. Ethical clearance originally provided by the Departments of Defence and Veterans

Affairs Human Research Ethics Committee. The views of the authors do not necessarily represent those of any other party.

NOTES

1. This research has been supported by the Trusted Autonomous Systems Defence Cooperative Research Centre.
2. As Stuart Hall (2011, 708) claims, neoliberal capitalist ideals come from the principles of 'classic' liberal economic and political theory: over the course of two centuries, "political ideas of 'liberty' became harnessed to economic ideas of the free market: one of liberalism's fault-lines which re-emerges within neoliberalism" (Hall 2011, 710). When referring to liberalism and neoliberalism, one does not involve a complete rejection of the practices of the other. In fact, "neoliberalism . . . evolves. It borrows and approximates extensively from classical liberal ideas; but each is given a further 'market' inflexion and conceptual revamp . . . neoliberalism performs a massive work of trans-coding while remaining in sight of the lexicon on which it draws" (Hall 2011, 711). We use "neoliberalism" to refer to the globalized and marketized *amplification of tensions* contained in classical liberalism. The amplification of these tensions on a global scale are reflected in the economic crisis characteristic of the post-Cold War period, where neoliberalism is primarily defined through a language of marketization, while not forgetting the "lexicon on which it draws," that is, the spirit of classical liberalism and its emphasis on equality, dignity, and rights for all. In line with neoliberalism's privileging of the unfettered market, security in this context is transformed from a public good into a commodity, packaged as a private service, delivered by private enterprise (Avant 2005).
3. Briefly, a governmentality approach is inspired by the writings of Michel Foucault. It traces the techniques of power that extend beyond the juridical functions of the state to penetrate the minds and hearts of those who are governed, thus shaping their conduct (Brock 2019, 6). As an approach to power, governmentality relies on the interchange between power and knowledge in a dynamic and mutually constitutive relation that shapes what can be known and how we can know it (Brock 2019, 6).
4. Sovereign power is a repressive, spectacular, and prohibitive form of power. Foucault claims that sovereignty was a central form of power prior to the modern era, is associated with the state, and is articulated in terms of law. Its preeminent form of expression is the execution of wrongdoers. Sovereignty is a main component of the liberal normative political project, which values autonomy and the achievement of agreement among a collectivity through communication and recognition. In contrast to sovereign power, biopolitical power is a productive power as far as it is aimed at cultivating positive effects. It is a subtler form of power that aims to enhance life by fixing on the management and administration of life via the health and well-being of the population.
5. Respondents were asked to rank incentives from least tempting to most tempting. Aside from financial incentives (increased salary and lump sum payments), other incentives included increased rank, enhanced opportunities for promotion and command, the availability of medals for robot service/combat, a more secure path/longer commission, reduced period of service, guaranteed opportunities to

transition to other categories of employment, and formal recognition of relevant training.

6. As McFarland et al. (forthcoming) show, the recruitment and retention challenges faced by the Royal Australian Navy (RAN) reflect the struggles of many other modern military forces. "The RAN is planning for the introduction of new platforms with new combat capabilities that feature significant advancements in technology with increased levels of complexity that will require increased levels of technical skills and competence" (Barb 2008). It is perhaps significant that, as well as presenting a recruitment challenge to armed forces, AI is sometimes also thought to alleviate the effects of a broader recruitment challenge. Given the difficulties of ensuring sufficient personnel quotas, the possibility of smaller crew sizes is one motivating factor in automation of combat systems.
7. That a flexible, agile, and lean military unit, coupled with unmanned systems is a pillar of the future orientation toward counterinsurgency and counterterrorism is unapologetically clear. Aside from the mildly ambiguous statement about the economic landscape informing the future of defense strategy, which for Panetta, necessitates a reduction in overall budget, it also produces an increase in investment. Technological capabilities will see greater investment, but investments in troop mobilization will be reduced.
8. This value reflects one respondent who created their own category of "maybe" in response to what was originally a yes or no question.

WORKS CITED

Abrahamsen, Rita and Michael J. Williams. 2009. "Security Beyond the State: Global Security Assemblages in International Politics." *International Political Sociology* 3 (1): pp. 1–17.

Adamsky, Dima. 2010. *The Culture of Military Innovation*. Stanford, CA: Stanford University Press.

Adey, Peter, Mark Whitehead, and Alison J. Williams. 2013. *From Above: War, Violence and Verticality*. Oxford: Oxford University Press.

Alexandra, Andrew, Deane-Peter Baker, and Marina Caparini (eds.). (2008). *Private Military and Security Companies: Ethics, Policies and Civil-Military Relations*. New York: Routledge.

Asad, Talal. 2007. *On Suicide Bombing*. New York: Columbia University Press.

Asaro, Peter M. 2013. "The Labor of Surveillance and Bureaucratized Killing: New Subjectivities of Military Drone Operators." *Social Semiotics* 23 (2): pp. 196–224.

Australian Army. 2017. *Land Warfare Doctrine*. Canberra.

Australian Army. 2018. *Robotic and Autonomous Systems Strategy*. Canberra: Future Land Warfare Branch, Australian Army.

Australian Department of Defence. 2016. *Defence White Paper*.

Avant, Deborah D. 2005. *The Market for Force: The Consequences of Privatizing Security*. New York: Cambridge University Press.

Avant, Deborah D. and Lee Sigelman. 2010. "Private Security and Democracy: Lessons From the Iraq." *Security Studies* 19 (2): pp. 230–265.

Baggiarini, Bianca. 2014. "Re-Making Soldier-Citizens: Military Privatization and the Biopolitics of Sacrifice." *St. Anthony's International Review* 9 (2): pp. 9–23.

Baggiarini, Bianca. 2015. "Military Privatization and the Gendered Politics of Sacrifice." In *Gender and Private Security in World Politics*, edited by Maya Eichler, pp. 37–54. Oxford: Oxford University Press.

Balint, Peter, and Ned Dobos. 2015. "Perpetuating the Military Myth–Why the Psychology of the 2014 Australian Defence Pay Deal Is Irrelevant." *Australian Journal of Public Administration* 74 (3): pp. 359–363.

Barb, Robert. 2008. "New Generation Navy: Personnel and Training—The Way Forward." *Australian Maritime Issues* 27 (SPC-A Annual): pp. 59–92.

Brock, Deborah R. 2019. *Governing the Social in Neoliberal Times*. Vancouver: UBC Press.

Brodie, Janine. 2008. "The Social in Social Citizenship." In *Recasting the Social in Citizenship*, edited by Engin F. Isin, pp. 20–44. Toronto: University of Toronto Press.

Brubaker, Rogers. 1992. *Citizenship and Nationhood in France and Germany*. Cambridge, MA: Harvard University Press.

Burchell, David. 2002. "Ancient Citizenship and Its Inheritors." In *Handbook of Citizenship Studies*, edited by Bryan S. Turner and Engin F. Isin, pp. 84–104. London: SAGE.

Chapa, Joseph O. 2017. "Remotely Piloted Aircraft, Risk, and Killing as Sacrifice: The Cost of Remote Warfare." *Journal of Military Ethics* 16 (3–4): pp. 256–271.

Cowen, Deborah. 2008. *Military Workfare: The Soldier and Social Citizenship in Canada*. Toronto: University of Toronto Press.

Dagger, Richard 2002. "Republican Citizenship." In *Handbook of Citizenship Studies*, edited by Bryan S. Turner and Engin F. Isin, pp. 145–158. London: SAGE.

Davis, Steven Edward. 2019. "Individual Differences in Operators' Trust in Autonomous Systems: A Review of the Literature." *Joint and Operations Analysis Division Defence Science and Technology Group*. Edinburgh: SA.

Dean, Mitchell. 1999. *Governmentality: Power and Rule in Modern Society*. Thousand Oaks, CA: SAGE.

Department of Defense. 2012. "Sustaining U.S. Global Leadership: Priorities for 21st Century Defense." *Defense Strategic Guidance*. Virginia: United States Department of Defense.

Dillon, Michael and Julian Reid. 2000. "Global Liberal Governance: Biopolitics, Security and War." *Millennium: Journal of International Studies* 30 (1): pp. 41–66.

Eichler, Maya. 2015. *Gender and Private Security in Global Politics*. Oxford: Oxford University Press.

Enemark, Christian. 2019. "Drones, Risk, and Moral Injury." *Critical Military Studies* 5 (2): pp. 150–167.

Foucault, Michel. 1991. "Governmentality." In *The Foucault Effect: Studies in Governmentality*, edited by Graham Burchell, Colin Gordon, and Peter Miller, pp. 87–104. Chicago: University of Chicago Press.

Galliott, Jai. 2016. *Military Robots: Mapping the Moral Landscape*. London: Routledge.

Galliott, Jai. 2017. "The Limits of Robotic Solutions to Human Challenges in the Land Domain." *Defence Studies* 17 (4): pp. 327–345.

Galliott, Jai. 2018. "The Soldier's Tolerance for Autonomous Systems." *Paladyn* 9 (1): pp. 124–136.

Graham, Stephen. 2008. "Imagining Urban Warfare." In *War, Citizenship, Territory*, edited by Deborah Cowen and Emily Gilbert, pp. 33–57. New York: Routledge.

Jabri, Vivienne. 2006. "War, Security, and the Liberal State." *Security Dialogue* 37 (1): pp. 47–64.

Jaume-Palasi, Lorena. 2019. "Why We Are Failing to Understand the Societal Impact of Artificial Intelligence." *Social Research: An International Quarterly* 86 (2): pp. 477–498.

Jevglevskaja, Natalia and Jai Galliott. 2019. "Airmen and Unmanned Aerial Vehicles." *The Air Force Journal of Indo-Pacific Affairs* 2 (3): pp. 33–65.

Lee, Peter. 2012. "Remoteness, Risk, and Aircrew Ethos." *Air Power Review* 15 (1): pp. 1–20.

Lutz, Catherine. 2002. "Making War at Home in the United States: Militarization and the Current Crisis." *American Anthropologist* 104 (3): pp. 723–773.

Mandel, Robert. 2004. *Security, Strategy, and the Quest for Bloodless War.* Boulder, CO: Lynne Rienner Publishers.

Manigart, Philippe. 2006. "Restructuring the Armed Forces." In *Handbook of the Sociology of the Military,* edited by Giuseppe Caforio and Marina Nuciari, pp. 323–343. New York: Springer.

Mbembé, Achille. 2003. "Necropolitics." Translated by Libby Meintjes. *Public Culture* 15 (1): pp. 11–40.

Millar, Katharine M. and Joanna Tidy. 2017. "Combat as a Moving Target: Masculinities, the Heroic Soldier Myth, and Normative Martial Violence." *Critical Military Studies* 3 (2): pp. 142–160.

Mills, C. Wright. 1959. *The Sociological Imagination.* New York: Oxford University Press.

Moskos, Charles C. 2000. "Toward a Postmodern Military: The United States as a Paradigm." In *The Postmodern Military,* edited by Charles C. Moskos, John Allen Williams, and David R. Segal, pp. 14–31. Oxford: Oxford University Press.

Moskos, Charles C., John Allen Williams, and David R. Segal (eds). 2000. *The Postmodern Military.* Oxford: Oxford University Press.

Muir, Bonnie. 1987. "Trust between Humans and Machines, and the Design of Decision Aids." *International Journal of Man-Machine Studies* 27(5–6): pp. 527–539.

Ong, Aihwa. 1999. *Flexible Citizenship: The Cultural Logics of Transnationality.* Durham, NC: Duke University Press.

Parenti, Christian. 2007. "Planet America: The Revolution in Military Affairs as Fantasy and Fetish." In *Exceptional State: Contemporary U.S. Culture and the New Imperialism,* edited by Ashley Dawson and Malini Johar Schueller, pp. 88–105. Durham, NC: Duke University Press.

Reid, Julian. 2006. *The Biopolitics of the War on Terror: Life Struggles, Liberal Modernity, and the Defence of Logistical Societies.* Manchester: Manchester University Press.

Renic, Neil C. 2018. "UAVs and the End of Heroism? Historicising the Ethical Challenge of Asymmetric Violence." *Journal of Military Ethics* 17 (4): pp. 188–197.

Roff, Heather and David Danks. 2018. "Trust but Verify: The Difficulty of Trusting Autonomous Weapons Systems." *Journal of Military Ethics* 17 (1): pp. 2–20.

Rose, Nikolas. 1999. *Powers of Freedom: Reframing Political Thought.* New York: Cambridge University Press.

Rosenblat, Alex. 2018. *Uberland: How Algorithms Are Rewriting the Rules of Work.* Oakland: University of California Press.

Sauer, Frank and Niklas Schörnig. 2012. "Killer Drones: The 'Silver Bullet' of Democratic Warfare?" *Security Dialogue* 43 (3): pp. 363–380.

Shimko, Keith L. 2010. *The Iraq Wars and America's Military Revolution.* Cambridge: Cambridge University Press.

Singer, Peter. 2005. "Outsourcing War." *Foreign Affairs* 84 (2): pp. 119–133.

US Government. 2014. *Unmanned Systems Integrated Roadmap FY2013–2038*. http://www.dtic.mil/dtic/tr/fulltext/u2/a592015.pdf.

Vallor, Shannon. 2013. The Future of Military Virtue: Autonomous Systems and the Moral Deskilling of the Military. In 2013 5th International Conference on Cyber Conflict. pp. 1–15.

Voas, David. 2014. "Towards a Sociology of Attitudes." *Sociological Research Online*. 19 (1): pp. 132–144.

Wedel, Janine R. 2008. "The Shadow Army: Privatization." In *Lessons from Iraq: Avoiding the Next war*, edited by Miriam Pemberton and William D. Hartung, pp. 116–124. Boulder, CO: Paradigm Publishers.

Wong, Leonard. 2006. "Combat Motivation in Today's Soldiers: US Army War College Strategic Studies Institute." *Armed Forces and Society* 32 (4): pp. 659–663.

Woodward, Rachel. 2008. "Not for Queen or Country or Any of That Shit . . . Reflections on Citizenship and Military Participation in Contemporary British Soldier Narratives." In *War, Citizenship, Territory*, edited by Deborah Cowen and Emily Gilbert, pp. 363–385. New York: Routledge.

10

The Automation of Authority: Discrepancies with *Jus Ad Bellum* Principles

DONOVAN PHILLIPS

10.1: INTRODUCTION

The changing nature of warfare presents unanswered questions about the legal and moral implications of the use of new technologies in the theater of war. International humanitarian law (IHL) establishes that the rights warring parties have in choosing the means and methods of warfare are not unlimited, and that there is a legal obligation for states to consider how advancements in weapons technologies will affect current and future conflicts[1]—specifically, they are required to consider if such advancements will be compatible with IHL. The character of technological advancement makes applying legal precedent difficult and, in many cases, it is unclear as to whether existing practices are sufficient to govern the scenarios in which new weapons will be implemented.[2] As this present volume is testament to, the development and use of lethal autonomous weapons systems (AWS) in particular is a current hotbed for these kinds of considerations.

Much attention has been paid to the question of whether or not AWS are capable of abiding by the *jus in bello* tenets of IHL: distinctness, necessity, and proportionality. The worry here is whether such systems can play by the rules, so to speak, once hostilities have commenced, in order that those who are not morally liable to harm come to none. Less attention has been paid to the question of whether the engagement of hostilities by AWS is in accord with the principles of *jus ad bellum*.[3] That is, whether the independent engagement in armed conflict by AWS without any human oversight can satisfy the requirements currently placed on the commencement of

Donovan Phillips, *The Automation of Authority: Discrepancies with* Jus Ad Bellum *Principles* In: *Lethal Autonomous Weapons*. Edited by: Jai Galliott, Duncan MacIntosh and Jens David Ohlin, © Oxford University Press (2021).
DOI: 10.1093/oso/9780197546048.003.0011

just conflicts: just cause, right intent, proper or legitimate authority, last resort, probability of success, and proportionality. The distinction is important. *In bello* considerations for AWS pertain to the practical implementation of humanitarian law within the circuitry of actual weapons systems, focusing on whether it is possible to program AWS such that they are capable of reliably abiding by the rules of warfare during engagements. *Ad bellum* considerations for AWS are one step removed from the battlefield, and, I take it, concern the conceptual tensions that AWS may have with IHL. Relinquishing the decision to engage in warfare to AWS, no matter how sophisticated, may, in principle conflict with the legal and ethical framework that currently governs the determination of just conflict.

In this chapter, I will consider how the adoption of AWS may affect *ad bellum* principles. In particular, I will focus on the use of AWS in non-international armed conflicts (NIAC). Given the proliferation of NIAC, the development and use of AWS will most likely be attuned, at least in part, to this specific theater of war. As warfare waged by modernized liberal democracies (those most likely to develop and employ AWS at present) increasingly moves toward a model of occupation and policing, which relies on targeted, individualized kill or capture objectives, how, if at all, will the principles by which we measure the justness of the commencement of such hostilities be affected by the introduction of AWS, and how will such hostilities stack up to current legal agreements[4] surrounding more traditional forms of engagement?

I will first detail Heather M. Roff's argument (2015) against the permissibility of using AWS to fight a defensive war based on the violation of the *ad bellum* principle of proportionality. However, contra Roff, I provide reasons that show why the use of AWS is not particularly problematic as far as proportionality is concerned. That being so, proportionality considerations give us no reason to think that the use of AWS cannot abide by IHL. Following that, I will present the emergent shift in the structure of modern warfare and consider how AWS might play a role in this new paradigm. In the final section I claim that, while arguments against AWS that stem from proportionality are unconvincing, it is unclear that the engagement of hostilities by AWS can conform to the *ad bellum* principle of proper authority.

Prima facie, there seems to be a tension between this principle of just war and the use of AWS. The proper authority requirement puts the decision to enter into a state of war within the purview of societies, states, or, more generally, political organizations.[5] However, when there is no human or association of humans (e.g., a legitimate government) involved in the decision-making processes of AWS, no human in the loop, the allocation of responsibility for the actions of those systems is uncertain. Consequently, I want to consider what implications the automation of authority has for IHL. If the current legal framework we have for determining just conflicts is violated, and yet nation-states still insist on developing and deploying AWS, as it seems they intend to do, then we must reconsider the principles that inform IHL so as to develop reasonable policies that ensure, or in any case make more likely, that AWS are employed within parameters that justice requires.

10.2: AWS AND *JUS AD BELLUM* PROPORTIONALITY

Roff claims that even in the clearest case "of a defensive war, we cannot satisfy the ad bellum principle of proportionality if we knowingly plan to use lethal autonomous systems during hostilities because of the likely effects on war termination and the achievement of one's just causes" (Roff 2015).[6] Her argument draws on Thomas Hurka's conception of the *jus ad bellum* principle of proportionality and what this principle requires of those who decide when and how to engage in armed conflict. According to Hurka, *ad bellum* proportionality conditions "say that a war . . . is wrong if the relevant harm it will cause is out of proportion to its relevant good" (Hurka 2005). Which is to say that, in deciding if going to war would be just or not, one must determine whether or not the resultant harms will be outweighed by the good that will come of waging it. Further, there are limits on *ad bellum* relevant goods. For example, if a war were to lift some state's economy out of economic depression, this good does not give that state the right to pursue military action even if it could be shown that the resultant economic upturn outweighed the evils done in the war. Conversely, there are no restrictions to the content of the evils relevant to proportionality: "that a war will boost the world's economy does not count in its favor, but that it will harm the economy surely counts against it" (Hurka 2005).

Roff takes Hurka's conception of *ad bellum* proportionality and carries it into the realm of AWS, specifically for when AWS are deployed as part of defensive use of force. Roff considers

> a case in which an unjust aggressor (State A) intentionally and without justification threatens the central rights of another state (State D), namely the rights of territorial integrity and/or state sovereignty. Under a forfeiture theory of self-defense State A loses its right not to be harmed by threatening an imminent violation [of] State D's rights. State D may inflict harm on State A to thwart an attack against it and to potentially restore State D's rights. The harm inflicted on State A must be necessary and proportionate. As noted above, only those benefits related to the just cause of defense will count in an *ad bellum* proportionality calculation, but *all* foreseen harms are included. (Roff 2015)

In response to such a threat, State D might consider using AWS as the first line of defense in efforts to check the aggression of State A. However, says Roff, the usual justification for retaliation to the threat presented by State A, that harm is imminent with respect to either state or citizen or both, is mitigated in the use of AWS. If the initial entities exposed to harm will be technologies that are not susceptible to lethal force (because they are not living), then the justification for retaliation is not accounted for. The worry is that it is incoherent to say that mechanized tools of warfare can be the bearers of harm in the same way that the living citizens of a nation can. The resultant harm from State A's aggression in this scenario amounts to little more than property damage and it is neither legal nor moral to respond to such damage with lethal force. And so, when a threat is initially brought against AWS, retaliation is not justified. However, I think we should find this initial foray unconvincing. The argument only shows that State D's proportionality calculation will include protecting its territorial integrity as the primary relevant good against which proportionality ought to be calculated. This ought then to be weighed against the foreseen harms of pursuing war with State A.

Roff anticipates this reply and is ready with one of her own: when pursued with AWS, such a war cannot meet the demands required by *ad bellum* proportionality because the calculations (including the relevant good of territorial integrity) are only satisfied when one round of hostilities is assumed. Roff says that, if we properly factor in the effect that pursuing war with AWS will have on subsequent rounds of hostilities, with an eye toward resolution of the conflict and restoration of peace and security, we will see that the goods produced by using AWS will be outweighed by the created harms.[7] This is for two reasons: (a) "the use of AWS will adversely affect the likelihood of peaceful settlement and the probability of achieving one's just causes . . . [and (b)] the use of AWS in conflict would breed a system wide AWS arms race" (Roff 2015). Regarding (a), Roff insists that AWS will inevitably lead to increased animosity by the belligerents who do not possess them, which in turn will lead to further conflict instead of resolution. For example, the US' employment of unmanned aerial vehicles (UAV, or drones) in Iraq, Pakistan, and Yemen suggests that even the use of these merely automated (rather than autonomous) weapons "breed[s] more animosity and acts as a recruiting strategy for terrorist organizations, thereby frustrating the U.S.'s goals" (Roff 2015). Given this, it seems likely that the use of AWS—fully autonomous systems—could make the situation even more caustic. Regarding (b), Roff argues that since, as per Hurka, we must consider all the negative outcomes from our pursuing war, we must consider the effect using AWS will have on the international community at large. For instance, other nations may decide it necessary to similarly arm themselves. The result "may actually tend to increase the use of violent means rather than minimize them. Autonomous war is thus more likely to occur as it becomes easier to execute" (Roff 2015).

I am sympathetic to the motivation behind these objections to the use of AWS. *Ad bellum* proportionality certainly requires that we take the long view and eschew short-sighted assessments when deciding if and how one goes to war. However, neither of these are particularly good reasons for thinking that the use of AWS cannot satisfy the requirements of *ad bellum* proportionality. Firstly contra (b), as Duncan MacIntosh argues, the proclivity to go to war if it becomes costless in terms of human sacrifice will not simply be due to the availability of AWS. Instead, this would owe to "not visualizing the consequences of actions, [or] lacking policy constraints" (MacIntosh, Unpublished (b), 13). If a state's first response to any and all aggression is deadly force (by AWS or otherwise), then, of course, there will be unnecessary conflict. But no one is suggesting that AWS be developed as a blanket solution to conflict, just as no one, to my knowledge, suggested that the development of firearms meant that they should be seen as the panacea for all disputes. *A fortiori*, since Roff appeals to Hurka's *ad bellum* principles, we may also do so, noting the so-called "last resort" condition for *jus ad bellum*. This condition states that "if the just causes can be achieved by less violent means such as diplomacy, fighting is wrong" (Hurka 2005). If states adhere at all to *ad bellum* principles when developing AWS, then we need not fear that the frequency of war would increase simply because it is easier to wage it, for there are other avenues to securing one's just causes, and ones which an impartial AI-governed AWS may be more likely to note and pursue than humans. Indeed, this condition might conceivably be so fundamental to the proportionality calculations of AWS that AWS *rarely* commence or engage in hostilities.

Roff might respond in the following manner: This not only shows that there will be more war, but worse, these wars will likely be unjust. States will simply ignore the last resort condition. But again, I think we have a convincing response to her worry. Given that the states who have the capabilities to develop and deploy such systems are those that have large stable democracies, which are not (at least in writing) committed to a state of unjust war, abuses will most likely be minimized due to abundant oversight. The bureaucracy surrounding AWS is going to be immense, which will help to safeguard against their rash use.[8] If the proliferation of AWS is really not such a negative thing after all, then counting it as a relevant evil to our proportionality calculation is an erroneous attribution.

Regarding (a), Roff says that "the means by which a state wages war—that is, the weapons and strategies it uses to prosecute (and end) its war—directly affect the proportionality calculations it makes when deciding to go to war" (Roff 2015). This is surely correct. If the means by which one wages war make achieving one's just cause more difficult, or impossible, to attain, then there is reason not to pursue war in such fashion. MacIntosh makes a similar point, saying that "part of successful warring is not attracting others to fight against you, so you must fight by rules that won't be found outrageous" (MacIntosh, Unpublished (b), 6). However, if one's cause is truly just, and if the resort to armed conflict deemed necessary, then one need not put so much stock in the opinions of one's opponent. Justice does not require that the wrongful party to conflict be immediately appeased in the conflict's resolution.

Although AWS may engender further animosity among those against which they are used, this is equally true when war is fought with any asymmetry whatsoever. Imbalances in numbers, favorable field position, strategy and tactics, as well as technology, all may induce resentment in the less well-equipped or prepared party to a conflict. This is a practical necessity of military action "more rooted in the sociology of conflict than in justice" (MacIntosh, Unpublished (b), 6). Further, given that the kinds of conflicts that are becoming most prevalent are non-international armed conflicts in which the belligerent parties are nonstate actors fighting in opposition to governmental militaries (of the home state but also often in conjunction with a foreign state military, e.g., Libya, Afghanistan, Syria), asymmetry is a baked-in characteristic of most modern wars. The imbalance of power in such conflicts is already often so wildly disproportionate that the addition of AWS by those who can develop them might not elevate the animus experienced by the sore party to hostilities. Adopting AWS might allow militaries to more effectively attain the just ends of war, while minimizing the risk to human life, without significantly raising the level of hatred the enemy has for them in virtue of their being engaged in the first place.

10.3: THE CHARACTER OF MODERN WARFARE

Prior asymmetries in conflict ought to be taken into consideration when the alteration of the means of warfare is on the table. With that in mind, I'll now entertain a brief digression on the character of the kinds of conflict that the entities most likely to develop AWS often find themselves engaged in. Understanding the operations that contemporary military action requires will better inform the discussion of whether AWS can plausibly play the role which a manned military currently does.

It is notable that international armed conflicts have been on the decline, at least in the modernized West. This is due in part to relative economic stability over the past half-century, distaste developed by Western societies for large scale warfare post-WWI and WWII, and the codification of IHL through charters and treaties. But this is certainly not to say that war has become an absent pursuit of Western nations; only rather to highlight that, especially since the turn of the century, the predominant mode of warfare is now non-international armed conflict. As Glenn J. Voelz notes, there is a "new mode of state warfare based on military power being applied directly to individual combatants" (2015); Gabriella Blum calls this "the individualization of war" (2013). The advent of individualized warfare can be seen as a result of "specific policy preferences and strategic choices in response to the threats posed by non-state actors" (Voelz 2015). Instead of fighting well-established militaries of other nation-states, the states of the West most often find themselves embroiled in battle against smaller, less cohesive armed groups. Even "individuals and groups of individuals are . . . capable of dealing physical blows on a magnitude previously reserved for regular armies" (Blum 2013) and, consequently, engagement with these individuals is necessary to prevent or minimize the harm they would seek to cause.

Nonstate military groups, or the individuals that comprise them, are often more disperse and less identifiable by conventional means, such as uniforms. Indeed, part of the relative success of such groups stems from anonymity. One of the main challenges in fighting against insurgencies is often simply identifying the enemy. This, in turn, leads to increased difficulty in respecting the *in bello* distinction between enemy combatants and civilians. To cope with these complications, state militaries battling insurgent or terrorist foes increasingly rely on intelligence gathering practices in order to clear this specific fog of war: "operational targeting has not only become individualized, but also *personalized* through the integration of identity functions" (Voelz 2015). The collection of data pertaining to "pattern of life" analysis (movement, association, family relations, financial transactions, and even biometric data) through surveillance allows militaries to "put a uniform on the enemy." Staggeringly, in Afghanistan between "2004 and 2011, US forces collected biometric data on more than 1.1 million individuals—equivalent to roughly one of six fighting age males" (Voelz 2015).

These practices characterize a split with former methods of warfare, where what made one liable to attack was membership in a state's armed forces. Now, we increasingly see that "targeting packages have more in common with police arrest warrants than with conventional targeting [practices]" (Voelz 2015). What makes one liable to incapacitation in modern NIAC are one's personal actions, "rather than [one's] affiliation or association" (Blum 2013). Furthermore, these targeting practices may apply outside of the active theater of war. As in the case of the war on terror, we see a " 'patient and relentless man-hunting campaign' waged by the US military against [individual] non-state actors" (Voelz 2015). This manhunt "extends beyond any active battlefield and follows Al Qaeda members and supporters wherever they are" (Blum 2013).

The picture that emerges is a stark one in which states engage in NIAC by occupying territory, mass surveillance, and "quasi-adjudicative judgments based on highly specific facts about the alleged actions of particular individuals" (Issacharoff and Pildes 2013). More often than not, force is brought to bear against these individuals via sophisticated drone strikes. The use of UAVs to surveil, target, and engage specific enemy combatants wherever they may be is now one of the most prevalent methods of, at least, the US military. It is estimated that "over 98% of non-battlefield targeted killings over the last decade have been conducted by [drones]" (Voelz 2015). In fact, the development of UAVs grew directly alongside the individualization of warfare, and their use is an expression of personalized targeting in its most pure form.

10.4: AWS IN AN IDEAL NON-INTERNATIONAL ARMED CONFLICT

While the use of drones in NIAC presents both advantages as well as concerns, the technology itself still requires human operation. There is always a human soldier who controls the action of a UAV, and consequently, those human operators, or the nations that they represent, retain responsibility for the actions that drones carry out. The targeting itself may be computer-aided but the decision of whom to target and when is still carried out by a human chain of command. UAVs are currently inert absent the will of the humans behind them. This would not be so in the case of AWS.

The appropriate question to ask is then: What might the implementation of a fire-and-forget weapon like an AWS actually look like in an NIAC? The very idea of mechanized or automated processes in war is not an entirely unfamiliar one. Many of the techniques that are integral to individualized warfare would be impossible without computerized data analysis simply because of the amount of data that informs them (Voelz 2015). Analysis, however, is not decision-making, and the goal of implementing AWS as difference makers in live combat will require that they be able to take on functions far beyond those of mere correlation and aggregation of data. There will be real-world consequences in allowing weapons systems to operate autonomously.

Recall (fn. 6) the second kind of deployment (B) for AWS, where, in a time of peace, or in a time where we know there are nonstate groups that mean to do our nation harm, but with whom we are not currently engaged, we have already deployed our AWS and there is no human on the loop. Suppose we have some component of the system devoted to monitoring the potential threats posed to our nation by nonstate actors around the world, and some other component that is the actionable part of the system capable of dealing with said threats once they arise. One day the intelligence gathering unit of this system puts together x, y, and z pieces of information and determines that there is an imminent threat that crosses some threshold of acceptable credibility.[9] (And a good thing too, because no human could have possibly waded through all that data.) Further, suppose that the threat is real, and, it is determined by the system, the threat cannot be dealt with diplomatically by the human-run government, this meaning that the principle of *ad bellum* last resort is respected. As a consequence, the AWS springs to action in order to neutralize the threat before harm can be done to innocent persons. Perhaps the system notifies that part of the military still run by humans so that they can tell the relevant authorities that the system has engaged enemy combatants, but they may not have time to respond given that AWS work very quickly out of necessity, and in any case, they would not be able to effectively change the course of the AWS because, after all, it is autonomous.

Now, the machines arrive on scene with access to all the relevant information needed regarding who is liable to harm and, respecting the rules of *jus in bello*, determine who is a civilian, who it is necessary to capture, who, if anyone at all, it is necessary to kill and at what cost each individual target should be pursued for either kill or capture. The machines execute the plan to the best possible outcome as initially determined, minimizing civilian casualties while ensuring all real threats are neutralized and peace and security can be maintained.

In the aftermath the rest of the military catches up, more data is gathered, prisoners are taken or handed over to the relevant authorities, and a localized (temporary?) occupation is established so that subsequent threats might be dealt with more effectively and with less bloodshed. Such a scenario is highly unlikely to play out so picturesquely, yet we ought to evaluate the best case the proponent of AWS has to see if, in principle, there is anything amiss. And this does seem to be the ideal case for AWS. This conflict risked no loss of life on the side using AWS, either civilian or combatant, and the AWS were able to neutralize an imminent threat to peace and security in the least costly and most efficient way.

10.5: AWS AND *JUS AD BELLUM* PROPER AUTHORITY

However, given this ideal scenario, one question is immediately pressing: Who went to war here? If the governing body of the nation who initializes an AWS is in the dark with respect to its moment to moment operations, then when the AWS engages in armed conflict, can it really be said that the nation has gone to war? Put another way, could robotized and autonomous targeted strikes against hostile armed groups, or specific individuals, be considered representative of the intentions of the state? Such questions not only have bearing upon jurisprudence and just war theory but also upon more practical implementations of IHL. For instance, given the common statist conception of the proper authority requirement, it is equally unclear whether the commencement of hostilities by AWS against nonstate groups constitutes an armed conflict that can legally be governed by the laws of IHL, and so those normally afforded its care during normal hostilities may not be afforded the protections that IHL is designed to give them.[10] Conflicts of this kind do not seem to invoke the mandate of any state whatsoever, for they are initiated without any governmental oversight against groups or individuals not recognized by the international community as representative of state interests.

The statist interpretation of the *ad bellum* requirement of proper authority maintains that just wars can only be initiated by "a legitimate authority: usually a state that represents its citizens and is recognized as such by the international community" (Benbaji 2015). Formulating proper authority in this way excludes certain actors from engaging in war justly. Individuals cannot wage war on this conception, and neither can failed states, evil dictatorships, or nonstate groups, which are generally not representative of the peoples of which they claim to be. In the case of our ideal scenario, wherein AWS make preemptive strikes against individuals in order to prevent harm from coming to those who are not morally liable to it, the governing body of the state that originally implemented the AWS is removed from the consideration of war altogether. It seems that, where the will of the state is absent, any war entered into is done so unjustly and unlawfully because it cannot be said that the state is the entity that decides to go to war. Therefore, adopting AWS that are truly autonomous, in that they act alone in the processes of target acquisition, tracking, and engagement, will necessarily violate the *ad bellum* requirement of proper authority. That is, AWS, in principle, cannot be a legitimate authority.

An obvious response to this position is to point out that AWS simply may engage in warfare in the name of the state, because they have been authorized by the state to do so. That a particular conflict was not foreseen by the state does not change the fact that the state conferred authority upon the AWS to protect its interests. Indeed, there is some precedent here to support the attribution of legal responsibility for the actions of nonstate entities to states that authorize those entities to act in their name.[11] Therefore, given the right kind of authorization, to be worked out through international agreement in accordance with restrictions on the development of new weapons, AWS can be said to conform to proper authority.

Nevertheless, this response does not seem open to the proponent of AWS. If we take them seriously in their conception of what the use of such weapons would come to, they often *ideally* would not conform to *ad bellum* proper authority as it has been laid out. Such wars would be fought, not to conform with the political will of a nation, but solely to preserve the rule of law. They would be fought *in nomine iustitae*, in the name of justice. As MacIntosh puts it, we could make robots "into perfect administrators and enforcers of law, unbiased and tireless engines of legal purpose. This is why so deploying them is the perfection of the rule of law and so required by rule of law values" (MacIntosh 2016).

Perhaps the problem lies not with the violation of *ad bellum* proper authority by the use of AWS. Instead, the possibility of automating the rule of law entails that the conception of *ad bellum* proper authority is no longer a necessary condition for just war. If a war meets all other criteria of *jus ad bellum*, then it ought not to matter who, or what, enters into it. The war ought to be fought by those who can carry it out effectively. If only AWS can attain the just ends of warfare, we ought not to worry that they will do so despite a lack of proper authority.[12] This position illustrates a direct tension between *ad bellum* proper authority and the specified use of AWS.[13] What is more, since wars that adhere to the requirement may still be unjust, autonomous weapons systems may, at least in principle, give us the best opportunity for avoiding the abuses of authority that have been characteristic of some modern conflicts. It is hard to imagine that, absent any human influence, the Iraq War would have been initiated by a sufficiently competent AWS.

Unfortunately, this position will not be found sufficiently plausible by those who support proper authority, and I want to acknowledge two responses before leaving off. Proponents of the requirement claim that allowing the mechanization of the rule of law, and with it the jettisoning of the proper authority requirement, will still tend to make wars fought by AWS more likely to be unjust than those fought when the proper authority requirement has been met. Proper authority is constituted by further sub-requirements: "political society authority," "beneficiary authority," and bearer authority" (Benbaji 2015). These sub-authorities correspond to the obligations that the instigating party has to those they represent, those they fight to benefit, and those who will bear the costs of their making war. The satisfaction of these sub-requirements works to ensure that wars pursued in compliance with them are just. I will discuss the first two sub-requirements. Firstly, political society authority maintains that "if a war is fought in the name of a group of individuals . . ., then this group is entitled to veto the war" (Benbaji 2015). The idea here is that if the society in whose name a war is pursued considers the actions of the state to be unjust, then it is likely that the state is acting without the interests of those it represents in mind, for example, for private reasons. Political society authority is then a good indication that *ad bellum* just cause is being respected. But the option to veto the actions of AWS in our considered scenario is not open to the state that originally authorizes their use. Consequently, AWS cannot meet the sub-requirement, they are not, and cannot be, authorized to represent the state in the right way, and so their use, in conflicting with *ad bellum* proper authority, will tend to result in unjust conflict.

Secondly, it is reasonable to assume that wars are "intended to secure a public good for a larger group (Beneficiary) on whose behalf the war is fought" (Benbaji 2015). For example, presumably, the Gulf War was entered into by the American government, in the name of the American people, not only to stop unjust aggression by Iraqi forces, but also to secure the public good of ridding unjust occupation for the people of Kuwait. The Kuwaiti peoples were the direct beneficiaries of that war. However, if the people of Kuwait objected to America's participation in the war, this would be a good indication that America pursued war unjustly despite its best calculations. The assumption here is that the "alleged beneficiaries are in a better position to assess the value of [the public good pursued via war]" (Benbaji 2015) than those would-be benefactors who calculate whether or not the pursuit of such a war is justified. What is required then, if this is so, is that the beneficiary of a war has the ability to veto its pursuit, but this could not be the case with an AWS. From a legal standpoint, these additional conditions, or the first of them in any case, may help to determine that a war is pursued illegally. If, say, a state was to pursue armed conflict, citing self-defense as just cause,[14] and its citizenry overwhelmingly declared that there was no need for such action, no need for self-defense because of no perceived imminent threat, then we have additional evidence from which to judge the unlawfulness of that pursuit.

10.6: CONCLUSION

One of the purposes of international regulation over the means and methods of warfare is to ensure that armed force shall not be used, save in the common interests of international peace and unity. If unconventional weapons are those most in need of regulation by the dictates of human institutions, then the most unconventional weapons of all are those that require no human to operate. Be that as it may, even when the use of new weapons comes into conflict with established moral justification and legal precedent, regulation need not necessitate prohibition. For the future is a fog of war through which such precedent simply cannot cut, and what is most amenable to the aims of IHL may not be most amenable to the current apparatus that supports it.

I have endeavored to show here that given the sorts of conflicts AWS are likely to be developed for, NIAC, it is an open question as to whether their implementation is compatible with the dictates of just war theory. Although it was seen that some arguments that stem from proportionality considerations do not cause issues for the use of AWS, in one very clear sense, autonomous weapons cannot respect current restrictions on the commencement of just conflicts. The automation of authority circumvents not only the moral requirements of just war theory, in the guise of the proper authority principle, but also many of the legal fail-safes we have in place to prevent armed conflict when possible and protect the innocent when not. That much is certain. What is necessary to decide now is whether or not such automation may constitute the basis for a reconsideration of the *jus ad bellum* justifications constraining international law.

NOTES

1. Art 35(1) and Art 36. Additional Protocol I (AP I). *Protocol Additional to the Geneva Conventions of August 12, 1949, and relating to the Protection of Victims of International Armed Conflicts,* 1125 UNTS 3, opened for signature June 8, 1977, entered into force December 7, 1978.
2. See https://www.icrc.org/en/war-and-law/weapons/ihl-and-new-technologies for discussion; also, the *International Review of the Red Cross: New Technologies and Warfare* 94 (886), 2012.
3. Grut (2013), to her credit, does discuss the issue of proper authority; however she focuses on where the assignment of moral responsibility for harm lies when lethal force is brought to bear by AWS. This is no doubt an important question; however, my focus in this paper differs, as will become clear below.
4. E.g., *Convention (III) relative to the Treatment of Prisoners of War.* 75 UNTS 135.
5. Benbaji (2015) claims that the common understanding of proper authority tends to favor sovereign states as the entities capable of entering into a state of just warfare for three reasons: (1) states have the right kind of status, one which makes declaration meaningful and possible; (2) the just cause requirement entails that the ends of war are attainable only by legitimate states (i.e., not by tyrannical governments etc.); (3) the authority of legitimate states explains why the *in bello* actions of individuals fighting in wars are governed by different rules. While the requirement of statehood has been relaxed since World War II, allowing for the legitimacy of civil wars or wars fought by smaller nonstate groups against oppressive regimes, the assumption here is still that these kinds of conflict are fought with the end of statehood in mind.
6. There is a discrepancy here between Roff's argument and the argument that I will make later on which must be immediately noted. Roff's argument pertains to our plans to use AWS "during hostilities," that is, when we have already been engaged by hostile forces. Her scenario requires that we make an ad bellum proportionality calculation with respect to the use of AWS of a certain kind. MacIntosh (this volume) implicitly correctly distinguishes two distinct uses of AWS: (a) once warfare has already broken out, wherein regular military personnel may presumably decide to deploy AWS, allowing them to carry out some given objective as they see fit; or (b) before warfare has broken out, wherein, having already been deployed with no objective in mind, AWS are allowed to decide the who, when, where, and how of engagement for themselves, without any further oversight (as could happen if, for example, AWS are tasked with determining when to retaliate against a sneak attack with nuclear weapons in mutually assured destruction scenarios). Roff's argument concerns the type (a) use of AWS, however as will become clear later on it is with their type (b) use where issues concerning *ad bellum* principles arise, and consequently where AWS fail to conform to preconceived legal notions of engaging in armed conflict.
7. Interestingly, Roff here collapses the *ad bellum* principle of "probability of success" with the principle of proportionality.

8. We have recourse here not only to the ethical *ad bellum* constraints, but also to universally accepted legislation requiring an attempt at the Pacific Settlement of disputes before the commencement of hostilities, for example, UN Charter chapter VI art 33, chapter VII art 41. Only after such attempts are reasonably made can the use of armed force be considered. There is no barrier, in principle, to the development of AWS that are capable of abiding by such legislation.
9. See Radin and Coats (2016) for discussion of the impact the use of AWS may have for the determination of whether or not a conflict can legally be considered an NIAC. Their focus is on the use of AWS by nonstate groups, but the applicability of the criteria that they highlight, namely, the level of organization of the parties to conflict and the intensity of conflict, are, as the authors note, equally relevant for states and their use of AWS (p. 134).
10. Radin and Coats (2016) consider this point in depth (pp. 137–138).
11. Yearbook of the International Law Commission on the work of its fifty-third session, (2001), vol II part 2, chapter 2 art 4(1): "The conduct of any State organ shall be considered an act of the State under international law, whether the organ exercises legislative, executive, judicial or any other functions, whatever position it holds in the organization of the State, and whatever its character as an organ of the central Government or of a territorial unit of the state"; art 4(2): "An organ includes any person or entity which has that status in accordance with the internal law of the State." Also see art 7 of the same report concerning the excess of authority or contravention of instructions, as well as article 9: "Conduct carried out in the absence or default of the official authorities."
12. Similar judgments, though more general (i.e., not stemming from tensions with AWS), can be found in Fabre (2008). There Fabre argues that the proper authority constraint ought to be dropped wholesale. So long as other *ad bellum* principles are respected, the fact that a just war is not waged by a proper authority does not thereby make it unjust.
13. Consequently, current international charters that rely on proper authority for the determination of the legality of conflict are also challenged by the introduction of AWS. The establishment of a UN Security Council, and the responsibilities of that international body, would be otiose if AWS are allowed the capability of circumventing them. See especially Charter of the United Nations, Chapters III–VII for the relevant statutes.
14. Self-defense is the only recognized recourse to war that sovereign states may appeal to without the approval of the UN Security Council: Charter of the United Nations, Chapter VII art 51.

WORKS CITED

Benbaji, Yitzhak. 2015. "Legitimate Authority in War." In *The Oxford Handbook of Ethics of War*, edited by Seth Lazar and Helen Frowe, pp. 294–314. New York: Oxford University Press.

Blum, Gabriella. 2013. "The Individualization of War: From War to Policing in the Regulation of Armed Conflicts." In *Law and War*, edited by Austin Sarat, Lawrence Douglas, and Martha Merill Umphrey, pp. 48–83. Stanford, CA: Stanford University Press.

Fabre, Cecil. 2008. "Cosmopolitanism, Just War Theory and Legitimate Authority." *International Affairs* 84 (5): pp. 963–976.

Grut, Chantal. 2013. "The Challenge of Autonomous Lethal Robotics to International Humanitarian Law." *Journal of Conflict and Security Law* 18 (5): pp. 5–23.

Hurka, Thomas. 2005. "Proportionality in the Morality of War." *Philosophy and Public Affairs* 33 (1): pp. 34–66.

Issacharoff, Samuel and Richard H. Pildes. 2013. "Targeted Warfare: Individuating Enemy Responsibility." *New York University Law Review* 88 (5): pp. 1521–1599.

MacIntosh, Duncan. 2016. "Autonomous Weapons and the Nature of Law and Morality: How Rule-of-Law-Values Require Automation of the Rule of Law." *Temple International and Comparative Law Journal* 30 (1): pp. 99–117.

MacIntosh, Duncan. This Volume. "Fire and Forget: A Moral Defense of the Use of Autonomous Weapons Systems in War and Peace."

MacIntosh, Duncan. Unpublished (b). *Autonomous Weapons and the Proper Character of War and Conflict (Or: Three Objections to Autonomous Weapons Mooted—They'll Destabilize Democracy, They'll Make Killing Too Easy, They'll Make War Fighting Unfair)*. Unpublished Manuscript. 2017. Halifax: Dalhousie University.

Radin, Sasha and Jason Coats. 2016. "Autonomous Weapon Systems and the Threshold of Non-International Armed Conflict." *Temple International and Comparative Law Journal* 30 (1): pp. 133–150.

Roff, Heather M. 2015. "Lethal Autonomous Weapons and Jus Ad Bellum Proportionality." *Case Western Reserve Journal of International Law* 47 (1): pp. 37–52.

Voelz, Glenn J. 2015. "The Individualization of American Warfare." *The US Army War College Quarterly Parameters* 45 (1): pp. 99–124.

PART II

The Rationality of Automaticity

11

Autonomous Weapons and the Future of Armed Conflict

ALEX LEVERINGHAUS

11.1: INTRODUCTION

In this contribution, I consider how Autonomous Weapons Systems (AWS) are likely to impact future armed conflicts. AWS remain a controversial topic because it is not clear how they are best defined, given that the concept of machine autonomy is contested. As a result, the repercussions of AWS for future armed conflicts are far from straightforward. Do AWS represent a new form of weapons technology with the potential to transform relations between belligerent parties (states and nonstate actors) and their representatives (combatants) on the battlefield, thereby challenging existing narratives about armed conflict? Or are AWS merely an extension of existing technologies and can thus be accommodated within existing narratives about armed conflict? Will practices and accompanying narratives of armed conflict be radically transformed through the advent of AWS? Or will future armed conflicts resemble the conflicts of the late twentieth and early twenty-first centuries, notwithstanding the introduction of AWS?[1]

While discussions of the future of armed conflict are necessarily speculative, they are not unreasonable, provided they have a sound starting point. Here, the starting point comprises two influential narratives that characterize contemporary armed conflict and which can be used as lenses to assess claims about its future. If there is a close fit between these narratives and AWS, AWS, *ceteris paribus*, are unlikely to be transformative. If there is no fit, the impact of AWS on the future of armed conflict is potentially profound. Naturally, narratives about armed conflict can have

Alex Leveringhaus, *Autonomous Weapons and the Future of Armed Conflict* In: *Lethal Autonomous Weapons*.
Edited by: Jai Galliott, Duncan MacIntosh and Jens David Ohlin, © Oxford University Press (2021).
DOI: 10.1093/oso/9780197546048.003.0012

strategic, geopolitical, historical, or political cores (or combinations thereof). The two narratives I utilize here have *normative* cores, focusing on how armed conflicts are and *should be* conducted. More precisely, they reflect a concern for the rights and moral status of civilians in armed conflict, as well as related principles of noncombatant immunity and proportionality. The question, then, is to what extent AWS fit in with existing normative narratives about the status of civilians in armed conflict, and whether or not their deployment would enhance their protection in the future.

In order to tackle this question, the chapter proceeds as follows. In the first part of the chapter, I offer some observations on the definition of AWS. This will be an opportunity for me to revise my own views on the subject. In the second part of the chapter, I look at AWS in relation to what I call the Humane Warfare Narrative. In the third part of the chapter, I investigate the relationship between AWS and the Humane Warfare Narrative's competitor, which I refer to as the Excessive Risk Narrative. In the fourth and final part of the chapter, I briefly put the abstract considerations from the chapter's preceding parts into a more practical context by applying them to the debate on military intervention.

11.2: SLIPPING THROUGH THE CRACKS: CONCEPTUAL ISSUES IN THE AWS DEBATE

As I mentioned above, the definition of AWS is contested. In what follows below, I respond to this problem with two suggestions. First, AWS should be seen as a particularly sophisticated form of automated weaponry. Second, while AWS are classifiable as automated weapons, they are not conceptually on a par with precision weaponry. Let me begin with some brief observations on why AWS are best classified as automated weapons systems. Without going into detail, central to the concept of a weapon is that weapons have been designed in order to produce a harmful effect, usually (but not exclusively) through the application of kinetic force to a target (Forge 2013; Leveringhaus 2016, 38–46). Note that this does not tell us anything about the legal or moral permissibility of creating and inflicting a particular type of harm on a specific target. It is also noteworthy that although there are many artifacts developed for the military that *contribute* to a harmful effect, they are not classifiable as weapons because they are not used to inflict harm themselves. Modern surveillance and reconnaissance technology, for instance, could be deployed in order to identify targets for an attack. But such systems are causally one step removed from the application of force to, and thus the infliction of harm on, a target. Weapons, by contrast, are directly causally involved in the infliction of harm. They are not one step removed from it.

To state the obvious, the distinguishing feature of AWS is that they inflict harm autonomously. Yet, as was pointed out earlier, it is not clear what machine autonomy in targeting consists in. True, it is sometimes argued that AWS are able to make decisions about targeting. But this response does not solve the problem. This is because it is rarely specified what decision-making by a machine would entail. Here, I think about decision-making along what I call the category-based approach to targeting (Leveringhaus 2016, 46–57). This approach assumes that AWS will be able to select individual targets from a prespecified target category, which will have been programmed into them by a human programmer. From a normative perspective, the human programmer has determined in advance whether the entities within a particular target category are deemed lawful targets under international humanitarian law (IHL). Imagine that an autonomous robot has been tasked with destroying artifacts that fall under the target category of enemy robots. The operator will have determined in advanced that enemy robots are legitimate targets under IHL. Acting autonomously, the robot, once deployed, is capable of locating, engaging, and destroying individual representatives of this target category, without further intervention from its programmer.

Critics could reply that the category-based approach neither (1) separates autonomous from automated weapons systems, nor (2) accounts for the decision-making capacities afforded by machine autonomy. Regarding the first criticism, AWS conceptually and technologically overlap with automated weapons. In other words, the conceptual and technological boundaries between the two types of weapons are fluid, rather than rigid. AWS are automated to a higher degree and are thus capable of carrying out more complex tasks than their automated relatives. As a result, the relevant differences are a matter of degree, rather than kind. In response to (2), without opening a philosophical can of worms, decision-making typically involves the capacity to choose between different options. At a higher level of automation, AWS have more options at their disposal about how to track, identify, and engage a particular target than less sophisticated automated systems. The robot from the above example might be capable of choosing from a variety of options on how to best detect and destroy enemy robots: when, how, and where to attack, for instance. It could also learn from its past behavior in order to increase its options and optimize its behavior in future missions. This suggests a much higher level of automation than typically found in simple "fire-and-forget" systems. The point, though, is that, like a less sophisticated automated weapons system, AWS only exercise and optimize their options within their assigned target category.

Still, at this stage of the analysis, I need to revise my own views on how to conceptualize AWS. In an earlier work, I argued that if AWS operate within preprogrammed targeting categories only, they are not only classifiable as automated weapons; they should also be treated as conceptually on a par with existing precision weaponry (Leveringhaus 2016, 31). But I no longer hold this view. This is because the relationship between AWS and the concept of precision is more problematic than I previously assumed. To make a start, it is useful to separate precision from automation and machine autonomy. The latter two concepts merely refer to a machine's capacity to accomplish tasks without the direct supervision of, or interference by, a human operator. They do not indicate whether a machine's behavior is precise in any meaningful sense of the word. It is, further, useful to draw a distinction between (1) precision or accuracy in the fulfillment of a preprogrammed task; and (2) the precision of the preprogrammed task itself as well as its effects. Number (1) denotes that an automated machine carries out its assigned task, rather than a (non-programmed) different task or a mixture of several (programmed and non-programmed) tasks. In the above example, the robot tasked with destroying enemy robots does just that, rather than tracking and engaging targets other than robots. That said, although a machine may be precise or accurate in carrying out its assigned task, the task and its effects may not be precise at all. Imagine a robot that has been deliberately programmed to shoot at anything it encounters. The robot may be precise and accurate in carrying out this task, but neither the task nor its effects are precise in any meaningful sense.

In what follows, I assume that AWS are precise and accurate in fulfilling their assigned task because they do not venture beyond preprogrammed target categories. Rather, it is the effects of their tasks, and their behavior in carrying them out, that pose a problem. To see why this is the case, it is worthwhile probing the concept of precision in more detail. The concept, I believe, involves three interrelated historical, normative, and technological elements.

- *Historical*: What counts as precision is historically relative. What counted as precision during the Vietnam War, for instance, is different from what counted as precision during the first Gulf War. During the Vietnam War, it might have been precise to drop a bomb within a target area measuring a square kilometer. Famously, in the first Gulf War, missiles were shown to enter a targeted building via its air conditioning shaft. Standards of precision, it is safe to say, are higher nowadays than they were in the past, though that does not render them unproblematic.
- *Normative*: Precision is normatively desirable because it enables higher degrees of compliance with relevant regulatory and normative frameworks, most notably IHL. At a minimum, better compliance is assessed against the legal and ethical principle of noncombatant immunity. In its orthodox form, the principle holds that civilians (1) are holders of rights not to be subjected to a direct and international attack, and (2) must not be exposed to disproportionate levels of harm as a side effect of an otherwise permissible military act (Walzer 2015). The concept of precision, then, reflects a belligerent's ability to apply force to a legitimate target without either directly engaging illegitimate targets (such as civilians and civilian infrastructure) or inflicting disproportionate harm on civilians as a side effect of an attack.
- *Technological*: Precision presupposes a belligerent's technological ability to model a weapon's likely kinetic effect; otherwise, it is hard to see how a particular weapon could enhance a belligerent's compliance with relevant regulatory frameworks. It needs to be relatively certain that a weapon will only attack legitimate targets and that any harm caused as a side effect in the course of doing so is unlikely to be disproportionate. Thus, the modeling of where, when, and against whom kinetic force is used matters legally, militarily, and ethically.

The historical element does not seem to pose problems for AWS. Historically, AWS are likely to be more precise than far blunter weaponry used in previous conflicts. The normative element does not seem to cause major problems, either. At least at first sight. This because AWS could be programmed to attack objects that are legally and normatively classifiable as legitimate targets. True, much of the debate on AWS has focused on whether this could include the category of human combatants. In principle, it can provide that human combatants would be clearly identifiable as such to an AWS. In practice, doubts remain. But even if the target category of human combatants is excluded, this still leaves plenty of scope for the deployment of

AWS against other and more readily identifiable categories of targets. Under those circumstances, AWS would prima facie satisfy the normative element of precision.

What remains problematic is the technological element. In advance, programmers will not know where, when, and how an AWS is likely to attack entities from its assigned target category. How exactly is it going to use the many options available to it? And how might it have optimized its options through machine learning? That is the price of cutting a machine loose and letting it operate, as the jargon goes, while being "out-of-the-loop." AWS, therefore, do not seem to satisfy the technological element of precision. Interestingly, this is likely to have a knock-on effect on the normative element. Without the ability to model an AWS's behavior, it becomes hard to determine (1) what the side effects of its use of kinetic force are for civilians located in its area of operations, and (2) whether these side effects are proportionate to any good achieved. This might constitute a strong argument against the development and deployment of *any* AWS, unless it can be shown that AWS would be deployed in defense domains where the side effects of their operation on civilians are zero. But I do not want to go quite as far (yet).

Instead, I emphasize that AWS seem to slip through conceptual and normative cracks. On the one hand, they are not the blunt and imprecise tools that have been used by states in armed conflict. On the other hand, given their unpredictable behavior and the resulting lack of ability to model their impact precisely, AWS cannot be readily classifiable as precision weapons, which diminishes their normative appeal somewhat. They are, then, something in between the blunt tools of war and precision weaponry. Not quite as bad as the blunt tools of war, but not quite as good as precision weaponry, either. This raises interesting questions for the main topic of this chapter, namely the extent to which existing normative narratives about armed conflict can be used as blueprints for future armed conflicts in which AWS might be deployed. The next two parts of the chapter explore these questions in detail.

11.3: AWS AND THE HUMANE WARFARE NARRATIVE

At the time of writing, it is the twentieth anniversary of NATO's Kosovo War. Among other things, the Kosovo campaign stood out because of its heavy reliance on airpower, especially the practice of high-altitude bombing and the bombing of dual infrastructure. It also featured the deep, and perhaps unprecedented, involvement of military lawyers in the making of targeting decisions. In response, two opposed normative narratives have emerged, which I refer to as the Humane Warfare Narrative and the Excessive Risk Narrative, respectively. Here, my goal is not to confirm or debunk either of the two narratives. Instead, I use them as lenses through which to assess the potential impact of AWS on the armed conflicts of the future. Before I do so, a word of caution is on order. Admittedly, given their roots in the Kosovo War, both narratives are limited to the military practices of powerful Western states, most notably the USA and its allies. However, since the USA and its allies are likely to be major players in the development of AWS, a focus on "the Western way of war" is legitimate, though it does not exhaust all facets of contemporary and future armed conflict.

Beginning with the Humane Warfare Narrative, this narrative assumes that, compared with earlier armed conflicts, contemporary warfare has become more restricted, with a greater concern for international legal norms, such as noncombatant immunity and proportionality (Coker 2001). This is not to say that the Kosovo War or any other Western-led armed conflicts post-Kosovo have not been destructive. They have. But the destructive effects of violence, the Humane Warfare Narrative contends, have been more restricted than in previous armed conflicts. From the perspective of the AWS debate, the Humane Warfare Narrative is not only interesting because of its emphasis on the ability of legal norms to restrict the damage caused by armed conflict; it is also interesting because it highlights the link between technological advances in weapons technology and the potential of emerging weapons systems to support greater compliance with relevant legal, and possibly also moral, norms. An armed conflict pursued with the "blunt tools" of war could hardly be humane. The availability of precision weaponry, by contrast, tips the balance in favor of the law and other normative restrictions on the use of force, rendering warfare humane.

The question, then, is whether AWS would reinforce or undermine the Humane Warfare Narrative's link between normative restrictions on warfare and advances in weapons technology. If the answer is positive, future wars in which AWS are deployed would be, *ceteris paribus*, humane wars, with higher targeting standards and less destruction overall. That is certainly how AWS are often presented. In order to support this claim, one does not necessarily have to endorse the famous "humans snap, robots don't" argument in favor of AWS (Arkin 2010). Surely, just as human soldiers have committed atrocities in armed conflict due to stress and other factors, the malfunctioning of *any* weapon can also have horrific consequences. Nor should one focus so much on the differences between human soldiers and machines. The "humans snap, robots don't" argument for AWS seems to presuppose that AWS are going to primarily replace human soldiers in theaters. But AWS are more likely to either replace less sophisticated automated weapons or allow for the automation of targeting practices and processes that it has hitherto been impossible to automate. For the Humane Warfare Narrative to retain its validity, AWS do not need to be perfect. They only need to outperform human soldiers and less sophisticated automated weaponry. The historical element within the concept of precision outlined earlier reinforces this point: it offers a comparative judgment, rather than an absolute one.

So, how would AWS potentially be better than existing weapons systems and possibly even human soldiers? It is hard to answer this question precisely because of the differences between systems and the purposes for which they are used. Yet, as a rule of thumb, there are roughly three relevant considerations.

First, how does the destructiveness of an AWS' kinetic effect compare to that of the systems it replaces? Let us return to the above example of the robot tasked with autonomously destroying and detecting enemy robots. Imagine that it had hitherto only been possible to attack the enemy robots from the air via a missile launched from a remotely piloted aircraft. The robot, however, can enter enemy territory with a low risk of detection and is able to engage the enemy robots in close combat. It is possible to argue that this method of destroying enemy robots is far less risky than the launch of a missile from a remotely piloted aircraft. In particular, any impact on civilians will be greatly reduced if the robot is deployed because the explosive yield of the missile would be far higher than the yield of a targeted shot by the robot. In this example, an AWS replaces a remotely piloted system, allowing for more targeted delivery of a smaller yield payload. Clearly, from the perspective of the Humane Warfare Narrative, the deployment of the robot is preferable.

The second consideration concerns an AWS' ability to adhere to its assigned target category. This issue harks back to my previous distinction between precision in the performance of a task and the precision of the actual task and its effects. AWS are precise in the performance of their task if they do not stray outside out of their preassigned target categories. Now, it would certainly be too much to demand that there must be no misapplications of force via an AWS whatsoever. Not even the Humane Warfare Narrative would go so far. Nor can it be said that more conventional precision weapons have never led to misapplications of force. Precision weaponry has been used to accidentally and wrongly target illegitimate targets. Yet this does not make precision weaponry normatively undesirable. The issue with regard to AWS is whether machine autonomy would introduce an element into a weapons system that undermined its precision in the fulfillment of its task, thereby making misapplications of force *more* likely than in the case of other weaponry. If it does, it would be hard to see how armed conflict pursued with AWS could resemble humane warfare. If it does not, the deployment of AWS could be one facet of humane warfare.

The third consideration opens up wider issues in the philosophy of war (Hurka 2005). Should belligerents only count the harms for which they are directly or indirectly responsible? Or should all harms be counted in an aggregate manner, regardless of who causes them? The two considerations I just outlined roughly correspond to the first question, as they are predominantly concerned with the harm caused by individual belligerents who seek to deploy AWS. The third consideration, by contrast, relates to the second question. Surely, AWS would be normatively desirable if they lowered the overall harm caused by armed conflict. One way in which this could be done is if all belligerents used AWS and adopted higher targeting standards. However, even if AWS are only deployed by one belligerent, their use could lower overall harm. For instance, AWS might be quicker in anticipating and deflecting an enemy attack, thereby ensuring that the enemy is not able to create or inflict harm. By preventing or intercepting enemy attacks, then, AWS would lower overall harm in armed conflict. Certainly, a war with less aggregate damage is more humane than an excessively destructive war.

Taken together, for the Humane Warfare Narrative to be prima facie applicable to future wars in which AWS are deployed, AWS need to pass three key tests:

(1) Are they less destructive and more effective than the weapons they replace?
(2) Are they precise in the performance of their task by adhering to preassigned target categories?
(3) Do they potentially lower the levels of aggregate harm caused by armed conflict?

If the answer to each of the three tests is positive, future wars in which AWS are deployed can be described, *ceteris paribus*, as humane wars. As a result, some future wars would resemble the wars of the late twentieth and early twenty-first centuries normatively. But unfortunately, this conclusion is premature, for two reasons.

The first reason goes to the Achilles heel of the Humane Warfare Narrative. Considering its origins in the Kosovo War, it implicitly assumes that Western states are militarily dominant on the battlefield. This is compounded by the fact that most wars fought by Western states were "wars of choice," rather than "wars of necessity." That is to say, these wars did not respond to an existential threat to the territorial integrity and political sovereignty of Western states. If faced with a war of necessity and an equally strong (or even stronger) adversary, would Western states stick to methods compatible with the Humane Warfare Narrative, or would they revert back to blunter tools when conducting armed conflicts? The same question arises in the context of AWS, albeit on a smaller scale. It is one thing to argue that belligerents deploying AWS would adopt higher targeting standards consistent with the Humane Warfare Narrative. It is quite another to maintain that they would do so, even if their opponents catch up—either by developing effective countermeasures against AWS or by developing and deploying effective AWS themselves. In such a case, adopting higher targeting standards associated with AWS would constitute a military disadvantage.

The second reason for why there is a tension between the Humane Warfare Narrative and AWS has to do with the thorny issue of precision. AWS might be precise in the fulfillment of their task by adhering to their preprogrammed target categories. Yet, as was pointed out earlier, the flexibility afforded by machine autonomy makes it hard to predict how AWS will behave once released onto a battlefield. In an ideal case, programmers can be confident that AWS will attack legitimate targets. What they do not know is when, how, and where AWS do so. However, as I argued above, some modeling of the effects of a weapon is necessary, not least to determine whether its impact on civilians would be proportionate. Without this ability, how can one be sure that AWS would, in reality, be less destructive than the weapons they replace? As a general rule of thumb, then, the further AWS are removed from the concept of precision weaponry, the harder it becomes to integrate them into the Humane Warfare Narrative. That narrative, after all, arose partly as a response to the deployment of precision weaponry. If future armed conflicts will be increasingly conducted with weapons systems that, because they operate with higher levels of automation, are more technologically sophisticated than existing precision weapons but "slip through conceptual cracks," it becomes hard to describe future conflicts as humane.

In sum, while the Humane Warfare Narrative has some relevance for the debate on AWS, there are forces pushing against extending it to future wars in which AWS are deployed. In the next part of the chapter, I assess whether the Humane Warfare Narrative's competitor, the Excessive Risk Narrative, can do a better job in accommodating AWS.

11.4: AWS AND THE EXCESSIVE RISK NARRATIVE

The Excessive Risk Narrative is in many ways the polar opposite of the Humane Warfare Narrative. Its key claim is that, despite advances in weapons technology and the involvement of military lawyers in targeting decisions, warfare has not become more humane. Rather, it remains excessively risky for civilians who get caught up in the crossfire. The Excessive Risk Narrative is not explicitly stated in normative terms because it flows from a more empirical analysis of armed conflict. That said, it has a normative core, which must contain a notion of proportionality and an understanding of the rights of civilians in armed conflict. If warfare is deemed excessively risky, it must be assessed against a normative standard of legitimate behavior in armed conflict, however vaguely articulated it might be.

The Excessive Risk Narrative, as I interpret it, has two versions. The first version focuses on the notion of risk transfer. Here, risks to (friendly) combatants are reduced while risks for civilians either remain static or increase (Shaw 2005). That is one of the reasons for why civilian casualty rates, as well as levels of non-lethal harm inflicted on civilians, remain high, especially when compared to levels of combatant casualties. Military technology, among other factors, has a key role to play in this regard. For instance, practices made possible by advances in the delivery of airpower, such as high-altitude bombing in Kosovo, keep friendly combatants out of way's harm way while not affording civilians a similar degree of protection. Remote-controlled combat technologies, most notably drones, seem to amplify this trend.

How, then, do AWS fare when viewed through the first version of the Excessive Risk Narrative? One general problem that makes such an assessment difficult is that the notion of risk transfer is obscure. To explain, it is useful to distinguish between risk reduction and risk transfer. In cases of risk reduction, an agent lowers levels of risk to himself while levels of risk remain the same for all other potentially affected parties. In cases of risk transfer, by contrast, an agent not only reduces risk to himself, but increases it for other potentially affected parties. A classic example is the difference between an airbag and an SUV with respect to road safety. Installing an airbag in my car, on one hand, reduces my risk of being killed in a frontal collision. The installation of the airbag does not affect the levels of risk for other participants in traffic. Buying an extremely large and heavy SUV, on the other hand, could be seen as an instance of risk transfer. The SUV might be better at protecting me during a collision than an airbag, but the consequences of colliding with my SUV are likely to be more severe for other participants in traffic. Risk reduction strategies, such as the installation of an airbag, are normatively relatively unproblematic. Risk transfers are not, not least because the agents to whom the risk is being transferred do usually not consent to this.

Naturally, AWS have the potential to *reduce* risk for friendly combatants. They increase the distance between combatants and the actual battlefield. They could be programmed in a relatively safe distance to combat action, for instance. On its own, it is hard to see what should be wrong with this, provided that risks remain roughly the same for other parties, especially civilians. An ideal scenario, which is undoubtedly on the minds of advocates of AWS, would be if risk decreased for both categories, friendly combatants and civilians. One should also bear in mind that increasing risks for friendly combatants does not necessarily lead to fewer risks for civilians. These risks might remain static or could even increase if combatants face higher risks to themselves. Hence, the fact that AWS allow militaries to reduce the risks faced by their own combatants is not sufficient to show that a war fought with AWS could automatically be described through the Excessive Risk Narrative. The use of AWS as a risk reduction strategy is fairly unproblematic.

The second version of the Excessive Risk Narrative, by contrast, is better at identifying potential problems with AWS. Here, the issue is not so much that AWS reduce risks for combatants. Rather, the point is that AWS are likely to be used in reckless ways and thus impose excessive risks on civilians (Cronin 2018). More precisely, the second version of the Excessive Risk Narrative not only assumes that the actions of militaries in contemporary armed conflicts involve risk transfers; their actions, rather, involve a high degree of recklessness. Perhaps this is the clearest indication that the Excessive Risk Narrative relies on normative foundations, notwithstanding its focus on the empirical analysis of armed conflict. For the attribution of recklessness to an agent involves a normative judgment. Recklessness typically signifies that an agent deliberately pursues a course of action that is extremely and unjustifiably risky, while being fully aware of the potential risks. Unless there are exculpating circumstances, the agent in question would be blameworthy for having engaged in reckless activities.

So, in what way can contemporary and future armed conflicts be seen as reckless? One prominent contribution to this discourse conceives of the issue as follows. True, existing precision weaponry is, historically speaking, more precise than the blunter tools of war. It is also true that military lawyers play an important part in the selection of targets. The problem, though, is that the technological superiority afforded by precision weaponry and the justificatory blanket provided by the law prompts states to engage in reckless acts. Admittedly, these acts may be legal because they fulfill the requirements of IHL. Yet, all things considered, they are reckless. To describe this phenomenon, I have, in a different writing, coined the term "legal recklessness": an otherwise legal military act may be normatively or ethically reckless (Leveringhaus 2019). Again, the Kosovo War serves as a good example. Controversially, it included widespread attacks on Serbian dual-use infrastructure (used by civilians and combatants). This may have been legal, but it raises questions about the risks that Serbian (and other) civilians faced as a result. Similarly, the use of sophisticated precision weaponry in densely populated urban environments may qualify as legal and is certainly preferable to the use of less sophisticated weapons. But overall, it may remain a reckless thing to do.

One can make similar arguments with regard to AWS. Their defenders would say that, just like precision weapons, AWS are technologically sophisticated and more precise than other forms of weaponry. While this is not a bad thing, it is exactly this kind of mindset that could mean that AWS are deployed in a legal yet recklessness manner. If they cause less damage than other means, why not, for example, deploy them in urban environments? Note that this is a contingent, rather than intrinsic, objection to AWS. The argument from legal recklessness focuses on the use of AWS, rather than their nature. Nor would it automatically advocate a ban of AWS or any precision weapons. For it might be possible to use AWS in contexts where their deployment is not reckless. The worry, however, is that AWS reinforce the same reckless mindsets as in the case of precision weaponry, thereby enabling significant risk transfers to civilians.

Interestingly, the above point about recklessness could also be turned into an intrinsic argument against AWS. This takes us back to the unpredictability of AWS and the problems with modeling their behavior accurately. Perhaps this means that all uses of AWS—and not only specific uses in urban environments or other unsuitable theaters—would automatically qualify as reckless. Releasing an armed machine into a theater with little idea of how exactly it is going to behave, apart from knowledge that it would adhere to its preassigned targeting categories, may just be *the* reckless thing to do in war.

To avoid such a conclusion, defenders of AWS could rightly point out that other methods of combat also involve degrees of unpredictability. There is no guarantee that a Cruise Missile might not veer off course and hit the wrong target. Granted, but the problem remains that the technology underpinning AWS is in its nature unpredictable. In any kind of weapons system, there will always be some potential for failure, be it because of human error or because of a technical malfunction. That cannot be avoided. What can be avoided, though, is deliberately sending a machine into the field that by its very nature is unpredictable.

Defenders of AWS might respond that human individuals are also unpredictable and may act in unforeseeable ways. But this response is not entirely successful, either. First, in armed conflict, states have to deploy humans at some stage; otherwise armed conflict would be impossible. States do, however, have some leeway regarding the types of weapons systems they develop and deploy. For armed conflict to be possible, one does not necessarily need AWS. Second, the argument seems to neglect that, if humans are unpredictable, those tasked with programming AWS may be unpredictable in their actions, too. They could, for instance, program AWS with an illegitimate target category. Finally, if humans are unpredictable in war, it does not make sense to introduce an even greater potential for unpredictability through the deployment of AWS. The aim should be to decrease unpredictability, not increase it. And this might make the use of less sophisticated but more predictable weapons technologies, such as existing precision weaponry, preferable to the deployment of AWS.

Overall, if the above observations are sound, the Excessive Risk Narrative has fewer difficulties in accommodating AWS than its competitor, the Humane Warfare Narrative. Arguably, this could be taken to indicate that future wars in which AWS are deployed are not too dissimilar from how the Excessive Risk Narrative describes armed conflicts. In short, future wars would be defined by high levels of risk for civilians, rather than any increase in "humaneness." That said, one should not discount the possibility that there might be some defense domains where the deployment of AWS neither results in risk transfer nor qualifies, all things considered, as reckless.

11.5: EMERGING WEAPONS TECHNOLOGIES AND THE FUTURE OF INTERVENTIONISM

Before I conclude this chapter, it is worthwhile exploring some of the rather abstract issues raised above in a more practical context. One context that is particularly interesting is the area of intervention. First, in the future, as a matter of state practice, states will reserve the option to intervene in another state's internal affairs. Whether these interventions are motivated by humanitarian values, *realpolitik* or some other consideration does not matter too much. The point is that interventions remain on the agenda. Second, insofar as humanitarian values are concerned, there is an officially recognized framework that governs intervention, which was ratified at the UN World Summit in 2005, namely the Responsibility to Protect (R2P). Whether, in light of recent failures by the international community to intervene in humanitarian disasters, R2P is sustainable and is an important question, which I shall not answer here. I would merely emphasize that, since 2005, the international community views itself at least under a moral obligation to prevent and halt atrocity crimes.

It is legitimate, therefore, to ask whether emerging military technologies would assist, or hinder, the international community in discharging its responsibilities. Third, as the example of the Kosovo War shows, in the discourse on intervention, the role of technology in armed conflict has been a prominent issue. Finally, the case of intervention is particularly good at illustrating the tensions between the Humane Warfare Narrative and the Excessive Risk Narrative. While I cannot offer a detailed discussion of intervention here, I want to flag up four relevant issues for the debate on AWS.

AWS and the role of intervening combatants: One issue that has bedeviled the discourse on intervention is the question of whether states should risk the lives of their own military personnel in order to intervene in another state's internal affairs. This problem is especially pertinent when one considers that interventions may be regarded as wars of choice, rather than necessity, making states reluctant to put the life and limb of their service personnel on the line. Ever since the USA's disastrous intervention in Somalia in 1992, states have been reluctant to commit ground troops during interventions. Hence, the ability to target from a distance is important for intervening states. It is hard to see, though, what AWS can add in this area. As the Kosovo campaign and the subsequent intervention in Libya (2011) showed, existing precision weaponry already gives states the ability to launch military strikes from a safe distance. Nor do AWS necessarily solve the other main issue arising from the reluctance of potential interveners to commit boots on the ground. In the end, someone has to control the territory of the target state, if only temporarily. This is a hurdle that precision-strike warfare, which is launched from afar, finds hard to overcome. At the time of writing, it is hard to fathom how AWS could enable states to automate the control of the territory of another state.

AWS and atrocity crimes: R2P assigns the international community responsibilities to prevent and halt atrocity crimes. Interestingly, autonomous technology could be useful for the prevention of atrocity crimes. One could imagine highly sophisticated surveillance and monitoring systems that do exactly the sorts of things Artificial Intelligence programming techniques are good at, namely detecting patterns in large data sets. It might become possible, then, to model and predict which behavioral patterns are likely to lead to atrocities. However, this is more a point about surveillance technology, not weapons technology. *Military* intervention has an inherent tension between the use of force, which is always risky, and the requirement to protect the vulnerable. The tension is reflected in the relationship between the Humane Warfare Narrative and Excessive Risk Narrative. On the one hand, the use of force needs to remain "humane" and must strictly adhere to legal norms. On the other hand, even the legal use of force during an intervention could still be excessively risky to the point of being reckless. Given that machine autonomy is unpredictable, one wonders how the deployment of AWS would result in increased protection for potential victims of atrocity crimes. If the use of existing precision weaponry has given rise to the Excessive Risk Narrative, then AWS are likely to reinforce this narrative in the context of intervention.

AWS, the Haves and the Have-Nots: In recent years, interventions have been carried out by strong states against states that could be described, by comparison, as militarily weak. AWS are likely to reinforce this weak-state vs. strong-state dynamic. They are likely to complement the arsenal of powerful states, with sufficient resources to invest into this type of technology. As such, in the area of intervention,

AWS are likely to reinforce the gap between those with access to sophisticated forms of combat technologies and those without.

AWS and jus ad vim: Interventions may not only be conducted for the reasons given by R2P. Sometimes national security interests may prompt states to intervene in another state's internal affairs. In 1971, India's intervention in East Pakistan to stem refugee flows into Indian territory was couched in terms of national security, rather than an appeal to humanitarian values. Israel's numerous interventions in the Syrian civil war (2011–present) serve as another good example here. Israel's actions were usually one-off strikes that sought to deny certain actors in the Syrian civil war the ability to attack Israel or otherwise harm Israeli interests in the region. In Israel's case, interventionist action fell below the threshold of what one would normally describe and conceptualize as war. The same could probably be said about targeted killings carried out via remote-controlled weapons, most notably remotely piloted aircraft. Some theorists argue that interventions that fall short of an armed conflict necessitate the creation of a new normative framework called *jus ad vim* (Brunstetter and Braun 2013). Leaving this issue aside, from a practical perspective, AWS may be a sound tool for exactly those operations. Since, unlike remote-controlled weapons, they do not depend on a live communications link with a human operator, they have a greater ability of entering enemy territory undetected. Arguably, they might also be quicker in doing so than comparable non-autonomous weapons systems. Perhaps it is here that, in the discourse on interventionism and armed conflict, AWS are going to have the widest impact. That said, they will build upon, and deepen, existing capacities rather than reinvent the wheel.

To sum up, at least insofar as the issue of interventionism is concerned, AWS seem far less revolutionary than the often abstract and futuristic discussions surrounding them suggest. Instead, they seek to reinforce existing trends in the area. They also encounter some of the same problems that existing weapons technologies have been unable to resolve, such as the continuing inability to control the territory of another state remotely. So, rather than wholeheartedly transforming the field of intervention, there is likely to be a high degree of continuity between past interventions and future ones in which AWS are deployed.

11.6: CONCLUSION

This chapter discussed how AWS might impact on future armed conflicts. To do so, I defined AWS as automated weapons systems that share some similarities with existing precision weaponry, but should not be classified as precision weapons themselves. With this in mind, I assessed AWS against two narratives used to describe contemporary armed conflict, the Humane Warfare Narrative and the Excessive Risk Narrative, respectively. The analysis yielded three takeaway points. First, both narratives have relevance for AWS and *vice versa*. As a result, aspects of the two narratives should be able to cover future armed conflicts in which AWS are going to be deployed. Second, while AWS have the potential to reduce the damage caused by armed conflict, the Humane Warfare Narrative struggles to accommodate them. This makes it unlikely that future wars fought with AWS would be "humane" wars. Third, the Excessive Risk Narrative finds it easier to accommodate AWS, pointing to the serious risks that may arise from their deployment. The use of AWS in future wars, therefore, could lead to further risk transfers and reckless military acts. This, however, is not unprecedented. Here, AWS appear to deepen trends seen in armed conflict since the late 1990s. My concluding analysis of AWS in the context of military intervention reinforces this point. AWS are unlikely to have a transformative effect on the practice of intervention. First, their deployment does not solve some of the long-standing problems with intervention. Second, AWS are likely to add to existing capabilities, rather than introduce radically new ones. In this sense, it is not unreasonable to believe that future wars in which AWS are deployed share many features and characteristics with the wars of the late twentieth and early twenty-first centuries.

NOTE

1. Research for this chapter was made possible via a grant for an Early Career Fellowship from the Leverhulme Trust (ECF-2016-643). I gratefully acknowledge the trust's support.

WORKS CITED

Arkin, Ronald. 2010. "The Case of Ethical Autonomy in Unmanned Systems." *Journal of Military Ethics* 9 (4): pp. 332–341.

Brunstetter, Daniel and Meghan Braun. 2013. "From Jus ad bellum to Jus ad vim: Recalibrating Our Understanding of the Moral Use of Force." *Ethics & International Affairs* 27 (1): pp. 87–106.

Coker, Christopher. 2001. *Humane Warfare*. London: Routledge.

Cronin, Bruce. 2018. *Bugsplat: The Politics of Collateral Damage in Western Armed Conflicts*. New York: Oxford University Press.

Forge, John. 2013. *Designed to Kill: The Case against Weapons Research*. Amsterdam: Springer.

Hurka, Thomas. 2005. "Proportionality in the Morality of War." *Philosophy & Public Affairs* 33 (1): pp. 34–66.

Leveringhaus, Alex. 2016. *Ethics and Autonomous Weapons*. London: Palgrave.

Leveringhaus, Alex. 2019. "Recklessness in Effects-based Military Operations: The Ethical Implications." *Journal of Genocide Research* 21 (2): pp. 274–279

Shaw, Martin. 2005. *The New Western Way of War: Risk Transfer War and Its Crisis in Iraq*. Cambridge: Polity.

Walzer, Michael. 2015. *Just and Unjust Wars: A Moral Argument with Historical Illustrations*. New York: Basic Books.

12

Autonomous Weapons and Reactive Attitudes

JENS DAVID OHLIN

12.1: INTRODUCTION

This chapter takes as its point of departure P.F. Strawson's famous discussion of our reactive attitudes in his essay "Freedom and Resentment," and applies these insights to the specific case of Autonomous Weapons Systems (AWS) (Strawson 1982). It is clear that AWS will demonstrate increasing levels of behavioral complexity in the coming decades. As that happens, it will become more and more difficult to understand and react to an AWS as a deterministic system, even though it may very well be constructed, designed, and programmed using deterministic processes. In previous work, I described what I called the "Combatant's Stance," the posture that soldiers must take toward a sophisticated AWS in order to understand its behavior—a process that necessarily involves positing beliefs and desires (and intentional states generally) in order to make sense of the behavior of the AWS (Ohlin 2016).[1]

The present chapter extends this analysis by now considering the reactive attitudes that an enemy soldier or civilian would take toward a sophisticated AWS. Given that an AWS is artificial, most enemy soldiers will endeavor to view an AWS dispassionately and not have any reactive attitudes toward it. In other words, an enemy soldier will endeavor not to resent an AWS that is trying to kill it and will endeavor not to feel gratitude toward an AWS that shows mercy. Strawson argued that even though the entire universe may function deterministically, human beings are mostly incapable of ridding themselves of reactive attitudes entirely—these

Jens David Ohlin, *Autonomous Weapons and Reactive Attitudes* In: *Lethal Autonomous Weapons*.
Edited by: Jai Galliott, Duncan MacIntosh and Jens David Ohlin, © Oxford University Press (2021).
DOI: 10.1093/oso/9780197546048.003.0013

feelings of gratitude and resentment are simply hardwired into the fabric of our emotional lives. They may be subject to some revision but not subject to wholesale elimination (Strawson 1982, 68).[2]

This chapter concludes that the same thing may be true of an AWS on the battlefield. Although soldiers will struggle to rid themselves of reactive attitudes with regard to an AWS (because it is a deterministic system), it may be impossible to fully revise our psychological dispositions in this way. I conclude with some practical implications for how battlefield interactions will unfold because of these philosophical insights.

12.2: THE PROMISE OF AWS

Imagine the following situation. A large state launches a military campaign against a nonstate actor located on the soil of a foreign state. For the sake of argument, let us assume that the actions of the nonstate actor cannot be attributed to the territorial state and that the territorial state objects to the military intervention on its territory. Furthermore, let us assume that the nonstate actor has launched acts of terrorism against the intervening state and that the intervening state has decided to exercise defensive force because the territorial state is unwilling or unable to resolve the threat on its own.[3]

In the course of these military operations, let us also assume that the intervening state will make use of air assets, both manned and unmanned, against the nonstate actors. Let us also assume that the assets of the nonstate actor, including its members, are located in dense, urban areas, and that drone strikes in those locations will inevitably result in significant collateral damage to innocent civilians.

So far, this story has tracked the details of many engagements that might have occurred by Western military powers against extremist organizations such as al-Qaeda or the Islamic State. In many of those engagements, the infliction of collateral damage has instilled great resentment among the local population (Gul and Royal 2006).[4] In some cases, the resentment has been so fierce that critics have worried that the animosity created by the (even lawful) collateral damage outweighs the security benefits of destroying the assets of the nonstate actor (Clarke 2004). In other words, military forces might kill twenty militants but in so doing, they might generate enough resentment that twenty or even more militants might rise up from the ranks of the local civilian population (Vogel 2010, 126).[5] From the perspective of strategy, this is a poor outcome.

But let us now inject a dose of mild futurism into the discussion. Assume that the military forces of the intervening state have an AWS that they are capable of deploying along with their unmanned aerial vehicles. The AWS makes the targeting calculations in order to determine both the military status of the intended target and also the permissibility of the attack given the anticipated collateral damage (Noone and Noone 2015, 29).[6] Specifically, the AWS determines, using its own algorithms, whether a particular target is a lawful target or not, that is, whether the target is a member of enemy military forces or a civilian who is directly participating in hostilities (DPH) (Chengeta 2016, 83–84).[7] Then, the AWS also calculates the expected collateral damage from destroying the target and weighs that against the expected military advantage to be gained from destroying the target.[8] The "weighing" process is fixed by an algorithm that ensures that envisioned collateral damage that is "clearly excessive" to the military advantage thereby results in the AWS canceling the strike and not engaging the target, at least not at that moment in time. Indeed, perhaps the AWS operates according to stricter Rules of Engagement (ROE) that are far more restrictive than the "clearly excessive" standard for collateral damage contained in the Rome Statute or the "excessive" standard contained in Additional Protocol I.[9] Consequently, according to these ROE, the AWS does not engage the target if the collateral damage reaches a preordained level that is deemed strategically unsatisfactory, regardless of whether it is "excessive" or not.[10]

From the perspective of the international humanitarian or criminal lawyer, the use of this Autonomous Weapon System (AWS) would seem to be advantageous (Hollis 2016, 13; Newton 2015, 5). And the advantages would seem to be numerous. First, the deployment of the AWS promises to routinize the target selection process so that instances of violations of the principle of proportionality (in collateral damage situations) are reduced or even eliminated entirely (Wagner 2012, 83).[11] From the perspective of civilians caught in the crossfire of an armed conflict, this would appear to be a great development. Second, one might even think that the use of the AWS might also squelch the possibility of resentment that promotes radicalism among the local population. Specifically, we noted earlier that sometimes collateral damage can be so extensive that it promotes so much resentment—and support for extremist causes—that it ends up outweighing any advantage conferred by killing the militants. If to kill a militant you need to kill a civilian who will inspire others to become militants, you have only kicked the can down the road rather than improved security in any meaningful or enduring way.

Now here is where the AWS itself might help matters. If the attacking force has dutifully constructed the AWS and then deploys it faithfully, the attacking force can reply to any criticism regarding collateral damage that the targeting decision was not made by the local commander on the field but, instead, the decision was carried out by the AWS in full compliance with both IHL and more restrictive ROEs. In theory, this should blunt the sharp edge of the resentment felt by the victims of collateral damage, since the collateral damage was not only lawful but was decided by a deterministic system operating in a sanitized and rational targeting environment, rather than operating from caprice or other inappropriate motivations. If *all* targeting were carried out by AWS systems of this kind, one might even envision a sanitized form of war that is carried out entirely within the legal and ethical constraints—a fully optimized "humane" war.[12] In such a world, the victims of collateral damage would have fewer objections to being on the receiving end of the collateral damage and would resent their victimization less than if the decision to fire was made by some local commander. The "procedural" objection that they might otherwise have for how they were selected would be muted (though a substantive objection regarding the outcome might remain).

I am not suggesting that a collateral damage victim (or the family of a collateral damage victim) would not complain about their victimization, simply because the targeting decision was made by the AWS. Instead, I am suggesting that victims of lethal targeting would complain *less*, as a comparative matter, if the targeting decision was made by an AWS rather than by a human agent, because the AWS would have made the decision to fire in a cool, calculated, unemotional, and lawful manner. The first reason why the victim might be less likely to resent the AWS attacker is that the decision to fire was not made by a human being at all but rather by an autonomous weapon. Usually, feelings of resentment or anger are reserved for our interactions with other human beings; computer systems, including autonomous ones, are less likely to generate these feelings for a variety of complicated reasons that will be explored in greater depth below. The second reason why the victim might be less likely to resent an AWS attacker is that the AWS would do its work dispassionately and without illegitimate motivations such as discrimination on the basis of race, religion, or nationality. The AWS makes determinations to fire based on its assessments of who is a military target, who is a civilian directly participating in hostilities, and when collateral damage is low enough such that it does not cross the threshold of being excessive (disproportionate). If the victim sees these as objective "calculations" rather than human "judgments," they are less likely to spark feelings of resentment.

For the moment, I wish to suspend any inquiry into whether this asymmetry between human and nonhuman judgments (i.e., resenting the human but not resenting the AWS) is rationally justified or not. Perhaps if the victims were thinking rationally, they *should* reason that it does not make a difference whether the decision to fire was made by a human being or by an autonomous system. But purely as a matter of fact, I think most observers would predict that the victims would be less likely to resent an autonomous system and more likely to resent a human being who makes the final decision to fire the weapon.

For the military force that deploys the AWS, this development might be significant. Recall above that the local population victimized by collateral damage might be radicalized and more likely to support extremist causes. However, if the targeting decision is made by the AWS, the attacking force would probably hope that the use of the AWS will blunt that possibility. In taking the targeting decision out of human hands and placing it with the AWS, the attacking force would be able to say, "We didn't decide to launch the strike, the AWS did, so you can't argue that the decision to fire was motivated by illegitimate considerations." The result would be less resentment, less radicalization, and less chance of building an insurgent attitude among the local population. This is a collateral benefit of the application of the AWS to this environment. Not only does it increase compliance with International Humanitarian Law (IHL) and ROE, but it also increases the perception of compliance in a way that reduces resentment on the part of the local population.

Now an important caveat is in order here. I am assuming that the AWS probably will not engage in any *jus ad bellum* analyses and that the targeting decision would be based purely on considerations internal to IHL and ROE, or perhaps criteria flowing from IHRL.[13] But it is probably not realistic to think that the AWS would make a *jus ad bellum* determination (Roff 2015, 39).[14] *That* determination would probably be made at the political level, outside of the military. So, for example, the political leaders would decide whether it is appropriate, all things considered, for their military to launch a military strike against a host state where a threatening NSA is located. And most importantly, the local population might resent *this jus ad bellum* decision because it is the cause for their misery, just as much as the collateral damage calculation and its associated tactical decision whether to strike or not.

In reality, it would seem that the local population's resentment will flow equally from considerations of *jus ad bellum* and *jus in bello,* such that the AWS's routinization of the IHL targeting questions would certainly reduce the complaints flowing from the local population. Indeed, the public (and global) discourse surrounding targeting has been dominated by IHL considerations while *jus ad bellum* considerations have, as a comparative matter, withered in public conversations (Moyn 2015).[15] One evidence of this fact is that lawyers focus on the "humanization" of armed conflict and members of the press debate whether an attack constitutes a war crime or not. In contrast, there is less and less public debate over whether a particular military campaign violates *jus ad bellum* or not (Moyn 2014).[16] There are many reasons for this disjunction, but one factor may be the relatively public and neutral criteria for determining IHL violations, while *jus ad bellum* standards, including articles 2 and 51 of the UN Charter, require far more application of the law to contested facts.

One might also imagine a situation where *soldiers* who are killed by an AWS targeting decision (as opposed to civilian collateral damage) would be less likely to resent the decision to kill them if the decision is made by a deterministic system, such as an AWS. Of course, soldiers are already less inclined than civilians to feel resentment toward their attacker, because they might feel some professional kinship with enemy soldiers because they share a common profession—a soldier who is tasked with carrying out the military policies of the state to whom they belong. This self-conception grants the soldier some immunity from feelings of resentment toward their attacker, but this feeling of professionalism is not absolute. In many situations, the soldier will resent the decision that was made to attack them. The knowledge that the decision to attack was made by a professionally programmed deterministic system would blunt those feelings of resentment. Consequently, the military goals of the operation could be accomplished while simultaneously reducing as far as possible negative feelings of resentment among the local population, whether civilian or military.

12.3: OUR REACTIVE ATTITUDES

In this section, I will complicate the story that I have just told and point out some reasons why the benefits of the AWS that I have outlined above may not come to pass. In short, I will argue that despite our earlier assumption that the victim of an AWS attack will feel less resentment because the attack was generated by an AWS, there are substantial reasons to doubt this hasty conclusion. In fact, it will be extremely hard for the victim to resist certain reactive attitudes, including feelings of resentment, as long as the AWS is sophisticated enough that its behavior seems similar to the decisions that a reasonably law-compliant human agent would make. There are several steps to this argument.

The first step requires explaining more about where reactive attitudes come from and delving into when they can, or cannot, be suspended. In "Freedom and Resentment," the philosopher Peter Strawson reminded us that human beings usually take a "reactive attitude" toward other human beings (Strawson 1982, 62).[17] By the phrase "reactive attitudes," Strawson was referring to emotional attitudes that one takes toward others in normal interpersonal engagements. So, for example, if a driver cuts you off on the roadway, you might naturally resent them for their lack of courtesy on the road. Similarly, if a stranger offers you a dollar when you are short on bills at a local merchant when you are trying to complete a cash transaction, you might feel grateful to them for their act of generosity. These feelings are a natural part of what it means to be a human being living in a functioning society with other human beings.

Reactive feelings logically presuppose that the object of one's reactive feeling is a free agent—someone that is responsible enough for their behavior to qualify for reward or punishment. We generally do not have reactive feelings to rocks or plants; we do not resent them if we are harmed by then, nor do we reward them when they make our lives better.[18] In other words, human beings have certain feelings toward other human beings—feelings of gratitude or resentment—that presume that other human beings are free agents, rather than deterministic entities. Those feelings of gratitude or resentment are the basis for a set of moral *practices*, such as praising or blaming other human beings who have helped or harmed us. In some instances, when dealing with infants or mentally ill patients, we might "suspend" this reactive stance and take an "objective" attitude toward these individuals because we do not take them to be proper subjects of praise and blame. Instead, we consider infants and mentally ill individuals to be appropriate subjects for practices associated with the objective attitude, such as treatment or management (Strawson 1982, 65). Mentally ill individuals should get treatment in a mental health facility, while children need proper management from a parent or other caregiver (Strawson 1982, 73).[19] Instead of seeing these individuals as 100% free agents, we view their behavior as being "caused" by factors outside of their own control. For this reason, we often approach them with an objective attitude rather than a reactive attitude.

Strawson distinguished between reactive and objective attitudes in order to make a particular intervention in the debate between free will and determinism (Strawson 1982, 68).[20] Strawson asked whether human beings would be able to respond to the alleged truth of universal determinism—the view that everything in the universe is determined rather than freely chosen—by foregoing the reactive stance entirely in favor of adopting the objective attitude in every single interpersonal reaction. Strawson suggested that this was highly improbable and that reactive attitudes were, to a certain extent, hardwired into our existence and our relationships with other human beings. And while we might drop the reactive attitude in favor of an objective attitude for particular persons (such as infants), those instances were always going to be exceptions to the general rule, rather than a mode of interaction that we could universalize (Strawson 1982, 68).

The Strawsonian intervention in the debate about universal determinism is not directly relevant for our inquiry about an AWS. But what *is* relevant is Strawson's intuition that giving up our reactive attitudes is not as easy as one might think. This is not to suggest that giving it up in any case is impossible—Strawson's intervention is limited to the idea that giving it up in *all* cases is impossible—but rather that giving it up, even in individual cases, might be *hard* to do. In other words, our reactive attitudes are difficult to forego in cases of interpersonal interactions.

Normally, we assume that an agent will first determine the truth of determinism with regard to any particular system, and then based on that decision, will either take a reactive attitude or an objective attitude toward that system. In other words, if one decides that a system is deterministic in some way, one will revise one's stance toward that system and approach it objectively. Conversely, if one decides that one is dealing with a free agent, then one will approach the system with a reactive attitude. The genius of Strawson was to teach us that this timeline should be questioned. It is unrealistic to think that an agent will *always* adjudicate the question of determinism first and then make a *decision* about how to approach an agent based on the results of the first inquiry. Reactive attitudes simply *happen*, and we must struggle to abandon them if we intellectually decide that they are inappropriate for some reason. Sometimes that abandonment is rather easy, but in other circumstances, it is far more difficult. When an individual is threatened with death at the hands of an AWS, it might be difficult for that individual to abandon those reactive attitudes, even if they are told that the AWS operates in a deterministic fashion.

In the following section, I will discuss the possibility that when targeted with an AWS, victims of a strike will be more likely than not to adopt a reactive attitude toward them. While revision is possible, and the objective stance is possible, it will be difficult. In some situations, it will be more natural to resent the AWS and its decision to fire, even if it is fundamentally a deterministic system.

12.4: REACTING TO AN AWS

What determines whether an individual will take a reactive or objective attitude toward an AWS? That will depend, in part, on the level of sophistication of the AWS. In a previous work, I argued that an AWS, in theory, could become so sophisticated that in order to understand its behavior, other human beings would need to adopt the Combatant's Stance in order to understand the behavior of the AWS (Ohlin 2016, 16).[21] In other words, other human beings would need to approach the AWS as a free agent, pursuing particular actions in order to satisfy particular goals. In this context, it would not matter whether the AWS was a free agent or not, because the behavior of the AWS might be functionally indistinguishable from that of a free agent. In order to understand its behavior, one might need to posit mental states to it, such as particular beliefs or desires, and that positing these mental states would be a prerequisite to making rational sense of its behavior (Ohlin 2016, 14; Turing 1950). Taking a purely objective point of view of the AWS would not be possible because the inner workings of the AWS would not only be inaccessible to other human beings but would be far too complex anyway to serve the demands of behavior interpretation. Only viewing the AWS as a free agent would suffice.

I will now extend this analysis to consider the *emotional* reaction that someone will have when they encounter the actions of that AWS. Although the victim of an AWS strike will not necessarily see the AWS, the temptation will be strong to resent whoever or whatever made the decision to fire the weapon in question. Even if the military forces announce that the decision to fire was made by an AWS—an AWS that complies with IHL and restrictive ROE—the individuals who are on the receiving end of the actions of the AWS might have a hard time adopting a purely objective attitude with regard to the AWS. There are several reasons for this.

First, it is especially hard to adopt the objective attitude when matters of life and death are at stake. If an individual is harmed by a falling rock, they are unlikely to feel resentment toward the rock. But this is a poor analogy. The better analogy would involve being harmed by an infant or by a psychotic aggressor.[22] In those cases, the victim might understand, rationally, that the source of the aggression is non-culpable and, therefore not an appropriate target of feelings of resentment and blame. However, foregoing the reactive approach might be extremely difficult for the victim, who might feel drawn, almost as if by nature, toward a reactive stance. The objective approach might be possible, but only after a significant amount of mental and emotional discipline; and in many cases, that discipline will be found wanting.

Second, the more complex the behavior, the more difficult it is to adopt the objective approach. A rock falling from the side of the mountain is a primitive event, easily explainable and understood using the laws of physics, without positing mental beliefs or desires or free agency, and therefore the emotional toll of adopting the objective approach is close to zero. In contrast, the behavior of the infant is more complex, yet still not complex enough that adopting the objective approach is impossible. It might require the positing of primitive mental states but not ones that are complicated. On the furthest side of the spectrum, the psychotic aggressor will exhibit the most complex of behaviors, and in that case adopting the objective approach is indeed very difficult. For this reason, it is sometimes the case that people rationally believe that they should not feel resentment toward a mentally ill person, yet they struggle with that realization, ultimately exhibiting reactive feelings of resentment anyway (Scheurich 2012).

If the behavior of an AWS is sufficiently complex, others on the battlefield may find it difficult to adopt an objective attitude toward the AWS. Moreover, and this is the key point, people may struggle to adopt the objective approach even if, at some level, they know that the AWS is a deterministic system. Even so, there is a gap between what one knows one should do rationally, and one's reactive attitudes. Given that these attitudes are constitutive of interpersonal relations, they can be suspended, but only after significant effort. And they cannot be suspended entirely, in every case.

An AWS decision to launch a strike involves a set of criteria that are so complex that an outsider is unlikely to make sense of the behavior without positing beliefs and desires to the AWS. That, in turn, will make it more likely that the victim will take a reactive attitude toward the AWS. This does not necessarily mean that the victim will argue that the AWS should be punished or that the victim will demand from the AWS a justification for its behavior. Rather, it simply means that the fact that the decision to kill was made by the AWS, rather than by a commander, will be cold comfort to the victim. The victim might still feel anger and resentment about the strike, even if the attacking military force tries to deflect blame by asserting that the decision to strike was made by the AWS.

At this point, one might object that I have not given sufficient credit to the capacity of individual human beings to switch between objective and reactive attitudes when circumstances warrant. After all, people do not get angry at websites or the decisions of a bank that are made by some complex algorithm. This much is true. The point is simply that reactive attitudes are hard to abandon, even when one learns that a particular system is deterministic in nature. The *temptation* to view the system as a free agent, and therefore the temptation to view it as an appropriate subject for feelings of blame or resentment, is incredibly strong and built into the human experience. Suspension of the reactive attitude is possible, but we should always remember that reactive attitudes constitute the baseline against which deviations toward an objective approach are then taken.

12.5: PRACTICAL IMPLICATIONS

What are the implications of this view for the conduct of hostilities (if any)? The key difference is that resentment among the local population might still be present, even if the decision to kill is made by an AWS rather than an individual soldier, and even if that decision is made in a way that is compliant with IHL. As noted above, collateral damage is consistent with IHL, and civilians on the receiving end of a strike might complain bitterly about the distributional harm that falls on their shoulders in the service of balancing military necessity and the principle of humanity (Schmitt 2010, 798). Even in the cool and calculated decision-making of a relatively "perfect" AWS, the local population might have difficulty suspending the reactive stance. Some feelings of resentment are inevitable even when the decision to kill is made by an entity that is arguably deterministic in nature.

The greatest significance of this insight will come in a counterinsurgency campaign. The goal of deploying an AWS in the counterinsurgency context would be to lower instances of collateral destruction in an attempt to win the "hearts and minds" of the local population, or at the very least not alienate them in the process of capturing and killing militants (Postma 2014, 303).[23] In addition to lowering the number of civilian deaths, the AWS might be deployed with the expectation that its detached and objective targeting protocols would lower resentment among the local population. While, in theory, this might be possible, there are uncertainties. Reactive attitudes are hard to abandon, and the mere fact that the AWS is a deterministic system might not be enough to cause the local population to abandon its reactive stance.

One might object that I have constructed a strawman in order to demolish it. If one does not expect AWS-controlled targeting to reduce resentment among the targets of an attack, then learning that the resentment will be hard to abandon is not much of a surprise. However, even if this particular insight is not particularly surprising, the reasons identified in this article might have a wider application in other situations. Along the way, we suggested that an AWS system, even if it is deterministic, might be so sophisticated that combatants on the battlefield approach it as a free agent—what I have called in other contexts the Combatant's Stance (Ohlin 2016, 14). In this essay, I have extended that analysis of behavior interpretation to include the emotional attitudes that go along with viewing someone or something as a free agent that is a legitimate target of feelings of gratitude or resentment.

To take just one example, soldiers on the battlefield sometimes have difficulty complying with the laws of war when they become overwhelmed with grief, anger, sorrow, PTSD, and other forms of psychological damage. Sometimes that psychological damage is caused by exposure to warfare and sometimes it predates deployment. These soldiers will sometimes snap and fail to live up to the demands of the law; they execute captured soldiers, desecrate the bodies of enemy soldiers, or shoot civilians for no good reason other than a general anger at a collective "enemy" that has inflicted harm on the soldier or his or her comrades. In this context, the existence of reactive attitudes run amok is of grave concern; not only does such a soldier resent the enemy, but the soldier is consumed by resentment to the point of acting irrationally and immorally. What we have learned from the present essay is that the existence of an AWS—to the extent that it is sophisticated enough to act like an enemy combatant—may generate these dangerous feelings of resentment. If one cares about reducing these horrific situations, the deployment of an AWS might not be a reliable tool to accomplish that result.

NOTES

1. Ohlin concludes that if "an AWS does everything that any other combatant does: engage enemy targets, attempt to destroy them, attempt as best as possible to comply with the core demands of IHL (if it is programmed to obey them) and most likely prioritize force protection over enemy civilians," then "an enemy combatant would be unable to distinguish the AWS from a natural human combatant."
2. Strawson concludes on page 68 that a "sustained objectivity of inter-personal attitude, and the human isolation which that would entail, does not seem to be something of which human beings would be capable, even if some general truth were a theoretical ground for it."
3. The "unwilling or unable" doctrine is the view that a state is entitled to use defensive force against a threatening nonstate actor located on the territory of a state that is either unwilling or unable to stop the nonstate actor. For a discussion of this doctrine, see Deeks 2012, 487.
4. Gul and Royal conclude that "military action which entails collateral damage . . . will probably encourage additional recruitment for terrorists."
5. Vogel notes that "[s]ome also assert that the military advantage of many of the drone attacks is minimal to nil, because either the importance of the target is often overstated or, more importantly, because the civilian losses generate increased hostility among the civilian population, thereby fueling and prolonging the hostilities."
6. Noone and Noone note that "[s]ome argue on behalf of AWS development and usage on the claim it can reduce human casualties, collateral damage, and war crimes by making war less inhumane through lessening the human element from warfare."
7. But Chengata asks "[w]hen is a person deemed to be directly participating in hostilities and will AWS be able to apply this complex standard?" and concludes that "the nature of contemporary armed conflicts constantly needs human judgment and discretion, both for the protection of civilians and not unfairly militating against the rights of combatants."
8. Several scholars have envisioned the possibility that an AWS could make a collateral damage estimation and also that a state might be responsible under international law for an AWS that engages in a deficient collateral damage calculation (Hammond 2015, 674).
9. "Intentionally launching an attack in the knowledge that such attack will cause incidental loss of life or injury to civilians . . . which would be clearly excessive in relation to the concrete and direct overall military advantage anticipated" (Rome Statute 1998). For a discussion of this provision, see Haque (2014, 215) and Akerson (2014, 215).
10. I am assuming here that the preordained amount would be stricter (permitting even less collateral damage) than what the ICL or ICL principle would require.
11. Wagner asks "whether AWS software is actually capable of making proportionality assessments."
12. However, some scholars have argued that the promise of a fully "humane" war is a dangerous ideal because it will make wars more frequent and difficult to end. In other words, the focus on "humaneness" has arguably sidelined questions of *jus ad bellum* and *jus contra bellum*. For example, see Moyn (2018).

13. The role of human rights law (as a body of law distinct from IHL) in armed conflict situations is the subject of intense legal discussion (Luban 2016; Ohlin 2016).
14. Roff notes that "AWS pose a distinct challenge to jus ad bellum principles, particularly the principle of proportionality" and concludes that "even in the case of a defensive war, we cannot satisfy the ad bellum principle of proportionality if we knowingly plan to use lethal autonomous systems during hostilities because of the likely effects on war termination and the achievement of one's just causes.".
15. Moyn laments "an imbalance in our attention to the conduct of the war on terror, rather than the initiation and continuation of the war itself."
16. Here Moyn concludes that legal discussions during the Vietnam era centered on *jus ad bellum*, whereas post-9/11 controversies have focused more on *jus in bello* questions.
17. Strawson states "[t]he central commonplace that I want to insist on is the very great importance that we attach to the attitudes and intentions towards us of other human beings, and the great extent to which our personal feelings and reactions depend upon, or involve, our beliefs about these attitudes and intentions."
18. For example, seeing a beautiful plant might make our day a little better but we wouldn't feel gratitude toward that plant—we would reserve that feeling exclusively to whoever is responsible for putting that plant there, for example, a gardener or a friend who gave us that plant.
19. See Strawson for a description of the objective view of the agent as "posing problems simply of intellectual understanding, management, treatment, and control").
20. Strawson concludes that the "human commitment to participation in ordinary inter-personal relationships is, I think, too thoroughgoing and deeply rooted for us to take seriously the thought that a general theoretical conviction might so charge our world that, in it, there were no longer any such things as inter-personal relationship as we normally understand them."
21. "[T]he standard for rational belligerency is whether an opposing combatant views the AWS as virtually indistinguishable from any other combatant, not in the sense of being physically indistinguishable (which is absurd), but rather functionally indistinguishable in the sense that the combatant is required to attribute beliefs and desires and other intentional states to the AWS in order to understand the entity and interact with it—not so much as a conversational agent but to interact with the AWS as an enemy combatant" (Ohlin 2016, 16).
22. George Fletcher first introduced the language of a "psychotic aggressor" as the *non-culpable* source of a threat or the source of a harm that requires the use of defensive force in response (Fletcher 1973).
23. Postma argues that "winning people's hearts and minds in a successful counterinsurgency requires capabilities beyond programmed algorithms."

WORKS CITED

Akerson, David. 2014. "Applying Jus in Bello Proportionality to Drone Warfare." *Oregon Review of International* Law 16 (2): pp. 173–224.

Chengeta, Thompson. 2016. "Measuring Autonomous Weapon Systems Against International Humanitarian Law Rules." *Journal of Law and Cyber Warfare* 5 (1c): pp. 63–137.

Clarke, Richard A. 2004. *Against All Enemies: Inside America's War on Terror.* New York: Free Press.

Deeks, Ashley S. 2012. "Unwilling or Unable: Toward a Normative Framework for Extraterritorial Self-Defense." *Virginia Journal of International Law* 52 (3): pp. 483–550.

Fletcher, George P. 1973. "Proportionality and the Psychotic Aggressor: A Vignette in Comparative Criminal Theory." *Israel Law Review* 8 (3): pp. 367–390.

Gul, Saad and Katherine M. Royal. 2006. "Burning the Barn to Roast the Pig? Proportionality Concerns in the War on Terror and the Damadola Incident." *Willamette Journal of International Law and Dispute Resolution* 14 (1): pp. 49–72.

Hammond, Daniel N. 2015. "Autonomous Weapons and the Problem of State Accountability." *Chicago Journal of International Law* 15 (2): pp. 652–687.

Haque, Adil Ahmad. 2014. "Protecting and Respecting Civilians: Correcting the Substantive and Structural Defects of the Rome Statute." *New Criminal Law Review* 14 (4): pp. 519–575.

Hollis, Duncan B. 2016. "Setting the Stage: Autonomous Legal Reasoning in International Humanitarian Law." *Temple International & Comparative Law* 30 (1): pp. 1–16.

Luban, David. 2016. "Acting as a Sovereign versus Acting as a Belligerent." In *Theoretical Boundaries of Armed Conflict and Human Rights*, edited by Jens David Ohlin, pp. 45–77. New York: University of Cambridge Press.

Moyn, Samuel. 2014. "From Antiwar Politics to Antitorture Politics." In *Law and War*, edited by Austin Sarat, Lawrence Douglas, and Martha Umphrey, pp. 154–197. Stanford, CA: Stanford University Press.

Moyn, Samuel. 2015. "Toward a History of Clean and Endless War." *Just Security*. October 9. https://www.justsecurity.org/26697/sanitizing-war-endlessness/.

Moyn, Samuel. 2018. "Humane: The Politics and Poetics of Endless War." Lecture at Duke University School of Law. September 7.

Newton, Michael A. 2015. "Back to the Future: Reflections on the Advent of Autonomous Weapons Systems." *Case Western Reserve Journal of International Law* 47 (1): pp. 5–23.

Noone, Gregory P. and Diana C. Noone. 2015. "The Debate Over Autonomous Weapons Systems." *Case Western Reserve Journal of International Law* 47 (1): pp. 25–35.

Ohlin, Jens David. 2016. "Acting as a Sovereign versus Acting as a Belligerent." In *Theoretical Boundaries of Armed Conflict and Human Rights*, edited by Jens David Ohlin, pp. 118–154. New York: University of Cambridge Press.

Postma, Peter B. 2014. "Regulating Lethal Autonomous Robots in Unconventional Warfare." *University of St. Thomas Law Journal* 11 (2): pp. 300–330.

Roff, Heather M. 2015. "Lethal Autonomous Weapons and Jus Ad Bellum Proportionality." *Case Western Reserve Journal of International Law* 47 (1): pp. 37–52.

Rome Statute of the International Criminal Court. Article 8(2)(b)(iv). A/CONF.183/9 (October 17, 1998, entered into force July 1, 2002).

Scheurich, Neil. 2012. "Moral Attitudes & Mental Disorders." *The Hastings Center Report* 32 (2): pp. 14–21.

Schmitt, Michael N. 2010. "Military Necessity and Humanity in International Humanitarian Law: Preserving the Delicate Balance." *Virginia Journal of International Law* 50 (450): pp. 795–839.

Strawson, Peter F. 1982. "Freedom and Resentment." In *Free Will*, edited by Gary Watson, pp. 59–80. Oxford: Oxford University Press.

Turing, Alan. 1950. "Computing Machinery and Intelligence." *Mind* 59 (235): pp. 433–460.

Vogel, Ryan J. 2010. "Drone Warfare and the Law of Armed Conflict." *Denver Journal of International Law and Policy* 39 (1): pp. 101–138.

Wagner, Markus. 2012. "Beyond the Drone Debate: Autonomy in Tomorrow's Battlespace." *America Society of International Law Proceedings* 106: pp. 80–84.

13

Blind Brains and Moral Machines: Neuroscience and Autonomous Weapon Systems

NICHOLAS G. EVANS

While the majority of neuroscience research promises novel therapies for treating dementia and post-traumatic stress disorder, among others, a lesser-known branch of neuroscientific research informs the construction of artificial intelligence inspired by human neurophysiology. The driving force behind these advances is the tremendous capacity of humans to interpret vast amounts of data into concrete action: a challenge that faces the development of autonomous robots, including autonomous weapons systems. For those concerned with the normative implications of autonomous weapons systems (AWS), however, a tension arises: that between the primary attraction of AWS are their theoretic capacity to make better decisions than humans in armed conflict, and the relatively low-hanging fruit of modeling machine intelligence on the very thing that causes humans to make (relatively) bad decisions—the human brain.

In this chapter, I examine human cognition as a model for machine intelligence, and some of its implications for AWS development. I first outline recent developments in neuroscience as drivers for advances in artificial intelligence. I then expand on a key distinction for the ethics of AWS: poor normative decisions that are a function of poor judgments given a certain set of inputs, and poor normative decisions that are a function of poor sets of inputs. I argue that given that there are cases in the second category of decisions in which we judge humans to have acted wrongly, we should likewise judge AWS platforms on a similar basis. Further, while

Nicholas G. Evans, *Blind Brains and Moral Machines: Neuroscience and Autonomous Weapon Systems* In: *Lethal Autonomous Weapons*. Edited by: Jai Galliott, Duncan MacIntosh and Jens David Ohlin, © Oxford University Press (2021). DOI: 10.1093/oso/9780197546048.003.0014 an AWS may in principle outperform humans in the former, it is an open question of *design* whether they can outperform humans in the latter, given the development of machine intelligence along human neurobiological lines. I then discuss what this means for the design and control of, and ultimately liability for AWS behavior, and sources of inspiration for the alternate design of AWS platforms.

13.1: INTRODUCTION

The potential emergence of lethal autonomous weapons system (LAWS) has given rise to, among other things, concern about the possibility of machines making decisions about when to kill, or when to refrain from killing. This concern is most acute in the idea of intelligent machines capable of thinking about killing in the vein of science fiction movies;[1] in more prosaic terms, it manifests in The Campaign to Stop Killer Robots (2018) and other forms of policy advocacy that make clear that the choice—however we understand that choice—to kill ought to remain in human hands, or with a "human in the loop" (Evans 2011). The former dovetails into long-standing concern with the rise of artificial intelligence (AI), or more appropriately artificial *general* intelligence (AGI). The latter with responsibility in war and fears of conflict escalation through autonomous drone warfare (Woodhams and Barrie 2018).

The chief argument for LAWS is the supposition that machines are, in principle, less fallible than humans. Machines do not get tired, do not get drunk, do not consume too many go-pills, and do not hate. Humans clearly do. Therefore, even a machine acting with human-like precision will make better decisions than an actual human. And, advocates would say, we can expect that LAWS will eventually surpass humans in their capacity for information processing and decision capacities (Arkin 2009).

In this chapter, my aim is not to argue whether or not we ought to use LAWS. That question has been asked a number of ways, with varying conclusions (Himmelreich 2019). Rather, I ask, even if we believe LAWS could, in principle, be justified technologies in armed conflict, what form should their decision process take? Not all decisions are created equal, and even advocates should be careful about the way their machines make decisions.

To advance this argument, I look at the connection between modern cognitive neuroscience and machine learning. The latter is clearly tied to LAWS as a subspecies of AI. The former, however, has not been explored, and I note how LAWS arguably benefit from civilian neuroscientific work into how the human brain processes large volumes of data and convert them to precise action.

From there, I argue that far from entailing achievement of human-like consciousness, this relationship between neuroscience and LAWS is modular, utilizing strategies common to human neural processing where it is advantageous to do so. This is similar to a view of functionalism that Scott Bakker has termed the "blind brain hypothesis." While I only sketch Bakker's view here, I note that a corollary of the blind brain hypothesis—and one Bakker has explored in detail—is how various neural processes can be instrumentalized in aid of other projects. Here, that other project is LAWS.

The crux of this is that the kind of process we choose to use in pursuing LAWS is important. I use two examples to show why this might be significant. The first is the gaze heuristic, a neuromotor function that undergirds how talented sportspeople, and apex predators such as birds of prey, perform spectacular catches. This is seemingly uncontroversial as a process and may, in fact, be beneficial for LAWS. The more controversial process is one Bakker demonstrates: the way "encapsulation" of information can allow for discrete decisions in the presence of extreme information loads. This is far more problematic, insofar as encapsulation allows for rapid information process, but does so in a way that reflects unknown or under-described bias.

The central thesis of my argument is this: if a process from cognitive neuroscience describing a human neural process is to be imported into LAWS, it ought to be a process that either (a) is good in its own right, or (b) is good in virtue of other elements of LAWS (even if it is not good for humans). If a process fails on both of these counts, it is a kind of process that LAWS ought not to have. I then conclude with a comment on how this might guide research into, and about LAWS.

13.2: HOW ROBOTS ~~THINK~~ BEHAVE

The term "neural net" is ubiquitous. Less known, however, is how strongly the *neural* in neural nets points to its inspiration and evolution. Neural nets are a subtype of these algorithms that take as their starting point the structure of human neural connections. In the brain, each neuron is connected to multiple others, allowing for the parallel processing of information, and the reinforcement of particular patterns as the brain learns. Neural networks start off as relatively homogeneous sets of weightings, but as information is added, the weightings between each connection begin to take the shape of the data provided, creating or eliminating pathways between multiple sets of properties in response to stimuli.

These kinds of algorithms are behavioral in nature but are often very limited in scope. AlphaGo was a deep learning algorithm designed to play the game Go, indigenous to Japan and China. Go is a game involving placing tiles on a 19 x 19 grid, in order to capture territory. The rules are very simple, but the large board size means that a game of Go has $2x10^{170}$ potential configurations. It was initially thought impossible for a machine to play Go at the same level as a human, but neural nets allowed for a machine, fed historical matches, to identify patterns and create strategies that would ultimately lead to the defeat of Ke Jie, the top Go player in the world (Google 2017).

Neuroscience has been an often-silent partner in the development of these algorithms. Much like Go, human behavior is very complex. Unlike Go, however, intelligence collection is highly multimodal: it involves a very broad range of signals, including social media, metadata, photographic, and audio recording. The task is to synthesize these into actionable data, determine the connections between them, and decide what matters. Here, neuroscience aids the processing of data through the creation of neural nets.

This relationship between neuroscience is self-reinforcing. On the one hand, insights from neuroscience provide a basis for thinking about designing algorithms to process data and make decisions. On the other, these algorithms can be trained to predict neural function. The Leifer Lab at Princeton University, for example, studies the dynamics of neural systems in *C. Elegans,* the nematode worm (Nguyen et al. 2017). The lab has constructed computational models, using optogenetics (in which genetically engineered worms' brains emit light as they process information), to describe all twenty-three neurons of a worm's brain. In case these seem trivial, let's put the kind of experiment in context: using computer science, the lab has created a near-perfect model of the neurology of a worm. This is a highly accurate model of a very simple brain—contrasted to human neuroscience, in which we tend to only provide rough models of one of the most complex brains on the planet.

What this collaboration between neuroscience and AI provides, at the level of neuroscience, is a set of tools to describe, and predict, the behavior of adversaries. A 2018 issue of *The Next Wave*, the National Security Agency's (NSA) technology review, noted that as researchers incorporate insights from neuroscience and AI into successive versions of the machine learning algorithms, they hoped to devise solutions to complex information processing tasks, with the goal of training machines to human-like proficiency and beyond. The goal here to train machines to perform much of the work of human analysts, but on scales that are too time consuming and/or complex for older forms of intelligence collection.

13.3: LEVERAGING THE HUMAN

As with intelligence collections, so with LAWS. A key impediment for self-governing robots is the capacity to generalize across object spaces. Neural nets are, in principle, great at finding things they already know about but find much more difficult the task—one that humans find very easy—to understand what new objects are when presented with conflicting data. A human could have only seen green frogs, for example, but understand that they are looking at a frog even if it is black and white striped. Not so, for many if not most neural nets.

This lack of generalizability has serious implications for targeting in LAWS. Human faces are notoriously difficult to parse. The set on which facial recognition AI are trained, moreover, are ethically problematic in their own right (Keyes et al. 2019). So, there is a strong incentive to develop neural nets that are capable of generalizing across and within object sets, even in the absence of strong data sets.

Enter neuroscience. Observations of rat brains, and later humans, have shown that one possible mechanism for generalization is a certain stochasticity, or randomness, in forming associations. Researchers at Purdue University showed in 2019 how the introduction of this randomness could form unexpected connections that allow for novel inferences, increasing the capacity for generalization.

This kind of randomness, inserted into the training of LAWS, could, in principle, generate inferential capacities that allow LAWS to better distinguish between combatants, or to perform some of the inferences about which critics of LAWS worry, such as distinguishing between ununiformed combatants and civilians. Although the algorithms that underlie actual LAWS development are (for understandable strategic reasons) not publicly available, we have reason to think that they may be.

The Defense Advanced Research Projects Agency (DARPA), for a start, has a strong connection to neuroscience, and an interest in developing AI that has the capacity for strong forms of generalization. The Agency's Science of Artificial Intelligence and Learning for Open-world Novelty (SAIL-ON) program has, as its core mission, developing AI that can rapidly generalize among object sets without the prohibitive cost of compiling data, which it identified during its AI Next campaign as a key sticking point to current approaches to AI. The agency, moreover, is deeply involved in neuroscience research, particularly around interpreting neural signals in deterministic ways for its brain-computer interfaces program. It also pursues the development of highly detailed models of insect brains similar to the Leifer lab's work to determine how insects generate complex behaviors from relatively simple neural systems, often only a few hundred neurons. Finally, DARPA has a broad program, the KAIROS program, which seeks to develop AI that can generate schemas to process information.

With such a range of projects, the general thrust of DARPA appears to be the creation of AI, inspired by or using human neural processes to perform tasks subservient to (in the loop), supervised by (on the loop), or independent of (out of the loop) human decision-making. This is not concrete proof, but DARPA's responses to particular operational applications are notoriously tight-lipped: a spokesperson for DARPA, after a 2015 test in which a woman used a brain-computer interface (BCI) to control a F-35 Joint Strike Fighter in simulation, refused to refer to the participant as a "test pilot" (Stockton 2015). This is understandable from an information security perspective (Evans 2021; Evans and Moreno 2017), but it shouldn't by itself stop us from making smart inferences about where DARPA is going with their technologies, especially given the long-standing US drive to develop autonomous weaponry (Evans 2011).

13.4: BLIND BRAINS AND MORAL MACHINES: REPLICATING STRENGTH OR WEAKNESS?

The relationship between neuroscience is ongoing and bidirectional and provides clear benefits in certain contexts. The development of neural nets has created a boom in information and data processing that allows large, disparate sets of data to be converted into actionable information. This has fed back into neuroscience, such as the development of broad models of human brain function and pathology in an effort to better describe and treat diseases such as Alzheimer's disease (Evans and Moreno 2014). It remains to be seen, however, whether this approach is productive in the case of LAWS.

A key problem for advocates of LAWS, or at least LAWS whose architecture is at least partly based on human neural states, is the degree to which the alleged failings of humans are dependent on the functional properties of human brains. For some, especially physicalists about the mind, the question may seem self-evident: all human behaviors, and their corresponding mental states, are based in the brain in some important sense. But the importance of this question is whether the *structure of human neurology*—and the neurology on which AI might be based—gives rise to some of the failings LAWS are meant to prevent.

To use an analogy from computer science—apropos given the connections between computer and cognitive science—some vulnerabilities a computer may have to exploitation are grounded in the flaws in software. Because software is highly malleable, it can be patched and secured against with relative ease. Some vulnerabilities, however, are grounded in the hardware, the physical circuitry of the computer. These are rarer but can be devastating if they can be exploited because they are much harder (though not impossible) to repair. The Meltdown vulnerability that primarily affected Intel microprocessors, discovered in January 2018, is an example of a hardware-based vulnerability, albeit one that had a software-based fix (Lipp et al. 2018).

In humans, we might have the same concerns. Some of our vulnerabilities, or failings, might be soft coded into us and subject to revision. Our propensity to hate people is arguably soft coded; even if it lies in the brain in some sense, the mental state and set of behaviors around hatred for particular individuals is certainly subject to revision: we can come to love, or at least stop hating our enemies.

Other behaviors, however, may be at least partially hard coded into our cognition, or even our neurology. These behaviors are likely those that are ubiquitous to humans, are present from an early age, and/or are kept for the majority of a human's life. They may be subject to development or refinement, and may exhibit natural variation among humans, but are grounded in aspects of human cognition that are by and large hardwired, including the possibility that they are part of neural development itself.

The most obvious behavior like this is the gaze heuristic. The gaze heuristic is common to humans but is shared with predators such as hawks (Hamlin 2017) and even dragonflies (Lin and Leonardo 2017). The heuristic relies on an agent orienting their gaze on the probable end path of an objective, relying on the change in angle an object has in your field of vision, and continuing to orient vision and bodily position until the object is intercepted. This is the process by which athletes intercept fast-moving balls in games such as baseball or cricket; anyone who has played (as this author was required to as part of Australian schooling) knows that to catch a ball you move where the ball *will be*, rather than toward where the ball is. Hamlin credits the "discovery" of the heuristic to the Royal Air Force (RAF) in the Second World War, but given the use of projectile weapons by indigenous Australians for almost 50 thousand years, and the presence of the heuristic in biological ancestors more than half a billion years distant from us (Peterson, Cotton, Gehling, and Pisani 2008), it is more likely that they discovered it *qua* heuristic that could be developed.

The gaze heuristic, likewise, is used in robotic systems. Often described in terms of "catching heuristics," the gaze heuristic has been used in humanoid robots or robotic arms trained to catch projectiles (Belousov et al. 2016; Kim, Shukla, and Billard 2014). Its use, however, gives lie to the idea that the gaze heuristic is only used in robots for catching. One author described the AIM9 Sidewinder missile, whose control logic uses the gaze heuristic, as the "one of the simplest systems either mechanical or biological that is capable of making decisions and completing a task autonomously" (Gigerenzer and Gray 2017). It is very easy to see how the use of the gaze heuristic in an AIM9 lends itself to LAWS.

The gaze heuristic is arguably unproblematic as a heuristic. One reason for this is that the heuristic is ontology independent: one does not have to know what it is one targeting to use the heuristic effectively. LAWS could use the gaze heuristic, modeled after human cognition, without compromising its purported benefits. LAWS could, in all likelihood, use the gaze heuristic more consistently than humans in targeting, for the reasons described by advocates above: it would not be distracted, tired, intoxicated, angry, and so on.

But it's not clear that this should necessarily apply to all human cognition. Some of the most sophisticated elements of human cognition might be profoundly maladaptive if what we care about are LAWS that better perform tasks according to the laws of war than humans do. To understand why requires a more thoroughgoing analysis of how the brain interprets data. I will only sketch this framework but do so in a way that highlights where these problems arise.

Scott Bakker provides a useful framework for thinking about how information is processed into sense data in mental states. The Blind Brain Hypothesis (BBT) is Bakker's early attempt to explain an account of the mind that takes as its basis the most recent findings in neuroscience and cognitive science (Bakker 2017). Bakker's work in philosophy of mind is similar to that of Churchland's (1989) work, as well as of other recent eliminativists, but the theory of mind itself is less interesting than the application of neuroscience to the human mind, and its further application to AI.

The problem, as set up by Bakker, is familiar to AI. The information available to an agent—agent here in a loose sense—is vast, well beyond what is necessary, or practically actionable. The human brain has a processing power of some 38 trillion operations a second, of which an agent only has access to the tiniest amount. A machine can compute an arbitrarily large amount of data, but formal calculation scales with complexity. So heuristics, and neurocognitive tricks, are necessary to fold this immense stream of data into the day-to-day functioning of an agent.

These tricks are, according to Bakker, "encapsulated" such that while they process information, the conscious brain has no access to them. A paradigm example Bakker gives of this encapsulation (and one that he claims is one-sided regarding information), is the visual field. The plain-language account of this claim is as such: Can you *see* the limits of your vision? The answer is, I presume, "no." There is no hard boundary between your sight and its limit; you cannot see not seeing. Your brain simply does not deliver you that information.

This, of course, is probably adaptive in a range of contexts. But this lack of information can have interesting consequences. Consider "flavor," the thing most people experience when eating. This is a conflation of the sense data of taste (tongue) and aroma (olfactory), such that flavors are a combination of both. Because we don't have knowledge of the boundaries of the information we receive from either, however, it is more or less impossible to determine in everyday activity what component of flavor arises in our tongue, and what in our nose. This is partly physical (the mouth and nasal passage are connected); it is also partly cognitive. We are not given access to the process by which the input data is converted to the signal we experience as sensation.

The problem for LAWS, I believe, is similar. The idea of a neural net is one in which the weightings of a neural net are encapsulated. That is, the value of the weights is divorced from the ream of data that an AI has been trained on. More importantly, the input of new data, if it changes those weights, is likewise atemporal. An AI trained on deep learning typically has no account of why its weights are the way they are. This is intentional on behalf of programmers, as it maintains the inferences generated through training without the processing or storage load of maintaining a database of thousands, millions, or even billions of datapoints from a training set and future experiences.

This is, in a way, how humans learn many tasks. We don't typically remember every instance of training we receive in a task, but rather only remember how to do that task and—if we're lucky or have good memories—certain memorable instances of our training: like our first success. But often this may be for orthogonal reasons to the training itself, like how good we felt at our success, not the technical aspects of the success.

These learning patterns, however, are vulnerable and maladaptive in virtue of their informational asymmetry and the way we are blind to their contours. Study of narrative, for example, has revealed that the narrative in which information is embedded can influence in favor of that information, even when we disagree with the propositional content it conveys (Bruneau, Dufour, and Saxe 2013; Bezdek 2015). The delivery-dependent form of terrorist messaging is a challenge for counterterrorism operations that need to track not simply hateful messaging, but the rhetorical and narrative forms that it takes (Casebeer 2005; 2014).

These kinds of effects, unlike the gaze heuristic, can be profoundly maladaptive. Our inability to know why we believe things, or know *that* we are coming to believe things, is a serious flaw in human cognition and behavior. The more we learn about human behavior, moreover, the more we become aware that the process of belief formation is rarely if ever rational or straightforward. We should be profoundly careful, then, if we are to incorporate these neurocognitive tricks into LAWS, even if they are efficacious from a programming side.

13.5: THE RESPONSIBILITY GAP AND HUMAN-INSPIRED LAWS

I have not described all possible neurocognitive tricks that might be transferred to LAWS from human cognition. What is more productive is to describe the kinds of impact tricks have in terms of what scholars on LAWS have referred to as the "responsibility gap"—the apparent disconnect between the consequences of a robot's actions, and the locus of responsibility for those acts (Matthias 2004; Sparrow 2007).

Like human cognition, robotic behavior is not holistic but modular. Unlike human cognition, however, designers have to make choices about which modules to include, and (to a degree) operators and their superiors have to make choices about which modules to lean on in an engagement. As systems become more complex the interactions become harder to anticipate, but there are still important choices to be made. At this level of discretion, the way LAWS are designed has implications for the responsibility gap.

Let's consider three kinds of scenarios.

13.5.1: Equivalence

In Equivalence, the same problems inherent to human neurobiology exist in some LAWS system. The robot's decision framework is less akratic than a human's, and thus not prone to moral wrongdoing caused by anger or hate. It, however, is still vulnerable to the features of the process that, like their human counterparts, are limited by design. For example, a robot's target recognition could be limited by the kinds and resolutions of identifying markings it can detect at speed. Here, as in human operations, responsibility is pushed toward the command structure that approves operations. In cases like the bombing of a hospital in Afghanistan in 2016, for example, operators attested that poor intelligence collection led to the ultimate failures that resulted in the bombing (Aisch, Keller, and Peçana 2016). LAWS in these contexts, armed with the same information, might not make the same errors, but if they did, we would look to the command and intelligence structures that caused this as we would with a human.

13.5.2: Trade-Off

At times, a robot might not suffer from the limitations of human neurobiology in its design, but rather some other nonhuman deficiency. This is not uncommon in existing robotic behavior. Some automatic sensors on restroom faucets that use infrared sensors can't "see" African Americans" (Hankerson 2017); Google's image recognition system famously categorized an African American couple as "gorillas" (Grush 2015); a HP camera that was meant to move to track faces as they moved around a frame could only do so with white faces, or faces washed in a particular glare (Hankerson 2017). These are cases, typically, of design choices related to how a computer detects edges, what facial morphologies are counted as sufficiently "human," and so on. Even with improvements in computing, these issues are unlikely to disappear. Just like the gaze heuristic or narratives, robots are programmed with heuristics and other neurocognitive tricks to process the huge amounts of information required to navigate the world. There's a prima facie case, however, that at least in a normative sense responsibility shifts to the designers of LAWS where the kinds of choices are impermissible and are anticipated or should reasonably be anticipated to arise. In choosing to introduce certain kinds of systems into LAWS, designers are responsible to the degree their choices are the determining factor in introducing these decision frameworks to the battlefield (e.g., Fichtelberg 2006), just as in the case of less-autonomous systems.

It is important to note, further, that trade-off designs provide a strong challenge to leadership over autonomous programs. Commanders are required to account for the disposition of their forces in operations, and it would be a mistake to consider LAWS as not holding dispositions in this sense. Even if they are not human, or possess agency or self-concept, LAWS are imbued with certain kinds of strengths and shortcomings. The challenge, as yet undiscussed, is the degree to which commanders are prepared to account for a set of reliable yet altogether *alien* shortcomings possessed by the AW.

13.5.3: Non-Inferiority

A case may arise where LAWS, in collaboration with neuroscience and cognitive science, are ultimately designed to be non-inferior to humans. That is, LAWS could be designed in a way that takes the best of human information processing and then designs out the "bugs" that are hardwired into us. This is the best option, but in some cases the most challenging.

In terms of responsibility, this seems, on the one hand, the most promising. In principle, you could design out otherwise morally blameworthy behavior from the robot. This is the kind of view put forward by Arkin and others, in which LAWS can do a better job at prosecuting war in line with military ethics and/or international humanitarian law than a human ever could.

Such a LAWS would seem, on first blush, to push liability back to command. After all, by designing out behavior that would otherwise cause the AW to act in ways that are similar to certain blameworthy actions by humans, it reduces the space of possible wrongdoing to things such as cyber perfidy to induce the AW to fail to recognize combatants as such (or noncombatants as such), for which belligerents are presumably responsible. Another example would be the problem of poorly framed orders by command, carried out faithfully by the machine.

On the other hand, if LAWS are non-inferior to humans, would one sense in which they would have to be so the (all too) human propensity to misplace our better natures, such as in the loyalty to others that leads individuals to prosecute illegal orders? These misplaced loyalties are at least in part determined by some of the tricks discussed above, such as the capacity to identify with factors orthogonal to a decision; or susceptibility to the narrative form of a story. Assuming these modules are one reason humans behave unethically on the battlefield an engineer may be obligated to design out these characteristics, and we would then anticipate that LAWS would be incapable in principle of following illegal orders.

If not incapable of, or at the very least highly resistant to following illegal orders, a LAWS would likely fail to be non-inferior to humans, but rather an example of Equivalence or Trade-Off above. In this case, the question lies in where the decision to introduce such a capacity exists. The decision could be that of the developers, or it could be *requested* by command or acquisition staff. That decision, however, should be identifiable.

The other alternative is that the capacity to follow illegal orders could be itself a result of a vulnerability introduced into the LAWS framework. Imagine a design scenario as follows. An autonomous, aerial vehicle is provided instructions about eliminating insurgents. Let's suppose that upon finding insurgents embedded in a civilian population (or maybe ahead of time), the LAWS messages command and asks for confirmation on whether to proceed. Legal actions *in bello* must, inter alia, be proportionate to the goals of the use of force. But let's suppose that the way a LAWS is designed is that a commander can simply enter a string or number to reflect the urgency or necessity of the operation. The commander, in order to compel the LAWS to act, types in some arbitrarily large number that they know, or through experience have inferred is large enough to always compel the LAWS to act. They are able to enter this, and have the LAWS "believe" them absent a request for evidence.

This would be a way that the input of certain diagnostics would comprise one of the blind spots Bakker talks about. By making the interpretive basis for certain reasons for action *unavailable* to LAWS, we risk making it vulnerable to precisely the same kinds of problems that plague human-centric operations. That is, many of the failings that plague human operators are not mere akratic actions, or actions taken in a reduced capacity. They are grounded, and framed, in our blind spots about our cognition and our reasons for action. Building those blind sports in to LAWS, informed by human neuroscience or not, is a pitfall of LAWS as a subset of general advances in robotics.

13.6: POLICIES MOVING FORWARD

In this chapter, I have argued that there are reasons to believe that the connection between cognitive science, and AI, poses challenges for LAWS. These are not unique to LAWS, but rather a particular class of problem that plagues AI. These problems are grounded in the capacity for our failings and/or shortcomings to be built in to the structure of LAWS.

This poses a design challenge for LAWS, and in closing, I provide a couple of potential options for thinking about LAWS governance, given the likely weaknesses of these platforms. The first and most obvious is to keep humans in the loop. That is, in light of the likely failings of LAWS, we ought to keep humans in the loop for oversight of the problem. While this is an attractive option, I think it is of limited utility. This is because, insofar as humans will often feature the same blind spots as LAWS (and possibly more), it is not clear that this kind of oversight is sufficient. Granted, serial observation of a problem can give us a higher true-positive rate, in the same way that an x-ray, followed by a blood test for cancer in case of a positive, is better than an x-ray alone. However, this implies the events are independent and serial. It is hard to see how, in practice, these events could be, given the predilection for humans to normalize and place trust in machines.

The second, however, would be to engage in what others have referred to as a process of "value sensitive design" (van den Hoven 1997). That is, to ensure that each technical component of LAWS is examined for the kinds of values it promotes, and its limits well-described both individually and as part of the system. These values can then be compared against human operation in war, and the standards set out by international humanitarian law. The key feature here, however, is to examine the components for their potential failings as well as their larger response.

Together, these two retain the possibility that LAWS could be used, in principle, so that any given action corresponds to the appropriate norms. It does not eschew further worries about conflict escalation and other principled opposition to LAWS, but it goes a long way to solving some of the individual act-level engineering problems that seem to arise when we set about the task of creating robots to fight on our behalf.

ACKNOWLEDGMENT

Research on this topic was funded by a Greenwall Foundation Making a Difference in Real-World Bioethics Dilemmas Mentored Project Grant, "Dual-Use Neurotechnologies and International Governance Arrangements," and a Greenwall Foundation President's Grant "Neurotechnological Candidates for Consideration in Periodic Revisions of the Biological and Toxin Weapons Convention and Chemical Weapons Convention." The work on AI was informed by NSF grant #1734521, "Ethical Algorithms in Autonomous Vehicles."

NOTE

1. Though, to the best of my knowledge, *The Terminator* franchise spends little to no time concerned with whether the T-series have mental states. They have operating systems, but there's a serious question about their self-concept (though I haven't seen *Dark Fate*).

WORKS CITED

Aisch, Gregor, Josh Keller, and S. Sergio Peçanha. 2016. "How a Cascade of Errors Led to the U.S. Airstrike on an Afghan Hospital." *New York Times*, April 29. Accessed August 8, 2019. https://www.nytimes.com/interactive/2015/11/25/world/asia/errors-us-airstrike-afghan-kunduz-msf-hospital.html.

Arkin, Ronald C. 2009. *Governing Lethal Behavior in Autonomous Robots*. London: Routledge.

Bakker, Scott R. 2017. *The Last Magic Show: A Blind Brain Theory of the Appearance of Consciousness*. Accessed September 10, 2019. https://www.academia.edu/1502945/The_Last_Magic_Show_A_Blind_Brain_Theory_of_the_Appearance_of_Consciousness?auto=download.

Belousov, Boris, Gerhard Neumann, Constantin A. Rothkopf, and Jan Peters. 2016. "Catching Heuristics Are Optimal Control Policies." In *30th Conference on Neural Information Processing Systems* (NIPS 2016). Barcelona, Spain.

Bezdek, Matt A., Richard J. Gerrig, William G. Wenzel, Jaemin Shin, Kate Pirog Revill, and Eric H. Schumacher. 2015. "Neural Evidence That Suspense Narrows Attentional Focus." *Neuroscience* 303: pp. 338–345. https://dx.doi.org/10.1016/j.neuroscience.2015.06.055

Bruneau, Emile, Nicholas Dufour, and Rebecca Saxe. 2013. "How We Know It Hurts: Item Analysis of Written Narratives Reveals Distinct Neural Responses to Others' Physical Pain and Emotional Suffering." *PLoS ONE* 8 (4). https://dx.doi.org/10.1371/journal.pone.0063085

Campaign to Stop Killer Robots. 2018. *Statement to the Convention on Conventional Weapons Meeting of High Contracting Parties*. Geneva: Meeting of High Contracting Parties. November 22. https://www.stopkillerrobots.org/wp-content/uploads/2018/11/KRC_StmtCCW_21Nov2018_AS-DELIVERED.pdf.

Casebeer, William D. and James A. Russell. 2005. "Storytelling and Terrorism: Towards a Comprehensive 'Counter-Narrative Strategy.'" *Strategic Insights* 4 (3): pp. 1–16.

Casebeer, William. 2014. "The Neuroscience of Enhancement: A Framework for Ethical Analysis." PowerPoint Slides. *Penn Neuroethics Series*. Philadelphia: University of Pensylvania.

Churchland, Paul M. 1989. *A Neurocomputational Perspective: The Nature of Mind and the Structure of Science*. Cambridge, MA: MIT Press.

DARPA. 2019. "AI Next Campaign." Washington, DC: Department of Defense. Accessed September 18 2019. https://www.darpa.mil/work-with-us/ai-next-campaign.

Evans, Nicholas G. 2011. "Emerging Military Technologies: A Case Study in Neurowarfare." In *New Wars and New Soldiers: Military Ethics in the Contemporary World*, edited by Paul Tripodi and Jessica Wolfendale, pp. 105–116. London: Ashgate.

Evans, Nicholas G. and Jonathan D. Moreno. 2017. "Neuroethics and Policy at the National Security Interface." In *Debates About Neuroethics: Perspectives on Its Development, Focus and Future*, edited by Eric Racine and John Aspler, pp. 141–160. Dordecht: Springer.

Evans, Nicholas G. Forthcoming 2020. *The Ethics of Neuroscience and National Security*. New York: Routledge.

Fichtelberg, Aaron. 2006. "Applying the Rules of Just War Theory to Engineers in the Arms Industry." *Science and Engineering Ethics* 12 (4): pp. 685–700. https://dx.doi.org/10.1007/s11948-006-0064-1

Gigerenzer, Gerd and Wayne D. Gray. 2017. "A Simple Heuristic Successfully Used by Humans, Animals, and Machines: The Story of the RAF and Luftwaffe, Hawks and Ducks, Dogs and Frisbees, Baseball Outfielders and Sidewinder Missiles—Oh My!" *Topics in Cognitive Science* 9 (2): pp. 260–263. https://dx.doi.org/10.1111/tops.12269.

Google. 2017. *AlphaGo*. Accessed January 24, 2020. http://deepmind.com

Grush, Loren. 2015. "Google Engineer Apologizes after Photos App Tags Two Black People as Gorillas." *The Verge*. July 1. Accessed July 12, 2019. https://www.theverge.com/2015/7/1/8880363/google-apologizes-photos-app-tags-two-black-people-gorillas.

Hamlin, Robert P. 2017. "The Gaze Heuristic:" Biography of an Adaptively Rational Decision Process." *Topics in Cognitive Science* 9 (2): pp. 264–288. https://dx.doi.org/10.1111/tops.12253

Hankerson, David, Andrea R. Marshall, Jennifer Booker, Houda El Mimouni, Imani Walker and Jennifer A. Rode. 2016. "Does Technology Have Race?" In *CHI EA '16 Proceedings of the 2016 CHI Conference Extended Abstracts on Human Factors in Computing Systems*. May. San Jose: Association for Computing Machinery, pp. 473–486.

Himmelreich, Johannes H. 2019. "Responsibility for Killer Robots." *Ethical Theory and Moral Practice* 22 (3): pp. 731–747. 10.1007/s10677-019-10007-9.

Keyes, Os, Nikki Stevens, and Jacqueline Wernimont. 2019. "The Government Is Using the Most Vulnerable People to Test Facial Recognition Software." *Slate*. March 17. Accessed September 18, 2019. https://slate.com/technology/2019/03/facial-recognition-nist-verification-testing-data-sets-children-immigrants-consent.html.

Kim, Seungsu, Ashwini Shukla, and Aude Billard. 2014. "Catching Objects in Flight." *IEEE Transactions on Robotics* 30 (5): pp. 1049–1065. https://dx.doi.org/10.1109/tro.2014.2316022.

Lin, Huai-Ti and Anthony Leonardo. 2017. "Heuristic Rules Underlying Dragonfly Prey Selection and Interception." *Current Biology* 27 (8): pp. 1124–1137. https://dx.doi.org/10.1016/j.cub.2017.03.010.

Lipp, Moritz, Michael Scwarz, Daniel Gruss, Thomas Prescher, Werner Haas, Anders Fogh, Jann Horn, Stefan Mangard, Paul Kocher, Daniel Genkin, Yuval Yarom, and Mike Hamburg. 2018. "Meltdown: Reading Kernel Memory from User Space." Accessed September 19, 2019. https://meltdownattack.com/meltdown.pdf.

Matthias, Andreas. 2004. "The Responsibility Gap: Ascribing Responsibility for the Actions of Learning Automata." *Ethics and Information Technology* 6 (3): pp. 175–183. https://dx.doi.org/10.1007/s10676-004-3422-1.

Nguyen Jeffrey P., Ashley N. Linder, George S. Plummer, Joshua W. Shaevitz, and Andrew M. Leifer. 2017. "Automatically Tracking Neurons in a Moving and Deforming Brain." *PLOS Computational Biology* 13 (5). https://doi.org/10.1371/journal.pcbi.1005517.

Onyshkevych, Boyan. 2019. "Knowledge-Directed Artificial Intelligence Reasoning Over Schemas (KAIROS)." *DARPA*. Accessed September 19, 2019. https://www.darpa.mil/program/knowledge-directed-artificial-intelligence-reasoning-over-schemas.

Peterson, Kevin J., James A. Cotton, James G. Gehling, and Davide Pisani. 2008. "The Ediacaran Emergence of Bilaterians: Congruence between the Genetic and the Geological Fossil Records." *Philosophical Transactions of the Royal Society B: Biological Sciences* 363 (1496): pp. 1435–1443. https://dx.doi.org/10.1098/rstb.2007.2233.

Sparrow, Robert. 2007. "Killer Robots." *Journal of Applied Philosophy* 24 (1): pp. 62–77. https://dx.doi.org/10.1111/j.1468-5930.2007.00346.x.

Stockton, Nick. 2015. "Woman Controls a Fighter Jet Sim Using Only Her Mind." *Wired*. May 3. Accessed August 2, 2019. https://www.wired.com/2015/03/woman-controls-fighter-jet-sim-using-mind/.

van den Hoven, Jeroen. 1997. "Computer Ethics and Moral Methodology." *Metaphilosophy* 28 (3): pp. 234–248. https://dx.doi.org/10.1111/1467-9973.00053.

Woodhams, George and John Barrie. 2018. *Armed UAVs in Conflict Escalation and Inter-State Crisis*. Geneva: UNIDIR Resources. Accessed September 13, 2019. http://www.unidir.org/files/publications/pdfs/armed-uav-in-conflict-escalation-and-inter-state-crisis-en-747.pdf#page17.

PART III

Developing Meaningful Human Control

14

Enforced Transparency: A Solution to Autonomous Weapons as Potentially Uncontrollable Weapons Similar to Bioweapons

ARMIN KRISHNAN

14.1: INTRODUCTION

AWS are based on the application of Artificial Intelligence (AI), which is designed to replicate intelligent human behavior. AWS are not merely automated in the sense that they can automatically engage targets under preprogrammed conditions with no direct human control, but they would be able to learn from experience and thereby improve their capacity to carry out a particular function with little or no need for human intervention. In other words, AWS would be able go beyond their original programming and would reprogram themselves by optimizing desirable outputs. However, the potential for unpredictable behavior of future AWS has alarmed academics, arms control activists, and also some governments.

UN Special Rapporteur Cristof Heyns warned that "[a]utonomous systems can function in an open environment, under unstructured and dynamic circumstances. As such their actions (like those of humans) may ultimately be unpredictable, especially in situations as chaotic as armed conflict, and even more so when they interact with other autonomous systems" (Heyns 2013, 8). The United Nations has held several meetings of a Group of Governmental Experts in connection to the Convention on Certain Conventional Weapons from 2014 with eighty governments participating, where a ban or regulation of Lethal Autonomous Weapons Systems (LAWS) has been discussed (Scharre 2018, 346). This indicates that governments

Armin Krishnan, *Enforced Transparency: A Solution to Autonomous Weapons as Potentially Uncontrollable Weapons Similar to Bioweapons* In: *Lethal Autonomous Weapons*. Edited by: Jai Galliott, Duncan MacIntosh and Jens David Ohlin, © Oxford University Press (2021). DOI: 10.1093/oso/9780197546048.003.0015 are aware of the potential dangers of the military application of AI and that they are willing to at least consider preventive arms control measures.

The challenge then becomes how to even approach the regulation of an emerging technology that is advancing at a rapid pace. The consensus among experts is that the key issue is to preserve *meaningful human control* over AWS (Heyns 2016, 15). Since AI is not a weapon as such and merely a method of control over any kind of machine or device, it may not be the best approach in terms of regulation to declare AWS to be a novel and distinctive class of weaponry, but rather to internationally regulate AI as a whole. The goal must be to reduce unpredictability and thereby enhance human ability to retain control for whatever function and capacity AI may be employed. As will be argued below, much can be learned from the challenge of international regulation in the area of biosecurity. The proposed solution is to have sufficient international transparency with respect to AI algorithms and to enforce transparency by way of state responsibility and product liability.

14.2: THE INHERENT UNPREDICTABILITY OF AI

A few decades ago, it was still possible to argue that computers were deterministic machines and could only do what they are programmed to do, making them, in theory, 100% predictable. Software was "frozen" or unable to modify itself. AI was at that time little more than an "expert system" that relied on heuristic rules programmed in a top-down approach into the machine, where the AI would only consist in the computer's ability to figure out which rule to apply in what kind of situation (Lee 2018, 7). This approach could still result in unpredictable behavior in situations not foreseen by the programmers, but more typically, the computer would just get stuck with the task and not do anything. Expert systems are still in use for dealing with certain narrow problems like assigning credit scores, but their main limitation is that they cannot improve their performance by themselves. The desire to overcome this limitation led to machine learning and neural network approaches in AI.

14.2.1: Neural Networks

Artificial neural networks (ANN) are modeled after the human brain. In a brain, neurons are connected to each other through synapses. These connections determine how neurons influence each other and how information flows in the form of a parallel processor (Alpaydin 2016, 86). It is a mechanism that allows the brain to acquire, store, and retrieve information efficiently. As the brain solves new tasks and learns, it changes as the neural connections change whenever information is processed, which is called brain plasticity. Such neural connections in the brain can be simulated on computers via neural network learning algorithms that try to optimize a performance criterion. "In a neural network, learning algorithms adjust the connection weights between neurons . . . the weight between two neurons gets reinforced if the two are active at the same time—the synaptic weight effectively learns the correlation between the two neurons" (Alpaydin 2016, 88–89). In other words, neural networks allow a software to change its programming in order to produce better results (Scharre 2018, 125).

14.2.2: Deep Learning

A major breakthrough occurred in AI in the last decade with the development of "deep learning," which applies neural network algorithms to "big data." Large data sets are used to train computers to solve a particular problem, such as recognizing the difference between a cat and a dog by optimizing "cat-ness" in a set of pictures. The process of machine learning can be supervised by humans to provide feedback to the computer as to how good the solutions are, which helps to improve the computer's ability to come up with correct solutions and reduce the percentage of incorrect solutions (Kaplan 2016, 30). The more data that can be fed to the computer for training, the better the results will be. A further advantage of allowing deep learning is that the AI is not limited by cognitive biases of humans and will, therefore, come up with solutions that are non-intuitive and that would not have been chosen by humans. In fact, the AI solutions may be better than solutions even the best human experts could find. Matthew Scherer has claimed that "the capability [of AI] to produce unforeseen actions may actually have been intended by the systems' designers and operators" (Scherer 2016, 365). In competitive situations such as chess games or trading on markets or on the battlefield, it can potentially provide a huge advantage to deploy AI that can "think" outside of the box and operate beyond the cognitive limitations of humans. As pointed out by Kenneth Payne, ANN "are free from biological constraints and evolved heuristics, both of which serve to aid human decision-making amid pressures of time and uncertainty but can also produce systematic errors of judgment" (Payne 2018, 171–172).

14.2.3: AI as a "Black Box"

Many AI researchers have warned that neural networks function like "black boxes" as inputs are not just manipulated by computer code that can be inspected but also interact with big data in a way that makes traceability and accountability very difficult (Etzioni and Etzioni 2017, 35). According to a report in *MIT Technology Review*,

> [y]ou can't just look inside a deep neural network to see how it works. A network's reasoning is embedded in the behavior of thousands of simulated neurons, arranged into dozens or even hundreds of intricately interconnected layers. The neurons in the first layer each receive an input, like the intensity of a pixel in an image, and then perform a calculation before outputting a new signal. These outputs are fed, in a complex web, to the neurons in the next layer, and so on, until an overall output is produced. Plus, there is a process known as back-propagation that tweaks the calculations of individual neurons in a way that lets the network learn to produce a desired output. (Knight 2017)

Payne similarly stated that "[t]he internal machinations of ANN are currently something of a mystery to humans—we can see the end result of calculations but cannot easily follow the logic inside the hierarchical stack of artificial neurons that produced it" (Payne 2018, 202). Even if AI researchers could understand every connection and process in a neural network, it would still not equate to achieving predictability of the AI system due to the complexity of feedback loops (Georges 2003,

66). This means AI developers cannot predict the behavior of an AI system in any other way than to run identical algorithms with identical data sets.

14.2.4: Evolving Robots

Louis Del Monte has discussed the dangers of deep learning AI to evolve and transcend their original programming by referencing an experiment carried out at the Swiss Federal Institute of Technology in Lausanne. Researchers at Lausanne built small-wheeled robots that were given basic behavioral rules and the ability to learn from experience. They had to avoid dark-colored rings that functioned as poisons and move toward light-colored rings that functioned as food. They were programmed to cooperate with each other by signaling others where the food or poison was. Performance was evaluated in terms of time spent near food vs. time spent near poison. After several hundred generations of these robots where the neural networks or "genomes" of successful robots got replicated and those of the unsuccessful ones got discarded, the robots learned to lure others to poisons and not to signal the location of food, which allowed them to get higher performance scores (Mitri, Floreano, and Keller 2009). In other words, AI researchers discovered that even "primitive artificially intelligent machines are capable of learning deceit, greed, and self-preservation without the researchers programming them to do so" (Del Monte 2018, 142). This is significant as self-learning robots could change their original programming and optimize or prioritize their own survival over other goals or objectives, such as completing a given mission or protecting friendly forces. It is important to keep in mind that circumventing programmed rules or learning deception would not require any self-awareness or human-level intelligence of an AI system but could emerge organically by way of the evolution of its neural network and the knowledge contained in it.

14.2.5: Danger of Inherently Unpredictable AI

There are three fairly obvious dangers of unpredictable AWS: (1) AWS may cause friendly fire incidents where they accidentally engage friendly forces or otherwise endanger or harm friendly forces (Scharre 2018, 141); (2) AWS may commit war crimes by engaging unlawful targets such as civilians or civilian objects or enemy soldiers who are hors de combat or who have signaled surrender. or AWS may cause disproportionate collateral damage (Sparrow 2015); and (3) AWS may lead to accidental wars or "flash wars," where AWS misinterpret the actions of the other side and take offensive action, resulting in out of control and "unforeseeable algorithm interactions" between different AWS with a high risk of escalation to war (Altmann and Sauer 2017, 130).

A particular concern is AWS turning war into "hyperwar," where humans could no longer meaningfully participate as warfare is leaving the "human space" "that is discernible to human senses" (Adams 2001, 1). Hyperwar is a term that was introduced by Air Force planners in the wake of the 1991 Gulf War and it refers to the expectation that future military engagements will take place at "unimaginably" and "unmanageably" fast speeds, thereby making it imperative that "machines will make and carry out battle decisions independent of their human counterparts" (Arnett 1992, 15). Hypersonic missiles and directed energy weapons can attack targets at speeds so great that no human operator could respond to a rapidly emerging threat that "pops up" on the battlefield. Furthermore, miniaturization of robots to micro- and even nano-scale means that autonomous weapons systems could be deployed in the millions, for example, as autonomous swarms that overwhelm targets by sheer numbers (Libicki 1997). "Both attack and defense will be completely automated, because humans are far too slow to participate" (Adams 2001, 9).

14.3: PROPOSED SOLUTIONS

AWS have raised concerns as to their ability to comply with the requirements of IHL in practice, but the issue as to whether AWS would be *in principle* unable to comply with HIS remains contentious. All nations are required to do a legal review of any new weapons system under Article 36 of the Additional Protocol I of the Geneva Convention, which would presumably prevent the introduction of weapons systems that are in violation of the requirements of IHL (Chengeta 2016). Governments have to make sure that any AWS they deploy are capable of being used in a manner that complies with all applicable customary and treaty law. Most importantly, it must be possible to use them in a manner that allows for discrimination and for the proportionate use of force (Schmitt and Thurnher 2013, 246). Furthermore, they would not be allowed to control weapons that violate other treaties such as the BWC, CWC, or CCW. Beyond that, it has been suggested that governments may opt for self-regulation in their military uses of AI to meet the standards set by IHL until the international community is willing to accept the international regulation of AWS, including the possibility of a comprehensive ban. Potential solutions for taming the unpredictability of AI are the "ethical governor," human-machine teaming, and testing and safety standards.

14.3.1: Ethical Governor Approach

Some analysts have claimed that AWS may be able to deliver better ethical outcomes than humans since they would be able to more consistently apply rules of engagement and act in accordance to the conventions of war than humans as they lack their own motivations and moral frailties. Roboticist Ronald Arkin has claimed that humans are prone to be emotional in combat and may therefore be more likely to commit war crimes than a machine that has an ethical programming. He wrote: "It is not my belief that an autonomous unmanned system will be able to be perfectly ethical in the battlefield, but I am convinced that they can perform more ethically than human soldiers are capable of" (Arkin 2009, 30–31). Amitai and Oren Etzioni have similarly called for the development of an "oversight AI" or "guardians" that "can ensure that the decisions made by autonomous weapons will stay within a predetermined set of parameters" (Etzioni and Etzioni 2017b). There are several problems with the oversight AI argument: (1) before an ethical AWS can be developed AI must first solve the "frame problem," namely the general inability of a machine to figure out which changes in a situation are relevant and which are not (Klincewicz 2015, 171); (2) if an AWS was "hardwired" never to attack certain targets such as children, hospitals, or places of worship, it would be straightforward for the enemy to exploit these behavioral limitations (Borenstein 2008, 7); and (3) machines may learn to circumvent rules that have been programmed into them, since the ethical governor would merely amount to a system of rules that runs on top of a self-learning AI system (Del Monte 2018, 143).

14.3.2: Human-Machine Teaming

The US military has frequently stated that they have no intention to move from "on-the-loop" systems to fully autonomous weapons (Friedberg 2016). According to US DoD Directive 3000.09, "[a]utonomus and semi-autonomous systems shall be designed to allow commanders and operators to exercise appropriate levels of human judgment over the use of force" (US DoD 2012, 2). The directive does not rule out the autonomous operation of weapons systems in every instance, but it does seem to impose a requirement for the human supervision of AWS and for the possibility of human intervention in the operation of an AWS at any time. The Pentagon wants to closely integrate humans with machines to combine the higher cognitive ability of humans with some of the main qualities of machines such as speed and greater survivability. This approach is called "centaur warfighting" after centaur chess, where human players work with an AI chess system to achieve a better gameplay than is possible by AI alone (Paul Scharre 2018, 321–322).

The underlying assumption is that human-robot teams would perform better than AWS would on their own. Apart from the chess example, there is actually little evidence for this. While IBM's Deep Blue victory over Gary Kasparov in 1997 was the result of human-machine collaboration where human chess experts trained the AI to beat the world champion, Google's AlphaGo used a deep learning neural network to defeat Go world champion Ke Jie in 2017 (Lee 2018, 1–4). Paul Scharre observed that "AlphaGo learned to play *go* without any human data to start with . . . AlphaGo taught itself to play" (Scharre 2018, 127). Besides, "human-machine collaboration and teamwork will become increasingly difficult as decision-making cycles of AWS shrink to micro-seconds" (Saxon 2016, 208). Some of these challenges could be addressed by integrating humans more closely with AWS by way of brain-machine interfaces that translate human threat perceptions and intentions in machine action in the matter of split seconds or by otherwise enhancing human performance through brain stimulation and other methods (Del Monte 2018, 193).

14.3.3: Testing and Safety Standards for AWS

George Lucas has suggested that the ethical risks that come with the deployment of an AWS could be addressed through responsibility for "due care" of the manufacturers of AWS and product liability (Lucas 2011). First of all, it would be a wrong expectation that AWS could be created that would never make any targeting mistakes or behave in a manner harmful to innocent bystanders. Instead one has to consider what is an acceptable failure rate and what are acceptable malfunctions for an AWS. It is usually assumed that an AWS should perform at least as well or better in making ethical decisions than a human soldier. One could even argue that the error rate for AWS must be substantially better than the error rate of humans and that a higher legal standard must be applied to AWS compared to human soldiers (Bhuta, Beck, and Geiß 2016, 374). AWS could make errors that have much more serious repercussions than errors made by humans, as decisions are made at a much faster rate with potentially self-reinforcing feedback loops and possible runaway interactions of different AI systems. Therefore, before any AWS could be deployed, it must be possible to adequately test the system to make sure it operates within acceptable margins of error. But as Heather Roff has pointed out,

> it is the very ability of a machine to overwrite its own code that makes it . . . unpredictable and uncontrollable. A great amount of "robot boot camp" would have to take place to generate a sufficient amount of experiential learning for LARs [Lethal Autonomous Robots], and even that would not guarantee that these machines would continue to act in accordance with such training once they encountered a new environment or new threat. (Roff 2014, 221)

As a result, an AWS must be tested and evaluated on a continuous basis (and not just before it is introduced into the armed forces) to make sure that its programming does not evolve in unexpected ways, leading to unpredictable behaviors (US DoD 2016, 15).

14.4: AWS AND ARMS CONTROL

An open letter by a group of technologists and scientists, most notably endorsed by Elon Musk, Bill Gates, Nick Bostrom, and Stephen Hawking, warned of the great dangers of AWS and advocated for "a ban of offensive autonomous weapons beyond meaningful human control" (Future of Life Institute 2015). Similarly, UN Secretary General Antonio Gueteres said in a recent speech addressing the Group of Governmental Experts before the March 2019 meeting that "machines with the power and discretion to take lives without human involvement are politically unacceptable, morally repugnant and should bc prohibited by international law" (UN 2019). The goal seems clear, but governments have yet to agree on how to handle the accelerating AI arms race.

14.4.1: Slow Progress

Several governments have remained skeptical about the need for regulating or banning AWS. For example, Russia has already rejected preventive arms control on the grounds that it was for now unnecessary, that key terms could not be adequately defined, and that a ban would harm the advancement of civilian applications of AI (Russian Federation 2017). At the UN expert meeting in Geneva in August 2018, a further attempt of banning AWS was blocked not only by Russia and Israel, but also by the United States (Hambling 2018). In a position paper submitted ahead of the meeting, the US government argued:

> that discussion of the possible options for addressing the humanitarian and international security challenges posed by emerging technologies in the area of lethal autonomous weapons systems in the context of the objectives

> and purpose of the Convention must involve consideration of how these technologies can be used to enhance the protection of the civilian population against the effects of hostilities. (UN 2018, Article 6)

The US government claims that there would be a net humanitarian benefit with respect to utilizing AI as it could enhance situational awareness and improve targeting. Up to now, only twenty-eight out of eighty participating governments have endorsed a ban while others prefer self-regulation or merely state that existing IHL would be adequate to deal with issues posed by AWS. Unless major military powers such as the United States, Russia, and China are part of an international regulation of AWS, there is little hope that any agreement reached would be meaningful.

14.4.2: If Not We Somebody Else Will Build AWS

The major military powers seem to believe that AI could lead to another revolution in military affairs, which makes it a risky option not to pursue it aggressively. According to a NATO-sponsored research led by Julian Lindley Finch:

> [a]rtificial Intelligence, deep learning, machine learning, computer vision, neuro-linguistic programming, virtual reality and augmented reality are all part of the future battlespace. They are all underpinned by potential advances in quantum computing that will create a conflict environment in which the decision-action loop will compress dramatically from days and hours to minutes and seconds . . . or even less. This development will perhaps witness the most revolutionary changes in conflict since the advent of atomic weaponry and in military technology since the 1906 launch of HMS Dreadnought. The United States is moving sharply in this direction in order to compete with similar investments being made by Russia and China, which has itself committed to a spending plan on artificial intelligence that far outstrips all the other players in this arena, including the United States. (Lindley-French 2017, 17)

Deep learning AI is part of the Pentagon's Third Offset strategy, which also includes human-machine collaborations (computer-assisted analysis), assisted human operations (wearable technology), human-machine combat teaming (soldiers partnered with AWS), and network-enabled semiautonomous technology (remotely operated systems) (Latiff 2017, 26). Even if the United States and other Western military powers could be persuaded to only operate on-the-loop robotic weapons systems or have ethical programming hardwired into them, there is little hope that others would follow the same standards. Amir Husain, a technology entrepreneur and inventor, suggested:

> How could such a ban be enforced? Is a statement by former secretary-general of the United Nations Ban Ki-moon going to stop North Korea from developing autonomous weapons? Or China from shipping CSS-2 missiles to unsavory governments in the Middle East? Or ISIS? It is simply not practical to expect that an agency or an international treaty will effectively monitor such

activity. I assert, once again, that the AI genie of innovation is out of the bottle; it cannot be stuffed back inside. (Husain 2017, 107)

China and Russia are also building numerous unmanned systems with varying degrees of autonomy. Paul Scharre has pointed out that the "Russian military has a casual attitude toward arming them [Unmanned Ground Vehicles] not seen in Western nations" and that "Russian programs are pushing the boundaries of what is possible with respect to robotic combat vehicles, building systems that could prove decisive in highly lethal tank-on-tank warfare" (Scharre 2018, 114).

14.4.3: The Long View

AWS seem to be inevitable as AI is increasingly transforming modern society. It would be unrealistic to expect that military organizations would not try to leverage a technology that is bound to become pervasive in the civilian sphere and that could result in greater efficiency and effectiveness across a wide range of societal sectors. Future regulation of AI, including military applications of AI, must focus on the reliability and predictability of AI to prevent bad outcomes. Futurists like Elon Musk, Ray Kurzweil, and Nick Bostrom think that progress in AI will eventually lead to artificial superintelligence (ASI), which could create an existential threat to humanity. Musk even compared the development of strong AI to summoning a demon (McFarland 2014).

As argued very convincingly by Nick Bostrom, superintelligence is inherently dangerous, regardless of whether it controls weapons or not (Bostrom 2014). He proposes several strategies for mitigating the dangers related to ASI, including boxing (containing AI in a way that its interaction with the outside world remains limited), using incentives (methods of rewarding good or desirable behavior), stunting (putting constraints on the cognitive abilities of AI), and tripwires (diagnostic methods that identify a dangerous activity so that the AI can be shut down in a timely manner) (Bostrom 2014, 175). These strategies could also be used for maintaining human control over less-than-super-intelligent military AI systems.

The key issue is to make sure AI behaves in the manner intended by its designers and operators and to have fail-safes in place that prevent any serious mistakes from occurring. It must also be possible to hold nations and other actors accountable for the failure to have sufficient safeguards for AI systems, regardless of whether they are military or civilian. Regulations of AWS should, therefore, focus on transparency in the development and deployment of AI for all major and consequential applications of AI. Attempts of regulating AWS through the Certain Conventional Weapons Convention on the grounds that they would be inhumane or indiscriminate weapons have not been successful so far and are unlikely to be more successful in the future.

14.5: LESSONS LEARNED FROM THE REGULATION OF BIOWARFARE/BIOSECURITY

Bioweapons and AWS have some interesting commonalities as they concern the problem of control. Bioweapons are also autonomous weapons in the sense that, once released, they can attack their targets with no need for human intervention. The parallels between the two classes of weapons (if one considers AWS as a distinctive class of weaponry) become more obvious when it comes to the comparison of cyber weapons and bioweapons. Indeed, a similar language is used for describing both with terms such as (computer) "viruses," "worms," "infection," the "mutation" and "evolution" of malware, and concepts such as "cyber immunity." There is even a growing overlap between the biosecurity and cybersecurity fields with biology inspiring new approaches to cybersecurity and digital tools enabling the creation of new biological organisms on a computer, making experiments with "wetware" unnecessary (CFR 2015). The defining component of an AWS is merely the software or the algorithm that turns data into decisions or behaviors. The regulation of AWS should therefore not be focused on the human-machine command relationship, but rather on the particular uses of AWS and their particular design principles to prevent negative outcomes. This requires transparency on the part of governments and the manufacturers as to what AI research they conduct and how the AI functions.

14.5.1: Offensive and Defensive AWS

Scharre has pointed out that AWS, defined as systems that can select and engage targets with no human intervention, already exist and that autonomy and intelligence are not directly connected: "[g]reater intelligence can be added into weapons without changing their autonomy" (Scharre 2018, 50). For example, the Phalanx close-in air defense system "must operate in a completely autonomous way" to be effective (Husain 2017, 101). Interestingly, despite the fact that Phalanx has been operational with the US Navy since 1980, the deployment and use of the system has not raised many ethical concerns. This has to do with the very narrow and defensive function of the weapons system. It, therefore, seems that there are indeed acceptable defensive roles for AWS, which would make a general ban of AWS unnecessary, if not undesirable (Wallach and Allen 2013, 134).

Amitai and Oren Etzioni have rejected the distinction of offensive and defensive weapons as impractical since even defensive systems can be used offensively by attacking from behind a defensive shield (Etzioni and Etzioni 2017a, 75). Nevertheless, this general distinction remains conceptionally important in an arms control context, where weapons are routinely characterized as being "defensive" or "offensive" in nature. Many arms control treaties have aimed at imposing limits on offensive weapons deemed particularly destabilizing due to their ability to enable a "first-strike." The 1932 League of Nations conference proposed banning "offensive weapons" conducive to war (Levy 1984, 220). Essentially, offensive weapons are those that enable an attack while defensive weapons *by themselves* do not.

The arms control effort in the area of biosecurity has, from the start, struggled with the difficulty of drawing a clear line between permissible defensive activities and prohibited offensive activities (Koblentz 2009, 67). States proclaim a right to conduct defensive biowarfare research under the BWC, including the limited production of biological agents and ammunition as part of a threat assessment (Leitenberg 2003, 225). Interestingly, the term "defensive research" does not even appear in the treaty text. As argued by Milton Leitenberg, whether an activity should be deemed offensive or defensive would depend on the strategic intent behind a biological program (Leitenberg 2003, 223). This means that even defensive preparations such as immunizing soldiers against certain biological agents can be (mis-) interpreted as offensive intent (Koblentz 2009, 68–69). It seems inevitable that any restrictions on offensive AWS would run into some very similar challenges as the BWC in terms of compliance monitoring and verification. Whether an AWS was defensive or offensive would, in part, depend on their offensive capability (range, payload, autonomy) and in part on strategic intent.

14.5.2: Incentives for Secrecy and Strategic Restraint

Biodefense research and military AI research have in common a strong propensity for secrecy, much of which is caused by public disdain but also by strategic considerations. As Gregory Koblentz has argued, "[s]tates developing defenses against biological weapons may need to keep certain aspects and characteristics of these activities secret to ensure the effectiveness of their preparations" (Koblentz 2009, 71). If an attacker was fully aware of the medical countermeasures available to the intended target, then these countermeasures could be undermined by exploiting vulnerabilities in the target's preparedness. Similarly, it has been argued by Henry Kissinger that "[w]ith AI, the other side's ignorance is one of your best weapons—sharing will be much more difficult" (MIT 2019). On the positive side, offensive weapons that rely mostly on secrecy and surprise for success such as bioweapons, cyber weapons, or AWS are unlikely to be used in any other than high-stakes situations. Any usage of such weapons gives the adversary the opportunity to analyze the attack and to develop effective countermeasures that reduce the chances that future attacks will be successful. It can be assumed that militaries will be reluctant to deploy and use AWS in limited wars, as it allows others to analyze the behavior of AWS and potentially find weaknesses in the way the AWS interpret and act on data. Greg Allen and Taniel Chan suggest that even "counter-AI" capabilities could be developed to exploit weaknesses in machine learning and in AI algorithms by feeding AI skewed data (Allen and Chan 2017, 63).

14.5.3: The Need for Transparency in AI Research and AI Applications

As there are more and more real-world applications of AI, ranging from high-frequency trading, facial recognition systems, and self-driving vehicles, it is inevitable that the number of legal issues related to AI will grow over time (Scherer 2016, 354–355). The AI industry is very aware of the many liability issues that could result from bad outcomes from unpredictable AI behavior. Making the inner workings of AI more transparent "could also make AI systems more secure, less susceptible to hacks or to being reverse-engineered by a terrorist" (Geib 2018). At a minimum, international safety standards and declarations of conformity to certain design principles can be used to mitigate these risks, as it has been proposed by a recent study sponsored by IBM (Arnold e.a. 2018). The study has identified four elements of trust in AI systems: 1) basic performance and reliability, including codified and standardized testing of AI; 2) safety, including the disclosure of information on training and test datasets, fairness, and explainability; 3) security or resistance to attacks aimed at modifying the behavior of AI; and 4) lineage or the tracking of all the data used or produced by the system (Arnold et al. 2018). Matthew Scherer has proposed an Artificial Intelligence Development Act (AIDA) as a mechanism for enforcing AI safety standards on a national level. The AIDA,

> would create an agency tasked with certifying the safety of AI systems. Instead of giving the new agency FDA-like powers to ban products it believes to be unsafe, AIDA would create a liability system under which the designers, manufacturers, and sellers of agency-certified AI programs would be subject to limited tort liability, while uncertified programs that are offered for commercial sale or use would be subject to strict joint and several liability. (Scherer 2016, 393)

Similar international standards can be established for the use of AWS, which may be overseen by a specialized international organization. Militaries can still compete in making their AIs faster or smarter than those of their military competitors, but they have to be sufficiently transparent about the inner workings of their AI. The main incentive for states to adhere to these standards is to avoid catastrophic failures resulting from unpredictable AI interactions and to be able to prove that catastrophic failures were not intentional, should they occur.

State parties that fail to declare conformity with safety and design principles for AI could be held accountable by the international community for any malfunctioning of their AWS. For example, the international regulation could require that AWS must be defensive in nature, that they must have built-in fail-safes that switch them off whenever they operate outside of acceptable parameters, and that they must be continuously tested to ensure their safe operation. The safe and secure operation of AWS would also require regular exchanges of test data to build trust and avoid accidents. International cooperation in AI development in view of increasing AI reliability and security must be encouraged. Given the inherent risks related to superintelligence, a ban or moratorium would seem reasonable (Del Monte 2018, 177).

14.5.4: Verification

It has been stated by many analysts that AI research does not require substantial resources and that it can be done discretely, creating challenges for the detection of such efforts and, subsequently the monitoring of arms control agreements that may seek to impose limits on such research. For example, Altmann and Sauer have argued that "AWS are much harder to regulate. With comparably fewer choke points that might be targeted by non-proliferation policies, AWS are potentially available to a wide range of state and non-state actors, not just those nation-states that are willing to muster the considerable resources needed for the robotic equivalent of the Manhattan Project" (Altmann and Sauer 2017, 125–126). Matthew Scherer even suggests that "a person does not need the resources and facilities of a large corporation to write computer code. Anyone with a reasonably modern personal computer (or even a smartphone) and an Internet connection can now contribute to AI-related projects" (Scherer 2016, 370).

While this may be true in principle and with respect to simpler applications of AI, the reality is that advanced AI is extremely resource intensive to develop. This clearly restricts the number of actors (governments and corporations) that can successfully enter or dominate the market for AI. Terrorists or lesser military powers may modify and weaponize commercial drones and equip them with some less complex AI to recognize targets to attack. However, when it comes to the development and operation of sophisticated military platforms and planning/battle management systems, it seems very unlikely that more than a few nations would have the resources and expertise to be competitive in this field. As Kai-Fu Lee has argued in his book, the main resource in the successful development of AI is data. Nations that are able to collect and exploit the most data will dominate AI development since they can build better AI. He wrote: "Deep learning's relationship with data fosters a virtuous circle for strengthening the best products and companies: more data leads to better products, which in turn attract more users, who generate more data that further improves the product," adding that he believes "China will soon match or overtake the United States in developing and deploying artificial intelligence" (Lee 2018, 18–20).

This results in two opportunities for international regulation: (1) the laboratories in the world that can develop cutting-edge AI due to access to talent, expertise, and data are not difficult to identify, which means there are good chances for monitoring compliance of any international AI regulation; (2) militaries will find it very challenging to collect meaningful data for deep learning in any other way than through extensive testing and exercises that can realistically simulate combat situations, which should also provide some opportunities to monitor such activities. Some of the testing can be done through simulations, but more important would be real-world field tests.

Similar confidence-building measures to enhance transparency are used in the biosecurity sector, which comprises regular exchanges of information regarding biological labs, ongoing research activities, disease outbreaks, past/present offensive or defensive biological programs, human vaccine production facilities, and implementation of relevant national legislation (Koblentz 2009, 60). As it would apply to AWS, states operating them should exchange information on their main AI development and test sites, AI research and testing activities, ongoing defensive AWS programs and other uses of military AI, and on relevant legislation and safety standards. This would build trust and prevent tragic accidents when AWS are inevitably deployed.

14.6: CONCLUSION

Governments have the right to develop and use AWS as they see fit, but the AI incorporated into these systems must be based on agreed design principles that enhance the observability, directability, predictability, and auditability of these systems, as suggested by the Defense Science Board Study (US DoD 2017). Governments should be encouraged that they issue declarations so that their AWS comply with international design standards. Confidence-building measures that increase transparency and trust in the development and employment of AI should be established in order to reduce the risks of misperception and miscalculation that may result from unpredictable AWS behavior and unpredictable AI interactions. If an accident related to the operation of an AWS occurs, the government at fault must be able to reliably demonstrate that there was no hostile intent on their part. Governments are ultimately responsible for the operation of AWS and they should be liable for any damages that result from faulty AWS behavior. This responsibility may be shared with the companies that develop and produce AWS. Most importantly, AWS should be restricted to defensive applications even if it will sometimes be difficult to determine the intent behind a national AI program or specific AWS.

WORKS CITED

Adams, Thomas K. 2001. "Future Warfare and the Decline of Human Decisionmaking." *Parameters* 41 (4): pp. 5–19.

Allen, Greg and Taniel Chan. 2017. *Artificial Intelligence and National Security.* Cambridge, MA: Harvard Belfer Center. https://www.belfercenter.org/sites/default/files/files/publication/AI%20NatSec%20-%20final.pdf.

Alpaydin, Ethem. 2016. *Machine Learning.* Cambridge, MA: MIT Press.

Altmann, Jürgen and Frank Sauer. 2017. "Autonomous Weapons Systems and Strategic Stability." *Survival* 59 (5): pp. 117–142. doi: 10.1080/00396338.2017.1375263.

Arkin, Ronald. 2009. *Governing Lethal Behavior in Autonomous Robots.* Boca Raton, FL: CRC Press.

Arnett, Erich K. 1992. "Welcome to Hyperwar." *Bulletin of American Scientists* 48 (7): pp. 14–21.

Arnold, Matthew, Rachel K. E. Bellamy, Michael Hind, Stephanie Houde, Sameep Mehta, Aleksandra Mojsilovic, Ravi Nair, Karthikeyan Natesan Ramamurthy, Darrell Reimer, Alexandra Olteanu, David Piorkowski, Jason Tsay, and Kush R. Varshney. 2018. "Factsheets: Increasing Trust in AI Services through Supplier's Declarations of Conformity." *IBM.* August 1–2. https://deeplearn.org/arxiv/62930/factsheets:-increasing-trust-in-ai-services-through-supplier's-declarations-of-conformity.

Bhuta, Nehal, Susanne Beck, Robin Geiß. "Present Futures: Concluding Reflections and Open Questions on Autonomous Weapons Systems." In *Autonomous Weapons Systems: Laws, Ethics, and Policy* edited by Nehal Bhuta, Susanne Beck, Robin Geiβ, Hin-Yan Liu, and Claus Kreβ, pp. 347–383 Cambridge: Cambridge University Press.

Borenstein, Jason. 2008. "The Ethics of Autonomous Military Robots." *Studies in Ethics, Law, and Technology* 2 (1): pp. 1–17. doi:10.2202/1941-6008.1036.

Bostrom, Nick. 2014. *Superintelligence: Paths, Dangers, Strategies.* Oxford: Oxford University Press.

CFR. 2015. "The Relationship Between the Biological Weapons Convention and Cybersecurity." Council on Foreign Relations: Digital and Cyberspace Policy Program. March 26. https://www.cfr.org/blog/relationship-between-biological-weapons-convention-and-cybersecurity.

Chengeta, Thompson. 2016. "Are Autonomous Weapons the Subject of Article 36 of Additional Protocol 1 to the Geneva Conventions?" *UC Davis Journal of International Law* 23 (1): pp. 65–99. doi:10.2139/ssrn.2755182.

Del Monte, Louis A. 2018. *Genius Weapons: Artificial Intelligence, Autonomous Weaponry, and the Future of Warfare.* New York: Prometheus Books.

Etzioni, Amitai, and Oren Etzioni. 2017a. "Pros and Cons of Autonomous Weapons." *Military Review* 97 (3): pp. 72–81.

Etzioni, Amitai and Oren Etzioni. 2017b. "Should Artificial Intelligence Be Regulated?" *Issues in Science and Technology* 33 (4): pp. 32–36.

Friedberg, Sydney. 2016. "Killer Robots? 'Never,' Defense Secretary Carter Says." *BreakingDefense.com*. September 15. https://breakingdefense.com/2016/09/killer-robots-never-says-defense-secretary-carter/.

Future of Life Institute. 2015. "Autonomous Weapons: an Open Letter from AI & Robotics Researchers." Accessed January 28, 2020. http://futureoflife.org/open-letter-autonomous-weapons/.

Geib, Claudia. 2018. "Making AI More Secret Could Prevent Us from Making It Better." *Futurism.com*. February 26. https://futurism.com/ai-secret-report/.

Georges, Thomas M. *Digital Soul: Intelligent Machines and Human Values*. Boulder, CO: Westview Press.

Hambling, David. 2018. "Why the US Is Backing Killer Robots." *Popular Mechanics*. September 14. https://www.popularmechanics.com/military/research/a23133118/us-ai-robots-warfare/.

Heyns, Christof. 2013. "Report of the Special Rapporteur on Extrajudicial, Summary or Arbitrary Executions, Christof Heyns." United Nations General Assembly: A/HRC/23/47. April 9. https://www.unog.ch/80256EDD006B8954/(httpAssets)/684AB3F3935B5C42C1257CC200429C7C/$file/Report+of+the+Special+Rapporteur+on+extrajudicial,.pdf.

Heyns, Cristof. 2016. "Joint Report of the Special Rapporteur on the Rights to Freedom of Peaceful Assembly and of Association and the Special Rapporteur on Extrajudicial, Summary or Arbitrary Executions on the Proper Management of Assemblies." United Nations General Assembly: A/HRC/31/66. February 40. https://undocs.org/es/A/HRC/31/66.

Husain, Amir. 2017. *The Sentient Machine: The Coming Age of Artificial Intelligence*. New York: Simon & Schuster.

Kaplan, Jerry. 2016. *Artificial Intelligence: What Everyone Needs to Know*. Oxford: Oxford University Press.

Klincewicz, Michal. 2015. "Autonomous Weapons Systems, the Frame Problem and Computer Security." *Journal of Military Ethics* 14 (2): pp. 162–176.

Knight, Will. 2017. "The Dark Secret at the Heart of AI." *MIT Technology Review*. April 11. https://www.technologyreview.com/s/604087/the-dark-secret-at-the-heart-of-ai/.

Koblentz, Gregory. 2009. *Living Weapons: Biological Warfare and International Security*. Ithaca, NY: Cornell University Press.

Latiff, Robert. 2017. *Future War: Preparing for the New Global Battlefield*. New York: Alfred A. Knopf.

Lee, Kai-Fu. 2018. *AI Superpowers: China, Silicon Valley, and the New World Order*. Boston: Houghton Mifflin Harcourt.

Leitenberg, Milton. 2003. "Distinguishing Offensive from Defensive Biological Weapons Research." *Critical Reviews in Microbiology* 29 (3): pp. 223–257.

Levy, Jack S. 1984. "The Offensive/ Defensive Balance of Military Technology: A Theoretical and Historical Analysis." *International Studies Quarterly* 28 (2): pp. 219–238.

Libicki, Martin. 1997. "The Small and the Many." In *In Athena's Camp: Preparing for Conflict in the Information Age* edited by John Arquilla and David Ronfeldt, pp. 191–216. Santa Monica, CA: RAND.

Lindley-French, Julian. 2017. "One Alliance: The Future Tasks of the Adapted Alliance." *Globsec NATO Adaptation Initiative*. November. https://www.globsec.org/wp-content/uploads/2017/11/GNAI-Final-Report-Nov-2017.pdf.

Lucas, George. 2011. "Industrial Challenges of Military Robotics." *Journal of Military Ethics 10* (4): pp. 274–295. doi: 10.1080/15027570.2011.639164.

McFarland, Matt. 2014. "Elon Musk: 'With Artificial Intelligence We Are Summoning the Demon.'" *Washington Post*. October 24. https://www.washingtonpost.com/news/innovations/wp/2014/10/24/elon-musk-with-artificial-intelligence-we-are-summoning-the-demon/?noredirect=on.

MIT. 2019. "AI Arms Control May Not Be Possible, Warns Henry Kissinger." *MIT Technology Review*. March 1. U78https://www.technologyreview.com/f/613059/ai-arms-control-may-not-be-possible-warns-henry-kissinger/.

Mitri, Sara, Dario Floreano, and Laurent Keller. 2009. "The Evolution of Information Suppression in Communicating Robots with Conflicting Interests." *PNAS* 106 (37): pp. 15786–15790. doi: 10.1073/pnas.0903152106.

Payne, Kenneth. 2018. *Strategy, Evolution, and War: From Apes to Artificial Intelligence*. Washington, DC: Georgetown University Press.

Roff, Heather. 2014. "The Strategic Robot Problem: Lethal Autonomous Weapons in War." *Journal of Military Ethics* 13 (3): pp. 211–227.

Roff, Heather. 2016. "To Ban or to Regulate Autonomous Weapons: A US Response." *Bulletin of the Atomic Scientists* 72 (2): pp. 122–124. doi:10.1080/00963402.2016.1145920.

Russian Federation. 2017. "Examination of Various Dimensions of Emerging Technologies in the Area of Lethal Autonomous Weapons Systems, in the Context of the Objectives and Purposes of the Convention." Geneva: Meeting of Group of Governmental Experts on LAWS. November 10. CCW/GGE.1/2017/WP8.

Saxon, Dan. 2016. 'A Human Touch: Autonomous Weapons, DoD Directive 3000.09 and the Interpretation of "Appropriate Levels of Human Judgment Over Force."' In *Autonomous Weapons Systems: Law, Ethics, Policy*, edited by Nehal Bhuta, Susanne Beck, Robin Geiβ, Hin-Yan Liu, and Claus Kreβ, pp. 185–208. Cambridge: Cambridge University Press.

Scharre, Paul. 2018. *Army of None: Autonomous Weapons and the Future of War*. New York: W.W. Norton & Co.

Scherer, Matthew U. 2016. "Regulating Artificial Intelligence Systems: Risks, Challenges, Competencies, and Strategies." *Harvard Journal of Law & Technology* 29 (2): pp. 353–400.

Schmitt, Michael and Jeffrey Thurnher. 2013. "'Out of the Loop': Autonomous Weapons Systems and the Law of Armed Conflict." *Harvard National Security Journal* 4: pp. 231–281.

Sparrow, Robert. 2015. "Twenty Seconds to Comply: Autonomous Weapons and the Recognition of Surrender." *International Law Studies* 91: 699–728.

U.S. DoD. 2012. "Autonomy in Weapons Systems." Directive Number 3000.09. November 21. https://www.esd.whs.mil/Portals/54/Documents/DD/issuances/dodd/300009p.pdf.

US DoD. 2017. *Summer Study on Autonomy*. Washington, DC: Defense Science Board. https://apps.dtic.mil/dtic/tr/fulltext/u2/1017790.pdf.

United Nations. 2018. "Humanitarian Benefits of Emerging Technologies in the Area of Lethal Autonomous Weapon Systems." Group of Governmental Experts of the High Contracting Parties to the Convention on Prohibitions or Restrictions on the

Use of Certain Conventional Weapons Which May Be Deemed to Be Excessively Injurious or to Have Indiscriminate Effects: CCW/GGE.1/2018/WP.4. March 28. https://unog.ch/80256EDD006B8954/(httpAssets)/7C177AE5BC10B588C125825F004B06BE/$file/CCW_GGE.1_2018_WP.4.pdf.

United Nations. 2019. "Autonomous Weapons That Kill Must Be Banned, Insists UN Chief." *UN Press Release*. March 25. https://news.un.org/en/story/2019/03/1035381.

Wallach, Wendell and Colin Allen. 2013. "Framing Robot Arms Control." *Ethics and Information Technology* 15 (2): pp. 125–135.

15

Normative Epistemology for Lethal Autonomous Weapons Systems

S. KATE DEVITT

15.1: INTRODUCTION

In *Army of None*, Paul Scharre (2018) tells the story of a little Afghan goat-herding girl who circled his sniper team, informing the Taliban of their location via radio. Scharre uses this story as an example of a combatant who he, and his peers did not target—but that a lethal autonomous weapon programmed to kill, might legally target. A central mismatch between humans and robots, it seems, is that humans know when an action is right, and a robot does not. In order for any Lethal Autonomous Weapon Systems (LAWS) to be ethical, it would need—at a minimum—to have situational understanding, to know right from wrong, and to be operated in accordance with this knowledge.

Lethal weapons of increasing autonomy are already utilized by militant groups, and they are likely to be increasingly used in Western democracies and in nations across the world (Arkin et al. 2019; Scharre 2018). Because they will be developed—with varying degrees of human-in-the-loop—we must ask what kind of design principles should be used to build them and what should direct that design? To trust LAWS we must trust that they know enough about the world, themselves, and their context of use to justify their actions. This chapter interrogates the concept of knowledge in the context of LAWS. The aim of the chapter is not to provide an ethical framework for their deployment, but to illustrate epistemological frameworks that could be used in conjunction with moral apparatus to guide the design and deployment of future systems.

S. Kate Devitt, *Normative Epistemology for Lethal Autonomous Weapons Systems* In: *Lethal Autonomous Weapons*.
Edited by: Jai Galliott, Duncan MacIntosh and Jens David Ohlin, © Oxford University Press (2021).
DOI: 10.1093/oso/9780197546048.003.0016

"Epistemology" is the study of knowledge (Moser 2005; Plato 380 B.C.; Quine 1969). Traditionally conceived, epistemology is the study of how humans come to know about the world via intuition, perception, introspection, memory, reason, and testimony. However, the rise of human-information systems, cybernetic systems, and increasingly autonomous systems requires the application of epistemic frameworks to machines and human-machine teams. Epistemology for machines asks the following: How do machines use sensors to know about the world? How do machines use feedback systems to know about their own systems including possible working regimes, machine conditions, failure modes, degradation patterns, history of operations? And how do machines communicate system states to users (Bagheri et al. 2015) and other machines? Epistemology for human-machine teams asks this: How do human-machine teams use sensors, perception, and reason to know about the world? How do human-machine teams share information and knowledge bidirectionally between human and machine? And how do human-machine teams communicate information states to other humans, machines, and systems?

Epistemic parameters provide a systematic way to evaluate whether a human, machine, or human-machine teams are trustworthy (Devitt 2018). Epistemic concepts underpin assessments that weapons do not result in superfluous injury or unnecessary suffering, weapons systems are able to discriminate between combatants and noncombatants, and weapons effects are controlled (Boothby 2016). The models discussed in this chapter aim to make Article 36 reviews of LAWS (Farrant and Ford 2017) systematic, expedient, and evaluable. Additionally, epistemic concepts can provide some of the apparatus to meet explainability and transparency requirements in the development, evaluation, deployment, and review of ethical AI (IEEE Global Initiative on Ethics of Autonomous and Intelligent Systems 2019; Jobin et al. 2019).

Epistemic principles apply to technology design, including automatic, autonomous, and adaptive systems, including how an artificial agent ought to modify and develop their own epistemic confidences as they learn and act in the world. These principles also guide system designers on how autonomous systems must communicate their doxastic states to humans. A doxastic state relates its agent's attitude to its beliefs, including its confidence, uncertainty, skepticism, and ignorance (Chignell 2018). Systems must communicate their representations of the world and their attitudes to these representations. Designers must program systems to act appropriately under different doxastic states to ensure trust.

Before setting off, I would like to acknowledge the limits of my own knowledge with regard to epistemology. This chapter will draw on the Western philosophical tradition in which I am trained, but I want to be clear that this is only one of many varied epistemologies in a wide range of cultural traditions (Mizumoto et al. 2018). The reader (and indeed the author) is recommended to explore alternate epistemologies on this topic such as ethnoepistemology (Maffie 2019) and the Geography of Philosophy project (Geography of Philosophy Project 2020). Additionally, there is a wide corpus of literature on military leadership that is relevant to epistemic discussions, particularly developing virtuous habits with regards to beliefs (e.g., Paparone and Reed 2008; Taylor et al. 2018). Note, I will not be addressing many ethical criticisms of LAWS such as the dignity argument (that death by autonomous weapons is undignified) or the distance argument (that human involvement in drone warfare is too psychologically and spatially distant for operators to act morally when LAWS are under their control).

This chapter, by introducing some foundational concepts and exploring a subset of epistemologies that will hopefully add to the debate on lethal autonomous weapons by highlighting the need for higher-order epistemic models to guide not only the design but also the training, evaluation, and regulation of lethal autonomous weapons systems irrespective of specific techniques and technologies used in their creation.

15.2: MOTIVATION

Meaningful human control is a critical concept in the current debates on how to constrain the design and implementation of LAWS. The 2018 Group of Governmental Experts on Lethal Autonomous Weapons Systems (LAWS) argued that,

> In the context of the deployment and use of a weapons system in an armed conflict, delegations noted that military personnel activate the weapons systems and monitor their functioning. This would require that the operator know the characteristics of the weapons system, is assured that they are appropriate to the environment in which it would be deployed and has sufficient and reliable information on them in order to make conscious decisions and ensure legal compliance. . . . [P]ositive measures are necessary to prevent indiscriminate action and injury by lethal autonomous weapons systems caused by a breakaway from human control. To develop such measures, concepts such as 'meaningful human control' and 'human judgment' need to be further elaborated and clarified. (Annex III, 18 CCW GGE LAWS 2018: 14)

"Meaningful human control" requires operators to *know* that systems are reliable and contextually appropriate. How should the parameters of human control and intervention be established? Researchers are grappling with the theoretical and practical parameters of meaningful human control to inform design criteria and legal obligation (Horowitz and Scharre 2015; Santoni de Sio and van den Hoven 2018). Santoni de Sio and van den Hoven (2018) argue that the analysis should be informed by the concept of "guidance control" from the free will and moral responsibility literature (Fischer and Ravizza 1998) translated into requirements for systems, engineering, and software design (van den Hoven 2013). In order to be morally responsible for an action X, a person or agent should possess "guidance control" over that action. Guidance control means that the person or agent is able to reason through an action in the lead-up to a decision, has sufficient breadth of reasoning capability to consider the ethical considerations (and change their actions on the basis of ethical considerations), and uses its own decisional mechanisms to make the decision.

A morally responsible agent has sensitive and flexible reasoning capabilities, is able to understand that its own actions affect the world, is sensitive to others' moral reactions toward it, and is in control of its own reasoning as opposed to being coerced, indoctrinated, or manipulated. An argument to ban LAWS is that a decision by a LAWS to initiate an attack—without human supervision—in an unstructured environment is not under meaningful human control because LAWS cannot track the *reasoning* required by international law (including necessity, discrimination, and proportionality), and they are not adaptive to changing morally relevant features of their operational environment (Asaro 2012; Sharkey 2012).

It is worth considering meaningful human control in terms of the trajectory of an action, from decision into consequences in the world. An expert archer shooting an arrow at a target has meaningful human control when they use their competence to set up the shot, to sense the changing wind, and fire during a lull. A novice archer is not in meaningful control because they lack the capacity to guide the arrow to the target—even though they may wish to hit the bullseye—and they fire rashly—without appropriate reflection on their own state or the environmental conditions that might affect their accuracy. The novice lacks full control. The trajectory of the arrow between the archer firing and it landing on the target is constrained both by the energy imbued within it from the archer and the vicissitudes of the wind that may blow it off course. Meaningful control over a projectile is affected by the amount of time it takes from a human making a decision to the outcomes and consequences of that decision and the uncertainties that could affect the outcome during the intervening period.

If an arrow was equipped with autonomous flight stabilizers to reorient itself to its human-programmed trajectory, then it is not controlled by a human, but it is operating in abidance with human intent. This is how Tomahawk cruise missiles and loitering munitions are programmed to persist to a human-selected target (Gettinger and Michel 2017; Raytheon 2019a). If the moral landscape changes in the time between launch and effect, for most of the history of weapons that operate at a distance, the shot lands and collateral damage is accepted as a terrible but not immoral consequence of the human action—because humans operated to the best of their capability and knowledge. Put another way, the projectile missed the legitimate target not due to human incompetence, but due to the manifestation of an unforeseen uncertainty, an unlucky intervention.

Suppose the collateral damage was a child walking into a targeted building. Would it be moral if the projectile was able to autonomously abort their mission, adjust its payload, or alter its trajectory on the basis of new information about the decision?—preventing harms seems just. What if the collateral damage of hitting one corner of the building could be calculated and contrasted with the collateral damage of hitting the other corner of the building faster than human thought for a time-critical mission. Could an autonomous weapon reason through the choice of which corner to strike to reduce harms? If the reasoning was robust, the ends seem to justify it. But, would this system still be in meaningful human control according to International Humanitarian Law (IHL)? Humans made the decision about the time sensitivity of the target in order to authorize the LAWS to adapt its target. Systems may be able to reason through many aspects of distinction and proportionality and eventually perhaps even necessity faster and more comprehensively than a human. Their timely knowledge advantage is a reason to consider their use as ethically justified.

Perhaps there are decisions for which humans should not be in meaningful control? As Hancock (2016: 289) asks,

> can we truly say that we always know best? If we examine our current record of planetary stewardship it is painfully obvious that we are lacking in both rationality and a necessary standard of care. It may well be possible that globally-interconnected operations are better conducted by quasi- and subsequently fully autonomous systems?

How many unjust harms could be mitigated with systems more knowledgeable than humans engaged in guarding civilians and defending protected objects (Scholz and Galliott 2018)?

What is relevant for this chapter is not to settle the debate on meaningful human control or abidance with IHL, but to illustrate the role of knowledge in the evaluation and acceptability of LAWS. In particular, it is about motivating the study of epistemic frameworks to understand why a particular deployment of LAWS may be deemed unethical due to it lacking the relevant knowledge to justify autonomous decision-making.

The structure of the chapter is as follows. First I will introduce the nuts and bolts of epistemology including the analysis of knowledge as 'justified true belief' and what that entails for different doxastic states of agents in conflict that might justify actions. I introduce cases where conditions of knowledge are threatened, called 'Gettier Cases' and explain why they are relevant in conflicts where parties are motivated to deceive. I will then work through the cognitive architecture of humans and artificial agents within which knowledge plays a functional role. The degree to which humans might trust LAWS in part depends on understanding how LAWS make decisions including how machines form, update and represent beliefs and how beliefs influence agent deliberation and action selection. The chapter finishes with a discussion of three normative epistemological frameworks: reliabilism, virtue epistemology, and Bayesian epistemology. Each of these offer design frameworks that LAWS can be evaluated against in their performance of tasks in accordance with commander's intent, IHL, and Laws of Armed Conflict (LOAC).

15.3: EPISTEMOLOGY

Epistemology is the study of how humans or agents come to know about the world. Knowledge might be innate (hardwired into a system), introspected, or learned (like Google maps dynamically updating bushfire information). The dominant conception of knowledge in the Western tradition is that a human knows *p* when she has justified true belief that *p* (Plato 369 B.C.). Under this framework, a Combatant (Ct) knows that the Person (P) is a Civilian (Cv) not a Belligerent (B) if the following are present.

15.3.1: Justified True Belief

a) Ct accurately identifies P as Cv,
b) Ct believes that they have accurately identified P as Cv, and
c) Ct is justified in believing that they have accurately identified P as Cv.

The enterprise of epistemology has typically involved trying to understand (1) What is it about people that enable them to form beliefs that are accurate, for example, what enables a combatant to identify a civilian versus a lawful target? (2) When are people justified in holding certain beliefs, for example, under what conditions are identification attributes in play and defensible? and (3) What warrants this justification, for example, what features about human perception, mission briefings, ISR, patterns of behavior, command structures, and so forth enable the combatant to have justified true beliefs? To better grasp the explanatory usefulness of knowledge as justified true belief, we can explore conditions where a combatant has false beliefs, does not believe, or has unjustified beliefs in order to tease out these component parts. Let's consider the same situation under the false belief, disbelief, and unjustified belief scenarios.

15.3.2: False Belief

a) Ct *inaccurately* identifies P as Cv instead of B,
b) Ct believes that they have accurately identified P as Cv, and
c) Ct is *not justified* in believing that they have accurately identified P as Cv.

False belief is the most significant threat to the combatant, as the misidentified belligerent may take advantage of the opportunity to aggress. If the combatant comes to harm, a post-event inquiry might find the combatant's own perceptual judgment faulty, or that the belligerent was able to conceal their status, such as by not wearing a uniform, traveling with a child, hiding their weapons, or spoofing intelligence networks.

15.3.3: Disbelief

a) Ct accurately identifies P as Cv,
b) Ct *does not believe* that they have accurately identified P as Cv, and
c) Ct is justified in believing that they have accurately identified P as Cv.

Disbelief may occur in "the fog of war," where evidence sufficient to justify a combatant's belief that a person is a civilian does not in fact influence their beliefs. Perhaps intelligence has identified the person as a civilian via methods or communication channels not trusted by the combatant—they may worry they're being spoofed. Or they doubt their own perceptual facilities—perhaps there really is a rifle inside the person's jacket? Disbelief can have multiple consequences; a cautious but diligent combatant may seek more evidence to support the case that the person is a civilian. Being cautious may have different impacts depending on the tempo of the conflict and the time criticality of the mission. If the combatant develops a false belief that the person is a belligerent, it may lead them to disobey IHL.

15.3.4: Unjustified Belief

a) Ct accurately identifies P as Cv,
b) Ct believes that they have accurately identified P as Cv, and
c) Ct is *not justified* in believing that they have accurately identified P as Cv.

Unjustified belief occurs when the combatant believes that the person is a civilian by accident, luck, or insufficient justification rather than via systematic application of reason and evidence. For example, the combatant sees the civilian being assisted by Médecins Sans Frontières. The person really is a civilian, so the belief is accurate, but it arose through unreliable means because both combatants and civilians are assisted by Médecins Sans Frontières (2019). The protection of civilians and the targeting process should not be accidental, lucky, or superficial. Combatants should operate within a reliable system of control that ensures that civilians and combatants can be identified with comprehensive justification—and indeed, many Nations abide by extensive systems of control, for example, the Australian government (2019). Consider a LAWS Unmanned Aerial Vehicle (UAV) that usually has multiple redundant mechanisms for identifying a target—say autonomous visual identification and classification, human operator, and ISR confirmation. If communication channels were knocked out so that UAV decisions were based on visual feed and internal mechanisms only, it might not be sufficient justification for knowledge, and the UAV may have to withdraw from the mission.

15.4: GETTIER CASES

Gettier cases occur in cases when achieving justified true belief is not said to produce knowledge (Gettier 1963). Imagine the combatant in a tank, receiving data on their surrounding environment through an ISR data feed that is usually reliable. They are taking aim at a building, a military target justified by their ROE and IHL. The data feed indicates that there are people walking in front of the building. Suppose the ISR feed was intercepted by an adversary, and this intercept went undetected by the combatant or their command. The false data feed is designed to trick the combatant, so warns them that civilians would be harmed if she takes the shot. As it happens, there *are* civilians walking past the building during the same time as the combatant is receiving the manipulated data feed. In this case, the following are possible.

15.4.1: Gettier Case

a) Ct accurately identifies P as Cv (because civilians are walking past the building),
b) Ct believes that they have accurately identified P as Cv, and
c) Ct is justified in believing that they have accurately identified P as Cv (because the ISR feed has been accurate and reliable in the past).

Epistemologists have created a "Gettier industry" to try and develop conceptions of knowledge that both explain and triumph over Gettier cases (Lycan 2006; O'Brien 2016). I am unable to cover all responses, but I will explore several epistemic models useful for designing LAWS and worthy of further investigation. Two approaches for solving Gettier cases are (1) the addition of different conditions for knowledge and (2) not requiring knowledge to obtain to justify belief. I explore both approaches in the following sections.

15.5: TRACKING

Nozick (1981) claims that Gettier cases can be resolved if the right sort of causal structure is in play for the attribution of knowledge. He calls this concept "tracking." Nozick supposes that to know, we must be using our facilities to track the structure of the world so that we are sensitive to factors that might affect knowledge attainment. So, for Nozick, for knowledge to occur for the combatant in the tank, the following conditions must be met:

a) P is a Cv (The person is a civilian);
ii) Ct believes that P is a Cv (the combatant believes that P is a Cv);
iii) If it were not the case that P is a Cv, then Ct would not believe that P is a Cv (if the person was not a civilian, the combatant would not believe that the person was a civilian);
iv) If it were the case that P is a Cv, then Ct would believe that P is a Cv (if the person was a civilian, then Ct would believe that the person is a civilian).

In this case, the combatant does not have knowledge because they would still believe that P was a civilian even if P was a combatant or even if P wasn't there at all. The lack of situational awareness of causal factors that affected beliefs explains the lack of knowledge. Adversaries will try to manipulate LAWS to believe the wrong state of the world, and thus significant efforts must be made to ensure LAWS' beliefs track to reality.

15.6: BELIEF

Core to the construction of knowledge is the concept of belief. It is worth being clear on what a belief is and what it does in order to understand how it might operate inside an autonomous system. In this chapter, I take "belief" to be a propositional attitude like "hope" and "desire," attached to a proposition such as "there is a hospital." So, I can believe that there is a hospital, but I can also hope that there is a hospital because I need medical attention. Beliefs can be understood in the functional architecture of the mind as enabling a human or an agent to act, because it is the propositional attitude we adopt when we take something to be true (Schwitzgebel 2011). In this chapter, beliefs are treated as both functional and representational. Functionalism about mental states is the view that beliefs are causally related to sensory stimulations, behaviors,and other mental states (Armstrong 1973; Fodor 1968). Representationalism is the view that beliefs represent how things stand in the world (Fodor 1975; Millikan 1984).

Typically, the study of knowledge has assumed that beliefs are all or nothing, rather than probabilistic (BonJour 1985; Conee and Feldman 2004; Goldman 1986). However, Pascal and Fermat argued that one should strive for rational decision-making, rather than truth—the probabilistic view (Hajek and Hartmann 2009). The all-or-nothing and probabilistic views are illustrated by the difference between Descartes's Cogito and Pascal's wager. In the Cogito, Descartes argues for a belief in God based on rational reflection and deductive reasoning. In the wager, Pascal argues for a belief in God based on outcomes evaluated probabilistically.

Robots and autonomous systems can be built with a functional architecture that imitates human belief structures called belief/desire/intention models (Georgeff et al. 1999). But, there are many cognitive architectures that can be built into a robot, and each may have different epistemic consequences and yield different trust relations (Wagner and Briscoe 2017). Mental states and mental models can be developed logically to enable artificial systems to instantiate beliefs as propositions (Felli et al. 2014) or probabilities (Goodrich and Yi 2013). The upshot is that the functional role of belief for humans can be mimicked by artificial systems—at least in theory. However, it is unclear whether the future of AI will aim to replicate human functional architecture or approach the challenge of knowledge quite differently.

15.7: THE REPRESENTATION OF KNOWLEDGE

How is knowledge represented and operated on within humans, autonomous systems, and human-machine teams? The ancient Greeks imagined that perceptual knowledge was recorded and stored in the mind, similarly to the way wax takes on the imprint of a seal (Plato 369 B.C.). Early twentieth-century thinkers used the metaphor of modern telephony, radio, and office workers to explain how signals from the world translated into thoughts, and thoughts were communicated between different brain regions (Draaisma 2000). The late twentieth century saw the rise of the computational model of the mind, supposing that humans store knowledge as representations akin to modern symbolic computers—allowing functions such as combining propositions using a language of thought and retrieving memories from storage (Fodor 1975). In the 1980s, the connectionist view of the mind arose based on neuroscience. Under connectionism, the mind is identified with the biological and functional substrate of the brain and simulated by building artificial neural networks (ANN) (Churchland 1989; Fodor and Pylyshyn 1988; Kiefer 2019). Connectionist networks such as deep learning succeed at tasks via networks of neurons arranged in a hierarchy. Each object, concept, or thought can be represented by a vector (LeCun 2015):

i) [-0.2, 0.3, -4.2, 5.1, . . .] represent the concept "cat";
ii) [-0.2, 0.4, -4.0, 5.1, . . .] represent the concept "dog."

Vectors, i) and ii) are similar because cats and dogs have many properties in common. Reasoning and planning consist of combining and transforming thought vectors. Vectors can be compared to answer questions, retrieve information, and filter content. Thoughts can be remembered by adding memory networks (simulating the hippocampal function in humans) (Weston et al. 2014). Grouping neurons into capsules allows retention of features of lower-level representations as vectors are moved up the ANN hierarchy (Lukic et al. 2019). Contrary to early critiques of "dumb connectionist networks," the complex structures and functionality of contemporary ANN meet the threshold required of sophisticated cognitive representations (Kiefer 2019)—although not yet contributing to explanations of consciousness, affect, volition, and perhaps reflective knowledge. Humans and technologies can represent the world, make judgments about propositions, and can be said to believe when they act as though propositions were true.

Knowledge might be about facts, but it is also about capabilities, the distinction between "knowing that" versus "knowing how" (Ryle 1949). *Knowing that* means the agent has an accurate representation of facts, such as the fact that medical trucks have red crosses on them, or that hospitals are protected places. *Knowing how* are skills, such as the ability to ride a bike, the ability of a Close in Weapons System (CIWS) to reliably track incoming missiles or loitering munition's ability to track a human-selected target (Israel Aerospace Industries 2019; Raytheon 2019b). *Knowledge how* describes the processes used to able humans or agents to perform tasks such as maneuvering around objects or juggling that may or may not be propositional in nature. *Knowledge how* can be acquired via explicit instruction, practice, and experience and can become an implicit capability over time. The reduction of cognitive load when an agent moves from learner to expert explains the gated trajectory through training programs for complex physical tasks such as military training.

Examples of *knowledge how* include the autopilot software on aircraft, or AI trained how to navigate a path or play a game regardless of whether specific facts are represented at any layer. An adaptive autonomous system can learn and improve *knowledge how in situ*. Any complex systems incorporating LAWS, such as human-autonomy teams (Demir et al. 2018) and manned-unmanned teams (Lim et al. 2018) must be assessed for how the system knows what it is doing and how it knows ethical action. *Knowledge how* is what a legal reviewer needs to assess in order to be sure LAWS are compliant with LOAC (Boothby 2016). *Knowledge how* is pertinent to any ethical evaluative layer, or ethical "governor" (Arkin et al. 2009). Evaluating *knowledge how* requires a testing environment simulating multiple actions, evaluating them against ethical requirements (Vanderelst and Winfield 2018). Many of the capabilities of LAWS are perhaps best understood as *knowledge how* rather than *knowledge that*, and our systems of assurance must be receptive to the right sort of behavioral evidence for their trustworthiness.

A concern for Article 36 reviews of LAWS is that they are a black box—that the precise mechanisms that justify action are hidden or obtuse to human scrutiny (Castelvecchi 2016). Not even AlphaGo's developer team is able to point out how AlphaGo evaluates the game position and picks its next move (Metz 2016). Three solutions emerge from the black box criticism of AI: (1) Unexplainable AI is unethical and must be banned; (2) Unexplainable AI is unethical, and yet we need to have it anyway; and (3) Unexplainable AI can be ethical under the right framework.

To sum up, so far I have examined the conditions of knowledge (justified true belief), belief, how beliefs are represented and used to make decisions. I now move to normative epistemology, theories that help designers of LAWS to ensure AI and artificial agents are developed with sufficient competency to justify their actions in conflict. Given the 'blackbox' issues with some artificial intelligence programming, I argue that reliabilism is an epistemic model that allows for systems to be tested, evaluated, and trusted despite some ignorance with regards to how any specific decision is made.

15.8: RELIABILISM

Skeptical arguments show that there are no necessary deductive or inductive relationships between beliefs and their evidential grounds or even their probability

(Greco 2000). In order to avoid skepticism, a different view of what constitutes good evidence must be found. Good evidence for a positive epistemology might be the reliable connection between what we believe about the world, and the way the world behaves (which is consistent with these beliefs), such that "the grounds for our beliefs are reliable indications of their truth" (Greco 2000, 4). Reliabilism supposes that a subject knows a proposition *p* when (a) *p* is true, (b) the subject believes *p*, and (c) the belief that *p* is the result of a reliable process. A key benefit of reliabilism is that beliefs formed reliably have epistemic value, regardless of whether an agent can justify or infer reasons for their reliability. Reliable beliefs, like the readings from a thermometer or thermostat, are externally verifiable. Cognitive agents are more complex than thermometers, however. Agents have higher-order reliability based on the reliability of subsystems. In complex agents, the *degree* of reliability of the process gives the *degree* to which a belief generated by it is justified (Sosa 1993). The most discussed variant of reliabilism is process (or paradigm) reliabilism: "S's belief in p is justified if it is caused (or causally sustained) by a reliable cognitive process, or a history of reliable processes" (Goldman 1994). An issue for reliabilists is a lack of sophistication about how cognitive processes actually operate—a similar problem for the internal processes of AI build by machine learning and deep learning.

15.9: VIRTUE EPISTEMOLOGY

Virtue epistemology is a variant of reliabilism in which the cognitive circumstances and abilities of an agent play a justificatory role.[1] In sympathy with rationalists (Descartes 1628/1988, 1–4, Rules II and III; Plato 380 B.C.), virtue epistemologists argue that there is a significant epistemic project to identify intellectual virtues that confer justification upon a true belief to make it knowledge. However, virtue epistemologists are open to empirical pressure on these theories. Virtue epistemology aims to identify the attributes of agents that justify knowledge claims. Like other traditional epistemologies, virtue epistemology cites normative standards that must be met in order for an agent's doxastic state to count as knowledge, the most important of which is truth. Other standards include reliability, motivation, or credibility. Of the many varieties of virtue epistemology (Greco 2010; Zagzebski 2012), I focus on Ernie Sosa's that specifies an iterative and hierarchical account of reliabilist justification (Sosa 2007; 2009; 2011), particularly useful when considering nonhuman artificial agents and the doxastic state of human-machine teams. Sosa's virtue epistemology considers two forms of reliabilist knowledge: animal and reflective.

15.9.1: Animal Knowledge

Animal knowledge is based on an agent's capacity to survive and thrive in the environment regardless of higher-order beliefs about its survival, without any reflection or understanding (Sosa 2007). An agent has animal knowledge if their beliefs are accurate, they have the skill (i.e., are adroit) at producing accurate beliefs, and their beliefs are apt (i.e., accurate due to adroit processes). Consider an archer shooting an arrow at a target. A shot is apt when it is accurate not because of luck or a fortuitous wind that pushes the arrow to the center, but because of the competence exhibited by the archer. Similarly an autonomous fire-fighting drone is apt when fire retardant is dropped on the fire due to sophisticated programming, and comprehensive test and evaluation. Sosa takes beliefs to be long-sustained performances exhibiting a combination of accuracy, adroitness, and aptness. Apt beliefs are accurate (true), adroit (produced by skillful processes), and are accurate *because* they are adroit. Aptness is a measure of performance success, and accidental beliefs are therefore not apt, even if the individual who holds those beliefs is adroit. Take, for example, a skilled archer who hits the bullseye due to a gust of wind rather than the precision of his shot.

Animal knowledge involves no reflection or understanding. However, animal knowledge can become reflective if the appropriate reflective stance targets it. For example, on one hand, a person might have animal knowledge that two combatants are inside an abandoned building, and when questioned, they reflect on their belief and form a reflective judgment that the people are combatants is in an abandoned building with the addition of explicit considerations of prior surveillance of this dwelling, prior experience tracking these combatants, footprints that match the boot tread of the belligerents' uniform, steam emerging from the window, and so forth. On the other hand, animal knowledge might "remain inarticulate" and yet yield "practically appropriate inferences" nevertheless, such as fighter pilot knowledge of how to evade detection, developed through hours of training and experience without the capacity to enunciate the parameters of this knowledge. The capacity to *explain* our knowledge is the domain of reflective knowledge.

15.9.2: Reflective Knowledge

Reflective knowledge is animal knowledge plus an "understanding of its place in a wider whole that includes one's belief and knowledge of it and how these come about" (Kornblith 2009, 128). Reflective knowledge draws on internalist ideas about justification (e.g., intuition, intellect, and so on) in order to bolster and improve the epistemic status brought via animal knowledge alone. Reflective knowledge encompasses all higher-order thinking (metacognition), including episodic memory, reflective inference, abstract ideas, and counterfactual reasoning. Animal and reflective knowledge comport with two distinct decision-making systems: (mostly) implicit System 1, and explicit System 2 (Evans and Frankish 2009; Kahneman 2011; Stanovich 1999; Stanovich and West 2000). System 1 operates automatically and quickly, with little or no effort and no sense of voluntary control. System 2 allocates attention to the effortful mental activities that demand it, including complex computations. The operations of System 2 are often associated with the subjective experience of agency, choice, and concentration. System 1 operates in the background of daily life, going hand in hand with animal knowledge. System 1 is activated in fast-tempo operational environments, where decision-making is instinctive and immediate. System 2 operates when decisions are high risk, ethically and legally challenging. System 2 is activated in slow-tempo operational environments where decisions are reviewed and authorized beyond an individual agent.

Virtue epistemology is particularly suited to autonomous systems that learn and adapt through experience. For example, autonomous systems, when first created, may perform fairly poorly and be untrustworthy in a range of contexts—perhaps every context. But, the expectation is that they are trained and deployed in a succession of constrained environments. Constrained environments are built with features and scenarios that AIs learn from, to build their competence and then they are exposed to more complexity and uncertainty as they build decision-making skills. Failure scenarios include unpredictable operating circumstances and operating in adversarial environments designed to trick machine learning algorithms and other experience-based AI. One way to improve decision-making under uncertainty is to allow beliefs to be expressed as a matter of degree, rather than certainty. This is the realm of Bayesian epistemology.

15.10: BAYESIAN EPISTEMOLOGY

Bayesian epistemology argues that typical beliefs exist (and are performed) in degrees, rather than absolutes, represented as credence functions (Christensen 2010; Dunn 2010; Friedman 2011; Joyce 2010). A credence function assigns a real number between 0 and 1 (inclusive) to every proposition in a set. The ideal degree of confidence an agent has in a proposition is the degree that is appropriate given the evidence and situation the agent is in. No agent is an ideally rational agent, capable of truly representing reality, so they must be programmed to revise and update their internal representations in response to confirming and disconfirming evidence, forging ahead toward ever more faithful reconstructions of reality.

Bayesian epistemology encourages a meek approach with regard to evidence and credences. As Hajek and Hartmann (2009) argue, "to rule out (probabilistically speaking) a priori some genuine logical possibility would be to pretend that one's evidence was stronger than it really was." Credences have value to an agent, even if they are considerably less than 1, and therefore are not spurned. Contrast this with the typical skeptic in traditional epistemology whose hunches, suppositions, and worries can accelerate the demise of a theory of knowledge, regardless of their likelihood. Even better than an abstract theory, the human mind, in many respects, operates in accordance with the tenants of Bayesian epistemology. Top-down predictions are compared against incoming signals, allowing the brain to adapt its model of the world (Clark 2015; Hohwy 2013; Kiefer 2019; Pezzulo et al. 2015).

Bayesian epistemology has several advantages over traditional epistemology in terms of its applicability to actual decision-making. Firstly, Bayesian epistemology incorporates decision theory, which uses subjective probabilities to guide rational action and (like virtue epistemology) takes account of both agent desires and opinions to dictate what they should do. Traditional epistemology, meanwhile, offers no decision theory, only parameters by which to judge final results. Secondly, Bayesian epistemology accommodates fine-grained mental states, rather than binaries of belief or knowledge. Finally, observations of the world rarely deliver certainties, and each experience of the world contributes to a graduated revision of beliefs. While traditional epistemology requires an unforgiving standard for doxastic states, Bayesian epistemology allows beliefs with low credences to play an evidential role in evaluating theories and evidence. In sum, the usefulness of Bayesian epistemology lies in its capacity to accommodate decision theory, fine-grained mental states, and uncertain observations of the world.

A comprehensive epistemology for LAWS will not merely specify the conditions in which beliefs are justified; it will also offer normative guidance for making rational decisions. Virtue epistemology and Bayesian epistemology (incorporating both confirmation theory and decision theory) provide parameters for design of LAWS that explain and justify actions and include a comprehensive theory of decision-making that links beliefs to the best course of action.

15.11: DISCUSSION

Imagine three autonomous systems: AS1, AS2, and AS3.

AS1: programmed according to virtue epistemology (AS1v),
AS2: programmed according to Bayesian epistemology (AS2b), and
AS3: programmed according to Bayesian virtue epistemology (AS3bv).

How will the three be deployed differently?

AS1v (autonomous systems with virtue epistemology) should only act when it knows, which means it must be trained to be highly competent in the specific domain of operation. This makes it highly reliable in a narrow window of operations. Automated countermeasures such as the Phalanx Close In Weapons System (CIWS) are excellent examples of reliable AS1v. When in automated mode, they search for, detect, track, engage, and confirm actions using computer-controlled radar systems. CIWS criteria for targeting include the following: Is the range of the target increasing or decreasing in relation to the ship? Is the contact capable of maneuvering to hit the ship? Is the contact traveling between the minimum and maximum velocities? These actions are safe because only human-made offensive weapons could meet the criteria to make the autonomous weapons system fire. If an incident does occur, then the parameters of the autonomous system are altered to ensure more competent safer operations.

AS2b (autonomous systems with Bayesian epistemology) acts when it has rational belief for action, and this may fall short of knowledge. Consider if AS2b was an autonomous logistics vehicle evaluating their surroundings. It plans an efficient route to a goal, predicts the paths of other objects, creates a map of better and worse paths based on collision avoidance, and updates the route to optimize its path and keep the environment safe (Leben 2019). There are many unknown scenarios for AS2b to manage because there are lots of situations where the robot might collide with objects if they move in a way the system is unable to predict and/or respond to. However, the risk of harmful collision might be deemed very low in a specific and constrained environment; thus it is certified to operate. A Bayesian human combatant operates in highly reliable conditions, but also in the "fog of war." Training, preparation and limited missions reduce the risk of error during lethal actions. But errors do occur, and these are managed so long as combatants have done their best to abide by IHL and the error was an unforeseen occurrence. Could a lethal autonomous weapons system AS2b be deployed similarly to a human combatant? It is likely that LAWS will face an asymmetric evaluation to a human operator. That is to say, the competence of the LAWS will be required to be many times higher if deployed under the same conditions as a human because incorrect task performance will not just affect one unit, but could be instantiated over hundreds or even thousands of implementations of the technology. This point has been made in the autonomous cars literature and is likely to be even more emotive in the regulation of LAWS (Scharre 2018).

AS3bv (autonomous system with Bayesian and virtue epistemology) acts in ways [B_m, $B_{n...}$] when it has rational belief for action and [V_m, $V_{n...}$] when it has knowledge. Suppose AS3bv is an autonomous drone. AS3bv performs low-risk actions using a Bayesian epistemology such as navigating the skies and AI classification of its visual feed even though it may not exist in a knowledge state. AS3bv considers many sorts of evidence, acknowledges uncertainty, is cautious, and will progress toward its mission even when uncertain. However, when AS3bv switches to a high-risk action, such as targeting with lethal intent, the epistemic mechanism flips to reflective knowledge as specified in Sosa's virtue epistemology. AS3bv will go through the relevant levels of reflective processing within its own systems and with appropriate human input and control under IHL.

A demonstration of AS3bv is the way humans have designed the Tomahawk subsonic cruise missile to self-correct by comparing the terrain beneath it to satellite-generated maps stored on-board. If its trajectory is altered, motors will move the wings to counter unforeseen difficulties on its journey. The tactical Tomahawk can be reprogrammed mid-flight remotely to a different target using GPS coordinates stored locally. Tomahawk engineers' and operators' competencies play a role in the success or failure of the missile to hit its target. If part of the guidance system fails, human decisions will affect how well the missile flies. Part of the reason why credences need to play a greater role in epistemology is that instances where knowledge does not obtain—yet competent processes are deployed—should not prevent action toward a goal.

It is possible that a future LAWS may achieve reflective knowledge via a hierarchy of Bayesian processes, known as Hierarchically Nested Probabilistic Models (HNPM). HNPM are structured, describing the relations between models and patterns of evidence in rigorous ways emulating higher-order "Type 2," reflective capabilities (Devitt 2013). HNPM achieve higher-order information processing using iterations of the same justificatory processes that underlie basic probabilistic processes. HNPM show that higher-order theories (e.g., about abstract ideas) can become inductive constraints on the interpretation of lower-level theories or *overhypotheses* (Goodman 1983; Kemp et al. 2007). HNPM can account for multiple levels of knowledge, including (1) abstract generalizations relating to higher level principles, (2) specific theories about a set of instances, and (3) particular experiences. If the human mind is, to a great degree, Bayesian, then building LAWS that operate similarly may build trust, explainability, understandability, and better human-machine systems. AS3bv systems will be more virtuous because they will move with assurance in their actions, declare their uncertainties, reflect on their beliefs, and be constrained within operations according to their obligations under IHL and Article 36 guidelines.

Then the question is, at what threshold of virtue and competence would any group or authority actually release AS3bv into combat operations or into a war scenario? As wars are increasingly operating in Grey Zones, they are becoming a virtual and physical conflagration between private individuals, economic agents, militarized groups, and government agencies. The future of war will need agents operating in complicated social environments that require a defensible epistemology for how they make decisions. Combining Bayesian epistemology with virtue epistemology enables LAWS to operate rationally and cautiously in uncertain environments with partial and changing information. This level of defensible adaptability is important in emerging battlefront situations where the enemy is not clear, and individuals who need to be targeted must be carefully thought through.

In sum, knowledge is the ideal epistemic state, but epistemic states where knowledge falls short may leave behind another justified epistemic state—rational belief—plus a feedback opportunity to increase knowledge (or the probability of knowledge) for future situations. Reliable processes create knowledge, but also improve the odds of future knowledge in different conditions. Instances of knowledge are valuable in that they inform the agent and those around them of the scale of their competencies. Whether any LAWS passes an Article 36 review depends on human confidence that the weapon is reliable and competent in normal or expected use. This outcome depends on whether an autonomous weapon can be used in compliance with laws of armed conflict and act in a manner that is predictable, reliable, and explainable. A Bayesian virtue epistemology values reliability and competence and skills; knowledge and credences. Epistemology becomes not just the study of justified true belief then, but also the study of the processes of belief revision in response to confirming or disconfirming evidence. Justification arises from the apt performance of reliable processes and their coherence and coordination with other beliefs (Devitt 2013).

15.12: CONCLUSION

This chapter has discussed higher-order design principles to guide the design, evaluation, deployment, and iteration of LAWS based on epistemic models to ensure that the lawfulness of LAWS is determined before they are developed, acquired, or otherwise incorporated into a States arsenal (International Committee of the Red Cross 2006). The design of lethal autonomous weapons ought to incorporate our highest standards for reflective knowledge. A targeting decision ought to be informed by the most accurate and fast information, justified over hierarchical levels of reliability enabling the best of human reasoning, compassion, and hypothetical considerations. Humans with meaningful control over LAWS ought to have knowledge that is safe, not lucky; contextually valid; and available for scrutiny. Our means of communicating the decision process, actions, and outcomes ought to be informed by normative models such as Bayesian and virtue epistemologies to ensure rational, knowledgeable, and ethical decisions.

NOTE

1. Contrast virtue epistemology with pure reliabilism or evidentialism where justification does not depend on agency.

WORKS CITED

Arkin, Ronald C., Leslie Kaelbling, Stuart Russell, Dorsa Sadigh, Paul Scharre, Bart Selman, and Toby Walsh. 2019. *Autonomous Weapon Systems: A Roadmapping*

Exercise. Atlanta: Georgia Institute of Technology, College of Computing. https://www.cc.gatech.edu/ai/robot-lab/online-publications/AWS.pdf.

Arkin, Ronald C., Patrick Ulam, and Brittany Duncan. 2009. *An Ethical Governor for Constraining Lethal Action in an Autonomous System*. Technical Report GIT-GVU-09-02. Atlanta: Georgia Institute of Technology, College of Computing.

Armstrong, David Mallet. 1973. *Belief, Truth, and Knowledge*. Cambridge: Cambridge University Press.

Asaro, Peter. 2012. "On Banning Autonomous Weapon Systems: Human Rights, Automation, and the Dehumanization of Lethal Decision-Making." *International Review of the Red Cross* 94 (886): pp. 687–709.

Australia. 2019. "Australia's System of Control and Applications for Autonomous Weapon Systems." Working Paper. Geneva: Meeting of Group of Governmental Experts on LAWS. March 26. CCW/GGE.1/2019/WP.2/Rev.1.

Bagheri, Behrad, Shanhu Yang, Hung-An Kao, and Jay Lee. 2015. "Cyber-Physical Systems Architecture for Self-Aware Machines in Industry 4.0 Environment." *IFAC-PapersOnLine* 48 (3): pp. 1622–1627.

BonJour, Laurence. 1985. *The Structure of Empirical Knowledge*. Cambridge, MA: Harvard University Press.

Boothby, William H. 2016. *Weapons and the Law of Armed Conflict*. Oxford: Oxford University Press.

Castelvecchi, Davide. 2016. "Can We Open the Black Box of AI?" *Nature News* 538 (7623): pp. 20–23.

GGE. 2018. *Report of the 2018 Session of the Group of Governmental Experts on Emerging Technologies in the Area of Lethal Autonomous Weapons Systems*. Geneva: United Nations Office at Geneva. 23 October. CCW/GGE.1/2018/3.

Chignell, Andrew. 2018. "The Ethics of Belief." *Stanford Encyclopedia of Philosophy*. Accessed August 5, 2019. https://plato.stanford.edu/archives/spr2018/entries/ethics-belief/.

Christensen, D. (2010). "Rational Reflection." *Philosophical Perspectives* 24(1): pp. 121–140. doi: 10.1111/j.1520-8583.2010.00187.x.

Churchland, Patricia Smith. 1989. *Neurophilosophy: Toward a Unified Science of the Mind-Brain*. Cambridge MA: MIT Press.

Clark, Andy. 2015. *Surfing Uncertainty: Prediction, Action, and the Embodied Mind*. New York: Oxford University Press.

Conee, Earl and Richard Feldman. 2004. *Evidentialism*. Oxford: Oxford University Press.

Demir, Mustafa, Nancy J. Cooke, and Polemnia G. Amazeen. 2018. "A Conceptual Model of Team Dynamical Behaviors and Performance in Human-Autonomy Teaming." *Cognitive Systems Research* 52: pp. 497–507.

Descartes, René. 1628/1988. "Rules for the Direction of Our Native Intelligence." In *Descartes: Selected Philosophical Writings*, edited by John Cottingham, Robert Stoothoff, Dugald Murdoch, and Anthony Kenny, pp. 1–19. Cambridge: Cambridge University Press.

Devitt, Susannah Kate. 2013. "Homeostatic Epistemology: Reliability, Coherence and Coordination in a Bayesian Virtue Epistemology." PhD dissertation. Rutgers The State University of New Jersey–New Brunswick. Available at https://eprints.qut.edu.au/62553/.

Devitt, Susannah Kate. 2018. "Trustworthiness of Autonomous Systems." In *Foundations of Trusted Autonomy*, edited by Hussein A. Abbass, Jason Scholz, and Darryn J. Reid, pp. 161–184. Cham, Switzerland: Springer International Publishing.

Draaisma, Douwe. 2000. *Metaphors of Memory: A History of Ideas about the Mind*. New York: Cambridge University Press.

Dunn, J.S. (2010). Bayesian Epistemology and Having Evidence. PhD, University of Massachusetts, Amherst. Retrieved from hyttp://scholarworks.umass.edu/open_acccess_dissertations/273/.

Evans, Jonathan and Keith Frankish (eds). 2009. *In Two Minds: Dual Processes and Beyond*. New York: Oxford University Press.

Farrant, James and Christopher M. Ford. 2017. "Autonomous Weapons and Weapon Reviews: The UK Second International Weapon Review Forum." *International Law Studies* 93 (1): pp. 389–422.

Felli, Paolo, Tim Miller, Christian Muise, Adrian R. Pearce, and Liz Sonenberg. 2014. "Artificial Social Reasoning: Computational Mechanisms for Reasoning about Others." In *Social Robotics: International Conference on Social Robotics. Sydney, NSW, Australia, October 27–29, 2014. Proceedings*, edited by Michael Beetz, Benjamin Johnston, and Mary-Anne Williams, pp. 146–155. Sydney: Springer Link.

Fischer, John Martin and Mark Ravizza. 1998. *Responsibility and Control: A Theory of Moral Responsibility*. New York: Cambridge University Press.

Fodor, Jerry A. 1968. *Psychological Explanation*. New York: Random House.

Fodor, Jerry A. 1975. *The Language of Thought*. Cambridge, MA: Harvard University Press.

Fodor, Jerry. A. and Zenon W. Pylyshyn. 1988. "Connectionism and Cognitive Architecture: A Critical Analysis." *Cognition* 28 (1–2): pp. 3–71.

Friedman, J. (2011). "Suspended Judgment." *Philosophical Studies* 162(2): pp. 165–181. doi:10.1007/s11098-011-9753-y.

Geography of Philosophy Project. 2020. "Go Philosophy." *Go Philosophy*. Accessed January 28, 2020. https://go-philosophy.com/category/research/knowledge/.

Georgeff, Michael, Barney Pell, Martha Pollack, Milind Tambe, and Michael Woolridge. 1999. "The Belief-Desire-Intention Model of Agency." In *Intelligent Agents V: Agents Theories, Architectures, and Languages. ATAL 1998. Lecture Notes in Computer Science*, edited by Jörg Müller, Munindar P. Singh, and Anand S. Rao, pp.1–10. Berlin: Springer.

Gettier, Edmund. 1963. "Is Justified True Belief Knowledge?" *Analysis* 23 (6): pp. 121–123.

Gettinger, Dan and Arthur Holland Michel. 2017. "Loitering Munitions." *Center for the Study of the Drone*. Accessed August 5, 2019. https://dronecenter.bard.edu/files/2017/02/CSD-Loitering-Munitions.pdf.

Goldman, Alvin I. 1986. *Epistemology and Cognition*. Cambridge, MA: Harvard University Press.

Goldman, Alvin I. 1994. "Naturalistic Epistemology and Reliabilism." In *Midwest Studies in Philosophy XIX: Philosophical Naturalism*, edited by Peter A. French, Theodore E. Uehling, and Howard K. Wettstein, pp. 301–320. Minneapolis: University of Minnesota Press.

Goodman, Nelson. 1983. *Fact, Fiction, and Forecast*. Cambridge, MA: Harvard University Press.

Goodrich, Michael A. and Daqing Yi. 2013. "Toward Task-Based Mental Models of Human-Robot Teaming: A Bayesian Approach." In *Virtual Augmented and Mixed*

Reality. Designing and Developing Augmented and Virtual Environments. VAMR 2013. Lecture Notes in Computer Science, edited by Randall Shumaker, pp. 267–276. Berlin: Springer.

Greco, John. 2000. *The Nature of Skeptical Arguments and Their Role in Philosophical Inquiry.* Cambridge: Cambridge University Press.

Greco, John. 2010. *Achieving Knowledge.* Cambridge: Cambridge University Press.

Hajek, Alan and Stephan Hartmann. 2009. "'Bayesian Epistemology." In *A Companion to Epistemology*, edited by Jonathan Dancy, Ernest Sosa, and Matthias Steup, pp. 93–105. Chicester: John Wiley & Sons, Ltd.

Hancock, Peter. A. 2016. "Imposing Limits on Autonomous Systems." *Ergonomics* 60 (2): pp. 284–291. doi: 0.1080/00140139.2016.1190035.

Hohwy, Jakob. 2013. *The Predictive Mind.* Oxford: Oxford University Press.

Horowitz, Michael C. and Paul Scharre. 2015. "Meaningful Human Control in Weapon Systems: A Primer." Working Paper. Washington, DC: Center for a New American Security (CNAS).

IEEE Global Initiative on Ethics of Autonomous and Intelligent Systems. 2019. "Ethically Aligned Design: A Vision for Prioritizing Human Well-Being with Autonomous and Intelligent Systems (EADe1)." *IEEE.*

International Committee of the Red Cross. 2006. "A Guide to the Legal Review of New Weapons, Means and Methods of Warfare: Measures to Implement Article 36 of Additional Protocol I of 1977." *International Review of the Red Cross* 88 (864): pp. 931–956.

Israel Aerospace Industries. 2019. "Harop: Loitering Munition System." Israel Aerospace Industries. Accessed 5 September. https://www.iai.co.il/p/harop.

Jobin, Anna, Marcello Ienca, and Effy Vayena. 2019. "Artificial Intelligence: The Global Landscape of Ethics Guidelines." *arXiv preprint.* arXiv:1906.11668.

Joyce, J.M., (2010). A Defence of Imprecise Credences in Inference and Decision Making. *Philosophical Perspectives* 24(1): pp. 281–323. doi:10.1111/j.1520-8583.2010.00194.x.

Kahneman, Daniel. 2011. *Thinking, Fast and Slow.* New York: Farrar, Straus and Giroux.

Kemp, Charles, Amy Perfors, and Joshua B. Tenenbaum. 2007. "Learning Overhypotheses with Hierarchical Bayesian Models." *Developmental Science* 10 (3): pp. 307–321.

Kiefer, Alex B. 2019. "A Defence of Pure Connectionism." PhD dissertation. City University of New York. Available at https://academicworks.cuny.edu/gc_etds/3036/.

Kornblith, Hilary. 2009. "Sosa in Perspective." *Philosophical Studies* 144 (1): pp. 127–136. doi: 10.1007/s11098-009-9377-7.

Leben, Derek. 2019. *Ethics for Robots: How to Design a Moral Algorithm.* New York: Routledge.

LeCun, Yann. 2015. "What's Wrong with Deep Learning?" Architecture of Computing Systems—ARCS 2015: 28th International Conference, March 24–27, 2015. Porto, Portugal.

Lim, Yixiang, Alessandro Gardi, Roberto Sabatini, Subramanian Ramasamy, Trevor Kistan, Neta Ezer, Julian Vince, and Robert Bolia. 2018. "Avionics Human-Machine Interfaces and Interactions for Manned and Unmanned Aircraft." *Progress in Aerospace Sciences* 102: pp. 1–46.

Lukic, V., Marcus Bruggen, Beatriz Mingo, Judith H. Croston, Gregor Kasieczka, and Phillip Best. 2019. "Morphological Classification of Radio Galaxies: Capsule

Networks versus Convolutional Neural Networks." *Monthly Notices of the Royal Astronomical Society* 487 (2): pp. 1729–1744.

Lycan, William. 2006. "On the Gettier Problem Problem." In *Epistemology Futures*, edited by Stephen Cade Hetherington, p. 148. Oxford: Clarendon Press.

Maffie, James. 2019. "Ethnoepistemology." *Internet Encyclopedia of Philosophy*. Accessed August 5, 2019. https://www.iep.utm.edu/ethno-ep/.

Médecins Sans Frontières. 2019. "Relief." *The Practical Guide to Humanitarian Law*. Accessed 10 September. https://guide-humanitarian-law.org/content/article/3/relief/.

Metz, Cade. 2016. "In Two Moves, AlphaGo and Lee Sedol Redefined the Future." *WIRED.com*. March 16. https://www.wired.com/2016/03/two-moves-alphago-lee-sedol-redefined-future/.

Millikan, Ruth. 1984. *Language, Thought, and Other Biological Categories*. Cambridge, MA: The MIT Press.

Mizumoto, Masaharu, Stephen P. Stich, and Eric McCready. 2018. *Epistemology for the Rest of the World*. Oxford: Oxford University Press.

Moser, Paul K. 2005. *The Oxford Handbook of Epistemology*. New York: Oxford University Press.

Nozick, Robert. 1981. *Philosophical Explanations*. Cambridge, MA: Harvard University Press.

O'Brien, Dan. 2016. *An Introduction to the Theory of Knowledge*, 2nd ed. Cambridge: Polity Press.

Paparone, Christopher R. and George E. Reed. 2008. "The Reflective Military Practitioner: How Military Professionals Think in Action." *Military Review* 8(2): pp. 67–77.

Pezzulo, Giovanni, Laura Barca, and Karl J. Friston. 2015. "Active Inference and Cognitive-Emotional Interactions in the Brain." *Behavioral and Brain Sciences* 38: p. 85.

Quine, W. V. 1969. "Epistemology Naturalized." In *Ontological Relativity and Other Essays*, edited by W. V. Quine, pp. 69–90. New York: Columbia University Press.

Raytheon. 2019a. "Tomahawk Cruise Missile." Accessed August 5, 2019. https://www.raytheon.com/capabilities/products/tomahawk.

Raytheon. 2019b. Raytheon. Phalanx Weapon System. Accessed August 2, 2019. https://www.raytheonmissilesanddefense.com/capabilities/products/phalanx-close-in-weapon-system.

Ryle, Gilbert. 1949. *The Concept of Mind*. Chicago: Chicago University Press.

Santoni de Sio, Filippo and Jeroen van den Hoven. 2018. "Meaningful Human Control over Autonomous Systems: A Philosophical Account." *Frontiers in Robotics and AI* 5: pp. 1–14.

Scharre, Paul. 2018. *Army of None: Autonomous Weapons and the Future of War*. New York: W. W. Norton & Company.

Scholz, Jason and Jai Galliott. 2018. "'AI in Weapons: The Moral Imperative for Minimally-Just Autonomy." In *International Conference on Science and Innovation for Land Power*. Adelaide, Australia.

Schwitzgebel, Eric. 2011. "Belief." In *The Stanford Encyclopedia of Philosophy*, edited by Edward N. Zalta. Accessed January 28, 2020. https://plato.stanford.edu/cgi-bin/encyclopedia/archinfo.cgi?entry=belief.

Sharkey, Noel. 2012. "Killing Made Easy: From Joysticks to Politics." In *Robot Ethics: The Ethical and Social Implications of Robotics*, edited by Keith Abney, George A. Bekey, and Patrick Lin, pp. 111–128. Cambridge MA: MIT Press.

Sosa, Ernest. 1993. "Proper Functionalism and Virtue Epistemology." *Noûs* 27 (1): pp. 51–65.

Sosa, Ernest. 2007. *A Virtue Epistemology: Apt Belief and Reflective Knowledge*, 2 vols. Oxford: Oxford University Press.

Sosa, Ernest. 2009. *Reflective Knowledge: Apt Belief and Reflective Knowledge*. Oxford: Oxford University Press.

Sosa, Ernest. 2011. *Knowing Full Well*. Princeton, NJ: Princeton University Press.

Stanovich, Keith E. 1999. *Who Is Rational?: Studies of Individual Differences in Reasoning*. Mahwah, NJ: Lawrence Erlbaum Associates.

Stanovich, Keith E. and Richard F. West. 2000. "Individual Differences in Reasoning: Implications for the Rationality Debate?" *Behavioral & Brain Sciences* 23 (5): pp. 645–665.

Taylor, Robert L., William E. Rosenbach, and Eric B. Rosenbach (eds). 2018. *Military Leadership: In Pursuit of Excellence*. New York: Routledge.

van den Hoven, Jeroen. 2013. "Value Sensitive Design and Responsible Innovation." In *Responsible Innovation*, edited by Richard Owen, John R. Bessant, and Maggy Heintz, pp. 75–84. Chichester, UK: John Wiley & Sons, Ltd.

Vanderelst, Dieter and Alan Winfield. 2018. "An Architecture for Ethical Robots Inspired by the Simulation Theory of Cognition." *Cognitive Systems Research* 48: pp. 56–66.

Wagner, Alan Richard and Erica J. Briscoe. 2017. "Psychological Modeling of Humans by Assistive Robots." In *Human Modeling for Bio-Inspired Robotics: Mechanical Engineering in Assistive Technologies*, edited by Jun Ueda and Yuichi Kurita, pp. 273–295. London: Academic Press.

Weston, Jason, Sumit Chopra, and Antoine Bordes. 2014. "Memory Networks." *arXiv preprint arXiv:1410.3916*.

Zagzebski, Linda. 2012. *Epistemic Authority: A Theory of Trust, Authority, and Autonomy in Belief*. New York: Oxford University Press.

16

Proposing a Regional Normative Framework for Limiting the Potential for Unintentional or Escalatory Engagements with Increasingly Autonomous Weapon Systems

AUSTIN WYATT AND JAI GALLIOTT

Media reports of fishermen being harassed by sleek black patrol vessels and clouds of quad rotor aircraft armed with less-than-lethal "pepper ball" rounds had spread like wildfire in the capital. Under increasing pressure from radio shock jocks and influential bloggers, the Kamerian president authorized the deployment of the *Repressor,* a recently refurbished destroyer on loan from their southern neighbor, to the waters around Argon Island, a volcanic outcrop at the center of overlapping traditional fishing grounds.

In the days since it had arrived on station at Argon, the *Repressor* had been repeatedly "buzzed" by small unmarked drones and black fast-boats, which they had been warned could be armed and did not respond to hails. The security detachment had already been mobilized twice in response to the seemingly random intrusions into the *Repressor*'s Ship Safety Zone. The captain reports that the constant tactical alerts had started to take a toll on the mentality of the sailors, none of whom had been able to get consistent sleep since arriving.

On the twelfth day of its deployment, the *Repressor* responded to a distress signal on the other side of Argon Island. Reports are unclear, but it appears that the distress signal was faked, and the *Repressor* was swarmed by small unmanned fast-boats and their communications system failed. By the time that fleet command was

Austin Wyatt and Jai Galliott, *Proposing a Regional Normative Framework for Limiting the Potential for Unintentional or Escalatory Engagements with Increasingly Autonomous Weapon Systems* In: *Lethal Autonomous Weapons.* Edited by: Jai Galliott, Duncan MacIntosh and Jens David Ohlin, © Oxford University Press (2021).
DOI: 10.1093/oso/9780197546048.003.0017

able to re-establish contact, the *Repressor*'s captain had taken the decision to ram one of the fast-boats that was allegedly blocking his escape from the area.

While the *Repressor* did not suffer significant damage or any casualties, the Kamerian government received a formal letter of protest from the Musorian embassy. According to the complaint, the vessels were manned civilian research vessels; the Musorians are demanding compensation and the Kamerian Navy publicly charge the *Repressor*'s captain with endangering shipping.

16.1: INTRODUCTION

This scenario illustrates how, in the absence of established international law or norms governing the deployment of unmanned weapon systems, an action taken by human agents against unmanned platforms can escalate tensions between neighboring states. While in this case the captain's intention was the safe extraction of his vessel, in other circumstances a state could decide to send a strong, coercive diplomatic message to a neighbor by destroying or capturing an unmanned platform with the assumption that this would not necessarily spark the level of escalatory response that would result from destroying a manned vessel. Without established international law, behavioral norms or even a common definition of "autonomous weapon system," capturing or destroying that unmanned platform could unexpectedly prompt an escalatory response.

However, rather than beginning with establishing mutually acceptable protocols for the safe interaction between unmanned and manned military assets in contested territory, the international process being conducted in Geneva has come to be dominated by the question of a preemptive ban on the development of Lethal Autonomous Weapon Systems (LAWS). This chapter argues in favor of a conceptual shift toward establishing these protocols first, even at a regional level, rather than continuing to push for binding international law.

Earlier chapters in this volume have engaged directly with some of the major legal, ethical, and moral questions that have underpinned the assumption that LAWS represent a novel or insurmountable barrier to the continued commitment of militaries to the principles of Just War and the Laws of Armed Conflict. Other authors have also provided clear explorations of the significant disagreement that remains as to whether meaningful human control can be maintained over autonomous and Artificial Intelligence (AI)-enabled systems, or even what "meaningful" means in practical terms.

By establishing that employing robotics and AI in warfare is not inherently offensive to the principles of international humanitarian law or fundamentally incompatible with the continued ethical use of force, this volume has laid the groundwork for a call to broaden the discourse beyond arguments over the merits or demerits of a preemptive ban.

While the Conference on Certain Conventional Weapons (CCW)-sponsored process has steadily slowed, and occasionally stalled, over the past five years, the pace of technological development in both the civilian and military spheres has accelerated. Furthermore, since the Meeting of Intergovernmental Experts process was formalized in 2016, we have seen the first use of a civilian remote-operated platform in the attempted assassination of a head of state (2018), a proxy force use unmanned aircraft to strike at the critical infrastructure of a key US ally (2019), and the first deployment of an armed unmanned ground vehicle into a combat zone (2018). While these cases used primarily remote-operated platforms, they are still concerning given that even civilian model drones have been brought to market in recent years with increasingly automated and autonomous capabilities.

Furthermore, state actors have continued to invest in pursuing increasingly autonomous systems and have been further embedding military applications of AI in their future force planning. Some of these states, such as the United States and Australia, have declined to formally support a ban and been upfront with their interest in utilizing these capabilities to enhance, augment, and even replace human soldiers. Other states have largely avoided committing to a position on the issue, despite clearly pursuing increasingly autonomous weapon systems (AWS) and armed remote-piloted aircraft.

Some smaller but well-resourced states see the potential to legitimately draw on systems that generate the mass and scalable effects they view as crucial to their continued security, while others are struggling to balance the military advantages of autonomous systems against the risk of unmanned platforms proliferating into the hands of rival states or nonstate actors. Therefore, for a large number of smaller and middle power states, especially in the Asia Pacific (which is the geographic focus of this chapter), there are strong disincentives against actively contributing to a centralized multilateral ban.

The end result is that the world is rapidly approaching a demonstration point for the "robotic dogs of war," to borrow a phrase from Baker, without an effective process for limiting the genuine risks associated with the rapid proliferation of a novel military technology, which we have already begun to see with drones.

Furthermore, without established international law, behavioral norms or even a common definition of "autonomous weapon system," there is no "playbook" for states to draw on when confronted with a security situation or violation of sovereignty involving an autonomous platform. Capturing or destroying that unmanned platform, while perceived to be a lower risk method of sending a coercive diplomatic message, could unexpectedly prompt an escalatory response from a state operating under a different "playbook."

In response, this chapter suggests the development of a normative framework that would establish common procedures and de-escalation channels between states within a given regional security cooperative prior to the demonstration point of truly AWS. Modeling itself on the *Guidelines for Air Military Encounters* and *Guidelines Maritime Interaction*, which were recently adopted by the Association of Southeast Asian Nations, the goal of this approach is to limit the destabilizing and escalatory potential of autonomous systems, which are expected to lower barriers to conflict and encourage brinkmanship while being difficult to definitively attribute.

Overall, this chapter focuses on the chief avenues by which ethical, moral, and legal concerns raised by the emergence of AWS could be addressed by the international community. Alongside a deeper understanding of the factors that influence how we perceive this innovation, there is value in examining whether the existing response options open to states are sufficient or effective. In the light of the observation that the multilateral negotiation process under the auspices of the CCW has effectively stalled, this chapter will offer an alternative approach that recognizes the value in encouraging middle power states to collectively pursue a common understanding of autonomous weapons, common technical standards and a set of de-escalatory behavioral norms.

16.2: AUTONOMOUS WEAPON SYSTEMS AND EXISTING INTERNATIONAL LAW

At the center of the ongoing debate surrounding AWS is the question of how they would interact with International Humanitarian Law (IHL), otherwise known as the Laws of Armed Conflict (LOAC). This debate has split scholars and ensured that the vast majority of published works have remained focused on whether International Humanitarian Law (IHL) can effectively regulate autonomous military technology, and whether a preemptive developmental ban is warranted.

Two major camps have formed in the scholarly community: those in favor of a ban, who are supported by multiple NGOs; and those against a developmental ban. The former argue that AWS violate international humanitarian law (Future of Life Institute 2015; Sauer 2016; Sharkey 2010; 2017) and international human rights law (Amnesty International 2015). In addition to prominent scholars, such as Asaro (2008; 2016), large NGOs (Docherty 2012) and the former UN Special Rapporteur on Extrajudicial Killings have published calls for a ban on the basis of ethical, moral, and legal objections to *killer robots* (Heyns 2013; 2017). At the forefront of the drive for a preemptive ban is a nongovernmental organization (NGO), the Campaign to Stop Killer Robots, extremely active advocates who have amassed support from large swaths of the academic and business community (Sample 2017). This group also keeps a list of country positions on LAWS that identifies states who are in favor of a developmental ban (Campaign to Stop Killer Robots 2017).

A smaller, but still substantial, body of scholarly work argues that a preemptive ban would not have the impact suggested by advocates. Those scholars who oppose a ban argue that a ban would be ineffective (Schmitt 2013), that the use of LAWS is sufficiently regulated by existing international laws and norms (Anderson et al. 2014), or that it is too late for a ban and that effective regulation is now needed (Sehrawat 2017). Among opposing scholars, the underlying logic is that responsible design and deployment within existing IHL and other normative frameworks is the most effective way to regulate the impact of LAWS. Anderson and Schmitt are both prominent academics who have argued in favor of alternative responses to a ban under IHL (Anderson et al. 2014; Schmitt 2013). As an example, Kastan argues that, while a ban is unnecessary, specialized military procedures and adaptions to IHL are needed (2013). This body of scholarly thought is more closely aligned with my perspective.

Advocating for a preemptive ban on autonomous military technology requires one to willfully minimize or ignore the dual-use, software-based nature of its enabling technologies. It also requires that one discount the fact that no weapon system currently exists (based on public knowledge) that crosses the line between "highly automated" and "autonomous," although admittedly there remains no universal agreement about where to draw that line or even how to objectively measure the autonomous capability of a given platform.

Furthermore, even if we were to ignore the limitations of current technology, it is difficult to support the related argument (Anderson 2016) that existing legal weapon review processes would be insufficient for evaluating whether AWS are a legal method (or tool) of warfare, which is distinct from whether a particular LAWS is deployed in a manner consistent with the principles of IHL.

Article 36 of Additional Protocol I of the 1949 Geneva Conventions already requires that states conduct a formal legal review before the procurement of any new weapon system to determine whether it inherently offends IHL (Schmitt 2013), as well as the risks posed in the event of misuse or malfunction (Geneva Academy 2014). As early as the April 2016 CCW Meeting of Governmental Experts on LAWS, multiple states publicly agreed that, as with any new weapon system, LAWS should be subject to legal review. It is not unusual for states to alter their process for conducting legal weapon reviews following the emergence of novel or evolutionary weapon systems (Anderson 2016). For example, Australia presented a detailed description of its System of Control and Applications for Autonomous Weapon Systems (which included legal review) as part of its submissions to the August 2019 Meeting of the CCW Group of Governmental Experts on LAWS.

Overall, the argument that existing legal review processes are insufficient in the case of increasingly AWS, or that LAWS inherently violate international humanitarian law does not reflect the focus of these standards, nor that the majority of (publicly acknowledged) unmanned systems (remote-operated, highly automated or even with limited autonomy) are generally platforms that carry legacy weaponry that has undergone previous legal review. For example, the South Korean Super-Aegis II is equipped with a 12.7 mm machine gun, versions of which have been regularly deployed by various militaries over the past sixty years.

Whether delegating the decision to end a human life to a machine would be ethically justifiable or not, while an important question, is not considered by these standards. Instead, some advocates of a preemptive ban have argued that these ethical concerns would be sufficient to violate the Martens Clause,[1] drawing parallels to the ban on blinding lasers, arguing that they also violated the principle of public conscience. Despite being an ongoing point of contention in the literature, it is difficult to evaluate the applicability of the Martens Clause simply because there is a dearth of large-scale studies of public opinion toward increasingly AWS.

Based on the available evidence, it seems clear that armed drones and LAWS are a legal method of warfare. However, ongoing legal reviews of individual emerging weapon systems are essential to ensure that new models do not individually violate these standards. Even when inherently legal as a method of warfare, weapons must be utilized in a manner that is consistent with the IHL principles of proportionality, necessity, distinction, and precautions in attack.

The principle of proportionality establishes that belligerents cannot launch attacks that could be expected to cause a level of civilian death or injury or damage to civilian property that is excessive compared to the specific military objective of that attack (Dinstein 2016). Attacks that recklessly cause excessive damage, or those launched with knowledge that the toll in civilian lives would be clearly excessive, constitute a war crime (Dinstein 2016). The test under customary international law applies a subjective "reasonable commander standard" based on the information available at the time (Geneva Academy 2014). To be deployed in a manner that complies with IHL, an autonomous platform would require the ability to reliably assess proportionality. Current generation AI is unable to satisfy a standard that was designed and interpreted as subjective (Geneva Academy 2014), although this could change as sensor technology develops (Arkin 2008).

The principle of military necessity reflects the philosophical conflict between applying lawful limitations to conflict and accepting the reality of warfare (Martin 2015). The principle of military necessity requires belligerents to limit armed attacks to "military objectives" that offer a "definite military advantage" (Martin 2015). Furthermore, attacks against civilian objects and destruction or seizure of property not "imperatively demanded by the necessities of war" are considered war crimes (Vogel 2010). This principle cannot be applied to a particular weapon platform as a whole; rather it must be considered on a case-by-case basis (Martin 2015).

The principle of distinction requires belligerents to distinguish between combatants and noncombatants as well as between military and civilian objects (including property) (Vogel 2010), and is the most challenging principle for a military to utilize LAWS in accordance with. At its core, an AWS is a series of sensors feeding into a processor; interpreting data to make an active identification and evaluation of a potential target (Stevenson et al. 2015). This is distinct from an automatic weapon, which fires once it encounters a particular stimulus, such as an individual's weight in the case of landmines. The technology does not currently exist that would allow LAWS to reliably identify illegitimate targets in a dynamic ground combat environment. A deployed LAWS would need a number of features including the ability to receive constant updates on the battlefield circumstances (Geneva Academy 2014); recognition software to recognize the difference between combatants and noncombatants as well as between allies and enemies in an environment where neither side always wears uniforms; and the ability to recognize when an enemy combatant has become hors de combat. There are too many variables on the modern battlefield, particularly in a counterinsurgency operation, for any sort of certainty that autonomous weapons will always make the same decision (Stevenson et al. 2015).

Overall, it is insufficient to push for the imposition of a development or deployment ban under IHL on an innovation that has not yet fully emerged. Beyond its questionable practicality, this push has become so central to the discourse surrounding LAWS that it is stifling progress toward arguably more effective outcomes such as: a standard function-based definition; a stronger understanding of the technological limitations among policymakers and end users; changes to operational procedures to improve accountability; or standardizing the benchmarks for Article 36 reviews of AI-enabled weapon platforms.

16.3: CHALLENGES TO REGULATING AUTONOMOUS AND AI-ENABLED SYSTEMS WITH TRADITIONAL MEASURES

There are two broad theoretical approaches for generating a framework for limiting the initial impact of major military proliferation. Firstly, the framework could be dictated and enforced by powerful states that gain a dominant early lead in the possession and development of AWS, albeit influenced by the persisting balance of power. However, as evidenced by previous revolutionary advances in military technology, including nuclear weapons, as the technology diffuses, the ability for the first mover or the dominant hegemonic power to control their use by other states diminishes. This effect is illustrative of the argument that "bad policy by a large nation ripples throughout the system," and that the chief cause of structural power shifts is generally "not the failure of weak states, but the policy failure of strong states" (Finnemore and Goldstein 2013).

This effect was also evident in the case of unmanned aerial vehicles. The United States enjoyed a sufficient comparative advantage in the early 2000s that it could have theoretically implemented a favorable normative framework and secured itself a dominant export market position. However, as described above, it failed to do so until 2015 and 2016, by which time diffusion and proliferation were already occurring, driven by both other states and the civilian market. While the United States maintained a significant technological advantage at that point, it was no longer sufficiently dominant in the production of UAVs to impose its will on the market and China's rise in the Asia Pacific was well underway. As a result, efforts by the United States to impose norms on the use of unmanned systems in 2015 and 2016 were only partially successful and had the unintended consequence of increasing the normative influence of China and Israel, who had assumed market dominance in the interim period.

In the absence of hegemonic leadership imposing a normative framework, we must turn attention to the international community. Supported by neoliberal institutionalist theory, the second potential source for norm generation would be a multinational institution (for example, the United Nations) led approach that aims to integrate controls under international humanitarian law. This approach recognizes the increasingly interlinked nature of the global community from an economic and security standpoint. This process started for AWS in 2014 with an informal meeting of experts, followed by more formal proceedings at CCW. In the absence of significant progress toward a common understanding how to meaningfully regulate AWS, with or without a developmental ban, this avenue toward an international normative framework does not appear promising.

Accepting that developing accepted international law to govern the deployment of increasingly autonomous unmanned platforms is unlikely to occur in the near future, and that neither the development of autonomous technology nor the proliferation of unmanned platforms are likely to cease during the process of pressuring the international community into action, the third approach would be for regional organizations and security communities to take a leading role in developing norms and common understanding around the deployment of unmanned systems.

16.4: POTENTIAL FORUMS FOR DEVELOPING A NORMATIVE LAWS FRAMEWORK AND BUILDING REGIONAL RESILIENCE TO POST-DEMONSTRATION POINT SECURITY SHOCK

There are four Association of Southeast Asian Nation (ASEAN)-led forums that could be utilized to formulate a regional normative framework for governing the use of AWS. These forums are the East Asia Summit, the ASEAN Regional Forum, the ASEAN Defence Ministers' Meeting, and the ADMM-Plus. These forums have the capacity to build on the stalled work of the CCW's group of governmental experts.

The first, and least suitable of these forums, would be the East Asia Summit (EAS), a strategic dialogue forum with a security and economic focus, which was established in 2005. EAS brings together high-level state representatives in a diplomatic environment that encourages private negotiation and informal cooperation. The dual purposes of the EAS were to draw major powers into the Southeast Asian security environment (Finnemore and Goldstein 2013) and to create a platform for ASEAN member states to maintain influence with those powers.

To this end, membership of the EAS extends beyond the ten ASEAN member states to include Australia, China, Japan, India, New Zealand, the Republic of Korea, Russia, and the United States (Department of Foreign Affairs and Trade 2019). These states are the primary actors in the region, representing a combined total of around 54% of the global population and 58% of global GDP (Department of Foreign Affairs and Trade 2019). Furthermore, five of these states are known to be developing increasingly AWS. As part of their induction, all members were required to have signed the *Treaty of Amity and Cooperation in Southeast Asia*, a multilateral peace treaty that prioritizes state sovereignty and the principle of noninterference, while renouncing the threat of violence (Goh 2003). However, its broad membership means that this forum would suffer from similar barriers to consensus as encountered in the UN-sponsored process. The inclusion of the United States, Russia, and China would negate any advantage that could be gained from shifting to a regional focus. Finally, the EAS was not designed with the same defense focus as the following forums. Instead, the EAS is built around leader-to-leader connections and the summit itself, leading to an inability to facilitate concrete multilateral defense cooperation (Bisley 2017).

The second forum to consider is the ASEAN Regional Forum (ARF), the first multilateral Southeast Asian security organization (Tang 2016). The ARF emerged in a post-Cold War environment, well before China had been widely recognized as a rising hegemonic competitor (Ba 2017). The ARF was intended to be an all-inclusive security community promoting discussion, peaceful conflict resolution, and preventative diplomacy (Ba 2017). While it has been used to promote regional efforts to reduce the illegal trade in small arms (Kingdom of Thailand 2017), the organization's noninterventionalist security focus and lack of institutional structure limit its utility as a forum for developing a normative LAWS framework.

The ARF lacks the capacity to facilitate effective discussions toward a regional LAWS normative framework and has proven incapable to develop concrete responses to traditional security threats in the region, leading to frustration among its extra-regional participants. Ironically, the external membership of the ARF, currently twenty-seven members (Tan 2017), has been the main factor in frustrating these efforts. While the ARF's inclusive approach was a noble (and politically expedient) sentiment, it has naturally steered discussion away from issues that would be sensitive to its members, contributing to its reputation as a "talk shop" (Tang 2016). Though the ARF has proven a useful tool for improving cooperation on nontraditional security issues and humanitarian aid, the participation of the United States and China has limited its capacity to meaningfully engage with major geopolitical flashpoints and has exposed divisions within the ASEAN membership (Kwok Song Lee 2015). Therefore, while the ARF has played an important role in shaping the regional security architecture, it would be unsuitable for developing a regional response to LAWS.

The third mechanism through which a normative framework could be developed is the ASEAN Defence Ministers' Meeting (ADMM). The establishment of the ADMM, and the complementary ADMM-Plus, was part of an institutional shift away from a diplomatic focus toward a functional one within the ASEAN Political Security Community (Tang 2016). These forums were established as part of an Indonesian-led effort to maintain ASEAN centrality in the face of alternative security communities being mooted by external partners that were frustrated with the ARF (chiefly Australia and the United States) (Ba 2017). The ADMM directly links senior military leadership, intelligence services, and security policy experts from each of the ten ASEAN member states through regular, formal meetings that then feed into the Expert Working Groups of the ADMM-Plus (Ba 2017).

There are two main reasons that the ADMM would be the best regional security forum through which to develop a normative framework that considers increasingly autonomous weapon systems. The first is that the ADMM is a comparatively neutral intra-regional institution that directly links the potential end users of AWS within ASEAN without directly involving either China or the United States. The second benefit of the ADMM is that its core purpose centers on building trust and intensifying intra-regional military cooperation within the deliberately narrowed constrains of regional nontraditional security issues. Finally, as discussed below, the ADMM has already successfully developed and adopted advisory normative guidelines for the interaction of aerial and naval forces on the high seas that incorporate mutual definitions, procedures, and practices to lower the risk of unintentional conflict or escalation in these domains, which a LAWS framework could be built around.

The final relevant forum is the ASEAN Defence Ministers' Meeting Plus, which is an extended, complementary version of the ADMM that incorporates the security services of eight extra-regional partner-states, but remains officially ASEAN-centered.[2] The ADMM-Plus is a multilateral orientated grouping that is focused on practical defense collaboration in six key areas, each of which has an Expert Working Group (Tang 2017). These areas of collaboration are maritime security, counterterrorism, military medicine, removal of mines, humanitarian and disaster relief, and peacekeeping operations (Tang 2017). Reviewing these focus areas highlights how ASEAN member states deliberately steered deliberations away from traditional security issues, reflecting the same geopolitical reality as in the ARF and EAS. However, the ADMM-Plus distinguishes itself with its role as a security-focused setting for defense policymakers to build trust, interoperability, and relationships (Tang 2016). Beyond policymaking, the ADMM-Plus facilitates valuable rotating collaborations between ASEAN and partner militaries to build trust directly between defense personnel (Searight 2018), which would be necessary for any LAWS normative framework to succeed. As with the ADMM, this forum has the benefit of a more defined institutional structure that is built around Expert Working Groups (EWG) in each of these areas. However, while the EWGs are co-chaired by an ASEAN member state and an external participant on a rotating basis (Searight 2018), the broader membership of the ADMM-Plus (particularly the United States and China) presents a greater risk of interference or delay in developing a normative framework than the more limited membership of the ADMM.

Overall, developing a normative framework for the safe deployment of autonomous and remote-operated weapon systems in Southeast Asia would be most likely to succeed if it was developed through a specifically established EWG within the ADMM forum. This would not be unprecedented, as the ADMM recently agreed to establish an EWG for cybersecurity. Unlike international law, there is no need for a region-specific normative framework to be formalized or publicly defended by participating states, nor would it need to be prescriptive or imposed on external actors. In this case, the fact that the ADMM is not a traditional security alliance would not diminish the chances of this success because the region would benefit significantly from even a shared definition of AWS and a common normative framework for the acceptable use and appropriate responses to unmanned platforms. The ADMM actually already performs a similar trust-building and stabilizing role within the region by facilitating direct defense diplomacy and multilateral training among the disparate Southeast Asian militaries and those of their external neighbors (Tang 2016).

16.5: ANALYZING RECENT ADMM GUIDELINES AS A MODEL

The ASEAN Defence Ministers' Meeting recently adopted two sets of relevant guidelines for military interaction on the high seas that provide valuable examples upon which a LAWS normative framework could be modeled. The *Guidelines on Air Military Encounters* were based on a concept paper written during the Philippines chairmanship (ADMM 2017), and the final document was published at the 12th ADMM the following year (while Singapore held the chair). This was followed by the *ADMM Guidelines for Maritime Interaction*, adopted in July 2019.

There are three important aspects of these guidelines that are worth considering when pondering potential ADMM *Guidelines for the Deployment of Unmanned or Autonomously Operating Platforms*. The first is that both documents repeatedly and specifically note that their contents are "non-binding and voluntary," and do not create any additional obligation under international law (ADMM 2019). Instead these guidelines are intended to reduce the risk of accidental or unintentional military escalation by establishing mutually agreed definitions and procedures that can be followed by member-state militaries and building mutual confidence between those militaries (ADMM 2018). Second, these guidelines make sensible use of existing international law and treaties as building blocks: deriving definitions, procedures, and even technical specifications from previously established sources that are widely utilized (such as the United Nations *Convention on the Law of the Sea* [UNCLOS] or the *International Regulations for Preventing Collisions at Sea* [COLREG]) (ADMM 2019) rather than "re-inventing the wheel." Finally, neither document applies to the territory of member states (a clear concession to sovereignty concerns). Instead these guidelines apply solely to military interactions in the high seas, which complicates its application given the ongoing territorial disputes in the broader region. Importantly though, this concession highlights the fact that any framework on the use of LAWS would be unlikely to be successfully adopted if it was perceived to infringe on sovereignty without a commensurate benefit.

This final aspect could be overcome by the inclusion of a technology-sharing regime alongside the normative framework to offset the sovereignty concessions. While less appealing for Singapore technology transfer, access, or even personnel exchange would be an influential offer to Indonesia, Vietnam, or Malaysia.

Further, both Indonesia and Singapore are making a concerted effort to further develop their domestic military production capability but have identified areas where pooling resources would be valuable, while ASEAN already facilitates broader cooperation between the defense industries of its member states. It is also worth considering that the exchange of technology and personnel, as well as multilateral exercises, are the most common and effective methods used to build interoperability and mutual trust among militaries, which would be vital for the safe deployment of LAWS.

Unfortunately, these guidelines were extremely short for multilateral policy documents. The *ADMM Guidelines for Maritime Interaction* is six pages long (ADMM 2019), while the *Guidelines for Air Military Encounters* is only seven pages in length (ADMM 2018). While the lack of detail in some points was discouraging, overall these guidelines still present concrete definitions and guidance on procedures. Given the comparative progress of underlying technology and the United Nations discussions, even this level of agreement would be a significant step forward for the continued stability of Southeast Asia.

16.6: CONCLUSION

Without meaningful progress toward a mechanism for limiting the diffusion of artificial intelligence-enabled autonomous weapon systems, or a normative framework for preventing unexpected escalation, there is an understandable level of concern in the academic, policy, and ethics spheres. Among the most common metaphors used to illustrate this anxiety in the early international debates was the comparison of LAWS to nuclear weapons. While this has largely dropped off in the scholarly literature, it remains a regular feature in the public discourse.

In addition to being conceptually problematic, this comparison placed an undue importance on international regulation, the only real institutional tool for multilateral organizations to contribute to the prevention of further proliferation of nuclear weapons. However, the failure of the CCW negation process over the past five years to establish even a common approach for determining whether a weapon would be covered by the proposed ban, should be taken as a strong indication that it is time for a new approach.

Instead of continuing to focus efforts on convincing superpower states and their allies to abandon a dual-use, enabling technology that they have come to view as central to the future warfare paradigm, the international community should refocus on developing the common standards, behavioral norms, communication, de-escalation protocols, and verifiable review processes that would limit the negative disruptive potential of increasingly AWS proliferation.

From a practical perspective, the initially conceptualized ban would no longer be effective, given that the core-enabling technologies for autonomous weapon platforms are dual use and being developed by dozens of state and nonstate entities. State policymakers and military leaders, therefore, have an ethical obligation to proactively pursue alternative approaches that minimize the potential for harm to civilian and the risk of unintentional escalation toward violence, even if this involves the creation of a "soft" or normative framework rather than established international law.

Generating a common understanding and increasing cooperation between states around unmanned platforms would reduce the short-term risk of escalation while the international community negotiates toward a more complete framework. This could remain a passive normative guidance framework (like the *ADMM Guidelines for Maritime Interaction*), or it could take a more proactive approach centered on a multilateral information and coordination agency modeled on the Regional Cooperation Agreement on Combating Piracy and Armed Robbery against ships in Asia.

As time goes on without an effective and enforceable international regulatory mechanism or ban, it will become increasingly important that the voices of the modern Melians are given greater weight. This chapter has demonstrated the applicability of a normative collaborative alternative that empowers regional states to regionally and internally regulate their use of increasingly autonomous technology, control the proliferation to violent nonstate actors, and maintain the intra-regional trust required to prevent unintentional conflict or provocation.

Concern about the potential negative impacts of autonomous weapons, however justifiable, should not be solely relied upon to support a position that autonomous weapon systems have no compensatory beneficial potential and should be preemptively banned. These are complex systems based on an emerging innovation, so let us take a step back and establish achievable, universally applicable guideposts for safe use now, rather than continue to pursue an international legal response while the development of increasingly autonomous systems continues unabated.

NOTES

1. The Martens Clause requires that the legality of new weapon systems be subject to the principles of humanity and the dictates of public conscience in cases that are not covered by established international law (ICRC 2014).
2. These extra-regional partners are: Australia, China, India, Japan, New Zealand, Russia, South Korea, and the United States.

WORKS CITED

Amnesty International. 2015. *Autonomous Weapons Systems: Five Key Human Rights Issues For Consideration*. London: Amnesty International.

Anderson, K. 2016. " Why the Hurry to Regulate Autonomous Weapon Systems—But Not Cyber-Weapons." *Temple International and Comparative Law Journal* 30 (1): pp. 17–42.

Anderson, K., D. Reisner and M. C. Waxman. 2014. "Adapting the Law of Armed Conflict to Autonomous Weapon Systems." *International Law Studies* 90 (1): pp. 386–411.

Arkin, R. C. 2008. "Governing Lethal Behavior: Embedding Ethics in a Hybrid Deliberative/Reactive Robot Architecture Part I: Motivation and Philosophy." In *3rd ACM/IEEE International Conference on Human-Robot Interaction*, pp. 121–128. The Netherlands: Association for Computing Machinery.

Asaro, P. M. 2008. "How Just Could a Robot War Be." In *Proceedings of the 2008 conference on Current Issues in Computing and Philosophy*, edited by Adam Briggle, Katinka Waelbers, and Phillip A. E. Brey, pp. 50–64. Netherlands: International Association of Computing and Philosophy.

Asaro, P. M. 2016. "The Liability Problem for Autonomous Artificial Agents." *In Ethical and Moral Considerations in Non-Human Agents, 2016 AAAI Spring Symposium Series*. Technical Report SS-16. Palo Alto, CA: The AAAI Press.

ASEAN Defence Ministers' Meeting (ADMM). 2017. *Concept Paper on the Guidelines for Maritime Interaction*. Manila: 11th ASEAN Defence Ministers' Meeting.

ASEAN Defence Ministers' Meeting (ADMM). 2019. *Guidelines for Maritime Interaction*. Bangkok: 13th ASEAN Defence Ministers' Meeting.

ASEAN Defence Ministers' Meeting (ADMM). 2018. *Guidelines for Air Military Encounters*. Singapore: 12th ASEAN Defence Ministers' Meeting.

Ba, A. D. 2017. "ASEAN and the Changing Regional Order: The ARF, ADMM, and ADMM-Plus." In *Building ASEAN Community: Political–Security and Socio-cultural Reflections*, edited by A. Baviera and L. Maramis, pp. 146–157. Jakarta: Economic Research Institute for ASEAN and East Asia.

Bisley, N. 2017. "The East Asia Summit and ASEAN: Potential and Problems." *Contemporary Southeast Asia: A Journal of International and Strategic Affairs* 39 (2): pp. 265–272.

Campaign to Stop Killer Robots. 2017. "Country Views on Killer Robots." October 11. https://www.stopkillerrobots.org/wp-content/uploads/2013/03/KRC_CountryViews_Oct2017.pdf.

Department of Foreign Affairs and Trade. 2019. "East Asia Summit Factsheet." July 1, 2019. https://www.dfat.gov.au/sites/default/files/eas-factsheet.pdf.

Dinstein, Y. 2016. *The Conduct of Hostilities Under the Law of International Armed Conflict*. Cambridge: Cambridge University Press.

Docherty, B. 2012. *Losing Humanity: The Case Against Killer Robots*. New York: Human Rights Watch.

Finnemore, M. and Goldstein, J. 2013. *Back to Basics: State Power in a Contemporary World*. Oxford: Oxford University Press.

Future of Life Institute. 2015. *Autonomous Weapons: An Open Letter from AI and Robotics Researchers*. Boston: Future of Life Institute.

Geneva Academy. 2014. *Academy Briefing 8: Autonomous Weapon Systems under International Law*. Geneva: Geneva Academy of International Humanitarian Law and Human Rights.

Goh, G. 2003. "The 'ASEAN Way': Non-Intervention and ASEAN's Role in Conflict Management." *Stanford Journal of East Asian Affairs* 3 (1): pp. 113–118.

Heyns, C. 2013. *Report of the Special Rapporteur on Extrajudicial, Summary or Arbitrary Executions*. A/HRC/23/47. Geneva: United Nations General Assembly.

Heyns, C. 2017. "Autonomous Weapons in Armed Conflict and the Right to a Dignified Life: An African Perspective." *South African Journal on Human Rights* 33 (1): pp.46–71.

ICRC. 2014. "Autonomous Weapon Systems: Technical, Military, Legal and Humanitarian Aspects." Briefing Paper. Geneva: Meeting of Group of Governmental Experts on LAWS. March 26–28.

Kastan, B. 2013. "Autonomous Weapons Systems: A Coming Legal 'Singularity?'" *Journal of Law, Technology & Policy* 45 (1): pp. 45–82.

Kwok Song Lee, J. 2015. *The Limits of the ASEAN Regional Forum*. Master of Arts in Security Studies (Far East, Southeast Asia, The Pacific). Monterey: Naval Postgraduate School.

Martin, C. 2015. "A Means-Methods Paradox and the Legality of Drone Strikes in Armed Conflict." *The International Journal of Human Rights* 19 (2): pp. 142–175.

Permanent Mission of The Kingdom of Thailand to The United Nations. 2017. *Statement delivered by H.E. Mr. Virachai Plasai, Ambassador and Permanent Representative of the Kingdom of Thailand to the United Nations at the General Debate of the First Committee (2nd Meeting of the First Committee)*. Seventy-second Session of the United Nations General Assembly. New York: United Nations General Assembly.

Sample, I. 2017. "Ban on Killer Robots Urgently Needed, Say Scientists." *The Guardian*. November 13. https://www.theguardian.com/science/2017/nov/13/ban-on-killer-robots-urgently-needed-say-scientists.

Sauer, F. 2016. "Stopping 'Killer Robots': Why Now Is the Time to Ban Autonomous Weapon Systems." Washington, DC: Arms Control Association. https://www.armscontrol.org/print/7713.

Schmitt, M. 2013. "Autonomous Weapon Systems and International Humanitarian Law: A Reply to the Critics." *Harvard National Security Journal Features*. February 5. https://harvardnsj.org/2013/02/autonomous-weapon-systems-and-international-humanitarian-law-a-reply-to-the-critics/.

Searight, A. 2018. *ADMM-Plus: The Promise and Pitfalls of an ASEAN-led Security Forum*. Washington, DC: Centre for Strategic & International Studies.

Sehrawat, V. 2017. "Autonomous Weapon System: Law of Armed Conflict (LOAC) and Other Legal Challenges." *Computer Law & Security Review* 33 (1): pp. 38–56.

Sharkey, N. 2010. "Saying 'No!'to Lethal Autonomous Targeting." *Journal of Military Ethics* 9 (4): pp. 369–383.

Sharkey, N. 2017. "Why Robots Should Not Be Delegated with the Decision to Kill." *Connection Science* 29 (2): pp. 177–186.

Stevenson, B., Sharkey, N., Marsh, N., and Crootof, R. 2015. "Special Session 10: How to Regulate Autonomous Weapon Systems." In *2015 EU Non-Proliferation and Disarmament Conference*. Brussels: International Institute for Strategic Studies.

Tan, S. S. 2017. "A Tale of Two Institutions: The ARF, ADMM-Plus and Security Regionalism in the Asia Pacific." *Contemporary Southeast Asia* 39 (2): pp. 259–264.

Tang, S. M. 2016. "ASEAN and the ADMM-Plus: Balancing between Strategic Imperatives and Functionality." *Asia Policy* 22 (1): pp. 76–82.

Tang, S.-M. 2018. "ASEAN's Tough Balancing Act." *Asia Policy* 25 (4): pp. 48–52.

Vogel, R. 2010. "Drone Warfare and the Laws of Armed Conflict." *Denver Journal of International Law and Policy* 45 (1): pp. 45–82.

17

The Human Role in Autonomous Weapon Design and Deployment

M.L. CUMMINGS

17.1: INTRODUCTION

Because of the increasing use of Unmanned Aerial Vehicles (UAVs, also commonly known as drones) in various military and paramilitary (i.e., CIA) settings, there has been increasing debate in the international community as to whether it is morally and ethically permissible to allow robots (flying or otherwise) the ability to decide when and where to take human life. In addition, there has been intense debate as to the legal aspects, particularly from a humanitarian law framework.[1]

In response to this growing international debate, the United States government released the Department of Defense (DoD) 3000.09 Directive (2011), which sets a policy for if and when autonomous weapons would be used in US military and paramilitary engagements. This US policy asserts that only "human-supervised autonomous weapon systems may be used to select and engage targets, with the exception of selecting humans as targets, for local defense. . . ."

This statement implies that outside of defensive applications, autonomous weapons will not be allowed to independently select and then fire upon targets without explicit approval from a human supervising the autonomous weapon system. Such a control architecture is known as human supervisory control, where a human remotely supervises an automated system (Sheridan 1992). The defense caveat in this policy is needed because the United States currently uses highly automated systems for defensive purposes, for example, Counter Rocket, Artillery, and Mortar (C-RAM) systems and Patriot anti-missile missiles.

M.L. Cummings, *The Human Role in Autonomous Weapon Design and Deployment* In: *Lethal Autonomous Weapons*. Edited by: Jai Galliott, Duncan MacIntosh and Jens David Ohlin, © Oxford University Press (2021).
DOI: 10.1093/oso/9780197546048.003.0018

Due to the time-critical nature of such environments (e.g., soldiers sleeping in barracks within easy reach of insurgent shoulder-launched missiles), these automated defensive systems cannot rely upon a human supervisor for permission because of the short engagement times and the inherent human neuromuscular lag, which means that even if a person is paying attention, there is approximately a half-second delay in hitting a firing button, which can mean the difference between life and death for the soldiers in the barracks.

So as of now, no US UAV (or any robot) will be able to launch any kind of weapon in an offensive environment without human direction and approval. However, the 3000.09 Directive does contain a clause that allows for this possibility in the future. This caveat states that the development of a weapon system that independently decides to launch a weapon is possible but first must be approved by the Under Secretary of Defense for Policy (USD(P)); the Under Secretary of Defense for Acquisition, Technology, and Logistics (USD(AT&L)); and the Chairman of the Joint Chiefs of Staff.

Not all stakeholders are happy with this policy that leaves the door open for what used to be considered science fiction. Many opponents of such uses of technologies call for either an outright ban on autonomous weaponized systems, or in some cases, autonomous systems in general (Human Rights Watch 2013, Future of Life Institute 2015, Chairperson of the Informal Meeting of Experts 2016). Such groups take the position that weapons systems should always be under "meaningful human control," but do not give a precise definition of what this means.

One issue in this debate that often is overlooked is that autonomy is not a discrete state, rather it is a continuum, and various weapons with different levels of autonomy have been in the US inventory for some time. Because of these ambiguities, it is often hard to draw the line between automated and autonomous systems. Present-day UAVs use the very same guidance, navigation, and control technology flown on commercial aircraft. Tomahawk missiles, which have been in the US inventory for more than thirty years, are highly automated weapons with accuracies of less than a meter. These offensive missiles can navigate by themselves with no GPS, thus exhibiting some autonomy by today's definitions. Global Hawk UAVs can find their way home and land on their own without any human intervention in the case of a communication failure.

The growth of the civilian UAV market is also a critical consideration in the debate as to whether these technologies should be banned outright. There is a $144.38B industry emerging for the commercial use of drones in agricultural settings, cargo delivery, first response, commercial photography, and the entertainment industry (Adroit Market Research 2019). More than $100 billion has been spent on driverless car development (Eisenstein 2018) in the past ten years and the autonomy used in driverless cars mirrors that inside autonomous weapons. So, it is an important distinction that UAVs are simply the platform for weapon delivery (autonomous or conventional), and that autonomous systems have many peaceful and commercial uses independent of military applications.

Given that advances in autonomy are pervasive across civilian and military technologies, this chapter will explain how current supervisory control systems, including weapons systems, are designed in terms of balancing authority between the human and the computer. A framework will be presented for how to conceptualize the human-computer balance for future autonomous systems, both civilian and military, and the specific implications for weaponized autonomous systems will be discussed.

17.2: BALANCING THE ROLE BETWEEN A HUMAN AND A COMPUTER

Human supervisory control (HSC) is the process by which a human operator intermittently interacts with a computer, receiving feedback from and providing commands, often remotely, to a system with varying degrees of embedded automation (Sheridan 1992). In supervisory control, a computer sits between the actual system and the human commanding the system. Not only do all UAVs, both military and civilian, operate at some level of supervisory control, but so do nuclear power plants, automated trains, and commercial passenger planes.

In developing any HSC system that involves the integration of human decision-making in concert with an automated system, the question often arises as to where, when, and how much humans versus automation should be in the decision-making loop? Allocating roles and functions between the human and the computer is critical in defining efficient and safe system architectures.

Getting this balance just right is not obvious for most system designers. The predominant engineering viewpoint across these systems is to automate as much as possible and minimize the amount of human interaction. Indeed, many controls engineers see the human as a mere disturbance in the system that can and should be designed out. Others may reluctantly recognize the human must play a role in such systems, either for regulatory requirements or low-probability event intervention (such as problems in nuclear reactors).

Striking the right balance between humans and computers in these complex systems is difficult. Most engineers have little to no training in human supervision of complex systems and do not know how to address the inherent variability that accompanies all human performance. They desire a set of rules and criteria that reduce the ambiguity in the design space, which for them typically means reducing the role of the human or at least constraining human behavior in an attempt to control it. Yet this is exactly what opponents of autonomous systems fear the most—that the human will be designed out of the system, which could create a significant moral and ethical shift in authority.

17.3: A HISTORICAL LOOK AT THE ROLE ALLOCATION DEBATE

Human Factors engineers have been addressing the human-computer role allocation conundrum since the early 1950s when radar was just coming online, and there was much discussion as to how to design what is now our current national air traffic control system (Fitts 1951). In part to help traditional engineers understand the nuances of how humans could interact with a complex automated system in a decision-making capacity, Levels of Automation (LOAs) have been proposed.

LOAs generally refer to the role allocation between automation and the human, particularly in the analysis and decision phases of a simplified information processing model of information acquisition, analysis, decision, and action phases (Parasuraman 2000; Parasuraman, Sheridan, and Wickens 2000; Sheridan and Verplank 1978). Sheridan and Verplank (1978) initially proposed that such LOAs could range from a fully manual system with no computer intervention to a fully automated system where the human is kept completely out of the loop, and this framework was later expanded to include ten LOAs (Table 17.1) (Parasuraman 2000).

For LOA scales like that in Table 17.1, the human is typically actively involved in the decision-making process at the lower levels. As the levels increase, the automation plays a more active role in decisions, increasingly removing the human from the decision-making loop. This scale addresses authority allocation, that is, who has the authority to make the final decision. Other taxonomies have proposed alternate but similar LOAs, attempting to highlight less rigid and more dynamic allocation structures (Endsley 1987; Kaber et al. 2005) as well as address the ability for humans and computers to coach and guide one another (Riley 1989).

In terms of weapons systems today, in keeping with the DoD 3000.09 Directive, there are no US offensive weapons that operate above LOA 5 per Table 17.1. Whether fired from manned or unmanned aircraft (or from a ship as in the case of a Tomahawk missile), an operator in the supervisory control loop may use a computer to assist in the targeting process, but a human always tells the computer when to fire and what to hit. It is important to note though that the United States does have defensive weapons that operate at LOAs 6 and above (as do other countries). These defensive higher levels are often called management by exception because the operator only interrupts the firing process that is commenced by the computer if desired. The only difference between an offensive or defensive automated weapon in the US inventory is the label we choose to give it and the human-driven policies that guide their deployment.

Table 17.1: Levels of Automation (Sheridan and Verplank 1978; Parasuraman, Sheridan and Wickens 2000).

Automation Level	Automation Description
1	The computer offers no assistance: human must make all decision and actions.
2	The computer offers a complete set of decision/action alternatives, or
3	narrows the selection down to a few, or
4	suggests one alternative, and
5	executes that suggestion if the human approves, or
6	allows the human a restricted time to veto before automatic execution, or
7	executes automatically, then necessarily informs humans, and
8	informs the human only if asked, or
9	informs the human only if it, the computer, decides to.
10	The computer decides everything and acts autonomously, ignoring the human.

17.4: AUTOMATED VS. AUTONOMOUS SYSTEMS

Despite their seemingly advanced technological status, the weapon systems described previously, as well as drones today, are more automated than autonomous. This seemingly nuanced description is far from trivial and is critical for the debate about future lethal autonomous systems. An automated system is one that acts according to a preprogrammed script for a task with defined entry/exit conditions. Take, for example, a house thermostat. There is a set of predetermined rules that guide the system (i.e., turn heat on at 68 degrees and keep the temperature there). The sensors on the thermostat are highly reliable, with a simple feedback loop that looks for rises or falls in the temperature, and there is very little chance for error or failure. Automated weapons work in a similar fashion, for example, home in on a set of GPS coordinates (or a laser designation), correct flight path when a disturbance is detected, and repeat until impact.

Autonomous systems represent a significant leap in complexity over automated systems primarily because of the role of probabilistic reasoning in such systems. An autonomous system is one that independently and dynamically determines if, when, and how to execute a task. Such a system will also contain many feedback loops, but the rule set is not clearly defined. In terms of the thermostat example, an autonomous thermostat is one that, for example, anticipates your arrival home and heats the house to your preference just prior to getting home. Such a system would need to guess at your arrival time, which could mean accessing traffic and weather reports as well as your smartphone calendar (indeed, such systems are just now coming on the market now). These systems will likely be correct most of the time, but your calendar or traffic reports may not be updated to reflect reality, causing the system to either heat too early or late.

While such an example is benign, the same logic applies to autonomous weapons systems. They will have to independently assess and reason about the world with their own sensors and have to check databases much more complex than a smartphone. For example, an autonomous UAV that launches its own weapons in the future will need to determine if a suspected target is friendly or hostile, and whether the current battle conditions meet the Rules of Engagement (ROE) for weapons release, and if so, the chances of collateral damage and a whole host of other possible issues.

Effectively such systems will ultimately have to make best guesses, just like humans do, particularly for target detection and identification, which remains a very difficult technological problem even by today's standards. This environment of having to make best guesses in the presence of significant uncertainty is what truly distinguishes an autonomous system from an automated one. And this difference is not discrete, but rather a continuum. The Global Hawk UAV, for example, is a highly automated UAV but has some low-level autonomy on-board that allows it to take itself home and lands when it senses a loss of communication.

Even though we have limited autonomy in some (but not all) UAVs, it is only a matter of time that this will increase. However, the role allocation problem, as discussed previously, will only get harder with autonomous systems because of the critical role that uncertainty plays. Because of the increasing need to reason probabilistically in these systems (called stochastic systems to distinguish them from the more rule-based deterministic automated systems), LOA frameworks provide little guidance in terms of balancing the human and computer roles (Cummings and Bruni 2009, Defense Science Board 2012). To address this gap, in the next section, I will discuss a framework to think about role allocation in autonomous systems, which highlights some of the obstacles in developing autonomous weapons system.

17.5: THE SKILLS, RULES, KNOWLEDGE, AND EXPERTISE FRAMEWORK FOR AUTONOMOUS SYSTEMS

Instead of thinking about role allocation as a function of whether the human or the computer is best suited for the task, Figure 17.1 depicts role allocation for both automated and autonomous systems based on the kind of reasoning needed for that task, independent of who (the human and/or the computer) performs it. This SRKE depiction (Cummings 2014) is an extension of Rasmussen's SRK (skills, rules, and knowledge-based behaviors) taxonomy (Rasmussen 1983).

In this taxonomy, skill-based behaviors are sensory-motor actions that are highly automatic, typically acquired after some period of training (Rasmussen 1983). Indeed, Rasmussen says, "motor output is a response to the observation of an error signal representing the difference between the actual state and the intended state in a time-space environment (1983, 259)." In Figure 17.1, an example of skill-based control for humans is the act of flying an aircraft. Student pilots spend the bulk of their training learning to scan dials and gauges so that they can instantly recognize the state of an aircraft and adjust if needed. Once this set of skills is acquired, pilots can then turn their attention (which is a scarce resource, particularly under high workload), to higher cognitive tasks.

Up the cognitive continuum in Figure 17.1 are rule-based behaviors, which are effectively those actions guided by subroutines, stored rules, or procedures.

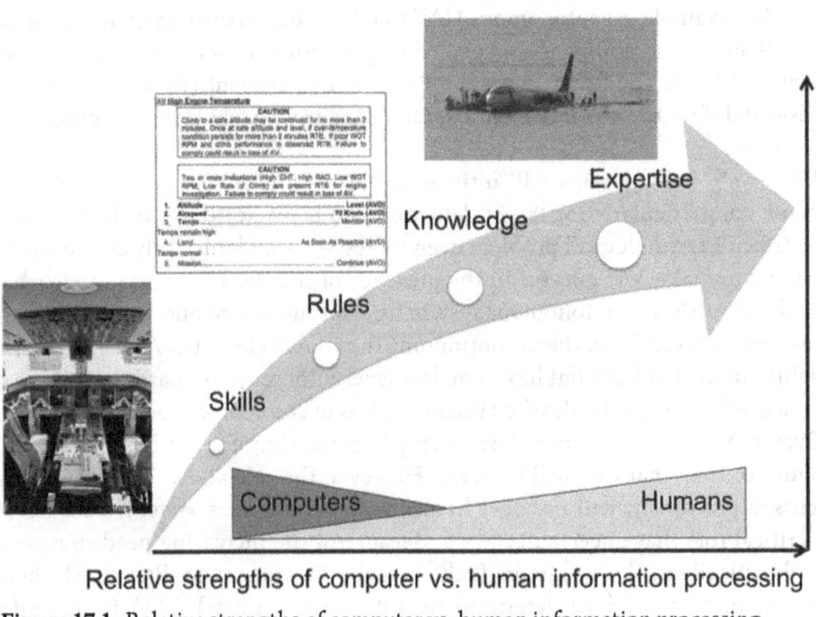

Figure 17.1 Relative strengths of computer vs. human information processing

Rasmussen likens rule-based behavior to following a cookbook recipe (Rasmussen 1983, 261). Difficulties for humans in rule-based environments often come from recognizing the correct goal in order to select the correct procedure or set of rules.

In Figure 17.1, in keeping with the aviation piloting example, pilots spend significant amounts of time learning to follow procedures. For example, when a fire light illuminates, pilots recognize that they should consult a manual to determine the correct procedure (since there are far too many procedures to be committed to memory), and then follow the steps to completion. Some interpretation is required, particularly for multiple system problems, which is common during a catastrophic failure like the loss of one engine.

The highest level of cognitive control is that of knowledge-based behaviors, where mental models built over time aid in the formulation and selection of plans for an explicit goal (Rasmussen 1983). The landing of USAIR 1549 in 2009 in the Hudson River, as depicted in Figure 17.1, is an example of a knowledge-based behavior in that the captain had to decide whether to ditch the aircraft or attempt to land it at a nearby airport. Given his mental model, the environment, and the state of the aircraft, the captain's very fast mental simulation made him choose the ditching option, with clear success.

The last behavior in the taxonomy is expertise, hence the name skills-rules-knowledge-expertise (SRKE) taxonomy. Figure 17.1 demonstrates that knowledge-based behaviors are a prerequisite for gaining expertise in a particular field, especially under significant uncertainty. Uncertainty occurs when a situation cannot precisely be determined, with potentially many unknown variables in a system that itself can be highly variable. Unfortunately, expertise cannot be achieved without substantial experience and exposure to degrees of uncertainty. Judgment and intuition are the key behaviors that allow experts to quickly assess an uncertain situation in a fast and frugal method (Gigerenzer, Todd, and Group 1999), without necessarily and laboriously comparing all possible plan outcomes.

As discussed previously, reasoning under uncertainty is a hallmark characteristic of an autonomous system, and can arise from exogenous sources such as the environment, that is, birds in the general vicinity of an airport that *might*, on rare occasion, be ingested in an engine. However, uncertainty can also be introduced from endogenous sources, either from human behaviors but also from computer/automation behaviors. The recent issues with the Boeing 737 MAX, where two fully loaded commercial planes crashed because of erroneous readings and poor software logic (Campbell 2019), are perfect examples of endogenous uncertainty.

17.6: AUTOMATION AND SKILL-BASED TASKS

When considering role allocation between humans and computers, it is useful to consider who or what can perform the skill, rule, knowledge, and expertise-based behaviors required for a given objective and associated set of tasks. For many skill-based tasks like flying an aircraft, automation in general easily outperforms humans. "Flying" in this sense is the act of keeping the aircraft on heading, altitude, and airspeed, that is, keeping the plane in balanced flight on a stable trajectory. Ever since the introduction of autopilots and, more recently, digital fly-by-wire control, computers are far more capable of keeping planes in stable flight for much longer periods of time than if flown manually by humans. Vigilance research is quite clear in this regard, in that it is very difficult for humans to sustain focused attention for more than twenty to thirty minutes (Warm, Dember, and Hancock 1996), and it is precisely sustained attention that is needed for flying, particularly for long duration flights.

There are other domains where the superiority of automated skill-based control is evident, such as autonomous trucks in mining industries. These trucks are designed to shuttle between pickup and drop-off points and can operate 24/7 in all weather conditions since they are not hampered by reduced vision at night and in bad weather. These trucks are so predictable in their operations that some uncertainty has to be programmed into them, or else they repeatedly drive over the same tracks, creating ruts in the road that make it difficult for manned vehicles to negotiate.

For many domains and tasks, automation is superior in skill-based tasks because such tasks are reduced to motor memory with a clear feedback loop to correct errors between a desired outcome and the observed state of the world. In flying and driving, the bulk of the work is a set of motor responses that become routine and nearly effortless with practice. The automaticity that humans can achieve in such tasks can, and arguably should, be replaced with automation, especially given human limitations like vigilance, fatigue, and the neuromuscular lag (Jagacinski and Flach 2003).

Understanding the neuromuscular lag is a critical consideration in understanding whether a human or a computer should be responsible for a task. Humans have an inherent time lag of approximately 0.5 seconds in their ability to detect and then respond to some stimulus, assuming they are paying perfect attention. If a task requires a response in less than that time, humans should not be the primary entity responsible for that task. The inability of the human to respond in less than 0.5 seconds is why a driverless car should not hand over control to a human during driving conditions (Cummings and Ryan 2014). It is also the reason that many defensive weapons are highly automated like the Phalanx, because many times humans simply cannot respond in time to counter incoming rockets and mortars (Cummings 2019.

The possibility of automating skill-based behaviors (and as we will later see, all behaviors) depends on the ability of the automation to sense the environment, which for a human happens typically through sight, hearing, and touch. This is not trivial for computers, but for aircraft, through the use of accelerometers and gyroscopes, inertial and satellite navigation systems, and engine sensors, the computer can use its sensors to determine with far greater precision and reliability, whether the plane is in stable flight and how to correct in microseconds if there is an anomaly.

This capability is why military and commercial planes have been landing themselves for years far more precisely and smoothly than humans. The act of landing requires the precise control of many dynamic variables, which the computer can do repeatedly without any influence from a lack of sleep or reduced visibility. The same is true for cars that can parallel park by themselves.

However, as previously mentioned, the ability to automate a skill-based task is highly dependent on the ability of the sensors to sense the environment and make adjustments accordingly, correcting for error as it arises. For many skill-based tasks like driving, vision (both foveal and peripheral) is critical for correct environment assessment. Unfortunately, computer vision, which is often a primary sensor for many autonomous systems, still lags far behind human capabilities, primarily due to the brittleness of embedded machine learning algorithms. Currently, such algorithms can only detect patterns or objects that have been seen before, and they struggle with uncertainty in the environment, which is what led to the death of the pedestrian struck by an Uber self-driving car (Laris 2018).

Figure 17.2 illustrates the limitations of deep learning algorithms used in computer vision. Three road vehicles (school bus, motor scooter, firetruck) are shown in normal poses, with three other unusual poses. Below each picture is the category of the algorithm's classification, along with its estimate of the probability this label is correct. So, for example, a bus on its side in Figure 17.2, column d, is seen as a snowplow with the algorithm 92% certain that it is correct. While a bus on its side may be a rare occurrence in normal driving circumstances (i.e., low uncertainty), such unusual poses are part of the typical battlefield environment (i.e., high uncertainty).

The inability of such algorithms to cope with uncertainty in autonomous systems is known as brittleness, which is a fundamental problem for computer vision based on deep learning. Thus, any weapon system that requires autonomous reasoning based on machine learning, either offensive or defensive, in uncertain

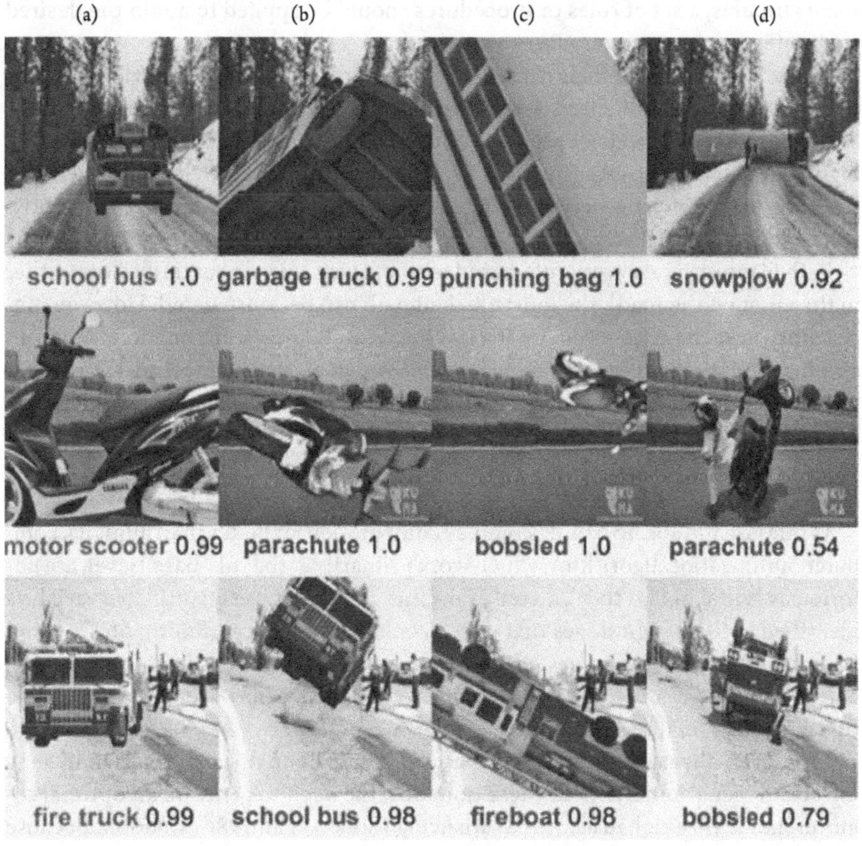

Figure 17.2 A deep learning algorithm prediction (probabilities follow the algorithm's label) for typical road vehicle poses in a 3D simulator (a) and for unusual poses (b-d) (Alcorn et al. 2018).)

situations has a high probability of failure. Such algorithms are also vulnerable to cybersecurity exploitation, which has been demonstrated with street signs (Evtimov et al. 2017) and face recognition (Sharif et al. 2016) applications.

Given these issues, any autonomous system that currently relies on computer vision systems to reason about dynamic and uncertain environments is likely to be extremely unreliable, especially in situations never before encountered by the system. Unfortunately, this is exactly the nature of warfare. Thus, for those skill-based tasks where computer vision is used, maintaining human control is critical, since the technology cannot handle uncertainty at this time. The one caveat to this is that it is possible for autonomous systems to accurately detect static targets with fewer errors than humans (Cummings in press). Static targets are much lower in uncertainty and, therefore, carry significantly less risk that an error can occur.

17.7: RULE-BASED TASKS AND AUTONOMY

As depicted in Figure 17.1, skill-based behaviors and tasks can be automated if the underlying sensors are adequate in building an accurate representation of the world, and uncertainty is low. Rule-based behaviors for humans, however, require higher levels of cognition since interpretation must occur to determine that given some stimulus, a set of rules or procedures should be applied to attain the desired goal state.

By the very nature of their if-then-else structures, rule-based behaviors are also potentially good candidates for automation, but again, uncertainty management is key. Significant aspects of process control plants, including nuclear reactors, are highly automated because the rules for making changes are well established and based on first principles, with highly reliable sensors that accurately represent the state of the physical plant.

Path planning is also very rule-based in that, given rules about traffic flow (either in the air or on the road), the most efficient path can be constructed. However, uncertainty in such domains makes it a less ideal candidate for automation. When an automated path planner is given a start and end goal, for the most part, the route generated is the best path in terms of least time (if that is the goal of the operator). However, many possibilities exist that automation may not have information about that cause such a path to be either suboptimal or even infeasible, such as in the case of accidents or bad weather.

While fast and able to handle complex computation far better than humans, computer optimization algorithms, which work primarily at the rule-based level, are notoriously brittle in that they can only take into account those quantifiable variables identified in the design stages that were deemed to be critical (Smith, McCoy, and Layton 1997). In complex systems with inherent uncertainties (weather impacts, enemy movement, etc.), it is not possible to include a priori every single variable that could impact the final solution.

Moreover, it is not clear exactly what characterizes an optimal solution in such uncertain scenarios. Often, in these domains, the need to generate an optimal solution should be weighed against a satisficing (Simon et al. 1986) solution. Because constraints and variables are often dynamic in complex environments, the definition of optimal is also a constantly changing concept. In those cases of time pressure, having a solution that is good enough, robust, and quickly reached is often preferable to one that requires complex computation and extended periods of time, which may not be accurate due to incorrect assumptions.

Another problem for automation of rule-based behaviors is similar to one for humans, which is the selection of the right rule or procedure for a given set of stimuli. Computers will reliably execute a procedure more consistently than any human, but the assumption is that the computer selects the correct procedure, which is highly dependent on the sensing aspect. As illustrated in the previous section, this can be problematic.

It is at the rule-based level of reasoning where the shift in applying automated versus autonomous reasoning in the presence of uncertainty is seen in current systems. The Global Hawk UAV works at a rule-based level when it is able to land itself when it loses communication. However, it is not yet been demonstrated that such an aircraft can reason under all situations it might encounter, which would require a higher level of reasoning, discussed in the next section.

17.8: KNOWLEDGE-BASED TASKS AND EXPERTISE

The most advanced form of cognitive reasoning occurs in domains where knowledge-based behaviors and expertise are required. These settings are also typically where uncertainty is highest, as depicted in Figure 17.1. While rules may assist decision-makers (whether human or computer) in aspects of knowledge-based decisions, such situations are, by definition, vague and ambiguous such that a mathematically optimal or satisficing solution is not available. Weapons release from any platform, manned or unmanned, requires knowledge-based reasoning, and autonomous weapon systems will have to be able to achieve this level of reasoning before they can be safely deployed.

It is precisely in these situations where the human power of induction is critical. Judgment and intuition are critical in these situations, as these are the weapons needed to combat uncertainty. Because of the aforementioned brittleness problems in the programming of computer algorithms and the inability to replicate the intangible concept of intuition, knowledge-based reasoning, and true expertise, for now, are outside the realm of computers. However, there is currently significant research underway to change this, particularly in the machine learning (sometimes called artificial intelligence) community, but progress is slow.

IBM's Watson, ninety servers each with a 3.5 GHz core processor (Deedrick 2011), is often touted as a computer with knowledge-based reasoning, but people confuse the ability of a computer to search vast databases to generate formulaic responses with knowledge. For Watson, which leverages natural language processing and pattern matching through machine learning, uncertainty is low. Indeed, when Watson was applied to medical diagnoses, it failed miserably, largely in part because of its inability to handle uncertainty (Strickland 2019).

This example highlights the probabilistic nature of knowledge-based reasoning. Whether humans or computers do it, both are guessing with incomplete information based on prior probabilities about an outcome. While the consequences for an autonomous thermostat guessing wrong about your arrival time at home are relatively trivial, the same cannot be said for autonomous weapons. Moreover, as illustrated in Figure 17.2, any higher-level reasoning that occurs vis-à-vis flawed deep learning at the skill- or rule-based level will likely be wrong so until this problem is addressed, knowledge-based reasoning should only be allocated to humans for the foreseeable future.

17.9: CONCLUSION

There is no question that robots of all shapes, sizes, and capabilities will become part of our everyday landscape in both military and commercial settings. But as these systems start to grow in numbers and complexity, it will be critical for engineers and policymakers to address the role allocation issue. To this end, this chapter presented a taxonomy for understanding what behaviors can be automated (skill-based), what behaviors can be autonomous (rule-based), and where humans should be leveraged, particularly in cases where inductive reasoning is needed and uncertainty is high (knowledge-based). It should be noted that these behaviors do not occur in discrete stages with clear thresholds, but rather are on a continuum.

Because computers cannot yet achieve knowledge-based reasoning, especially for the task of target detection and identification where uncertainty is very high, autonomous weapons simply are not achievable with any guarantees of reliability. Of course, this technological obstacle may not stop other nations and terrorist states from attempting to build such systems, which is why it is critical that policymakers understand the clear technological gap between what is desired and what is achievable.

This raises the question of technical competence for policymakers who must approve the use of autonomous weapons. The United States has designated the Under Secretary of Defense for Policy, the Under Secretary of Defense for Acquisition, Technology, and Logistics, and the Chairman of the Joint Chiefs of Staff as decision-makers with the authority to approve autonomous weapons launches. Such systems will be highly sophisticated with incredibly advanced levels of probabilistic reasoning never before seen in weapon systems. It has been well established that humans are not effective decision-makers when faced with even simple probabilistic information (Tversky and Kahneman 1974). So, this begs the question of whether these four individuals, or any person overseeing such complex systems who is not a statistician or roboticist, will be able to effectively judge whether the benefit of launching an autonomous weapon platform is worth the risk.

Since the invention of the longbow, soldiers have been trying to increase the distance for killing, and UAVs in their current form are simply another technological advance along this continuum. However, autonomous weapons represent an entirely new dimension where a computer, imbued with probabilistic reasoning codified by humans with incomplete information, must make life and death decisions with even more incomplete information in a time-critical setting. As many have discussed (Anderson and Waxman 2013; Cummings 2004; Human Rights Watch 2013; International Committee for the Red Cross 2014), autonomous weapons raise issues of accountability as well as moral and ethical agency, and the technical issues outlined here further highlight the need to continue this debate.

NOTE

1. This paper is a derivative of an earlier work: Mary L. Cummings, 2017. "Artificial Intelligence and the Future of Warfare." International Security Department and US and the Americas Programme. London: Chatham House.

WORKS CITED

Adroit Market Research. 2019. "Drones Market Will Grow at a CAGR of 40.7% to Hit $144.38 Billion by 2025." *GlobeNewswire.* May 10. https://www.globenewswire.com/news-release/2019/05/10/1821560/0/en/Drones-Market-will-grow-at-a-CAGR-of-40-7-to-hit-144-38-Billion-by-2025-Analysis-by-Trends-Size-Share-Growth-Drivers-and-Business-Opportunities-Adroit-Market-Research.html.

Alcorn, Michael A., Qi Li, Zhitao Gong, Chengfei Wang, Long Mai, Wei-Shinn Ku, and Anh Nguyen. 2018. "Strike (with) a Pose: Neural Networks Are Easily Fooled by Strange Poses of Familiar Objects." Poster at the 2019 Conference on Computer Vision and Pattern Recognition. *arXiv: 1811.11553.*

Anderson, Kenneth and Matthew Waxman. 2013. *Law and Ethics for Autonomous Weapon Systems: Why a Ban Won't Work and How the Laws of War Can.* Jean Perkins Task Force on National Security and Law. Stanford, CA: Hoover Institution.

Campbell, Darryl. 2019. "Redline: The Many Human Errors That Brought Down the Boeing 737 MAX." *The Verge.* May 2. Accessed May 17. https://www.theverge.com/2019/5/2/18518176/boeing-737-max-crash-problems-human-error-mcas-faa.

Chairperson of the Informal Meeting of Experts. 2016. *Report of the 2016 Informal Meeting of Experts on Lethal Autonomous Weapons Systems (LAWS).* Geneva: United Nations Office at Geneva.

Cummings, Mary L. 2004. "Creating Moral Buffers in Weapon Control Interface Design." *IEEE Technology and Society* 23 (3): pp. 28–33.

Cummings, Mary L. 2014. "Man vs. Machine or Man + Machine?" *IEEE Intelligent Systems* 29 (5): pp. 62–69.

Cummings, Mary L. 2019. "Lethal Autonomous Weapons: Meaningful Human Control or Meaningful Human Certification?" *IEEE Technology and Society.* December 5. Accessed January 28, 2020. https://ieeexplore.ieee.org/document/8924577.

Cummings, Mary L. and Jason C. Ryan. 2014. "Who Is in Charge? Promises and Pitfalls of Driverless Cars." *TR News* 292 (May–June): pp. 25–30.

Cummings, Mary L. and Sylvain Bruni. 2009. "Collaborative Human Computer Decision Making." In *Handbook of Automation,* edited by Shimon Y. Nof, pp. 437–447. New York: Springer.

Deedrick, Tami. 2011. "It's Technical, Dear Watson." *IBM Systems Magazine.* February. Accessed January 28, 2020. http://archive.ibmsystemsmag.com/ibmi/trends/whatsnew/it%E2%80%99s-technical,-dear-watson/.

Defense Science Board. 2012. *The Role of Autonomy in DoD Systems.* Washington, DC: Department of Defense. https://fas.org/irp/agency/dod/dsb/autonomy.pdf.

Eisenstein, Paul A. 2018. "Not Everyone Is Ready to Ride as Autonomous Vehicles Take to the Road in Ever-Increasing Numbers." *CNBC.* October 15. Accessed August 23, 2019. https://www.cnbc.com/2018/10/14/self-driving-cars-take-to-the-road-but-not-everyone-is-ready-to-ride.html.

Endsley, Mica. 1987. "The Application of Human Factors to the Development of Expert Systems for Advanced Cockpits." In *31st Annual Meeting*. Santa Monica, CA: Human Factors Society

Evtimov, Ivan, Kevin Eykholt, Earlence Fernandes, Tadayoshi Kohno, Bo Li, Atul Prakash, Amir Rahmati, and Dawn Song. 2017. "Robust Physical-World Attacks on Deep Learning Models." *arXiv preprint 1707.08945*.

Fitts, Paul M. 1951. *Human Engineering for an Effective Air Navigation and Traffic Control system*. Washington, DC: National Research Council. https://apps.dtic.mil/dtic/tr/fulltext/u2/b815893.pdf.

Future of Life Institute. 2015. "Autonomous Weapons: An Open Letter from AI & Robotics Researchers." Accessed January 28, 2020. http://futureoflife.org/open-letter-autonomous-weapons/.

Gigerenzer, Gerd, Peter M. Todd and The ABC Research Group. 1999. *Simple Heuristics That Make Us Smart*. Oxford: Oxford University Press.

Human Rights Watch. 2013. "Arms: New Campaign to Stop Killer Robots." Human Rights Watch. April 23. Accessed January 28, 2020. https://www.hrw.org/news/2013/04/23/arms-new-campaign-stop-killer-robots.

International Committee for the Red Cross. 2014. "Report of the ICRC Expert Meeting on 'Autonomous Weapon Systems: Technical, Military, Legal, and Humanitarian Aspects." Working Paper. March 26–28. Geneva: ICRC. https://www.icrc.org/en/download/file/1707/4221-002-autonomous-weapons-systems-full-report.pdf.

Jagacinski, Richard J. and John M. Flach. 2003. *Control Theory for Humans: Quantitative Approaches to Modeling Performance*. Mahwah, NJ: Lawrence Erlbaum Associates.

Kaber, David. B., Melanie C. Wright, Lawrence. J. Printzel III, and Michael P. Clamann. 2005. "Adaptive Automation of Human-Machine System Information-Processing Functions." *Human Factors* 47 (4): pp. 730–741.

Laris, Michael. 2018. "Fatal Uber Crash Spurs Debate about Regulation of Driverless Vehicles." *Washington Post*. March 23. https://www.washingtonpost.com/local/trafficandcommuting/deadly-driverless-uber-crash-spurs-debate-on-role-of-regulation/2018/03/23/2574b49a-2ed6-11e8-8688-e053ba58f1e4_story.html.

Parasuraman, Raja. 2000. "Designing Automation for Human Use: Empirical Studies and Quantitative Models." *Ergonomics* 43 (7): pp. 931–951.

Parasuraman, Raja, Thomas B. Sheridan, and Chris D. Wickens. 2000. "A Model for Types and Levels of Human Interaction with Automation." *IEEE Transactions on Systems, Man, and Cybernetics—Part A: Systems and Humans* 30 (3): pp. 286–297.

Rasmussen, Jens. 1983. "Skills, Rules, and Knowledge: Signals, Signs, and Symbols, and Other Distinctions in Human Performance Models." *IEEE Transactions on Systems, Man, and Cybernetics* 13 (3): pp. 257–266.

Riley, Victor A. 1989. "A General Model of Mixed-Initiative Human-Machine Systems." In *33rd Annual Meeting*. Denver, CO.: Human Factors Society.

Sharif, Mahmood, Sruti Bhagavatula, Lujo Bauer, and Michael K. Reiter. 2016. "Accessorize to a Crime: Real and Stealthy Attacks on State-of-the-Art Face Recognition." In *ACM SIGSAC Conference on Computer and Communications Security*. Vienna, Austria: Association for Computing Machinery.

Sheridan, Thomas B. 1992. *Telerobotics, Automation and Human Supervisory Control*. Cambridge, MA: MIT Press.

Sheridan, Thomas B. and William Verplank. 1978. *Human and Computer Control of Undersea Teleoperators*. Man-Machine Systems Laboratory, Department of Mechanical Engineering. Cambridge, MA: MIT Press.

Simon, Herbert A., Robin Hogarth, Charles R. Piott, Howard Raiffa, Thomas C. Schelling, Richard Thaier, Amos Tversky, Kenneth Shepsle, and Sidney Winter. 1986. "Report of the Research Briefing Panel on Decision Making and Problem Solving." In *Research Briefings 1986*, edited by National Academy of Sciences, pp. 17–36. Washington, DC: National Academy Press.

Smith, Phil J., C. Elaine McCoy, and Charles F. Layton. 1997. "Brittleness in the Design of Cooperative Problem-Solving Systems: The Effects on User Performance." *IEEE Transactions on Systems, Man and Cybernetics, Part A: Systems and Humans* 27 (3): pp. 360–371.

Strickland, Eliza. 2019. "IBM Watson, Heal Thyself." *IEEE Spectrum* 56 (4): pp. 24–31.

Tversky, Amos and Daniel Kahneman. 1974. "Judgment under Uncertainty: Heuristics and Biases." *Science* 185 (4157): pp. 1124–1131.

US Department of Defense. 2011. *DoD Directive 3000.09: Autonomy in Weapon Systems.* Fort Eustis, VA: Army Capabilities Integration Center, U.S. Army Training and Doctrine Command. fas.org/irp/doddir/dod/d3000_09.pdf.

Warm, Joel S., William N. Dember, and Peter A. Hancock. 1996. "Vigilance and Workload in Automated Systems." In *Automation and Human Performance: Theory and Applications*, edited by Raja Parasuraman and Mustapha Mouloua, pp. 183–200. Mahwah, NJ: Lawrence Erlbaum Associates.

INDEX

For the benefit of digital users, indexed terms that span two pages (e.g., 52–53) may, on occasion, appear on only one of those pages.

Tables are indicated by *t* following the page number